# Internet and Smartphone Addiction: An Evidence-Based Approach

# Internet and Smartphone Addiction: An Evidence-Based Approach

Editor: Henry Taylor

AMERICAN
MEDICAL PUBLISHERS
www.americanmedicalpublishers.com

AMERICAN
MEDICAL PUBLISHERS
www.americanmedicalpublishers.com

**Cataloging-in-Publication Data**

Internet and smartphone addiction : an evidence-based approach / edited by Henry Taylor.
p. cm.
Includes bibliographical references and index.
ISBN 979-8-88740-220-8
1. Internet addiction. 2. Smartphones--Psychological aspects. 3. Nomophobia.
4. Digital media--Psychological aspects. 5. Compulsive behavior. 6. Psychiatry.
I. Taylor, Henry.
RC569.5.I54 I58 2023
616.858 4--dc23



American Medical Publishers,
41 Flatbush Avenue,
1st Floor, New York,
NY 11217, USA

ISBN 979-8-88740-220-8 (Hardback)

# Contents

# Contents

# Preface

Smartphone addiction refers to a behavioral condition that involves the obsessive use of a smartphone. It is often fueled by an internet addiction disorder. The addiction occurs due to electronic gadgets, as well as the applications, games and internet that connect the people with virtual world. The symptoms of internet addiction disorder manifest in both physical and emotional forms. Depression, isolation, agitation, defensiveness, no sense of time, avoidance of work, fear, loneliness, procrastination, mood swings and anxiety are some of the emotional symptoms of internet and smartphone addiction. Some physical signs and symptoms include backache, insomnia, neck pain, weight gain or loss, dry eyes and other vision problems. Cognitive behavior therapy, group therapy and psychotherapy are some common treatment methods for internet and smartphone addiction. This book provides an evidence based approach to help develop a better understanding of internet and smartphone addiction. It is a resource guide for experts as well as students.

This book is a result of research of several months to collate the most relevant data in the field.

When I was approached with the idea of this book and the proposal to edit it, I was overwhelmed. It gave me an opportunity to reach out to all those who share a common interest with me in this field. I had 3 main parameters for editing this text:

1. Accuracy - The data and information provided in this book should be up-to-date and valuable to the readers.

2. Structure - The data must be presented in a structured format for easy understanding and better grasping of the readers.

3. Universal Approach - This book not only targets students but also experts and innovators in the field, thus my aim was to present topics which are of use to all.

Thus, it took me a couple of months to finish the editing of this book.

I would like to make a special mention of my publisher who considered me worthy of this opportunity and also supported me throughout the editing process. I would also like to thank the editing team at the back-end who extended their help whenever required.

**Editor**

1

# Profiles of Problematic Internet Use and its Impact on Adolescents' Health-Related Quality of Life

**Juan M. Machimbarrena [1], Joaquín González-Cabrera [2,*], Jéssica Ortega-Barón [2], Marta Beranuy-Fargues [2], Aitor Álvarez-Bardón [2] and Blanca Tejero [2]**

1 Faculty of Psychology, University of the Basque Country (UPV/EHU), 20018 Donostia-San Sebastian, Spain; juanmanuel.machimbarrena@ehu.eus

2 Faculty of Education, Universidad Internacional de la Rioja (UNIR), 26006 Logrono, Spain; jessica.ortega@unir.net (J.O.-B.); marta.beranuy@unir.net (M.B.-F.); aitor.alvarez@unir.net (A.Á.-B.); blanca.tejero@unir.net (B.T.)

* Correspondence: joaquin.gonzalez@unir.net

**Abstract:** The internet has been a breakthrough for adolescents in many ways, but its use can also become dysfunctional and problematic, leading to consequences for personal well-being. The main objective is to analyze profiles related to problematic internet use and its relationship with health-related quality of life (HRQoL). An analytical and cross-sectional study was carried out in a region of northern Spain. The sample comprised 12,285 participants. Sampling was random and representative. Mean age and standard deviation was 14.69 ± 1.73 (11–18 years). The Spanish versions of the Problematic and Generalized Internet Use Scale (GPIUS2) and of the Health-Related Quality of Life (KIDSCREEN-27) were used. Four profiles were detected (non-problematic use, mood regulator, problematic internet use, and severe problematic use). The prevalence of these last two profiles was 18.5% and 4.9%, respectively. Problematic internet use correlated negatively and significantly with HRQoL. The severe problematic use profile presented a significant decrease in all dimensions of HRQoL. Analyses were carried out to extract a cut-off point for GPIUS2 (52 points). The results and practical implications are discussed.

**Keywords:** problematic internet use; health-related quality of life; adolescent; cut-off point; internet addiction

---

## 1. Introduction

Digital society is a source of development and opportunities for people, because it allows them to communicate, obtain information, and develop projects in a way that was previously unthinkable. However, despite all the advantages it implies, digital society also poses risks, especially for younger people. Currently, adolescents live in a very different way from other generations, and young people have a complex and bidirectional relationship between what is occurring online and offline, and, according to the model of co-construction, adolescents shape their reality by connecting their offline and online worlds, the latter frequently predominating [1]. People born since the year 2000 have received the name of the Z-generation, the postmillennial or centennial generation, and one of the elements that has clearly differentiated them from other generations is the massive use of internet on mobile phones [2]. This can be seen in international surveys that reveal that up to 24% of adolescents between 13 and 17 years of age are constantly connected to the internet [3] or in the Spanish context, where it has been found that, among more than 25,000 adolescents between 11 and 18 years, almost 96% own a smartphone, and of them, 87% claim to use it daily [4]. This higher exposure increases the chances that many of the classic psychosocial problems (abuse, violence, and addictions) will have quickly found their online equivalent (cyberbullying, sexting, problematic internet use, nomophobia, etc.), and their prevalence is increasing [1,5,6].

Currently, the DSM-5 [7] does not include internet addiction or intensive internet use as an addictive disorder, nor does it include internet consumption in general within the "behavioral addictions". Notwithstanding, there have been several important approaches to internet use in the last two decades. Thus, Tokunaga and Rains [8] refer to three great traditions such as: (a) problematic internet use (PIU) as an impulse control disorder (these authors have conceptualized it as a product of inadequate control over impulsive thoughts or feelings); (b) PIU as a substance dependence (this has been regarded as analogous to a chemical addiction and is defined as internet dependency); and (c) PIU as a deficit of relational and relationship-building resources (negative effects of this internet use in the person's life).

This study has focused on this last approach to PIU, which involves emphasizing the possible dysfunctions entailed by the consumption of internet in the individual's life [9–11]. According to this theoretical approach, PIU must be understood as a preference for online social interaction and for mood regulation through the internet, which increases the probability of presenting deficient self-regulation (either due to compulsive internet use or to excessive concern about it) and which leads to various negative consequences in the person's life [9]. We must also consider that maladaptive cognitions about oneself and the world are considered part of the concept of PIU. These thoughts generate a feeling of inefficiency in offline social interactions and the possibility to overcome it through online relations [9,12]. In fact, it has been observed that online behavior carried out by adolescents with high social anxiety and low skills is mainly motivated by the desire to make friends [13]. There is also a tendency to think about online social interactions when the internet is not available, or to anticipate what will happen when one reconnects, which is a concern for the individual. To finalize this approach, we indicate that deficits in relationship-building resources lead to aversive moods, which makes people feel isolated and withdrawn [11,12,14].

Irrespective of the still controversial conceptualization of PIU, epidemiological studies report prevalence rates that demonstrate the clinical and social relevance of inappropriate internet use, especially when it entails risks and problems for a person [5,15–18]. Although it is difficult to talk about the general prevalence of PIU because of the many tools and ways of defining the construct [8,19], we note some studies in the international context such as that of Cha and Seo [20], who reported that almost 17% of adolescents present problematic use of the internet and/or the smartphone, and that up to 31% present risk of an addiction. In European studies, the prevalence reported is very variable: ranging from 4.4% of pathological internet use and 13.5% of maladaptive internet use (MIU) [21] up to between 14.3% and 54.9% [22]. In the Spanish context, Carbonell et al. (2012) found 6.1% of frequent problems due to internet use in a sample that included an age ranging from preadolescence to young people [23]. González–Cabrera et al. (2017) noted prevalences close to 4% in adolescents who presented PIU, and almost 40% presented occasional problematic use in the last seven months [4]. Other studies have found data with similar values to the ones presented [5,24]. However, other Spanish [25] authors suggest higher prevalences, indicating that up to 19.9% of Spanish adolescents present PIU, and, in another study with a very broad sample, 16.3% [26]. Finally, some studies have tried to establish groups of users according to adolescents' profile of internet usage [27–30]. The results of these studies are not unanimous, although they often find profiles related to the ones proposed by Brandtzæg (2010) depending on the frequency of use, ranging from low use (sporadics), average use (lurkers/instrumental users/socializers) to high use (advanced users). In a Spanish study, Rial et al., (2015) replicated this taxonomy, finding four user profiles similar to the sporadics, socializers, instrumental, and advanced users of Brandtzæg [28], which they called first steppers, trainees, sensible users, and heavy users, respectively [30].

With regard to gender, some studies point out that PIU is higher in boys than in girls [21,31] whereas, in other investigations, it is higher in girls than in boys [5,18,24,26]. With regard to age, PIU seems to increase with age [32]. Studies with samples of adolescents suggest that post-compulsory students (late adolescence) present more PIU than the early courses (10–12 years) [26], although other authors find no age-related differences [24]. If young people are compared with middle aged people, the former have higher levels of PIU [18].

The problematic use that some adolescents make of the internet has also been shown and it has been reported to have a negative impact on health including changes in health habits (sleep, eating, physical activity, etc.) and their interference in the family, social, and academic life indicated in several studies [33,34]. Some variables associated with an increased risk of manifesting problematic internet-related behaviors have also been identified. Specifically, it has been associated with cyberbullying [24,35], with some personality traits, such as higher neuroticism and lower responsibility, openness to change, and agreeableness [16], as well as with loss of control, feelings of anger, stress symptoms, social isolation, family conflicts [33], and anxiety and depression [19].

In relation to the instruments that have evaluated PIU, there is a wide variety (cfr. Rial et al., 2016, [36] for a more thorough review of this and other internet-related constructs). In particular, instruments such as the Generalized and Problematic Internet Use Scale-2 (GPIUS2) [9–11], the OCS [14], and the PIUS [37] have been designed based on the above perspective of considering PIU as a relational resource deficit [8]. Of these three, the GPIUS2 [9,10] is the most complete, as it integrates the dimensions of uncontrolled internet use, use preoccupation, mood alteration, online efficacy, and negative outcomes. Neither the GPIUS2 nor any of the other instruments present the dimension of tolerance/withdrawal [8]. The GPIUS2 is one of the most widely used in relation to this approximation to PIU and it currently presents the limitation of a lack of cut-off points for the detection of problematic use [10]. Few studies have focused on establishing cut-off points, because the samples are generally not sufficiently large or representative [23,38,39]. In Spanish, the only known case of a tool that presents cut-off points is that of Gómez et al. [25]. However, their tool is far from the conceptualization of Caplan [9,11].

Health-related quality of life (HRQoL) is a complex construct for which there is no accepted definition [40]. Nevertheless, there is a clear consensus to not define it as an absence of disease or disorder but instead from a more holistic point of view that integrates physical, psychological, emotional, and social aspects. Moreover, well-being must be perceived by the subject him—or herself—and also by those around him or her [40–42]. HRQoL has been widely studied in adult population in numerous medical pathologies, and many instruments have been developed to measure it [43]. Recently, the European KIDSCREEN instruments, aimed at the evaluation of HRQoL in children and adolescents, were developed [41]. During childhood–adolescence, evidence has revealed that girls suffer a greater loss of physical and psychological HRQoL than do boys [44]. Some of the psychosocial problems that are beginning to be assessed in relation to HRQoL are those associated with violence. These include abuse [45], bullying [46], or cyberbullying [47].

Therefore, at present, PIU has hardly been related to HRQoL. Although there is evidence that adaptive internet use has positive effects on children's psychological well-being [48,49], currently research focuses on problems related to problematic, addictive, or maladaptive use related to the loss of HRQoL or of psychological well-being. Despite the evidence that has been found, there is currently great heterogeneity in the way we define and evaluate the two constructs. Thus, lower HRQoL has been reported in adolescents and young adults with PIU than in those without PIU [50,51]. This relationship between inadequate internet use and poorer HRQoL has also been observed in primary education students [52]. There is evidence of the inverse relationship between PIU and HRQoL [53] and between internet addiction and HRQoL [54]. Other studies have explored the use of social media, and online games are related to poorer psychological well-being, especially among girls [55]. From Caplan's approach to PIU, it could be considered that online social preference and mood regulation through the internet generate social interactions that provoke feelings of emotional loneliness even if the individual apparently has social support, because this kind of communication lacks the sensory richness that human beings need [56,57]. This is also supported by studies indicating the two-way relationship between emotional loneliness and PIU, especially when the use of social media is predominant [58,59].

Considering the above, the present study has as its main objectives: (1) to analyze the profiles related to PIU and (2) to analyze the relationship between problematic use and HRQoL in a broad sample of adolescents. In addition, we had the following secondary objectives: (1) to analyze sex and age in relation to PIU; (2) to analyze the prevalence of PIU in adolescents; (3) to compare HRQoL as a function of the profile of PIU; and (4) to establish a cut-off point for PIU.

The study had the following hypotheses: (H1) there will be significant and inverse relationships between PIU and HRQoL; (H2) the greater the level of PIU, especially if it is severe, the worse will be HRQoL [54].

## 2. Materials and Methods

### *2.1. Design and Participants*

An analytical and cross-sectional study was carried out in an autonomous community in northern Spain. The sample comprised 12,285 participants of whom 49.1% were boys (*n* = 6032) and 50.3% girls (*n* = 6181); 72 participants did not provide this datum (0.6%). The sample obtained in the study is representative of students enrolled in public and concerted centers. With a 99% confidence level, a sampling error of 1% for a population variance of 0.50, the representative sample comprises 11,853 participants. In addition, sample selection was random, taking into account the number of students of each stage, the proportionality of centers in each location, and the type of center. Mean age and standard deviation was 14.69 ± 1.73 with a range of 11–18 years. Concerning age, 40% (*n* = 4912) of the sample was between 11–13 years old, 37.3% (*n* = 4580) between 14–15 years, and 22.45% (*n* = 2766) between 16–18 years, with 27 (0.2%) participants who did not provide this datum. Fifty-nine schools participated, and more than 90% of the students of the centers were recruited. Concerning ownership, 16 schools were private schools (*n* = 3381; 27.25%) and 43 were public schools (*n* = 8904; 72.5%). The average socioeconomic and cultural index (ISEC) of the schools of the sample is similar to the mean ISEC of the autonomous community to which they belong, according to data obtained from the diagnostic assessments in the 2009–2014 period.

### *2.2. Instruments*

The participants provided information about demographic variables such as sex, grade, school, and age. For the analysis of the variables under study, the following instruments were used in relation to the previous five months (start of the course).

Spanish version of the GPIUS2 [9,10]. It has 15 items divided into five factors: preference for online social interaction (e.g., "I prefer to interact with other people through the internet rather than communicating face to face"), mood regulation (e.g., "I've used the internet to talk to others when I've felt lonely"), Negative consequences (e.g., "My use of the internet has hindered the control of my life"), cognitive concern (e.g., "I would feel lost if I couldn't connect to the internet"), and compulsive use (e.g., "When I'm not on the internet, it's hard to resist the urge to connect"). Agreement with the items is rated on a six-point Likert scale ranging from 1 (completely disagree) to 6 (completely agree). The reliability ratings can be seen in Table 5.

For the evaluation of HRQoL, we used the Spanish version of the KIDSCREEN-27 [41] for children and adolescents aged 8 to 18 years. This version evaluates five dimensions through 27 items: physical well-being (e.g., "Have you felt well and fit?"), psychological well-being (e.g., "Have you felt sad?"), autonomy and relationship with parents (e.g., "Have your parents had enough time for you?"), friends and social support (e.g., "Have you and your friends helped each other?"), and school environment (e.g., "Have you done well in school?"). The development of the KIDSCREEN was based on the probabilistic partial credit model (PCM), which belongs to the family of Rasch models. PCM tries to explain the actual behavior of the respondents in the testing situation by the estimated the person parameter and the location of the item-response-category-thresholds. The PCM assumes all items of a scale to be indicators of a single unidimensional latent trait [41]. For the KIDSCREEN-27, the mean scores varied around 50 ($SD = 10$) due to $T$-value standardization. There are standardized data for the Spanish infant-juvenile population. The reliability indexes can be seen in Table 5.

*2.3. Procedure*

The application of the questionnaires to the students of the different classrooms was supervised by the tutor, aided by the Guidance Department and the school direction. A rigorous procedure was established for data collection through the Survey Monkey® online platform, using the computer labs of each school. We emphasized the importance of responding sincerely, individually, and reflectively, but without taking too much time on each item. The average response time for the questionnaire battery was approximately 12 minutes. Collaboration was voluntary, anonymous, and disinterested.

The study was carried out with the authorization of the participants, the schools, and the political-educational institution of the autonomous community. Through the official communication channels with the families, the schools sent a passive consent form that informed the legal tutors about the purpose of the study and its characteristics, its promoters and their right not to participate. Those parents/tutors who did not wish to allow participation returned the signed consent refusing participation. This occurred in less than 1% of the sample. The project was approved by the Ethics Committee of the Principality of Asturias (Ref.59/17), and the juvenile Prosecutor's Office was informed, following the legal regulations in force. There were no exclusion criteria, except for the refusal to participate by the legal guardians or by the students themselves.

*2.4. Data Analysis*

Statistical analyses were carried out using the Statistical Package for the Social Sciences (SPSS) [60], the R software program [61], and the Pysch [62] and Mclust [63] package. Firstly, to determine the internal consistency of the instruments used, Cronbach alphas [64] and omega coefficients [65] were estimated. Then, we checked the assumptions of normality of the target variables of the study (Shapiro-Wilks statistic), as well as the homogeneity of variances to compare the groups (Levene test).

The following analyses were carried out on the GPIUS2 scores: (1) Student's $t$ for dependent and independent samples to determine possible sex differences in the GPIUS2 dimensions; (2) ANOVA with post-hoc Bonferroni comparisons to determine age group differences; (3) Latent Profile Analysis (LPA) to identify profiles of internet use, taking into account the five dimensions of the GPIUS2; for this purpose, exploratorily, we compared different solutions according to the Bayesian criterion information (BIC) and the Akaike information criterion (AIC). Latent profile analysis (LPA) tries to identify clusters of individuals based on responses to a series of continuous variables. LPA assumes that there are unobserved latent profiles that generate patterns of responses on indicator items. The resulting profiles can then inform behavioral or other important outcome differences and help explain inconsistencies in prior research [66]; (4) Chi-square analysis and analysis of the adjusted standardized residuals to identify the distribution of sex and age in the profiles; (5) receiving operating characteristic (ROC) curve analysis, using the "severe problematic use" profile as the gold standard to distinguish between two binary elements (i.e., severe PIU and non-problematic internet use). The ROC curve analysis identified the cut-off points based on their sensitivity (i.e., the percentage of true positives among problematic users) and their specificity (i.e., the percentage of true negatives among users with non-problematic use). We also analyzed the GPIUS2's likelihood of making a correct diagnosis through positive (PV+) and negative predictive values (PV−), and lastly, its overall accuracy or efficiency (ACC), indicating the proportion of valid results among all the results.

To determine the relation between the GPIU and its effects on HRQoL, the following analyses were carried out; (1) partial Pearson correlations for both sexes (with age as control variable) between the five GPIUS2 dimensions and the five KIDSCREEN dimensions; (2) ANOVA with post-hoc Bonferroni comparisons of the profiles obtained with LPA (independent variable) and the scores obtained in the five KIDSCREEN dimensions to analyze HRQoL differences as a function of PIU. A value of less than $p = 0.05$ was considered significant.

## 3. Results

### 3.1. Differences in PIU as a Function of Sex and Age

Sex and age differences in problematic use are shown in Table 1. Girls obtained significantly higher scores in the total GPIU than boys, although the size of the effect was small ($t = -7.23$, $p < 0.001$, $d = 0.015$). More specifically, girls showed significantly higher scores in the variables: mood regulation, cognitive preoccupation, and compulsive use. Age-based analyses revealed significant differences in GPIUS2 ($F$ (2,12280) = 127.12, $p < 0.001$, $\eta_p^2 = 0.020$) and its five dimensions. In particular, the group of 11–13-year-olds obtained lower scores in all the dimensions, whereas the group of 14–15-year-olds obtained the highest scores.

### 3.2. Profiles of Internet Use and Effects on Quality of Life

To compare the scores obtained in the GPIUS2 and its five dimensions and their relationship with HRQoL, we performed LPA. Table 2 shows the values obtained for the different models. Inspection of the fit indices suggests a four-profile solution as the best fit, as the fit indices began to level off after additional profiles. The Bootstrap Likelihood Ratio Test provided a significant $p$-Value, indicating a good fit for the four-profile solution, which ceased to be significant when adding more profiles. This solution offered high values of entropy and the average posterior probabilities for the membership in each latent profile were high (from 0.85 for "mood regulation use" to 0.96 for the "severe problematic problem").

The mean (standardized) scores obtained in the dimensions of the GPIUS2 are shown in Figure 1, and their respective scores in Table 3.

The profile that comprised the largest number of participants was the "non-problematic" profile, characterized by scores below the average in all five GPIUS2 dimensions. Next, two profiles emerged with a similar number of participants, but with different usage patterns: the "mood regulator" profile showed a high level of usage for mood regulation and high online preference, but it obtained scores below the average in the rest of the dimensions. The "problematic internet use" profile showed above average values in all the GPIUS2 dimensions, but much lower scores than the last profile, "severe problematic-compulsive use", which obtained the highest scores in all GPIUS2 dimensions, with particularly high scores in negative consequences, cognitive preoccupation, and compulsive use.

Table 4 shows the profiles according to sex and age. Chi-square analyses yielded significant differences for both variables. The analysis of the standardized residuals indicated a higher number of boys in the non-problematic users group and a higher number of girls in the problematic users and severe problematic users groups. Regarding age, the standardized residuals indicated a smaller number of 11–13-year-olds and a larger number of 16–17-year-olds in the three profiles related to dysfunctional use. However, more 11–13-year-olds and fewer 14–15- and 16–17-year-olds than expected were found in the non-problematic use profile.

**Table 1.** Differences as a function of the variables sex and age groups (11–13 years, 14–15 years, and 16–18 years) in the Generalized and Problematic Internet Use Scale-2 (GPIUS2) dimensions.

| | Boys | Girls | $t$ ($p$) | $d$ | 11–13 Years [a] | 14–15 Years [b] | 16–18 Years [c] | $F$ ($p$) | $\eta^2$ | Post Hoc |
|---|---|---|---|---|---|---|---|---|---|---|
| | $M$ ($SD$) | $M$ ($SD$) | | | $M$ ($SD$) | $M$ ($SD$) | $M$ ($SD$) | | | |
| Online Preference | 5.60 (3.33) | 5.56 (3.35) | 0.696 (0.486) | 0.01 | 5.23 (3.15) | 5.73 (3.37) | 5.71 (3.43) | 27.99 (0.000) | 0.005 | a < b; a < c |
| Mood Regulation | 7.81 (4.48) | 8.39 (4.59) | 7.01 (0.001) | 0.13 | 7.19 (4.39) | 8.23 (4.58) | 8.75 (4.49) | 119.04 (0.000) | 0.019 | a < b < c |
| Negative Consequences | 4.55 (2.67) | 4.63 (2.76) | 1.61 (0.107) | 0.02 | 4.16 (2.39) | 4.63 (2.74) | 4.91 (2.88) | 77.20 (0.000) | 0.012 | a < b < c |
| Cognitive Preoccupation | 5.28 (3.15) | 5.85 (3.44) | 8.61 (0.000) | 0.17 | 4.92 (3.01) | 5.73 (3.35) | 5.96 (3.44) | 92.67 (0.000) | 0.015 | a < b < c |
| Compulsive Use | 6.28 (3.73) | 6.88 (4.04) | 7.26 (0.001) | 0.15 | 6.01 (3.69) | 6.69 (3.96) | 6.96 (3.95) | 61.31 (0.000) | 0.010 | a < b < c |

Note: Boys ($n$ = 6032); girls ($n$ = 6181); 11–13 years ($n$ = 4912), 14–15 years ($n$ = 4580); 16–18 years ($n$ = 2766), $t$ = Student's $t$; $p$ = significance; $d$ = Cohen's $d$; $F$ = Fishers $F$; $\eta^2$ = partial eta squared; Post hoc = Bonferroni's post hoc comparison.

**Table 2.** Fit of the 2–5 profile models based on the GPIUS2 dimensions.

| Profile | AIC | BIC | Sample Size Adjusted BIC | LL | $p$-Value for BLRTS | Entropy | $n$ Per Profile | | | | |
|---|---|---|---|---|---|---|---|---|---|---|---|
| | | | | | | | 1 | 2 | 3 | 4 | 5 |
| 2 | 153,323.079 | 153,441.738 | 153,390.891 | 76,645.540 | 0.001 | 0.98 | 9645 | 2640 | | | |
| 3 | 146,752.960 | 146,916.115 | 146,846.201 | 73,354.480 | 0.001 | 0.95 | 9383 | 3071 | 831 | | |
| **4** | **144,715.491** | **144,923.143** | **144,834.162** | **72,329.745** | **0.001** | **0.90** | **7107** | **2300** | **2277** | **609** | |
| 5 | 144,730.976 | 144,983.124 | 144,875.076 | 72,331.488 | 1.0 | 0.66 | - | - | - | - | - |

AIC = Akaike information criterion; BIC = Bayesian information criterion; LL = likelihood logarithm; BLRT = bootstrapped likelihood ratio test sequential. The selected model (four-profile model) is shown in boldface.

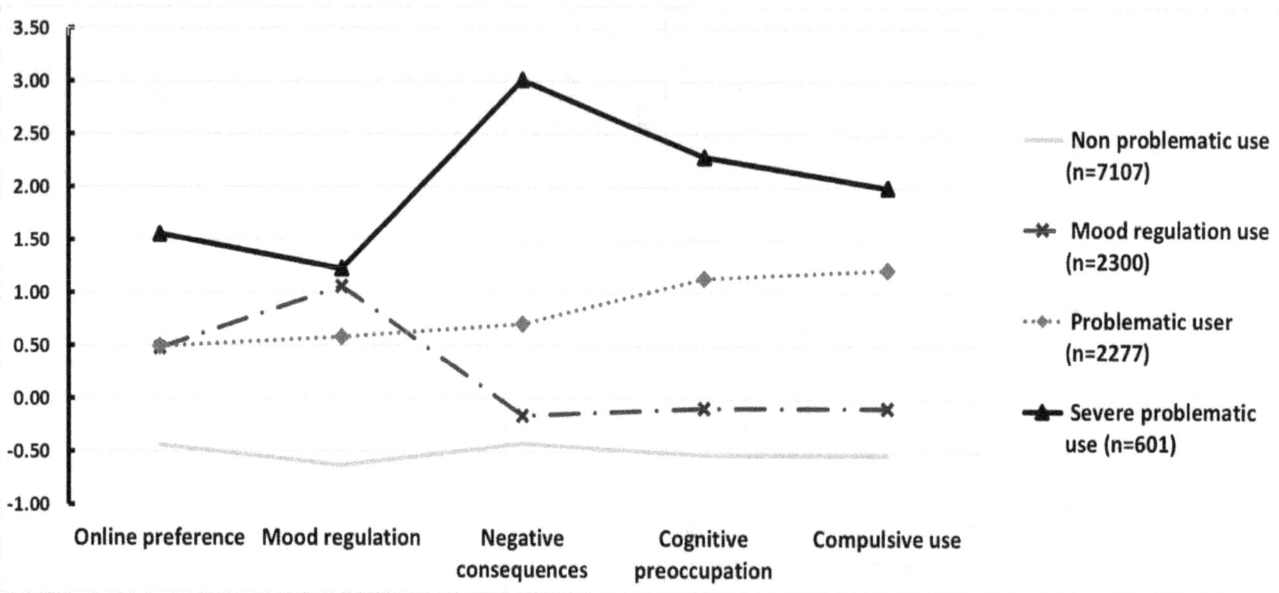


**Figure 1.** Profiles of problematic internet use (standardized scores).

**Table 3.** Differences in the dimensions of the GPIUS-2 as a function internet usage profile ($n$ = 12,258).

| GPIUS Profile | Online Preference | | Mood Regulation | | Negative Consequences | | Cognitive Preoccupation | | Compulsive Use | |
|---|---|---|---|---|---|---|---|---|---|---|
| | *M (SD)* | | *M (SD)* | | *M (SD)* | | *M (SD)* | | *M (SD)* | |
| No problem [a] | 4.10 | 1.84 | 5.22 | 2.51 | 3.43 | 1.02 | 3.81 | 1.35 | 4.52 | 2.15 |
| Mood regulation use [b] | 7.17 | 3.63 | 12.92 | 2.81 | 4.16 | 1.60 | 5.27 | 1.94 | 6.23 | 2.52 |
| Problematic use [c] | 7.22 | 3.49 | 10.74 | 3.96 | 6.50 | 2.45 | 9.34 | 2.80 | 11.33 | 2.65 |
| Severe problematic use [d] | 10.77 | 4.29 | 13.67 | 3.63 | 12.77 | 2.85 | 13.16 | 3.26 | 14.37 | 2.90 |
| *F (df)* $\eta^2$ | *F* (4,12281) = 1919.67 ***; $\eta^2$ = 0.319; | | *F* (4,12281) = 5646.19 ***; $\eta^2$ = 0.580; | | *F* (4,12281) = 7925.33 ***; $\eta^2$ = 0.648; | | *F* (4,12281) = 7952.08; $\eta^2$ = 0.660 ***; | | *F* (4,12281) = 7090.52 ***; $\eta^2$ = 0.634; | |
| Post hoc Bonferroni (Cohen's *d*) | a < b (1.27);<br>a < c (1.33);<br>a < d (3.12);<br>b < d (0.95);<br>c < d (0.97); | | a < b (2.98);<br>a < c (1.88);<br>a < d (3.23);<br>b > c (0.64);<br>b < d (0.25);<br>c < d (0.75); | | a < b (0.61);<br>a < c (2.05);<br>a < d (7.40);<br>b < c (1.10)<br>b < d (4.47);<br>c < d (2.40); | | a < b (0.80);<br>a < c (2.16);<br>a < d (3.74);<br>b < c (1.69);<br>b < d (3.46);<br>c < d (1.32); | | a < b (0.80);<br>a < c (2.16);<br>a < d (3.74);<br>b < c (1.69);<br>b < d (3.46);<br>c < d (1.32); | |

Note: M = arithmetic mean; SD = standard deviation; $p$ = significance; $F$ = Fishers $F$; df = degrees of freedom; $\eta^2$ = eta squared; *** = $p < 0.001$.

### *3.3. Relationship between GPIU and HRQoL*

Next, we examined the relation between the GPIU and HRQoL. The correlations between the five GPIUS2 dimensions and the five HRQoL dimensions, controlling age for both sexes, are presented in Table 5. In the sample as a whole, significant negative correlations were observed between the GPIUS2 dimensions and KIDSCREEN dimensions, with values ranging between $r = -0.101$ (cognitive preoccupation and peer relations) and $r = -0.334$ (mood regulation and psychological well-being). As can be seen in Table 5, the partial correlations were weaker than those obtained with the sample as a whole, particularly in the case of boys in the parents relations and autonomy dimension and online preference ($r = -0.069$), whereas girls obtained higher correlations between the School environment dimension and the five GPIUS2 dimensions.

**Table 4.** Sex and age distribution in the GPIU profiles.

| GPIU Profile | Male ($n$ = 6032) | Female ($n$ = 6181) | $\chi^2$ (3) | 11–13 years ($n$ = 3606) | 14–15 years ($n$ = 4516) | 16–17 years ($n$ = 4160) | $\chi^2$ (6) |
|---|---|---|---|---|---|---|---|
| | $f$ (%) [a] | $f$ (%) | | $f$ (%) [b] | $f$ (%) | $f$ (%) | |
| Non problematic use ($n$ = 7107) | 3643 (60.4) * | 3424 (55.4) ** | 42.96 (<0.001) | 2448 (67.90) * | 2503 (55.4) ** | 2156 (51.8) ** | 255.80 (<0.001) |
| Mood regulation use ($n$ = 2300) | 1123 (18.6) | 1167 (18.9) | | 541 (15.0) ** | 895 (19.8) * | 864 (20.8) * | |
| Problematic use ($n$ = 2277) | 1007 (16.7) ** | 1250 (20.2) * | | 495 (13.7) ** | 883 (19.5) * | 899 (21.6) * | |
| Severe problematic use ($n$ = 601) | 259 (4.3) ** | 272 (3.1) * | | 122 (3.4) ** | 236 (4.1) | 207 (5.8) * | |

Note: $f$ = frequency; % = percentage; $\chi^2$ (df); Chi Squared (degrees of freedom); [a] percentage indicated over each column (sex); [b] percentage indicated over each column (age group). * Adjusted standardized residuals > 1.96. ** Adjusted standardized residuals < −1.96.

**Table 5.** Partial correlations (controlling for age) between the GPIUS2 dimensions and the five KIDSCREEN-27 dimensions in boys and girls. Means and standard deviations are included for the study sample ($n$ = 12,285).

| | | 1. | 2. | 3. | 4. | 5. | 6. | 7. | 8. | 9. | 10. | $M$ ($SD$) | $\alpha$ | $\omega$ |
|---|---|---|---|---|---|---|---|---|---|---|---|---|---|---|
| GPIUS–2 Dimensions | 1. Online preference | — | 0.468 | 0.392 | 0.412 | 0.350 | −0.207 | −0.292 | −0.213 | −0.218 | −0.221 | 5.58 (3.34) | 0.85 | 0.85 |
| | 2. Mood regulation | 0.471 | — | 0.367 | 0.456 | 0.404 | −0.214 | −0.358 | −0.262 | −0.185 | −0.271 | 8.10 (4.54) | 0.82 | 0.83 |
| | 3. Negative consequences | 0.432 | 0.365 | — | 0.562 | 0.593 | −0.206 | −0.293 | −0.241 | −0.205 | −0.260 | 4.59 (2.71) | 0.76 | 0.77 |
| | 4. Cognitive preoccupation | 0.460 | 0.451 | 0.609 | — | 0.734 | −0.172 | −0.228 | −0.175 | −0.089 | −0.224 | 5.57 (3.31) | 0.79 | 0.79 |
| | 5. Compulsive use | 0.422 | 0.419 | 0.611 | 0.702 | — | −0.190 | −0.229 | −0.188 | −0.091 | −0.234 | 6.58 (3.90) | 0.82 | 0.84 |
| KIDSCREEN Dimensions | 6. Physical well–being | −0.183 | −0.144 | −0.169 | −0.132 | −0.175 | — | 0.453 | 0.376 | 0.321 | 0.415 | 49.14 (12.00) | 0.87 | 0.88 |
| | 7. Psychological well–being | −0.251 | −0.301 | −0.291 | −0.250 | −0.251 | 0.401 | — | 0.546 | 0.504 | 0.544 | 48.53 (10.13) | 0.86 | 0.86 |
| | 8. Parents relations and autonomy | −0.169 | −0.204 | −0.219 | −0.181 | −0.212 | 0.358 | 0.480 | — | 0.440 | 0.490 | 52.83 (10.91) | 0.84 | 0.84 |
| | 9. Social support and peers | −0.189 | −0.131 | −0.151 | −0.121 | −0.143 | 0.367 | 0.490 | 0.475 | — | 0.386 | 54.09 (10.34) | 0.85 | 0.85 |
| | 10. School environment | −0.150 | −0.183 | −0.202 | −0.179 | −0.207 | 0.299 | 0.425 | 0.459 | 0.373 | — | 49.73 (10.32) | 0.80 | 0.81 |

Note: The correlations for boys are shown below the diagonal, and for girls above it. All correlations were significant at the level $p < 0.001$. M = arithmetic mean; $SD$ = standard deviation; $\alpha$ = Cronbach's alpha; $\omega$ = McDonald's omega.

Then, ANOVAs were carried out to compare the scores in the five HRQoL dimensions as a function of the LPA profiles of PIU. The results can be seen in Table 6.

**Table 6.** Differences in the KIDSCREEN-27 dimensions as a function of the internet use profile ($n$ = 12,258).

| GPIU Profile | Phy-wb *M (SD)* | Psy-wb *M (SD)* | Pr&A *M (SD)* | SS&P *M (SD)* | SchEn *M (SD)* |
|---|---|---|---|---|---|
| No problem [a] | 51.30 (11.89) | 51.36 (9.89) | 55.19 (10.88) | 55.64 (10.15) | 52.02 (10.42) |
| Mood regulation use [b] | 47.51 (11.13) | 45.54 (8.90) | 50.54 (10.13) | 52.61 (9.87) | 47.66 (9.07) |
| Problematic use [c] | 45.76 (11.12) | 44.79 (8.69) | 49.28 (9.66) | 52.01 (10.04) | 46.32 (8.77) |
| Severe problematic use [d] | 42.61 (13.24) | 40.64 (9.46) | 47.24 (11.23) | 49.47 (11.95) | 43.51 (11.21) |
| *F(df)* $\eta^2$ | $F$ (3,12226) = 221.22 ***; $\eta^2$ = 0.051; | $F$ (3,12144) = 534.34 ***; $\eta^2$ = 0.117; | $F$ (3,12173) = 293.87 ***; $\eta^2$ = 0.068; | $F$ (3,12263) = 143.94 ***; $\eta^2$ = 0.034; | $F$ (3,12236) = 326.01 ***; $\eta^2$ = 0.074; |
| Post hoc Bonferroni *(Cohen's d)* | a > b (0.33); a > c (0.47); a > d (0.72); b > c (0.16); b > d (0.40); c > d (0.27); | a > b (0.62); a > c (0.71); a > d (1.10); b > d (0.53); c > d (0.46) | a > b (0.44); a > c (0.57); a > d (0.71); b > d (0.30); c > d (0.20) | a > b (0.30); a > c (0.36); a > d (0.60); b > d (0.31); c > d (0.25) | a > b (0.43); a > c (0.57); a > d (0.81); b > c (0.15); b > d (0.43); c > d (0.30) |

Note: Phy-wb = physical well-being; Psy-wb = psychological well-being; Pr&A = parents relations and autonomy; SS&P = social support and Peers; SchEn= school environment; M = arithmetic mean; SD = standard deviation; $p$ = significance; $F$ = Fisher's $F$; $\eta^2$ = eta squared. df = degrees of freedom; *** = $p < 0.001$.

### 3.4. *GPIUS-2 Cut-Off Point*

In order to create a cut-off point for the GPIUS2, a ROC curve analysis was performed. The result of this analysis showed an area under the curve (AUC) of 0.975, indicating a suitable potential of the GPIUS2 to discriminate between problematic and non-problematic internet users (see Figure

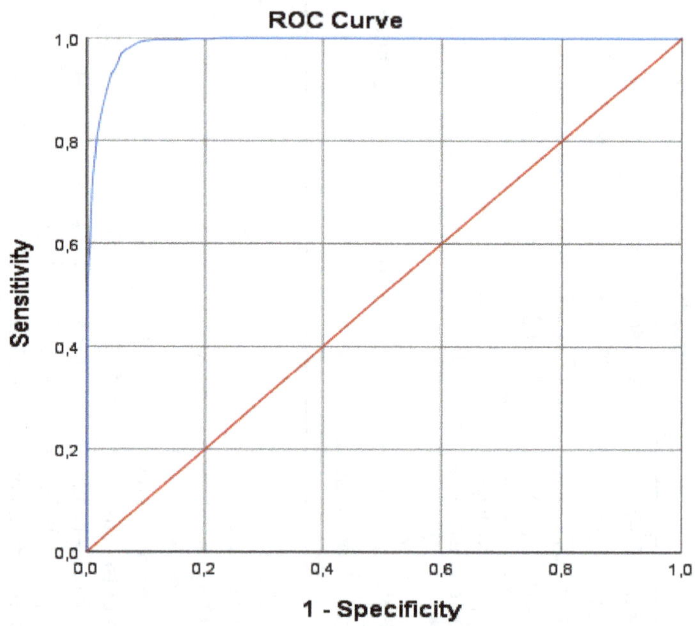


**Figure 2.** The receiver operating characteristic (ROC) curve of the Spanish version of GPIUS2.

Table 7 shows the sensitivity, specificity, PV+, PV−, and ACC of the GPIUS2 and its different cut-off points, calculated using the profile of "severe problematic users" as the gold standard. The analysis led to a number of possibilities based on the authors' decisions, in which a specific approach was prioritized due to the low prevalence of the problem and the primary interest of avoiding the generation of false positives. Hence, the value of 52 was proposed as a cut-off point to differentiate users with

PIU from those who do not have this problem. At this point, a specificity of 96% and a sensitivity of 93% were obtained. PV− was higher than 99%, so less than 1% of those who were not classified as problematic users were misdiagnosed. Finally, the ACC for the cut-off point 52 was 96%.

**Table 7.** Cut-off point for GPIUS-2 based on the "severe problematic users" profile obtained through LPA.

| Cut-Point | TP | TN | FP | FN | Sens. | Spec. | PV+ | PV− | ACC |
|---|---|---|---|---|---|---|---|---|---|
| 46 | 598 | 10,491 | 1193 | 3 | 99.50% | 89.79% | 33.39% | 99.97% | 90.26% |
| 47 | 596 | 10,654 | 1030 | 5 | 99.17% | 91.18% | 36.65% | 99.95% | 91.58% |
| 48 | 592 | 10,772 | 912 | 9 | 98.50% | 92.19% | 39.36% | 99.92% | 92.50% |
| 49 | 588 | 10,887 | 787 | 13 | 97.84% | 93.26% | 42.76% | 99.88% | 93.41% |
| 50 | 583 | 10,998 | 686 | 18 | 97.00% | 94.13% | 45.94% | 99.84% | 94.27% |
| 51 | 568 | 11,101 | 583 | 33 | 94.51% | 95.01% | 49.35% | 99.70% | 94.99% |
| 52 | 559 | 11,196 | 488 | 42 | 93.01% | 95.82% | 53.39% | 99.63% | 95.69% |
| 53 | 542 | 11,279 | 405 | 59 | 90.18% | 96.53% | 57.23% | 99.48% | 96.22% |
| 54 | 525 | 11,350 | 334 | 76 | 87.35% | 97.14% | 61.12% | 99.33% | 96.66% |
| 55 | 510 | 11,411 | 273 | 91 | 84.86% | 97.66% | 65.13% | 99.21% | 97.04% |
| 56 | 486 | 11,484 | 200 | 115 | 80.87% | 98.29% | 70.85% | 99.01% | 97.44% |
| 57 | 465 | 11,520 | 136 | 164 | 73.93% | 98.83% | 77.37% | 98.60% | 97.56% |

Note: TP = True Positive; TN = True Negative; FP = False Positive; FN = False Negative; Sens= Sensitivity; Spec= Specificity; PV+ = Positive Predictive Value; PV− = Negative Predictive Value; ACC = Accuracy.

## 4. Discussion

This paper contributes to our knowledge of adolescents' PIU and HRQoL. It also delves into a little-explored reality by analyzing differences in HRQoL as a function of the level of severity associated with PIU and it provides a cut-off point for a widely used tool in this topic.

Although it has used a conceptualization of PIU that considers it an artifact of relational and relationship-building resource deficits, the data obtained are consistent with those found in other studies. Approximately 5% of the study sample presented severe problems, which coincides with previous studies in the Spanish context [4,5,23,24]. If the problematic use and the severe problematic use profiles are considered jointly, the prevalence is about 23%, which is consistent with other studies in the national [25,26] or in European contexts [22]. In relation to sex and PIU, the data show that there are more problems in girls than in boys, as had been reported in previous studies [5,18,24,26,55]. However, this is a controversial issue, as other studies indicate the opposite [21,31]. Part of these differences may be due to the conceptualization of PIU, especially if the focus is on internet addiction or on specific problematic internet uses such as online gambling [18]. Another possible explanation is related to the evaluation of PIU in girls, particularly focused on the use of social media [55,67]. Boys generally present higher levels of other internet uses such as online video games [68]. The data also suggest that there is lower prevalence of problematic use during early adolescence (10–12 years), in line with other studies [26,52,55].

Various studies have linked the inappropriate use of the internet with psychological problems such as psychological stress and symptoms of mental disorders [38], behavioral problems, hyperactivity, impact on daily life activities, depression, and poor physical health [69]. Other authors have pointed out that inadequate use of the internet is related to low scores on the HRQoL, as well as to lower self-perceived social support and more friends known only through the internet [52,70]. In this same line, the data from this study provide evidence of the relationship between HRQoL and PIU, from the perspective of Caplan [9,11], which placed special emphasis on mood regulation through the internet and the preference for online relationships. However, the data are also convergent with other approaches [47,50–53]. The most important (inverse and significant) relationships were found between mood regulation and negative consequences and psychological well-being. The loss of psychological well-being in those adolescents with problematic use and, especially, with severe problematic use, is very acute (a bit more than one total standard deviation). These data confirm the first and second hypotheses (H1 significant and inverse relationships between PIU and HRQoL; and H2 the greater the level of PIU, especially if it is severe, the worse will be HRQoL) of the manuscript. It is possible that excess emotion regulation and online social preference are associated with high levels of emotional loneliness, which would influence psychological well-being [56].

LPA identified four subgroups, three of which were expected based on the literature [5,28,30]: non-problematic use, problematic use, and severe problematic use. However, a profile emerged that was called "mood regulator" which presents high scores in the dimension of mood regulation and online preference and low scores in the remaining dimensions. This is evidence of the interest in applying new statistical techniques to already established knowledge [66]. The characteristics of the "mood regulator" profile use match the theoretical model proposed by Caplan [9,11] but without problems due to negative consequences. As shown in the results, the impact on the KIDSCREEN-27 dimensions increases as the use of the internet becomes more problematic. Inspection of the affected dimensions in the mood regulator profile shows that this style could be prior to—or derive in—more problematic internet usage, depending on other factors such as connection time, gratifying experiences, and its influence in the academic-work, family, or social areas. In turn, these results are consistent with other studies that identify different types of users [28,30], although they consider additional variables. In particular, the no-problem group would be equivalent to the first steppers or sporadic groups, the group of mood regulator users could resemble the group of entertainment users, whereas the problematic user or severe problematic user profiles would be related to the heavy users or advanced user groups. This expands a future line of research, as prevention and intervention programs could focus on these profiles and analyze their evolution over time and through motives for change.

This work obtained a cut-off point (52), which represents a unique contribution to the literature. There are few works in this line that establish cut-off points to differentiate people with or without problems in internet contexts [25,68]. We sought a balance between all the indicators, while being especially cautious when making decisions because of the diagnostic implications that are associated with labeling [71,72]. Thus, a high level of specificity of the test prevailed, as a specific test is useful when it is positive, and this is especially important in problems with low prevalence, such as severe problematic use (about 5%). In similar vein, the chosen cut-off point has an especially high negative predictive value (99.6%), which means that almost 100% of the subjects who were classified as negative do not, in fact, have a severe problem. We chose this conservative usage to favor the diagnosis of clearly severe cases and to avoid over-diagnosis.

However, the study is not exempt from limitations. First, the results are based on self-reports with the entailed response bias. In the future, additional measures are proposed such as sociograms or parent/teacher/peer reports. This is a cross-sectional study, which does not allow establishing causal relationships between the study dimensions, so, in the future, studies should propose longitudinal designs. Although the sample is broad and representative of a Spanish region, we must be cautious when extrapolating the results to other cultural contexts. The cut-off point was not estimated by any external measure (e.g., another validated PIU screening tool and/or practitioner's diagnosis/judgement), although a similar methodology has been used elsewhere in the scientific literature [68]. Future studies will be necessary to re-examine these results and use other external measures. Although this is not a limitation in itself, it must be taken into account that PIU was conceptualized in a certain way, following the model of Caplan [9,11], not contemplating other theoretical formulations, and this makes the comparison of data with other studies more difficult. It is also possible that "mood regulating" users are more than entertainment users, as too much mood regulation through external activities may be linked to psychopathology, and this was not evaluated. We also note that a multilevel analysis could have been considered, taking into account the possible variability between classes and schools, but this was not possible because the data were not collected by classes, but only by schools due to the planning of the study with the educational authorities. It would also be advisable in the future to include other instruments, especially those with validations in many languages, to facilitate the comparison of results and to compare theoretical proposals of PIU. Constructs related to internet gaming disorder or online gambling could also be introduced as specific problems in order to analyze their influence on HRQoL and other constructs related to psychological well-being.

The study has several practical implications for professionals in the educational and clinical field. The GPIUS2 can be administered quickly as of 10 years of age and can provide an idea of whether or not the person presents problematic use problems. The evidence of more PIU in girls and in older adolescents reveals a reality that should be considered in order to adapt the different interventions in this problem. Likewise, the cut-off point reached in this study clearly establishes the score above which we can consider an adolescent to present PIU, with the practical, educational, and clinical implications that this entails. Also, the loss of HRQoL in adolescence without a medical cause may be associated with psychosocial problems such as those explored in this study and can be considered from the perspective of health professionals (pediatricians, psychologists, etc.). Similarly, prevention strategies and programs related to internet problems should increasingly focus on the problematic uses of the internet or even, as has been shown, its use as a mood-regulator. It is expected that adequate prevention will reduce these problems and help adolescents to make a healthier and more positive use of the internet.

## 5. Conclusions

Four internet profiles were found in terms of adolescent usage habits. There is a negative relationship between PIU and HRQoL. In particular, adolescents with severe PIU showed a greater impact on their HRQoL, although those who used the internet as a mood-regulator and those who presented problematic use also showed impaired HRQoL. In addition, the score of 52 in the GPIUS is proposed as a cut-off point to distinguish users with severe PIU.

**Author Contributions:** Conceptualization, J.M.M. and J.G.-C.; formal analysis, J.M.M. and J.G.-C.; funding acquisition, J.G.-C.; investigation, J.M.M., J.G.-C., J.O.-B., M.B.-F., A.Á.-B. and B.T.; methodology, J.M.M. and J.G.-C.; project administration, J.G.-C.; Resources, J.M.M., J.O.-B., M.B.-F., A.Á.-B. and B.T.; supervision, J.G.-C.; Validation, J.O.-B., M.B.-F., A.Á.-B. and B.T.; writing—original draft, J.M.M. and J.G.-C.; writing—review and editing, J.M.M., J.G.-C., J.O.-B. and M.B.-F.

**Acknowledgments:** We wish to thank the participating schools, their management teams, faculty and, especially, the students and their families for realizing the importance of the study. We are especially grateful to the "Dirección General de Ordenación Académica e Innovación Educativa (Consejería de Educación y Cultura del Principado de Asturias, España]).

## References

1. Subrahmanyam, K.; Smahel, D. Connecting Online Behavior to Adolescent Development: A Theoretical Framework. In *Digital Youth: The Role of Media in Development*; Springer-Verlag: New York, NY, USA, 2011; pp. 27–40. ISBN 978-1-4419-6277-5.
2. Lee, S.-Y.; Lee, D.; Nam, C.R.; Kim, D.Y.; Park, S.; Kwon, J.-G.; Kweon, Y.-S.; Lee, Y.; Kim, D.J.; Choi, J.-S. Distinct patterns of Internet and smartphone-related problems among adolescents by gender: Latent class analysis. *J. Behav. Addict.* **2018**, *7*, 454–465. [CrossRef] [PubMed]
3. Lenhart, A. *Teens, Social Media and Technology Overview 2015: Smartphones Facilitate Shifts in Communication Landscape for Teens*; Pew Research Center: Washington, DC, USA, 2015.
4. González-Cabrera, J.; Balea, A.; Vallina, M.; Moya, A.; Laviana, O. *Informe Ejecutivo del Proyecto CIBERASTUR [CYBERASTUR Project Executive Report]*; Educastur: Asturias, Spain, 2017.
5. Machimbarrena, J.M.; Calvete, E.; Fernández-González, L.; Álvarez-Bardón, A.; Álvarez-Fernández, L.; González-Cabrera, J. Internet Risks: An Overview of Victimization in Cyberbullying, Cyber Dating Abuse, Sexting, Online Grooming and Problematic Internet Use. *Int. J. Environ. Res. Public Health* **2018**, *15*, 2471. [CrossRef] [PubMed]
6. Villacampa, C.; Gómez, M. Nuevas tecnologías y victimización sexual de menores por online grooming [New technologies and sexual victimization of minors by online grooming]. *Rev. Electrónica Cienc. Penal y Criminol.* **2016**, *2*. Available online: http://criminet.ugr.es/recpc/18/recpc18-02.pdf (accessed on 12 October 2019).

7. American Psychiatric Association. *Diagnostic and Statistical Manual of Mental Disorders: DSM-5*; American Psychiatric Association: Philadelphia, PA, USA, 2013; ISBN 9780890425541.
8. Tokunaga, R.S.; Rains, S.A. A Review and Meta-Analysis Examining Conceptual and Operational Definitions of Problematic Internet Use. *Hum. Commun. Res.* **2016**, *42*, 165–199. [CrossRef]
9. Caplan, S. Theory and Measurement of Generalized Problematic Internet use: A Two-step Approach. *Comput. Hum. Behav.* **2010**, *26*, 1089–1097. [CrossRef]
10. Gámez-Guadix, M.; Orue, I.; Calvete, E. Evaluation of the Cognitive-behavioral Model of Generalized and Problematic Internet Use in Spanish adolescents. *Psicothema* **2013**, *25*, 299–306. [PubMed]
11. Caplan, S. Problematic Internet use and psychosocial well-being: Development of a theory-based cognitive–behavioral measurement instrument. *Comput. Hum. Behav.* **2002**, *18*, 553–575. [CrossRef]
12. Davis, R. A cognitive-behavioral model of pathological Internet use. *Comput. Hum. Behav.* **2001**, *17*, 187–195. [CrossRef]
13. Navarro, R.; Yubero, S. Impact of Social Anxiety, Social Skills and Cyberbullying on Online Communication. *Escritos Psicol./Psychol. Writ.* **2012**, *5*, 4–15. [CrossRef]
14. Davis, R.; Flett, G.; Besser, A. Validation of a New Scale for Measuring Problematic Internet Use: Implications for Pre-employment Screening. *Cyberpsychol. Behav.* **2002**, *5*, 331–345. [CrossRef]
15. Cheng, C.; Li, A.Y. Internet Addiction Prevalence and Quality of (Real) Life: A Meta-Analysis of 31 Nations Across Seven World Regions. *Cyberpsychol. Behav. Soc. Netw.* **2014**, *17*, 755–760. [CrossRef] [PubMed]
16. Kuss, D.J.; Van Rooij, A.J.; Shorter, G.W.; Griffiths, M.D.; Van De Mheen, D. Internet addiction in adolescents: Prevalence and risk factors. *Comput. Hum. Behav.* **2013**, *29*, 1987–1996. [CrossRef]
17. Müller, K.W.; Glaesmer, H.; Brähler, E.; Woelfling, K.; Beutel, M.E. Prevalence of internet addiction in the general population: Results from a German population-based survey. *Behav. Inf. Technol.* **2014**, *33*, 757–766. [CrossRef]
18. Lopez-Fernandez, O. Generalised Versus Specific Internet Use-Related Addiction Problems: A Mixed Methods Study on Internet, Gaming, and Social Networking Behaviours. *Int. J. Environ. Res. Public Health* **2018**, *15*, 2913. [CrossRef] [PubMed]
19. Tokunaga, R.S. A meta-analysis of the relationships between psychosocial problems and internet habits: Synthesizing internet addiction, problematic internet use, and deficient self-regulation research. *Commun. Monogr.* **2017**, *84*, 423–446. [CrossRef]
20. Cha, S.S.; Seo, B.K. Smartphone use and smartphone addiction in middle school students in Korea: Prevalence, social networking service, and game use. *Health Psychol. Open* **2018**, *5*. [CrossRef] [PubMed]
21. Durkee, T.; Kaess, M.; Carli, V.; Parzer, P.; Wasserman, C.; Floderus, B.; Apter, A.; Balazs, J.; Barzilay, S.; Bobes, J.; et al. Prevalence of pathological internet use among adolescents in Europe: Demographic and social factors. *Addiction* **2012**, *107*, 2210–2222. [CrossRef] [PubMed]
22. Laconi, S.; Kaliszewska-Czeremska, K.; Gnisci, A.; Sergi, I.; Barke, A.; Jeromin, F.; Groth, J.; Gámez-Guadix, M.; Ozcan, N.K.; Demetrovics, Z.; et al. Cross-cultural study of Problematic Internet Use in nine European countries. *Comput. Hum. Behav.* **2018**, *84*, 430–440. [CrossRef]
23. Carbonell, X.; Chamarro, A.; Griffiths, M.; Oberst, U.; Cladellas, R.; Talarn, A. Problematic Internet an Cellphones. *An. Psicol.* **2012**, *28*, 789–796.
24. Yudes-Gómez, C.; Baridon-Chauvie, D.; González-Cabrera, J.-M. Cyberbullying and Problematic Internet Use in Colombia, Uruguay and Spain: Cross-cultural Study. *Comunicar* **2018**, *26*, 49–58. [CrossRef]
25. Gómez, P.; Rial, A.; Braña, T.; Varela, J.; Barreiro, C. Evaluation and early detection of problematic Internet use in adolescents. *Psicothema* **2014**, *26*, 21–26.
26. Gómez, P.; Rial, A.; Braña, T.; Golpe, S.; Varela, J. Screening of Problematic Internet Use Among Spanish Adolescents: Prevalence and Related Variables. *Cyberpsychol. Behav. Soc. Netw.* **2017**, *20*, 259–267. [CrossRef] [PubMed]
27. Hill, W.W.; Beatty, S.E.; Walsh, G. A segmentation of adolescent online users and shoppers. *J. Serv. Mark.* **2013**, *27*, 347–360. [CrossRef]
28. Brandtzæg, P.B. Towards a unified Media-User Typology (MUT): A meta-analysis and review of the research literature on media-user typologies. *Comput. Hum. Behav.* **2010**, *26*, 940–956. [CrossRef]

29. Gómez, P.; Harris, S.K.; Barreiro, C.; Isorna, M.; Rial, A. Profiles of Internet use and parental involvement, and rates of online risks and problematic Internet use among Spanish adolescents. *Comput. Hum. Behav.* **2017**, *75*, 826–833. [CrossRef]
30. Rial, A.; Gómez, P.; Picón, E.; Braña, T.; Varela, J. Identification and Characterization of Adolescent Internet User's Profiles. *Span. J. Psychol.* **2015**, *18*, E50. [CrossRef]
31. Munno, D.; Cappellin, F.; Saroldi, M.; Bechon, E.; Guglielmucci, F.; Passera, R.; Zullo, G. Internet Addiction Disorder: Personality characteristics and risk of pathological overuse in adolescents. *Psychiatry Res.* **2017**, *248*, 1–5. [CrossRef]
32. Carbonell, X.; Chamarro, A.; Oberst, U.; Rodrigo, B.; Prades, M. Problematic Use of the Internet and Smartphones in University Students: 2006–2017. *Int. J. Environ. Res. Public Health* **2018**, *15*, 475. [CrossRef]
33. Cerniglia, L.; Zoratto, F.; Cimino, S.; Laviola, G.; Ammaniti, M.; Adriani, W. Internet Addiction in adolescence: Neurobiological, psychosocial and clinical issues. *Neurosci. Biobehav. Rev.* **2017**, *76*, 174–184. [CrossRef]
34. Muñoz-Rivas, M.J.; Fernández, L.; Gámez-Guadix, M. Analysis of the indicators of pathological internet use in spanish university students. *Span. J. Psychol.* **2010**, *13*, 697–707. [CrossRef]
35. Martínez-Ferrer, B.; Moreno, D.; Musitu, G. Are adolescents engaged in the problematic use of social networking sites more involved in peer aggression and victimization? *Front. Psychol.* **2018**, *9*, 801. [CrossRef] [PubMed]
36. Rial, A.; Gómez, P.; Isorna, M.; Araujo, M.; Varela, J. PIUS-a: Problematic Internet Use Scale in adolescents. Development and psychometric validation. *Adicciones* **2016**, *27*, 47.
37. Ceyhan, E.; Ceyhan, A.A.; Gürcan, A. The Validity and Reliability of the Problematic Internet Usage Scale. *Educ. Sci. Theory Pract.* **2007**, *7*, 411–416.
38. Beranuy-Fargues, M.; Chamarro, A.; Graner, C.; Carbonell, X. Validation of two brief scales for Internet addiction and mobile phone problem use. *Psicothema* **2009**, *21*, 480–485. [PubMed]
39. Jenaro, C.; Flores, N.; Gómez-Vela, M.; González-Gil, F.; Caballo, C. Problematic internet and cell-phone use: Psychological, behavioral, and health correlates. *Addict. Res. Theory* **2007**, *15*, 309–320. [CrossRef]
40. Wallander, J.L.; Koot, H.M. Quality of life in children: A critical examination of concepts, approaches, issues, and future directions. *Clin. Psychol. Rev.* **2016**, *45*, 131–143. [CrossRef]
41. The Kidscreen Group Europe. *The KIDSCREEN Questionnaires—Quality of Life Questionnaires for Children and Adolescents. Handbook*; Pabst Science Publishers: Lengerich, Germany, 2006; ISBN 9783899673340.
42. Ravens-Sieberer, U.; Gosch, A.; Rajmil, L.; Erhart, M.; Bruil, J.; Power, M.; Duer, W.; Auquier, P.; Cloetta, B.; Czemy, L.; et al. The KIDSCREEN-52 Quality of Life Measure for Children and Adolescents: Psychometric Results from a Cross-Cultural Survey in 13 European Countries. *Value Health* **2008**, *11*, 645–658. [CrossRef]
43. Lin, X.J.; Lin, I.M.; Fan, S.Y. Methodological issues in measuring health-related quality of life. *Tzu Chi Med. J.* **2013**, *25*, 8–12. [CrossRef]
44. Vélez Galárraga, R.; López Aguilà, S.; Rajmil, L. Gender and self-perceived health in childhood and adolescence in Spain. *Gac. Sanit.* **2009**, *23*, 433–439. [CrossRef]
45. da Silva-Júnior, I.F.; Hartwig, A.D.; Demarco, G.T.; Stüermer, V.M.; Scobernatti, G.; Goettems, M.L.; Azevedo, M.S. Health-related quality of life of maltreated children and adolescents who attended a service center in Brazil. *Qual. Life Res.* **2018**, *27*, 2157–2164. [CrossRef]
46. Hidalgo-Rasmussen, C.; Molina, T.; Molina, R.; Sepúlveda, R.; Martínez, V.; Montaño, R.; González, E.; George, M. Influence of bullying on the quality of life perception of Chilean students. *Rev. Med. Chil.* **2015**, *143*, 716–723. [CrossRef] [PubMed]
47. González-Cabrera, J.; León-Mejía, A.; Beranuy-Fargues, M.; Gutiérrez-Ortega, M.; Alvarez-Bardón, A.; Machimbarrena, J.M. Relationship between cyberbullying and health-related quality of life in a sample of children and adolescents. *Qual. Life Res.* **2018**, *27*, 2609–2618. [CrossRef] [PubMed]
48. Shaw, L.H.; Gant, L.M. In defense of the internet: The relationship between internet communication and depression, loneliness, self-esteem, and perceived social support. *Cyberpsychol. Behav.* **2002**, *5*, 157–171. [CrossRef] [PubMed]
49. Valkenburg, P.M.; Peter, J.; Schouten, A.P. Friend networking sites and their relationship to adolescents' well-being and social self-esteem. *Cyberpsychol. Behav.* **2006**, *9*, 584–590. [CrossRef] [PubMed]

50. Cao, H.; Sun, Y.; Wan, Y.; Hao, J.; Tao, F. Problematic Internet use in Chinese adolescents and its relation to psychosomatic symptoms and life satisfaction. *BMC Public Health* **2011**, *11*, 802. [CrossRef] [PubMed]
51. Mei, S.; Yau, Y.H.C.; Chai, J.; Guo, J.; Potenza, M.N. Problematic Internet use, well-being, self-esteem and self-control: Data from a high-school survey in China. *Addict. Behav.* **2016**, *61*, 74–79. [CrossRef] [PubMed]
52. Takahashi, M.; Adachi, M.; Nishimura, T.; Hirota, T.; Yasuda, S.; Kuribayashi, M.; Nakamura, K. Prevalence of pathological and maladaptive Internet use and the association with depression and health-related quality of life in Japanese elementary and junior high school-aged children. *Soc. Psychiatry Psychiatr. Epidemiol.* **2018**, *53*, 1349–1359. [CrossRef]
53. Vadher, S.B.; Panchal, B.N.; Vala, A.U.; Ratnani, I.J.; Vasava, K.J.; Desai, R.S.; Shah, A.H. Predictors of problematic Internet use in school going adolescents of Bhavnagar, India. *Int. J. Soc. Psychiatry* **2019**, *65*, 151–157. [CrossRef]
54. Tran, B.X.; Huong, L.T.; Hinh, N.D.; Nguyen, L.H.; Le, B.N.; Nong, V.M.; Thuc, V.T.M.; Tho, T.D.; Latkin, C.; Zhang, M.W.; et al. A study on the influence of internet addiction and online interpersonal influences on health-related quality of life in young Vietnamese. *BMC Public Health* **2017**, *17*, 138. [CrossRef]
55. Devine, P.; Lloyd, K. Internet Use and Psychological Well-being among 10-year-old and 11-year-old Children. *Child Care Pract.* **2012**, *18*, 5–22. [CrossRef]
56. Costa, R.M.; Patrão, I.; Machado, M. Problematic internet use and feelings of loneliness. *Int. J. Psychiatry Clin. Pract.* **2019**, *23*, 160–162. [CrossRef] [PubMed]
57. González-Cabrera, J.; Pérez-Sancho, C.; Calvete, E. Diseño y validación de la "Escala de inteligencia emocional en internet" (EIEI) para adolescentes. *Behav. Psychol./Psicol. Conduct.* **2016**, *24*, 93–105.
58. Zhang, S.; Tian, Y.; Sui, Y.; Zhang, D.; Shi, J.; Wang, P.; Meng, W.; Si, Y. Relationships between social support, loneliness, and internet addiction in Chinese postsecondary students: A longitudinal cross-lagged analysis. *Front. Psychol.* **2018**, *9*, 1707. [CrossRef] [PubMed]
59. Yao, M.Z.; Zhong, Z.J. Loneliness, social contacts and Internet addiction: A cross-lagged panel study. *Comput. Hum. Behav.* **2014**, *30*, 164–170. [CrossRef]
60. IBM Corp. *Statistical Package for the Social Sciences for Windows*; IBM Corp: Armonk, NY, USA, 2015.
61. R Core Team. *R: A Language and Environment for Statistical Computing*; R Foundation for Statistical Computing: Vienna, Austria, 2015.
62. Revelle, W. *Psych: Procedures for Personality and Psychological Research*; Northwestern University: Evanston, IL, USA, 2018.
63. Scrucca, L.; Fop, M.; Murphy, T.B.; Raftery, A.E. mclust 5: Clustering, classification and density estimation using Gaussian finite mixture models. *R J.* **2016**, *8*, 205–233. [CrossRef]
64. Cronbach, L.J. Coefficient alpha and the internal structure of tests. *Psychometrika* **1951**, *16*, 297–334. [CrossRef]
65. McDonald, R.P. *Test Theory: A Unified Treatment*; Lawrence Erlbaum Associates Publishers: Mahwah, NJ, USA, 1999; ISBN 0-8058-3075-8.
66. Zyphur, M.J. When Mindsets Collide: Switching Analytical Mindsets to Advance Organization Science. *Acad. Manag. Rev.* **2017**, *34*, 677–688.
67. Montag, C.; Bey, K.; Sha, P.; Li, M.; Chen, Y.F.; Liu, W.Y.; Zhu, Y.K.; Li, C.B.; Markett, S.; Keiper, J.; et al. Is it meaningful to distinguish between generalized and specific Internet addiction? Evidence from a cross-cultural study from Germany, Sweden, Taiwan and China. *Asia-Pac. Psychiatry* **2015**, *7*, 20–26. [CrossRef]
68. Fuster, H.; Carbonell, X.; Pontes, H.M.; Griffiths, M.D. Spanish validation of the Internet Gaming Disorder-20 (IGD-20) Test. *Comput. Hum. Behav.* **2016**, *56*, 215–224. [CrossRef]
69. El Asam, A.; Samara, M.; Terry, P. Problematic internet use and mental health among British children and adolescents. *Addict. Behav.* **2019**, *90*, 428–436. [CrossRef]
70. Barayan, S.S.; Al Dabal, B.K.; Abdelwahab, M.M.; Shafey, M.M.; Al Omar, R.S. Health-related quality of life among female university students in Dammam district: Is Internet use related? *J. Fam. Community Med.* **2018**, *25*, 20–28.

71. Echeburúa, E.; Salaberría, K.; Cruz-Sáez, M. Aportaciones y limitaciones del DSM-5 desde la Psicología Clínica [Contributions and limitations of DSM-5 from Clinical Psychology]. *Ter. Psicol.* **2014**, *32*, 65–74. [CrossRef]
72. Frances, A. The past, present and future of psychiatric diagnosis. *World Psychiatry* **2013**, *12*, 111–112. [CrossRef] [PubMed]

# 2

# Personal Factors, Internet Characteristics, and Environmental Factors Contributing to Adolescent Internet Addiction: A Public Health Perspective

**Sulki Chung [1,*], Jaekyoung Lee [2] and Hae Kook Lee [3]**

1 Department of Social Welfare, Chung-Ang University, Seoul 06974, Korea
2 Korea Center on Gambling Problems, Research and Development Team, Seoul 04554, Korea; jklee@kcgp.or.kr
3 Uijeongbu St. Mary's Hospital, The Catholic University of Korea, Uijeongbu-si 11765, Korea; nplhk@catholic.ac.kr
* Correspondence: chungs@cau.ac.kr

**Abstract:** Individual characteristics, family- and school-related variables, and environmental variables have equal importance in understanding Internet addiction. Most previous studies on Internet addiction have focused on individual factors; those that considered environmental influence typically only examined the proximal environment. Effective prevention and intervention of Internet addiction require a framework that integrates individual- and environmental-level factors. This study examined the relationships between personal factors, family/school factors, perceived Internet characteristics, and environmental variables as they contribute to Internet addiction among adolescents based on the public health model. A representative sample of 1628 junior high school students from 56 regions in Seoul and Gyeonggi-do participated in the study via questionnaires with the cooperation of the Ministry of Health and Welfare and the district office of education. The study analyzed psychological factors, family cohesion, attitudes toward academic activities, Internet characteristics, accessibility to PC cafés, and exposure to Internet game advertising. About 6% of the adolescents were categorized as being in the severely addicted group. Between-group comparisons showed that the addicted group had started using the Internet earlier; had higher levels of depression, compulsivity, and aggressiveness as well as lower family cohesion; and reported higher accessibility to PC cafés and exposure to Internet game advertising. Multiple logistic regression indicated that for adolescents, environmental factors had a greater influence than family or school-related factors. Policy implications for prevention and intervention are discussed.

**Keywords:** Internet addiction; public health model; Internet game advertising; accessibility; environmental factors

---

## 1. Introduction

As Internet usage has rapidly increased, it has become a part of our lives and is both a medium for providing a wealth of information and an important tool for connecting with others around the globe [1]. The advent of smartphones and easy access to the Internet have brought about many advantages. However, many people have developed concerns about such ease of access and social networking, particularly for adolescents; one concern is Internet addiction. Although not a formal diagnosis, Internet addiction is becoming widely accepted as a problem that may require professional treatment [2]. There is a lack of consensus regarding the definition of Internet addiction, and the term has been used in different studies with different connotations. In general, Internet addiction is defined as excessive use of the Internet accompanied by withdrawal, tolerance, and negative repercussions [3]. For consistency reasons, we utilize the term Internet addiction throughout this paper to represent a pathological state that occurs due to Internet overuse. A school-based survey for 9th and 10th grade students in seven European countries (Greece, Spain, Poland, Germany, Romania, the Netherlands, and Iceland) revealed that 0.8% to 1.7% of the students were suspected to have Internet addiction using Young's Internet addiction test [4]. A meta-analysis that reviewed studies from 31 nations reported that the global occurrence of Internet addiction was estimated at 6% [5]. However, higher estimates of the problem have been reported in Korea. Reportedly, almost 100% of South Korean adolescents are Internet users [6], and Internet addiction is a serious public health issue among Korean adolescents [7,8]. According to a national survey, adolescents had the highest proportion of high-risk Internet dependence (13.1%), followed by adults (5.8%), and then children (5.0%) [9]. Survey results from different countries also reported that adolescents as a group are the most vulnerable to Internet addiction [10]. Children and adolescents, having grown up in the digital technology era, have been familiar with digital devices and the Internet from an early age. A typical 15-year-old in 2015 would have been using the Internet since age 10 and the hours spent on the Internet is noticeably increasing among Organization for Economic Co-operation and Development countries [11]. Research studies in addiction have indicated that exposure to substance use at an earlier age increases the risk for addiction and risky behaviors later in life [12,13]. This can also be said for Internet use at an early age, and there is a concern that early access to electronic devices could lead to escalated risks for addiction [14]. Also of importance is the contents of the Internet. Different contents of the Internet affect young people to engage in overuse of the Internet. For instance, Greenfield [15] suggests that the most addictive aspects of the Internet are sexual content and computer gaming. Although these content areas are not limited to the Internet, when these are accessed using the Internet, the addictive potential of the contents are known to be amplified. A recent study also reported that people who frequently engage in web surfing experience the same psychological effects as those who are hooked on gambling [16].

Mental health experts believe that Internet addiction may manifest the same troubling effects as substance abuse or gambling disorders [17]. Internet addiction has been associated with various physical and psychological problems, and Internet addiction mostly manifests in adolescents as social withdrawal, loneliness, low motivation, and low educational performance [18].

Many studies have been conducted to identify the factors associated with Internet addiction. Of these, a number of studies have documented personal risk factors, typically psychological factors. These include depression [18–21], anxiety [20,21], aggression [22], impulsivity [23], and low self-esteem [21,24]. Among many personal risk factors of Internet addiction, depression, aggression, and impulsivity are of particular interest due to their association with other clinical subtypes. Depression is related to emotional vulnerability or internalizing problems, and aggression and impulsivity are related to externalizing problems such as attention deficit hyperactivity disorder, which are both known to increase the risk for Internet addiction [25]. There is strong evidence that individuals with higher levels of depression are more vulnerable to developing Internet addiction [19,26–29]. A recent longitudinal study also confirmed that depression is a positive predictor of adolescent Internet addiction [30]. Some studies have identified aggression as a predictor of Internet addiction. In a cross-sectional study of Lebanese adolescents, higher levels of aggression were associated with a higher level of Internet addiction [27]. A similar pattern was witnessed for young people in Taiwan and Korea [22,31]. Impulsivity is another psychological trait that is positively associated with Internet addiction. Several studies have discussed the correlation between high impulsivity and Internet addiction among adolescents [32,33], and a similar finding was reported among young people with internet gaming disorder [34].

Some studies addressed the extent to which interpersonal variables contribute to Internet addiction. They sought to explain Internet addiction in terms of interpersonal difficulties, and confirmed the role of family- and school-related variables in relation to Internet addiction among adolescents. For instance, conflict with parents, family functioning, and family resilience have been identified to influence Internet addiction [35–37]. School-related variables such as teacher's support and attitude toward school life are also associated with young people's Internet addiction. This is especially true for Korean adolescents, where there is enormous pressure for high academic achievement [38].

Another set of factors that has received relatively less attention is related to the characteristics of the Internet and its influence on addictive behavior. Few studies explicate Internet addiction by understanding what factors of the Internet enhance or reduce a user's excessive form of use. Several researchers have discussed the seductive and gratifying properties specific to the Internet that attract users [39–41]. They claim that certain properties of the Internet are associated with an elevated risk for Internet addiction. For instance, Turkle [42] isolated two dimensions of the Internet that are seductive to the Net generation: the pleasure of control and the perceived fluidity of identity [41]. Several other seductive factors were identified such as self-presentation, diversion, relationship building, and virtual community to name a few [40,41].

Most existing literature on Internet addiction has focused on individual and psychological factors and the proximal environment such as family and peer groups. Extensive meta-analysis or systematic review studies on risk factors of Internet addiction focused mainly on intrapersonal or interpersonal variables [10,31,43], and social environmental factors have received relatively less attention. The studies that have explored environmental factors mostly focused on the proximal environment such as family- and school-related variables [36,38,44]. Only a few studies examined social factors or larger environmental variables (such as exposure to advertisements and accessibility) as they contribute to Internet addiction among young people [45–47]. For instance, in alcohol-related research, factors such as availability of alcohol and exposure to alcohol are known environmental factors that influence young people's drinking behavior [48,49]. It is not difficult to assume that availability and accessibility to the Internet may also affect Internet addiction. However, such factors were infrequently explored in Internet addiction research [46]. Internet addiction is a broader concept that encompasses Internet game addiction. Although this study focuses on Internet addiction in general, we believe that examining the influence of Internet game advertisements as an environmental factor is legitimate given that a large part of Korean adolescents' Internet use is allocated to playing online games [9].

As discussed above, personal variables, family- and school-related variables, characteristics of the Internet, and environmental variables all contribute to the risk of Internet addiction. Effective prevention and intervention of Internet addiction requires a framework that integrates individual- and environmental-level factors. This is well reflected in the public health model or the epidemiologic triangle based on the public health perspective. Originally designed as a model for infectious disease, the public health model considers three areas of causes in understanding and intervening with any health problems [50,51]. One is the external agent that may contain certain destructive potential. Second is the host, who has individual susceptibility. The last factor is the environment that promotes or discourages certain health-related behavior. Applying the model to Internet addiction, the model focuses on the importance of the host (individual characteristics), agent (characteristics of the Internet), and the environment (i.e., social influence and accessibility) in the manifestation of Internet addiction. The public health model posits that any health problem is a result of the interactions among the three factors. Therefore, the development of effective public health measures for prevention and intervention usually requires assessment of all three components and their interactions [51]. To date, few studies have examined Internet addiction from a public health perspective. An awareness of the influence of these three factors may have a significant impact on intervention, prevention, and policy efforts.

The aim of the current study is to fill the gap in addiction literature by examining Internet addiction among adolescents based on a public health framework. Specifically, the study will explore the relationship among individual variables, family/school variables, the Internet characteristics, and environmental factors as they contribute to Internet addiction. The goal is to identify factors that are more influential when all areas are considered within the framework. To achieve this goal, the study utilizes the Internet addiction test (IAT) developed by Young [52,53]. The IAT has been used extensively in many studies to assess Internet addiction in both the clinical and research fields [54]. It has also been used to identify risk factors [31,43]. However, it should be noted that the IAT is not a diagnostic tool and that categorizing addiction based on the IAT does not define a clinical diagnosis.

The following research questions will be addressed using a representative community sample: (1) Are there any differences between the addict and the non-addict group in regard to psychological factors, family- and school-related factors, perceived Internet characteristics, and environmental factors? (2) Which factors that reflect the agent, host, and environment in a public health model are more important than others in predicting Internet addiction?

## 2. Materials and Methods

### 2.1. Participants

This study utilized a community-based cross-sectional survey. The survey subjects were junior-high-school students who reported the highest risk of Internet addiction in Korea [9]. A representative sample of 1871 middle (junior-high) school students participated in the study. We randomly selected one school from each of the 56 regions in Seoul and Gyeonggi-do that represented both urban and rural districts. Coeducational schools were selected to ensure equal allocation of genders. All students in one randomly selected classroom from each school were asked to participate in the survey between 1 December and 27 December 2015. Questionnaires were mailed to schools with cooperation from the Ministry of Health and Welfare and the district office of education. The study received approval from the Institutional Review Board. Only students who signed the informed consent participated in the survey. Of the 1871 students who responded to the questionnaire, 1628 were included in the analysis after excluding 243 that had at least one missing value in demographic and Internet use behavior variables. Of the 1628 participants, 52.0% ($n = 847$) were male and 47.0% ($n = 781$) were female, and the mean age was 14.9 ($SD = 0.34$).

### 2.2. Measures

#### 2.2.1. Internet Addiction

Young's 20-item Internet addiction test was used to measure Internet addiction [52]. Each item was measured on a five-point Likert scale. Responses for each item were added to obtain a final score. Many years after the initial development of the IAT, Young proposed a new cut-off point [53]. People who score more than 50 on the IAT are thought to be experiencing frequent problems because of Internet use. For those who score above 80, Internet use is thought to be causing significant problems with their lives. Because the purpose of this study is to examine risk factors associated with the higher risk of Internet addiction, we used the addiction category based on the IAT rather than the overall score. Young proposed four groups of Internet addiction: normal range: 0–30; mild: 31–49; moderate: 50–79; and severe: 80–100. In order to focus on more severe cases, the normal range and mild addiction (low risk) group were combined into one group. Therefore, respondents were categorized into three groups: normal use: 0–49; moderate addiction: 50–79; and severe addiction: 80–100. The IAT in this study held a good internal consistency with a Cronbach's alpha ($\propto$) of 0.94.

#### 2.2.2. Psychological Variables

The tool used in the study was developed and validated by the National Information Society Agency to identify Internet addiction and coexisting disorders in a national survey on Internet addiction [55]. Each scale consisted of eight questions measured on a four-point Likert scale ranging from one (not at all) to four (very often). Scores were summed for each of the three features with a higher score reflecting a greater degree of impulsivity (e.g., "act on spur of the moment"), depression (e.g., "feeling hopeless"), and aggressiveness (e.g., "have trouble controlling temper"). All three measures possessed good internal consistency (the Cronbach's alpha was 0.86 for impulsivity, 0.91 for depression, and 0.91 for aggressiveness).

#### 2.2.3. Family and School Factors

The Family Cohesion and Adaptability Evaluation Scales (FACES III) was used to measure family relationship. This scale was originally developed by Olson and colleagues [56], and a Korean version of the scale [57] was utilized in the current study. The family cohesion scale in the FACES III consists of ten questions on a five-point Likert scale that measure emotional ties, family support, time spent together, and interest in leisure time with family. Higher scores reflect higher family cohesion, and the Cronbach's alpha (∝) was 0.96.

A school adaptation scale developed for Korean students [58] was employed to examine school-related factors. The scale evaluates the degree of adaptation to the school environment, which includes questions about the relationship with teachers, the relationship with schoolmates, attitude toward academic activities, and school participation. The tool consists of four subscales and 14 questions on a five-point Likert scale. Higher total scores indicate a positive assessment of school life. The Cronbach's alpha (∝) for the subscales were acceptable: 0.94 for relationship with teachers, 0.90 for relationship with schoolmates, 0.62 for attitude toward academic activities, and 0.61 for school participation.

#### 2.2.4. Perceived Internet Characteristics

The agent characteristics in the public health model refer to the traits of the medium in relation to a given problem. In this study, Internet characteristics are defined as the properties of the Internet perceived by individuals in relation to Internet use. Perceived Internet characteristics were measured by the Internet characteristics scale developed by Chung et al. [59] that was designed to identify the characteristics of the Internet perceived by adolescents. It consists of eight factors with 27 items including entertainment, interpersonal relationship, accessibility, profitability, anonymity, immersion, competition, and escape. Based on a previous study that identified three factors to predict young people's Internet addiction [59], our study included three factors as perceived Internet characteristics: namely, interpersonal relationship (four items; e.g., "the Internet provides opportunities to meet with diverse people"), anonymity (four items; e.g., "People can attract attention without revealing themselves"), and entertainment/pleasure (five items; e.g., "the Internet provides entertainment"). Each item was measured using a five-point Likert scale, from strongly disagree to strongly agree. The interpersonal relationship characteristic of the Internet refers to the perception of the Internet as grounds for building relationships; anonymity refers to the perception of the Internet as a site where people can act freely without identifying themselves; entertainment refers to the perception that the Internet provides fun and excitement. The measures for interpersonal relationships, anonymity, and entertainment showed good internal consistency (∝ = 0.85, 0.86, and 0.87, respectively).

#### 2.2.5. Environmental Factors

Social environmental factors consisted of accessibility to PC cafés and exposure to Internet game advertisements. Previous studies have identified access to PC cafés as a risk factor for Internet addiction among Korean adolescents [47]. PC cafés, a unique feature in Korea, are well-equipped with advanced computers and are optimized for playing Internet games, which attracts many young people. We measured the accessibility to PC cafés using the scale reconstructed by Nam and Lee [60] that consists of a three-item (i.e., There is a nearby PC café for Internet use; I have easy access to PC cafés; there are many PC cafés near my home or school) five-point Likert scale. A higher total score indicated higher accessibility to PC cafés. The Cronbach's alpha (∝) was 0.85.

We also included exposure to Internet game advertisements as a major environmental factor. Exposure to Internet game advertisements consists of exposure and acceptability. To our understanding, there is no known instrument with which to measure exposure to Internet game advertisements. We used the tool that examined exposure to alcohol advertisements [61,62], except we restructured it to fit Internet game advertisement exposure. Two questions about respondent's exposure to Internet game advertisements (i.e., How often do you see Internet game advertisements? In the past month, how often did you see Internet game advertisements in the medium that you frequently use?) and the frequency of exposure were measured on a four-point Likert scale. The Cronbach's alpha (∝) was 0.88.

The advertisement acceptability questions used to determine alcohol use among youths were adopted for the current study [62,63]. However, for the purposes of our study, the questions were modified to assess the acceptability of Internet game advertisements. Two questions were asked: the number of game ads they had seen in various media over the past month and the number of memorable ads that they remember.

### 2.3. Statistical Analysis

To verify the differences between sociodemographic characteristics according to Internet use, a chi-square test ($\chi^2$) was performed. Between-group comparisons of the variables based on the public health model according to the presence of Internet addiction were analyzed using analysis of variance. A logistic regression analysis was utilized to identify the factors associated with Internet addiction. All statistical analyses were performed using SPSS version 20.0 (IBM Corp. Released, Armonk, NY, USA).

## 3. Results

### 3.1. Sociodemographic Characteristics

Adolescents' demographic profiles were assessed using four survey items, namely gender, residing region, living with parents, and parents' working status (Table 1). Based on the Internet addiction test cut-off scores, 455 (27.9%) were identified as normal Internet users, 1067 (65.5%) belonged to the moderate-addiction or addiction-risk group, and 106 (6.5%) belonged to the severe addiction group. The group differences according to sociodemographic characteristics showed that 6.6% male and 6.4% female students were in the addiction group, and 66.7% male and 64.3% female students were deemed at risk for addiction (moderate addiction). There were no significant differences between three groups in regard to sociodemographic characteristics.

**Table 1.** Sociodemographic characteristics ($N$ = 1628).

| | | $n$ (%)/mean | Internet Addiction | | | $\chi^2$ |
|---|---|---|---|---|---|---|
| | | | Normal Use ($n$ = 455) | Moderate Addiction ($n$ = 1067) | Severe Addiction ($n$ = 106) | |
| Gender | | | | | | 1.406 |
| | Male | 847 (52.0) | 226 (26.7) | 565 (66.7) | 56 (6.6) | (df = 2) |
| | Female | 781 (48.0) | 229 (29.3) | 502 (64.3) | 50 (6.4) | $p$ = 0.495 |
| Region | | | | | | 1.552 |
| | Seoul | 698 (42.9) | 187 (26.8) | 469 (67.2) | 42 (6.0) | (df = 2) |
| | Gyeonggi | 930 (57.1) | 268 (28.8) | 598 (64.3) | 64 (6.9) | $p$ = 0.460 |
| Living with parents | | | | | | |
| | Both | 1496 (91.9) | 415 (27.7) | 987 (66.0) | 94 (6.3) | 7.019 |
| | Father | 41 (2.5) | 17 (41.5) | 21 (51.2) | 3 (7.3) | (df = 6) |
| | Mother | 82 (5.0) | 22 (26.8) | 52 (63.4) | 8 (9.8) | $p$ = 0.319 |
| | Other | 9 (0.6) | 1 (11.1) | 7 (77.8) | 1 (11.1) | |
| Both parents working | | | | | | 0.796 |
| | Yes | 1075 (66.0) | 304 (28.3) | 705 (65.6) | 66 (6.1) | (df = 2) |
| | No | 553 (34.0) | 151 (27.3) | 362 (65.5) | 40 (7.2) | $p$ = 0.672 |

### 3.2. Internet Use Behaviors

Table 2 summarizes Internet use behaviors between normal use, moderate addiction, and severe addiction groups. About 74% of students had started using the Internet in grade school, and 19.7%

had started using it while of preschool age. Of those who started using the Internet as early as before preschool, 9.4% were identified as addicted, compared to 10.0% and 5.4% who started using the Internet at preschool age and grade-school age, respectively. These group differences were statistically significant. More adolescents in the normal-use group reported a later age of first Internet use. Of the normal-use group, 81.3% ($n$ = 370) started using the Internet in grade school (vs. 71.8% and 61.3% for the moderate addiction and addiction groups, respectively) (% not shown in Table 2). When students were asked to choose what Internet content they used regularly, the most frequently reported answers were webtoons, movies, or television (91.8%) and Social Networking Service or messenger (91.5%), followed by games (82.1%). Significant group differences were found for games and web surfing, with a higher percentage in the moderate addiction and severe addiction groups compared to the normal-use group.

**Table 2.** Internet use behavior ($N$ = 1628).

| | Totaln (%) | Internet Addiction (n, %) | | | $\chi^2$ | $\omega$ |
|---|---|---|---|---|---|---|
| | | **Normal Use ($n$ = 455)** | **Moderate Addiction ($n$ = 1067)** | **Severe Addiction ($n$ = 106)** | | |
| Age of first Internet use | | | | | | |
| Before preschool | 53 (3.2) | 12 (22.7) | 36 (67.9) | 5 (9.4) | 36.060 *** (df = 6) | 0.15 |
| Preschool age | 320 (19.7) | 52 (16.2) | 236 (73.8) | 32 (10.0) | | |
| Grade-school age | 1201 (73.8) | 370 (30.8) | 766 (63.8) | 65 (5.4) | | |
| Other | 54 (3.3) | 21 (38.9) | 29 (53.7) | 4 (7.4) | | |
| Internet contents | | | | | | |
| Game | 1337 (82.1) | 339 (74.5) | 913 (85.6) | 85 (80.2) | 26.877 *** (df = 2) | 0.13 |
| Web toon/movie/TV | 1495 (91.8) | 409 (89.9) | 990 (92.8) | 96 (90.6) | 3.801 (df = 2) | |
| Adult materials | 168 (10.3) | 39 (8.6) | 116 (10.9) | 13 (12.3) | 2.287 (df = 2) | |
| SNS, messenger | 1489 (91.5) | 409 (89.9) | 985 (92.3) | 95 (89.6) | 2.893 (df = 2) | |
| Web surfing | 860 (52.8) | 214 (47.0) | 576 (54.0) | 70 (66.0) | 14.125 ** (df = 2) | 0.09 |

Note: Multiple answers were allowed for Internet contents. ** $p < 0.01$; *** $p < 0.001$. Effect size ($\omega$) = 0.10 (small), 0.30 (medium), 0.50 (large) [64].

### *3.3. Relationship between Psychological, Family/School, the Internet, and Environmental Characteristics and Internet Addiction*

Table 3 summarizes the group differences in domains based on the public health model, namely psychological features, family/school factors, environmental factors, and Internet characteristics. For each domain, we focused on the variables that previous research had indicated were predictors of Internet addiction. One-way analysis of variance between groups was applied to examine differences between the normal use, moderate addiction, and severe addiction groups, followed by Tukey's post-hoc test. Normality and homogeneity of variance assumptions were assessed. We first tested the normality through Shapiro–Wilk test and examined skewness and kurtosis. Shapiro–Wilk test rejected the null hypothesis and the absolute value for skewness and kurtosis did not exceed 2, which assumes a normal distribution of the variables. Levene's test was performed to assess the homogeneity of variance and the results of the Games–Howell analysis were presented as a post hoc test for variables that do not assume equal variance. In order to confirm the differences among these groups, effect size was suggested. When adolescents in three groups were compared, the severe addiction group consistently had the highest level in all psychological features followed by the moderate addiction group and the normal use group. The differences were significant at the $p < 0.001$ level, although the effect size ranged from 0.01 to 0.24.

**Table 3.** Relationship between psychological, family/school, Internet, and environmental characteristics, and Internet addiction ($N = 1628$).

| | Min | Max | Mean | SD | Internet Addiction Mean (SD) | | | F | $\eta^2$ |
|---|---|---|---|---|---|---|---|---|---|
| | | | | | Normal (a) | Moderate Addiction (b) | Severe Addiction (c) | | |
| Psychological factors | | | | | | | | | |
| Impulsivity | 8 | 32 | 15.6 | 4.6 | 12.2 (4.2) | 16.6 (4.0) | 20.2 (4.1) | 259.7 *** a < b < c ($df = 2$) | 0.24 |
| Depression | 8 | 32 | 13.0 | 4.6 | 10.5 (3.7) | 13.8 (4.3) | 16.6 (5.0) | 134.4 *** a < b < c ($df = 2$) | 0.14 |
| Aggressiveness | 8 | 32 | 13.8 | 5.1 | 10.8 (4.1) | 14.7 (4.7) | 18.4 (5.2) | 171.4 *** a < b < c ($df = 2$) | 0.18 |
| Family/school factors | | | | | | | | | |
| Family cohesion | 10 | 50 | 37.3 | 8.2 | 38.8 (9.8) | 36.7 (7.4) | 36.2 (8.0) | 11.5 *** a > b, c ($df = 2$) | 0.01 |
| Relationship with teachers | 3 | 15 | 10.9 | 2.6 | 11.5 (3.0) | 10.6 (2.4) | 10.6 (2.5) | 20.1 *** a > b, c ($df = 2$) | 0.02 |
| Peer relationships | 3 | 15 | 11.6 | 2.6 | 12.1 (2.8) | 11.3 (2.5) | 11.5 (2.5) | 15.3 *** a > b ($df = 2$) | 0.02 |
| Academic activities | 5 | 25 | 16.8 | 3.1 | 17.6 (3.7) | 16.5 (2.8) | 17.1 (2.9) | 20.2 *** a > b ($df = 2$) | 0.02 |
| School participation | 3 | 15 | 10.5 | 2.1 | 11.0 (2.4) | 10.2 (2.0) | 10.8 (2.2) | 25.8 *** a > b, b>c ($df = 2$) | 0.03 |
| Perceived Internet characteristics | | | | | | | | | |
| Relationship | 4 | 20 | 10.1 | 4.1 | 8.0 (4.0) | 10.8 (3.7) | 13.2 (4.0) | 125.8 *** a < b < c ($df = 2$) | 0.14 |
| Anonymity | 4 | 20 | 9.2 | 4.0 | 6.6 (3.5) | 10.0 (3.6) | 12.5 (4.1) | 189.8 *** a < b < c ($df = 2$) | 0.19 |
| Entertainment | 5 | 25 | 13.2 | 5.5 | 10.1 (5.3) | 14.3 (4.9) | 16.2 (6.0) | 122.0 *** a < b < c ($df = 2$) | 0.13 |
| Environmental factors | | | | | | | | | |
| Accessibility of PC cafés | 3 | 15 | 10.2 | 3.3 | 9.4 (3.6) | 10.4 (3.2) | 11.4 (3.1) | 21.8 *** a < b < c ($df = 2$) | 0.03 |
| Exposure to Internet game ads | 2 | 8 | 5.9 | 1.4 | 5.6 (1.6) | 6.0 (1.3) | 6.5 (1.3) | 26.5 *** a < b < c ($df = 2$) | 0.03 |
| Acceptability of Internet game ads | 1 | 10 | 5.6 | 3.0 | 5.2 (3.0) | 5.7 (3.0) | 6.4 (3.1) | 8.0 *** a < b < c ($df = 2$) | 0.01 |

Note: *** $p < 0.001$. Effect size ($\eta^2$) = 0.01 (small), 0.06 (medium), 0.14 (large) [64].

A comparison of family and school factors between the three groups showed a similar pattern. Students in the normal use group showed a significantly higher level of family cohesion, relationship with teachers, relationship with peers, attitude toward academic activities, and school participation. All differences were statistically significant.

The characteristics of the Internet content to which adolescents are drawn were compared. Mean scores in interpersonal relationship, anonymity, and entertainment characteristics were highest in the severe addiction group, followed by the moderate addiction group and then the normal use group, with the differences being statistically significant ($p < 0.001$).

Lastly, three environmental factors were compared between normal use, moderate addiction, and severe addiction groups, namely accessibility to PC cafés, exposure to Internet advertisements, and acceptability of Internet game advertisements. The mean score between the three groups was statistically significant ($p < 0.001$). Adolescents with addiction reported higher levels of accessibility to PC cafés, exposure to Internet ads, and acceptability of Internet game ads compared to the two other groups.

### *3.4. Factors Influencing Internet Addiction*

Logistic regression was performed to determine the effect of variables in psychological, parent/school, environmental, and agent domains on the likelihood of having Internet addiction (Table 4). The severe addiction group was tested against the rest of the sample (moderate addiction and normal use groups) in order to determine the risk factors for the higher degree of Internet addiction. The logistic regression model was statistically significant ($\chi^2$ (26) = 231.29, $p < 0.001$), explaining 38.0% of the variance in Internet addiction among adolescents. Controlling for demographic and Internet use characteristics (gender, region, living with parents, age at first exposure to the Internet, etc.), six variables were found to increase the likelihood of Internet addiction. Among psychological factors, impulsiveness (Wald = 36.14, $p < 0.001$, Exp (B) = 1.277) and aggression (Wald = 4.42, $p < 0.05$, Exp (B) = 1.077) were identified as increasing the risk of Internet addiction. Among perceived Internet characteristics, a high perception of the Internet's potential to build relationships (Wald = 12.17, $p < 0.001$, Exp (B) = 1.186) and anonymity (Wald = 8.80, $p < 0.01$, Exp (B) = 1.150) increased the risk of Internet addiction. Family and school factors were not significant predictors of Internet addiction. Two environmental factors, namely accessibility to PC cafés (Wald = 5.58, $p < 0.05$, Exp (B) = 1.116) and exposure to Internet game ads (Wald = 3.91, $p < 0.05$, Exp (B) = 1.26) were significant predictors of Internet addiction. Adolescents with higher accessibility to PC cafés and increased exposure to Internet game ads were respectively 1.12 and 1.26 times more likely to become addicted to the Internet.

**Table 4.** Logistic regression analysis of factors influencing Internet addiction.

| | *B* | *S. E.* | *Wald* | *OR* | *Exp (B) 95% CI* | |
|---|---|---|---|---|---|---|
| | | | | | **Lower** | **Upper** |
| Psychological factors | | | | | | |
| Impulsivity | 0.244 | 0.041 | 36.140 | 1.277 *** | 1.179 | 1.382 |
| Depression | 0.024 | 0.036 | 0.464 | 1.025 | 0.956 | 1.098 |
| Aggressiveness | 0.075 | 0.035 | 4.417 | 1.077 * | 1.005 | 1.155 |
| Family/school factors | | | | | | |
| Family cohesion | 0.026 | 0.020 | 1.622 | 1.026 | 0.986 | 1.067 |
| Relationship with teachers | −0.058 | 0.067 | 0.746 | 0.943 | 0.827 | 1.077 |
| Peer relationship | 0.001 | 0.060 | 0.001 | 1.001 | 0.891 | 1.125 |
| Academic activities | 0.070 | 0.060 | 1.336 | 1.072 | 0.953 | 1.207 |
| School participation | −0.031 | 0.079 | 0.155 | 0.970 | 0.831 | 1.131 |
| Internet characteristics | | | | | | |
| Relationship | 0.170 | 0.049 | 12.174 | 1.186 *** | 1.078 | 1.305 |
| Anonymity | 0.140 | 0.047 | 8.796 | 1.150 ** | 1.049 | 1.261 |
| Entertainment | −0.014 | .032 | 0.186 | 0.986 | 0.926 | 1.050 |
| Environmental factors | | | | | | |
| Accessibility to PC café | 0.110 | 0.047 | 5.581 | 1.116 * | 1.019 | 1.223 |
| Exposure to Internet game ads | 0.230 | 0.116 | 3.914 | 1.259 * | 1.002 | 1.581 |
| Acceptability of Internet game ads | −0.017 | 0.045 | 0.135 | 0.984 | 0.900 | 1.075 |
| Gender (Male = 1) | −0.418 | 0.309 | 1.837 | 0.658 | 0.360 | 1.205 |
| Region (Seoul = 1) | −0.507 | 0.266 | 3.616 | 0.603 | 0.358 | 1.016 |
| Live with parents | −0.472 | 0.393 | 1.445 | 0.624 | 0.289 | 1.347 |
| Both parents working | −0.237 | 0.267 | 0.784 | 0.789 | 0.468 | 1.332 |

**Table 4.** *Cont.*

| | *B* | *S. E.* | *Wald* | *OR* | *Exp (B)* 95% *CI* | |
|---|---|---|---|---|---|---|
| | | | | | Lower | Upper |
| Age of first Internet use 1 | 0.259 | 0.875 | 0.088 | 1.296 | 0.233 | 7.208 |
| Age of first Internet use 2 | −0.285 | 0.696 | 0.168 | 0.752 | 0.192 | 2.942 |
| Age of first Internet use 3 | −0.651 | 0.669 | 0.946 | 0.522 | 0.140 | 1.936 |
| Game | −1.097 | 0.385 | 8.105 | 0.334 ** | 0.157 | 0.710 |
| Web toon/movie/TV | −0.388 | 0.485 | 0.642 | 0.678 | 0.262 | 1.753 |
| Adult materials | −0.171 | 0.422 | 0.165 | 0.843 | 0.368 | 1.927 |
| SNS/messenger | −0.606 | 0.440 | 1.899 | 0.546 | 0.230 | 1.292 |
| Web surfing | 0.538 | 0.282 | 3.653 | 1.713 | 0.986 | 2.976 |
| $\chi^2$ | | | 231.287 ($df$ = 26) *** | | | |
| −2*LL* | | | 472.806 | | | |
| *Nagelkerke* $R^2$ | | | 0.380 | | | |

Note: Age of Internet use was dummy coded as the following: Age of first Internet use 1 = before preschool; Age of first Internet use 2 = preschool age; Age of first Internet use 3 = grade school; *B* = coefficient; *SE* = standard error of the coefficient; *OR* = odds ratio; *CI* = confidence interval; * $p < 0.05$; ** $p < 0.01$; *** $p < 0.001$.

## 4. Discussion

The present study investigated the predictors of Internet addiction based on the public health model using a representative sample of middle-school students in two major regions in Korea. More than half (72%) of Korean Adolescents in the study were categorized as moderate and severe addiction group, indicating that Internet addiction is a public health concern. Applying the public health model, several factors were found to be related to Internet addiction.

In regard to psychological factors, depressive symptoms, impulsivity, and aggressiveness were consistently higher among the addiction and moderate addiction groups compared to the normal use group. This finding is consistent with previous research that discussed the correlation between depression [18,28], impulsivity [23,31,65–68], aggression [22,27], and Internet addiction among young people. However, when other domains of the public health model were introduced, impulsivity and aggressiveness were found to predict Internet addiction. These associations are not surprising and are in line with extensive research on addictive behaviors, as cited in the introduction. Impulsivity is related to craving and dysfunctional coping with affective mood state, thereby increasing the risk of addictive behavior [67,68]. Impulsivity is one of the key symptoms of ADHD. The high comorbidity between ADHD and Internet addiction may be mediated by impulsivity [69]. With respect to aggressiveness, results are also consistent with past research showing that individuals with a high level of aggression also had a higher tendency toward Internet addiction [22,27]. However, since the study design is cross-sectional, it is difficult to determine whether the two traits were significant predictors for Internet addiction or the result of addiction. That is, impulsivity and aggressiveness may result from excessive Internet use and related problems. Future investigations are required to conclude whether impulsivity or aggressiveness result from, or are significant risk factors for, Internet addiction. Interestingly, the influence of depression became non-significant. One possible explanation could be that within the public health framework, depression does not affect one's likelihood for Internet addiction as much as characteristics of the Internet or environmental factors.

This is similar to what we found regarding family and school-related variables. Findings from the bivariate analysis showed that adolescents who used the Internet without problems had a higher level of family cohesion and a more positive attitude toward academic activities compared to the addicted group. Previous studies also indicated that family factors were predictors of Internet addiction. For instance, for Italian adolescents, family members' affective involvement has found to be associated with lower levels of Internet addiction [70]. Another study confirmed that inter-parental conflict predicted the incidence of Internet addiction among Taiwanese adolescents [35]. However, when other domains of the public health model were controlled for, the influence of family and school related variables became non-significant. Again, a possible explanation for this discrepancy may be related to the importance of environmental variables. Although the family and school environment is an important part of their life, larger environmental context related to the Internet may be more crucial in the development of Internet addiction among young people. Adolescents who experience lower family cohesion or find school life stressful may find refuge in nearby PC cafés where they can indulge themselves in games and Internet activities without distraction. This may be especially true for Korean youths, who are constantly under pressure for academic performance both in the family and at school.

Examination of the Internet's characteristics in relation to addiction showed that the addicted group reported a higher level of entertainment (pleasure), anonymity, and interpersonal relationship factors. When other factors of the public health model were controlled, interpersonal relationships and anonymity were found to be associated with Internet addiction. Adolescents who perceived the Internet as a platform for socialization or building relationships were more likely to indulge in Internet use. This may indicate that the Internet is particularly compelling for those who otherwise find it hard to socialize. This result is in line with Chen and Kim's [40] study that found the relationship building property to be positively related to problematic use of social network sites. Those who believe that acting freely without revealing their identity is an attractive aspect of the Internet were at increased risk for addiction. This may be similar to the discussion of having a fluid identity in online life as one of the seductive properties of the Internet [41]. These findings indicate that the characteristics of the Internet can affect adolescents' Internet use behavior. To date, studies examining the influence of the Internet characteristics on Internet addiction within a public health framework are quite limited. More studies are needed to better understand the influence of traits of the Internet on Internet addiction.

Finally, our study results indicated that environmental factors are good predictors of Internet addiction in adolescents. The addicted adolescents reported higher accessibility to PC cafés and greater exposure to Internet game advertising. This held true after controlling for all other domains, namely individual, family and school, and Internet factors. PC café accessibility refers to the physical spaces in which the Internet can be used. Our findings support previous studies that have verified the effect of easy access to PC cafés on Internet addiction among Korean adolescents [47,60]. Availability and accessibility are well documented in substance abuse literature as risk factors for addictive behavior [48,49,71], and the current study's results are consistent with the existing literature [72]. In addition, the influence of exposure to advertising is consistent with previous studies [73,74]. Our study revealed that adolescents who have more exposure to Internet game advertising and those who are more accepting of advertisements are more likely to become addicted. As a major public health policy, the World Health Organization emphasized regulating the availability and marketing of alcohol to prevent drinking-related problems [75]. We believe that the same can be applied to Internet addiction. For example, regulating the density of PC cafés and mandatory staff training to recognize and cope with excessive users can be suggested. Over the past ten years, there has been a tremendous increase in online game marketing in Korea. Despite this rapid growth, there are no regulations regarding the content of advertisements (e.g., violence, adult materials, etc.) or advertising models [76]. Adolescents are frequently exposed to Internet game ads with inappropriate and violent content. In addition, online game advertisements that feature popular actors are increasing significantly, which will likely attract young people. The current study results speak to the need for public policy that considers the effects of these environmental factors.

Most studies on Internet addiction have focused on individual factors, and even those that considered environmental influences were likely to examine the proximal environment such as familial and peer influence. One strength of this study is that it examined the broader environment such as accessibility to PC cafés and the exposure to advertisements that adolescents experienced in their community, which are common in Korea and some Asian countries. The findings confirmed the importance of the environmental influence on adolescents' Internet addiction. At the same time, because PC cafés are unique to only some countries, the findings are applicable to the Korean context and few other cultures. When applying the model, researchers need to explore unique environmental features of the culture. Another limitation of the study is related to the definition of Internet characteristics. We included seductive properties of the Internet as the agent factor in the public health model. However, these properties may reflect the individual's perception rather than the Internet itself. More research and further corroboration is needed to determine the characteristics of the Internet as the agent in relation to addiction. Since this study design was cross-sectional and could not illustrate a causal relationship, its results should be interpreted cautiously. There exists a possibility that some variables found to be influential such as impulsivity, aggressiveness, and the acceptability of online game ads may have been the result of Internet addiction. Further studies should examine whether these are risk factors for Internet addiction, the result of Internet addiction, or both. Despite its limitations, this study fills the gap in addiction literature by attempting to explain adolescents' Internet addiction from a public health perspective.

## 5. Conclusions

Our study revealed several risk factors in the individual, Internet, and environmental domains. Although misuse of the Internet may be an individual's choice, the current study speaks to the role of other factors such as the characteristics of the Internet and the environment in which individuals make their choice. Since these environmental factors are related to the profit-seeking of related industries, prevention efforts require a social policy approach. That is, strategies should target both changing individuals' behaviors and setting the public health goal of reducing harmful Internet use at the country level. These may include regulations on PC café opening hours for adolescents and restrictions on the promotion and sponsorship of online games in youth activities. In 2019, the World Health Organization announced the inclusion of internet gaming disorder in the International Classification of Diaseses-11, and identified it as a health problem that requires a public health initiative. Further research is needed on intervention policies that specifically target individual and environmental risks based on the public health model. Findings of the current study may help in the planning of suitable strategies geared toward adolescent health.

**Author Contributions:** S.C. and J.L. conceptualized the study; all authors validated the study; S.C. and J.L. prepared the original draft; all authors contributed to review and editing; S.C. and H.K.L. contributed to funding acquisition.

**Acknowledgments:** Authors would like to thank doctoral students, Suyoung Lee, Soo Bi Lee, Jiseon Kim, for their efforts in administrative and technical support for the original project.

## References

1. Young, K.S.; de Abreu, C.N. *Internet Addiction: A Handbook and Guide to Evaluation and Treatment*; John Wiley & Sons Inc.: Hoboken, NJ, USA, 2011.
2. Pies, R. Should DSM-V designate "Internet addiction" a mental disorder? *Psychiatry* **2009**, *6*, 31–37. [PubMed]
3. Young, K.S. Internet Addiction: Diagnosis and treatment considerations. *J. Contemp. Psychother.* **2009**, *39*, 241–246. [CrossRef]
4. Tsitsika, A.; Janikian, M.; Schoenmakers, T.M.; Tzavela, E.C.; Olafsson, K.; Wójcik, S.; Macarie, G.F.; Tzavara, C.; Richardson, C. Internet addictive behavior in adolescence: A cross sectional study in seven European countries. *Cyberpsychol. Behav. Soc. Netw.* **2014**, *17*, 528–535. [CrossRef] [PubMed]
5. Cheng, C.; Li, A.Y.-L. Internet addiction prevalence and quality of (real) life: A meta-analysis of 31 nations across seven world regions. *Cyberpsychol. Behav. Soc. Netw.* **2014**, *17*, 755–760. [CrossRef]
6. Lee, C.S.; McKenzie, K. Socioeconomic and geographic inequalities of internet addiction in Korean adolescents. *Psychiat. Investig.* **2015**, *12*, 559–562. [CrossRef]
7. Ryu, H.; Lee, J.Y.; Choi, A.R.; Chung, S.J.; Park, M.; Bhang, S.; Kwon, J.; Kweon, Y.; Choi, J. Application of Diagnostic Interview for internet addiction (DIA) in clinical practice for Korean adolescents. *J. Clin. Med.* **2019**, *8*, 202. [CrossRef]
8. Ministry of Gender Equality and Family. *2018 Adolescents White Paper*; MOGEF: Seoul, Korea, 2018.
9. National Information Society Agency. *The Survey on Internet Overdependence 2015*; NIA: Seoul, Korea, 2016.

10. Nakayama, H.; Mihara, S.; Higuchi, S. Treatment and risk factors of internet use disorders. *Psychiatry Clin. Neuros.* **2017**, *71*, 492–505. [CrossRef]
11. OECD. *Children & Young People's Mental Health in the Digital Age Shaping the Future*; OECD Publishing: Paris, France, 2018.
12. Odgers, C.L.; Caspi, A.; Nagin, D.S.; Piquero, A.R.; Slutske, W.S.; Milne, B.J.; Dickson, N.; Poulton, R.; Moffitt, T.E. Is It Important to Prevent Early Exposure to Drugs and Alcohol Among Adolescents? *Psychol. Sci.* **2008**, *19*, 1037–1044. [CrossRef]
13. Jordan, C.J.; Andersen, S.L. Sensitive periods of substance abuse: Early risk for the transition to dependence. *Dev. Cogn. Neurosci.* **2017**, *25*, 29–44. [CrossRef]
14. Moon, Y.I.; Koo, H.Y.; Park, H.R. Scope of Internet Addiction and Predictors of Addiction in Korean Children in Early Elementary School. *Korean J. Child Health Nurs.* **2005**, *11*, 263–272.
15. Greenfield, D. The addictive properties of Internet usage. In *Internet Addiction: A Handbook and Guide to Evaluation and Treatment*; Young, K.S., de Abreu, C.N., Eds.; John Wiley & Sons: Hoboken, NJ, USA, 2011; pp. 135–153.
16. Reed, P.; Romano, M.; Re, F.; Roaro, A.; Osborne, L.A.; Viganò, C.; Truzoli, R. Differential physiological changes following internet exposure in higher and lower problematic internet users. *PLoS ONE* **2017**, *12*, 1–11. [CrossRef] [PubMed]
17. Kishore, A.; Pan, T.; Naskar, N.N. Internet addiction and its associated factors: Study among the students of a public health school of Kolkata. *Int. J. Health Allied Sci.* **2019**, *8*, 159–163.
18. Bazrafshan, M.; Jokar, M.; Rahmati, M.; Ahmadi, S.; Kavi, E.; Sookhak, F.; Aliabadi, S.H. The relationship between depression and internet addiction among paramedical students in Larestan, Iran. *J. Clin. Diagn. Res.* **2019**, *13*, 16–19. [CrossRef]
19. Young, K.S.; Rogers, R.C. The relationship between depression and internet addiction. *Cyberpsychol. Behav.* **1998**, *1*, 25–28. [CrossRef]
20. Ho, R.C.; Zhang, M.W.B.; Tsang, T.Y.; Toh, A.H.; Pan, F.; Lu, Y.; Mak, K.-K. The association between internet addiction and psychiatric co-morbidity: A meta-analysis. *BMC Psychiatry* **2014**, *14*, 284–306. [CrossRef] [PubMed]
21. Abdul, A.M.; Wan, I.W.S.; Bahar, N.; Mahadevan, R.; Azhar, S.S. Internet addiction among secondary school students in Klang Valley, Malaysia: What is the Association with depressive symptoms, anxiety symptoms, and self-esteem? *Int. Med. J. Malaysia* **2018**, *17*, 17–25.
22. Ko, C.H.; Yen, J.Y.; Liu, S.C.; Hang, C.F.; Yen, C.F. The associations between aggressive behaviours and internet addiction and online activities in adolescents. *J. Adolescent Health* **2009**, *44*, 598–605. [CrossRef] [PubMed]
23. Lee, H.W.; Choi, J.S.; Shin, Y.; Lee, J.; Jung, H.Y.; Kwon, J.S. Impulsivity in internet addiction: A comparison with pathological gambling. *Cyberpsychol. Behav. Soc. Netw.* **2012**, *15*, 373–377. [CrossRef]
24. Stieger, S.; Burger, C. Implicit and explicit self-esteem in the context of internet addiction. *Cyberpsychol. Behav. Soc. Netw.* **2010**, *13*, 681–688. [CrossRef]
25. Lee, S.-Y.; Lee, H.K.; Choo, H. Typology of Internet gaming disorder and its clinical implications. *Psychiatry Clin. Neurosci.* **2017**, *71*, 479–491. [CrossRef]
26. Yen, J.; Lin, H.; Chou, W.; Liu, T.; Ko, C. Associations among resilience, stress, depression, and Internet gaming disorder in young adults. *Int. J. Environ. Res. Public Health* **2019**, *16*, 3181. [CrossRef] [PubMed]
27. Obeid, S.; Saade, S.; Haddad, C.; Sacre, H.; Khansa, W.; Al Hajj, R.; Kheir, N.; Hallit, S. Internet addiction among Lebanese adolescents: The role of self-esteem, anger, depression, anxiety, social anxiety and fear, impulsivity, and aggression—A cross-sectional study. *J. Nerv. Ment. Dis.* **2019**, *207*, 838–846. [CrossRef] [PubMed]
28. Przepiorka, A.; Blachnio, A.; Cudo, A. The role of depression, personality, and future time perspective in internet addiction in adolescents and emerging adults. *Psychiatry Res.* **2019**, *272*, 340–348. [CrossRef] [PubMed]
29. Kim, Y.J.; Jang, H.M.; Lee, Y.; Lee, D.; Kim, D.J. Effects of internet and smartphone addictions on depression and anxiety based on propensity score matching analysis. *Int. J. Environ. Res. Public Health* **2018**, *15*, 859. [CrossRef]
30. Li, G.; Hou, G.; Yang, D.; Jian, H.; Wang, W. Relationship between anxiety, depression, sex, obesity, and internet addiction in Chinese adolescents: A short-term longitudinal study. *Addict. Behav.* **2019**, *90*, 421–427. [CrossRef]

31. Koo, H.J.; Kwon, J.H. Risk and protective factors of internet addiction: A meta-analysis of empirical studies in Korea. *Yonsei Med. J.* **2014**, *55*, 1691–1711. [CrossRef]
32. Lin, M.-P.; Ko, H.-C.; Wu, J.Y.-W. Prevalence and psychosocial risk factors associated with Internet addiction in a nationally representative sample of college students in Taiwan. *Cyberpsychol. Behav. Soc. Netw.* **2011**, *14*, 741–746. [CrossRef] [PubMed]
33. Liu, S.-J.; Lan, Y.; Wu, L.; Yan, W.-S. Profiles of impulsivity in problematic internet users and cigarette smokers. *Front. Psychol.* **2019**, *10*, 772. [CrossRef]
34. Ryu, H.; Lee, J.Y.; Choi, A.; Park, S.; Kim, D.J.; Choi, J.S. The Relationship between Impulsivity and Internet Gaming Disorder in young adults: Mediating effects of interpersonal relationships and depression. *Int. J. Environ. Res. Public Health* **2018**, *15*, 458. [CrossRef]
35. Ko, C.H.; Wang, P.W.; Liu, T.L.; Yen, C.F.; Chen, C.S.; Yen, J.Y. Bidirectional associations between family factors and internet addiction among adolescents in a prospective investigation. *Psychiatry Clin. Neuros.* **2015**, *69*, 192–200. [CrossRef]
36. Yu, L.; Shek, D.T.-L. Internet addiction in Hong Kong Adolescents: A three-year longitudinal study. *J. Pediatr. Adolesc. Gynec.* **2013**, *26*, S10–S17. [CrossRef] [PubMed]
37. Kim, M.K. Relationship of multicultural adolescents' stress, depression, family resilience and internet game addiction. *J. Korea Converg. Soc.* **2016**, *7*, 205–210. [CrossRef]
38. Jang, S.H.; Park, Y.J. Effects of teenagers' ego-identity, school life adaptation, and stress on internet addiction. *J. Hum.* **2010**, *15*, 195–226.
39. Song, I.; Larose, R.; Eastin, M.S.; Lin, C.A. Internet gratifications and internet addiction: On the uses and abuses of new media. *Cyberpsychol. Behav.* **2004**, *7*, 384–394. [CrossRef] [PubMed]
40. Chen, H.-T.; Kim, Y. Problematic use of social network sites: The interactive relationship between gratifications sought and privacy concerns. *Cyberpsychol. Behav. Soc. Netw.* **2013**, *16*, 806–812. [CrossRef] [PubMed]
41. Leung, L. Net-generation attributes and seductive properties of the internet as predictors of online activities and internet addiction. *Cyberpsychol. Behav.* **2004**, *7*, 333–348. [CrossRef] [PubMed]
42. Turkle, S. *Life on the Screen*; Sion & Schuster: New York, NY, USA, 1995.
43. Lam, L.T. Risk factors of Internet addiction and the health effect of internet addiction on adolescents: A systematic review of longitudinal and prospective studies. *Curr. Psychiatry Rep.* **2014**, *16*, 508. [CrossRef]
44. Yuh, J. Aggression, social environment, and Internet gaming addiction among Korean adolescents. *Soc. Behav. Pers.* **2018**, *46*, 127–138. [CrossRef]
45. Hur, M.H. Demographic, habitual, and socioeconomic determinants of Internet addiction disorder: An empirical study of Korean teenagers. *Cyberpsychol. Behav.* **2006**, *9*, 514–525. [CrossRef]
46. Durkee, T.; Kaess, M.; Carli, V.; Parzer, P.; Wasserman, C.; Floderus, B.; Mandelli, L.; Apter, A.; Balazs, J.; Barzilay, S.; et al. Prevalence of pathological internet use among adolescents in Europe: Demographic and social factors. *Addiction* **2012**, *107*, 2210–2222. [CrossRef]
47. Ju, S.J. A comparative study on risk factors and protective factors for the internet addiction of adolescents from the regional characteristics. *J. Future Oriented Youth Soc.* **2011**, *8*, 121–147.
48. Gruenewald, P.J. Regulating availability: How access to alcohol affects drinking and problems in youth and adults. *Alcohol. Res. Health* **2011**, *34*, 248–256. [PubMed]
49. Paschall, M.J.; Grube, J.W.; Thomas, S.; Cannon, C.; Treffers, R. Relationships between local enforcement, alcohol availability, drinking norms, and adolescent alcohol use in 50 California cities. *J. Stud. Alcohol Drugs* **2012**, *73*, 657–665. [CrossRef] [PubMed]
50. Hester, R.K.; Miller, W.R. *Handbook of Alcoholism Treatment Approaches*, 3rd ed.; Allyn and Bacon: Boston, MA, USA, 2003.
51. Dicker, R.; Coronado, F.; Koo, D.; Parrish, R.G. *Principles of Epidemiology in Public Health Practice*, 3rd ed.; U.S. Department of Health and Human Services: Atlanta, GA, USA, 2006.
52. Young, K.S. Internet addiction: The emergence of a new clinical disorder. *Cyberpsychol. Behav.* **1998**, *1*, 237–244. [CrossRef]
53. Young, K. Clinical assessment of Internet-addicted clients. In *Internet Addiction: A Handbook and Guide to Evaluation and Treatment*; Young, K.S., de Abreu, C.N., Eds.; John Wiley & Sons: Hoboken, NJ, USA, 2011; pp. 19–34.
54. Moon, S.J.; Hwang, J.S.; Kim, J.Y.; Shin, A.L.; Bae, S.M.; Kim, J.W. Psychometric properties of the Internet Addiction Test: A systematic review and meta-analysis. *Cyberpsychol. Behav. Soc. Netw.* **2018**, *21*, 473–484. [CrossRef] [PubMed]

55. National Information Society Agency. *The Survey on Internet Addiction 2011*; NIA: Seoul, Korea, 2012.
56. Olson, D.H.; Portner, J.; Lavee, Y. *FACES III Manual*; University of Minnesota: St. Paul, MN, USA, 1985.
57. Choi, Y.S. A Review of studies of Family Adaptability and Cohesion Evaluation Scales (FACES). *J. Korean Home Manag. Assoc.* **1996**, *14*, 131–145.
58. Son, H.S. A Study on the Adolescents' Needs for School Social Work Services Dependent on their Living Environments. Master's Thesis, Daegu University, Daegu, Korea, 2002.
59. Chung, S.; Kim, Y.S.; Yoo, H.S.; Lee, J.K.; Lee, S.; Lee, S.B. *Public Health Model Development of Internet Game Addiction and Prevalence of Related Harm*; Korea Ministry of Health and Welfare: Seoul, Korea, 2016.
60. Nam, Y.O.; Lee, S.J. Risk and protective factors, and mental health in youth's internet addiction by the addiction types. *Korean J. Soc. Welfare* **2005**, *57*, 195–222.
61. Schooler, C.; Feighery, E.; Flora, J.A. Seventh graders' self-reported exposure to cigarette marketing and its relationship to their smoking behavior. *Am. J. Public Health* **1996**, *86*, 1216–1221. [CrossRef]
62. Unger, J.B.; Schuster, D.; Zogg, J.; Dent, C.W.; Stacy, A.W. Alcohol advertising exposure and adolescent alcohol use: A comparison of exposure measures. *Addict. Res. Theory* **2003**, *11*, 177–193. [CrossRef]
63. Pierce, J.P.; Gilpin, E.A.; Emery, S.L.; Farkas, A.J.; Zhu, S.H.; Choi, W.S.; Berry, C.C.; Distefan, J.M.; White, M.M.; Soroko, S.; et al. *Tobacco Control in California: Who's Winning the War? An Evaluation of the Tobacco Control Program, 1989–1996*; University of California: San Diego, CA, USA, 1998.
64. Cohen, J. *Statistical Power Analysis for the Behavioral Sciences*, 2nd ed.; Lawrence Erlbaum Associates: New York, NY, USA, 1988.
65. Cao, F.; Su, L.; Liu, T.Q.; Gao, X. The Relationship between impulsivity and internet addiction in a sample of Chinese adolescents. *Eur. Psychiat.* **2007**, *22*, 466–471. [CrossRef]
66. Chen, S.; Lo, M.; Lin, S.S.-J. Impulsivity as a Precedent Factor for Problematic Internet Use: How Can We Be Sure? *Int. J. Psychol.* **2017**, *52*, 389–397. [CrossRef] [PubMed]
67. Antons, S.; Mueller, S.M.; Wegmann, E.; Trotzke, P.; Schulte, M.M.; Brand, M. Facets of impulsivity and related aspects differentiate among recreational and unregulated use of Internet pornography. *J. Behav. Addict.* **2019**, *8*, 223–233. [CrossRef] [PubMed]
68. Brand, M.; Young, K.S.; Laier, C.; Wölfling, K.; Potenza, M.N. Integrating psychological and neurobiological considerations regarding the development and maintenance of specific Internet-use disorders: An Interaction of Person-Affect-Cognition-Execution (I-PACE) model. *Neurosci. Biobehav. Rev.* **2016**, *71*, 252–266. [CrossRef] [PubMed]
69. Wang, B.Q.; Yao, N.Q.; Zhou, X.; Liu, J.; Lv, Z.T. The association between attention deficit/hyperactivity disorder and internet addiction: A systematic review and meta-analysis. *BMC Psychiatry* **2017**, *17*, 260. [CrossRef] [PubMed]
70. Cacioppo, M.; Barni, D.; Correale, C.; Mangialavori, S.; Danioni, F.; Gori, A. Do attachment styles and family functioning predict adolescents' problematic internet use? A relative weight analysis. *J. Child Fam. Stud.* **2019**, *28*, 1263–1271. [CrossRef]
71. Broman, C. The availability of substances in adolescence: Influences in emerging adulthood. *J. Child Adoles. Subst.* **2016**, *25*, 487–495. [CrossRef] [PubMed]
72. Dhir, A.; Chen, S.; Nieminen, M. Predicting adolescent internet addiction: The roles of demographics, technology accessibility, unwillingness to communicate and sought internet gratifications. *Comput. Hum. Behav.* **2015**, *51*, 24–33. [CrossRef]
73. Esser, M.B.; Jernigan, D.H. Policy approaches for regulating alcohol marketing in a global context: A public health perspective. *Annu. Rev. Public Health* **2018**, *39*, 385–401. [CrossRef]
74. Jernigan, D.; Noel, J.; Landon, J.; Thornton, N.; Lobstein, T. Alcohol marketing and youth alcohol consumption: A systematic review of longitudinal studies published since 2008. *Addiction* **2016**, *112*, 7–20. [CrossRef]
75. World Health Organization. *Global Status Report on Alcohol and Health 2018*; World Health Organization: Geneva, Switzerland, 2018.
76. Ministry of Science, ICT and Future Planning. *2016 Online Advertising Law System Guide*; KISA: Seoul, Korea, 2016.

# 3

# Mind over Matter: Testing the Efficacy of an Online Randomized Controlled Trial to Reduce Distraction from Smartphone Use

**Melina A. Throuvala [1,*], Mark D. Griffiths [1], Mike Rennoldson [2] and Daria J. Kuss [1]**

[1] International Gaming Research Unit, Psychology Department, Nottingham Trent University, Nottingham NG1 4FQ, UK; mark.griffiths@ntu.ac.uk (M.D.G.); daria.kuss@ntu.ac.uk (D.J.K.)

[2] Psychology Department, Nottingham Trent University, Nottingham NG1 4FQ, UK; mike.rennoldson@ntu.ac.uk

* Correspondence: melina.throuvala@ntu.ac.uk

**Abstract:** Evidence suggests a growing call for the prevention of excessive smartphone and social media use and the ensuing distraction that arises affecting academic achievement and productivity. A ten-day online randomized controlled trial with the use of smartphone apps, engaging participants in mindfulness exercises, self-monitoring and mood tracking, was implemented amongst UK university students ($n = 143$). Participants were asked to complete online pre- and post-intervention assessments. Results indicated high effect sizes in reduction of smartphone distraction and improvement scores on a number of self-reported secondary psychological outcomes. The intervention was not effective in reducing habitual behaviours, nomophobia, or time spent on social media. Mediation analyses demonstrated that: (i) emotional self-awareness but not mindful attention mediated the relationship between intervention effects and smartphone distraction, and (ii) online vigilance mediated the relationship between smartphone distraction and problematic social media use. The present study provides preliminary evidence of the efficacy of an intervention for decreased smartphone distraction and highlights psychological processes involved in this emergent phenomenon in the smartphone literature. Online interventions may serve as complementary strategies to reduce distraction levels and promote insight into online engagement. More research is required to elucidate the mechanisms of digital distraction and assess its implications in problematic use.

**Keywords:** distraction; smartphones; social media; intervention; randomized controlled trial; social media addiction

## 1. Introduction

Attentional focus is one of the most fundamental resources and a key to successful and high-order work [1]. In the attention economy [2], multiple online and offline activities compete for an alternative share of attention [3]. This trend is expected to grow in the face of increasing communication complexity and information overload [4], which is becoming even more prevalent partially due to the vast online accessibility, immediacy and convenience of smartphones, acting as a major motivational pull for engagement [5] and prompting constant multitasking and frequent attentional loss [6]. There are currently more than 3.5 billion smartphone users [7] and smartphone use is an emergent area of research [8–10]. Emerging evidence on cognitive function has shown that smartphone availability and daily interruptions compete with higher-level cognitive processes creating a cognitive interference effect [11–15], associated with poorer cognitive functioning [16–19], performance impairments in daily life [20] and potential supplanting of analytical thinking skills by "offloading thinking to the device" [21] (p. 473). In spite of such initial evidence, there are cognitive correlates within the smartphone context, such as distraction, which have been less explored in the literature. Studies report that students use their smartphones for more than 25% of effective class duration, and smartphone distractions occur every 3–4 min, for over a minute in duration [22]. Student focus on any single task is reported to last 3–5 min [23] with excessive smartphone use hindering academic performance as a result of allowing goal-irrelevant information to compete with goal-relevant tasks [24,25]. Therefore, examining the processes involved in the occurrence of distraction as well as protective strategies for its containment is timely. The present study evaluates the efficacy of evidence-based mediating strategies in reducing distraction employed in an online randomized controlled trial.

Distraction is an emotion regulation coping strategy used to deflect attention from the task at hand in order to relieve emotional distress, reflected as difficulty in concentrating and maintaining goal-focused behaviour, with an adaptive function in negative affect situations [26–30]. Smartphone distraction constitutes an emergent concern, operationally defined as the disruption in attention due to: (i) external cues received (i.e., notifications), (ii) cognitive salience (i.e., internal cues) of the smartphone and social media, or (iii) cognitive avoidance (i.e., coping mechanism) for emotion regulation [17,31–33]. Checking behaviours, frequently engaged in during smartphone use, are associated with repeated external or internal interruptions, leading to attentional micro-disengagements and distraction [20,31,34]. According to the control model of social media engagement [5], this may occur as need to control online content, relationships and self-presentation produces an attentional conflict (offline vs. online or platform/activity switch), arousal and distraction, leading either to facilitation (by the presence of online others) [35,36] and heightened engagement or shallow processing, when engaged in parallel cognitively demanding tasks. Therefore, constant disruptions may cause a rise in attention problems and hyperactivity levels [37] as a result of allowing goal-irrelevant information to compete with goal-relevant tasks [24,25] with impacts on wellbeing, productivity and academic achievement, particularly amongst young people [22,38–41]. A large contributor to this effect is excessive social media use, which has been suggested as a vulnerability factor for problematic smartphone use [42–44]. To date, the effects of smartphone use on student outcomes may still be small [45].

### 1.1. Distraction and Its Relation to Other Psychological Constructs in the Smartphone Literature

*Online vigilance.* Distraction by smartphone use appears to be activated by internal thoughts or external cues interfering with other tasks, which may be driven by online vigilance—a constant preoccupation with online content, leading to salience, monitoring and prompting urges to check [46], resulting in strong habitual behaviour [47,48]. Salience of online content has been found to be negatively associated with affective wellbeing and life satisfaction, particularly when thoughts are negative [49].

*Attention impulsiveness and habitual smartphone use.* Attention impulsiveness has also been implicated in smartphone distraction, reinforced by rewarding, habitual checking behaviours [47], and has a significant relationship with problematic smartphone use [50]. Recent evidence also suggests symptom severity of problematic social media use to be mainly associated with attention impulsiveness and difficulties with inhibitory control or executive control functions [51], task performance [52] and chronic media multitasking [25]. This is intensified in a low interest academic context, reducing lecture comprehension [53], level of motivation, and fluid intelligence [54].

*Fear of Missing Out (FoMO) and Nomophobia (NoMO).* FoMO—the fear of being excluded from rewarding social experiences – and NoMO – the fear of no access to a mobile device—have both been evidenced in the smartphone literature as triggering a need to be in constant contact and reinforcing use [55–62]. Therefore, FoMO could be a main driver of distraction due to the propensity to be present in the positive experiences others are having, depicted in online content. FoMO has been associated with depression, smartphone addiction, anxiety, mindfulness and wellbeing [63], negative affectivity, problematic smartphone use, and levels of online social engagement [60].

*Stress, anxiety, emotion regulation and problematic use.* Socio-emotional correlates of FoMO have included negative affect, rejection sensitivity, and high stress levels [64], and reviews have suggested a small-to-medium association between smartphone use and stress and anxiety [65]. Therefore, negative emotional states may be a precursor to smartphone distraction and its use may be motivated by emotion regulation. Relief of negative emotions and psychological states along with emotional gains from smartphone use have been found to be significantly higher for Generation Z (individuals born between 1995 and 2015) [66] and could be an outcome of difficulties with emotion regulation, creating a vicious cycle sustaining overreliance for coping [67] and dysfunctional metacognitive beliefs among problematic users [68]. Smartphone unavailability and intolerance of uncertainty have been evidenced in problematic smartphone use [69,70], and affect perceived stress and mental wellbeing [71]. Concerns for the emotional and behavioural consequences of excessive smartphone and social media use have been addressed [9,72–75]. However, what constitutes problematic online behaviour needs constant conceptual and methodological re-evaluation [76] as engagement with new products/platforms emerges.

*Mindfulness, self-monitoring and mood tracking.* Self-monitoring of social media activity, self-exclusion from specific platforms, and the practice of mindfulness are considered successful wellbeing practices [77,78]. Mindfulness, defined as the purposeful, non-judgemental awareness of the presenting experience [79], facilitates the sustaining of on-task behaviours [80], affecting attention, affect regulation, body awareness, and self-perception [81–83], and has been used in gambling harm-reduction and substance use disorders, with intervention effects reducing cravings, post-traumatic symptoms, and negative affect [84–90]. Mindfulness has been negatively associated with distraction, suggesting that one's awareness of own thought wandering (meta-awareness) may decrease the frequency of distraction [17] and aid academic attainment [91]. Self-monitoring of mood (also defined as mood tracking) has been found to boost overall emotional self-awareness [92], which can in turn lead to improvements in emotional self-regulation [93]. Therefore, these strategies could be trialled to help diminish attentional bias occurring within the context of social media and smartphone use [94,95].

### *1.2. Smartphone Mental Health Apps (MHapps) and Online Randomized Controlled Trials*

Digital wellbeing apps or MHapps (apps that track an individual's behaviour, i.e., time spent online, or that aid cognitive, emotional and/or behavioural wellbeing) [96] have been suggested as supporting self-awareness and self-regulation [97] and utilized in mental healthcare given their functionality, accessibility, higher adherence rates, real-time assessment, low-cost and for their intervention potential [98,99]. The literature suggests that evidence-based apps may be efficacious in raising self-awareness, mental health literacy and wellbeing, self-efficacy, and ability to cope [96,100–102]. Online psychological interventions are becoming more prominent in the digital age [103], rendering numerous positive health outcomes [102,104–108], complementing service provision and recognized by governmental health institutions (e.g., National Institute for Health and Care Excellence (NICE) in the UK) [109]. However, more research is required to determine the comparative effectiveness of these therapies and their components [110] in improving mental health and wellbeing and rigorous objective evaluation beyond their developers is required.

To date, there have been a small number of internet-based interventions associated with device use in university settings. Distraction is not considered a dysfunctional construct by itself, but has been implicated in emotion regulation, ADHD, and other disorders [111–113], and has been minimally examined in the context of the digital environment with no evidence to date as to strategies that could ameliorate its occurrence [114]. Therefore, the aim of the present study was to test the preliminary efficacy of an online intervention based on cognitive behavioural principles (i.e., self-monitoring, mood tracking, and mindfulness) to reduce distraction and related psychological outcomes (i.e., stress) among university students. Given: (i) young adults are keen users of smartphone apps, with increased vulnerability to self-regulation and technology use [74], (ii) the high stakes for academic achievement, and (iii) the similarity in processes observed between gambling addiction and social media overuse [115], the strategies of *mindfulness, activity monitoring*, and *mood tracking* utilized in gambling harm-reduction [86,116,117] are employed in the present study. These strategies were delivered and facilitated through the use of smartphone MHapps and were tested for their efficacy in reducing levels of distraction and related psychological outcomes and their role in inducing changes in wellbeing [118–120]. The following hypotheses were formulated:

**Hypothesis 1** (H1). *Compared to the control condition at follow-up, students receiving the intervention would report: (i) lower rates of smartphone distraction, smartphone and social media use duration, impulsivity, stress, problematic social media use, FoMO and NoMO and (ii) higher levels of mindful attention, emotional self-awareness, and self-efficacy.*

**Hypothesis 2** (H2). *At follow-up, high distractors (HDs) compared to low distractors (LDs) (based on a median-split analysis) would show a greater reduction in distraction and significant improvement in outcomes.*

**Hypothesis 3** (H3). *The intervention will mediate the relationship between (i) mindful attention and smartphone distraction, and (ii) emotional awareness and smartphone distraction. Additionally, online vigilance will mediate the relationship between smartphone distraction and problematic social media use.*

To the authors' knowledge and given the novelty of the construct of smartphone distraction, this is the first study to examine a preliminary online randomized controlled trial via MHapps for the reduction of smartphone distraction. The present study fills a gap in the smartphone literature by assessing the efficacy of engaging with behaviour change strategies (i.e., mindfulness, self-monitoring, and mood-tracking) used successfully in gambling harm prevention for the reduction of distraction.

## 2. Materials and Methods

### 2.1. Design

The present study tested the efficacy of a ten-day online app-delivered randomized controlled trial (RCT) based on cognitive-behavioural principles to reduce distraction (primary outcome) and a number of secondary psychological outcomes: self-awareness, mindful attention, FoMO, anxiety, and depression among university students. RCTs are considered the gold standard in intervention effectiveness despite limitations addressed by scholars [121,122], primarily for the lack of external validity or methodological choices [123]. A pragmatic psychosocial intervention with an RCT design was chosen [124]. The duration of the intervention was set given a pragmatic consideration of the free use period of one of the apps (*Headspace*) and, secondly, due to the preliminary nature of this investigation. Consolidated Standards of Reporting Trials (CONSORT) guidelines were followed in the protocol and the procedures and reporting of the intervention [125].

The intervention involved the active engagement for the period of ten consecutive days with three smartphone apps serving three different functions: to assess smartphone and social media use, conduct mindfulness sessions with an emphasis on eliminating distraction, and track mood and assess its impact on distraction, stress, self-regulation, and other measures. Interaction with apps was encouraged to: (i) raise emotional awareness of common mood states, such as feeling down, worried, or stressed through mindfulness, (ii) guide basic smartphone monitoring, focusing skills, and awareness, and (iii) provide insight through mood tracking (Table 1). To further support active engagement with these intervention components, eligible participants were asked to keep a daily online activity log for the duration of the intervention (i.e., the number of screen-unlocks and the time of day and number of minutes for which the smartphone was used, usefulness of apps, etc.), to aid time perception of daily activities, raise awareness levels, and help increase the accuracy of self-reporting and adherence to the intervention [126,127]. Promoting self-awareness of media use and understanding of own behaviour was a key target of the intervention in order to curb distraction. The study was reviewed and approved (No. 2018/226) by the research team's university ethics committee.

**Table 1.** The three components of the intervention.

| Intervention Components | Smartphone App Used | Evidence-Based Benefits | Psychological Evidence for Benefits |
|---|---|---|---|
| | | Mindfulness | |
| Brief mindfulness sessions | Headspace app | • Mindfulness practice and mood tracking offer benefits in emotion regulation, attention, stress and low mood levels & meta-awareness<br>• Evidence for replenishing students' focused engagement in mental tasks (i.e., homework) | [128]<br>[80]<br>[82,83]<br>[129] |
| | | Self-monitoring and Self-exclusion | |
| Social media and smartphone use Abstinence option | Anti-Social app | • Self-monitoring & exclusion (minutes on social media, times of unlocking smart phone each day, favourite and most time consuming and accessed apps) aid emotion regulation<br>• Reflection on dependence on smartphone, extent of use, lost attention, checking frequency<br>• Performance feedback & meta-awareness | [130]<br>[131]<br>[77]<br>[132]<br>[133]<br>[134]<br>[101] |
| | | Mood-tracking | |
| | Pacifica app | • Mood tracking can boost overall emotional self-awareness which can in turn lead to improvements in emotional self-regulation | [93]<br>[135]<br>[136] |

Daily reminders and messages via blogging were sent as a reminder to maintain routine and reflect on levels of activity [126,137].

*2.2. Participants*

Participants were recruited using convenience and snowball sampling techniques. After gaining institutional ethical approval, the study was advertised to students through the research credit scheme, in university lectures and labs, and to the public through social media as an online intervention to assess the reduction of smartphone distraction. This experimental intervention demanded a significant time involvement and offering incentives increased the chances of participation and completion of the full ten-day intervention. In return for participation, students were offered either research credits or entry in a prize draw (£50 gift cards). Participants were included in the study based on two screening criteria: regular smartphone and social media usage. Only those affirming both and granting consent were able to continue with participation. Following the completion of the survey, participants were allocated to one of the two conditions (intervention [IG] or control [CG]) and further instructions for participation in the intervention were provided depending on the allocation condition. After initially providing age and gender demographics, participants responded to survey items regarding habitual smartphone and social media behaviour (estimates of duration of use), smartphone distraction severity, trait self-regulation, trait mindfulness and other psychological constructs (detailed in "Materials"). The survey took approximately 25 min to complete.

A total of 261 participants were recruited who participated in the baseline assessment. Of these, 155 were undergraduate Psychology students in the UK (59.3%). The sample comprised 47 males (18%) and 214 females (82%), with an age range of 18 to 32 years ($M$ = 20.72, $SD$ = 3.12). Figure 1 depicts the flow of participants through the study procedures. After the baseline assessment, during the intervention period two individuals of the intervention group withdrew from the study and were not considered in the analysis. From the 259 remaining participants, seven were removed due to providing 90% incomplete data. The final sample considered at baseline was 252 participants (intention to treat (ITT) group) and included 123 participants in the intervention group and 129 in the control group. Participants who completed both assessments were considered in the per-protocol analysis (PP) ($n$ = 143, 56% of the original sample), with 72 participants comprising the IG and 71 participants the CG.

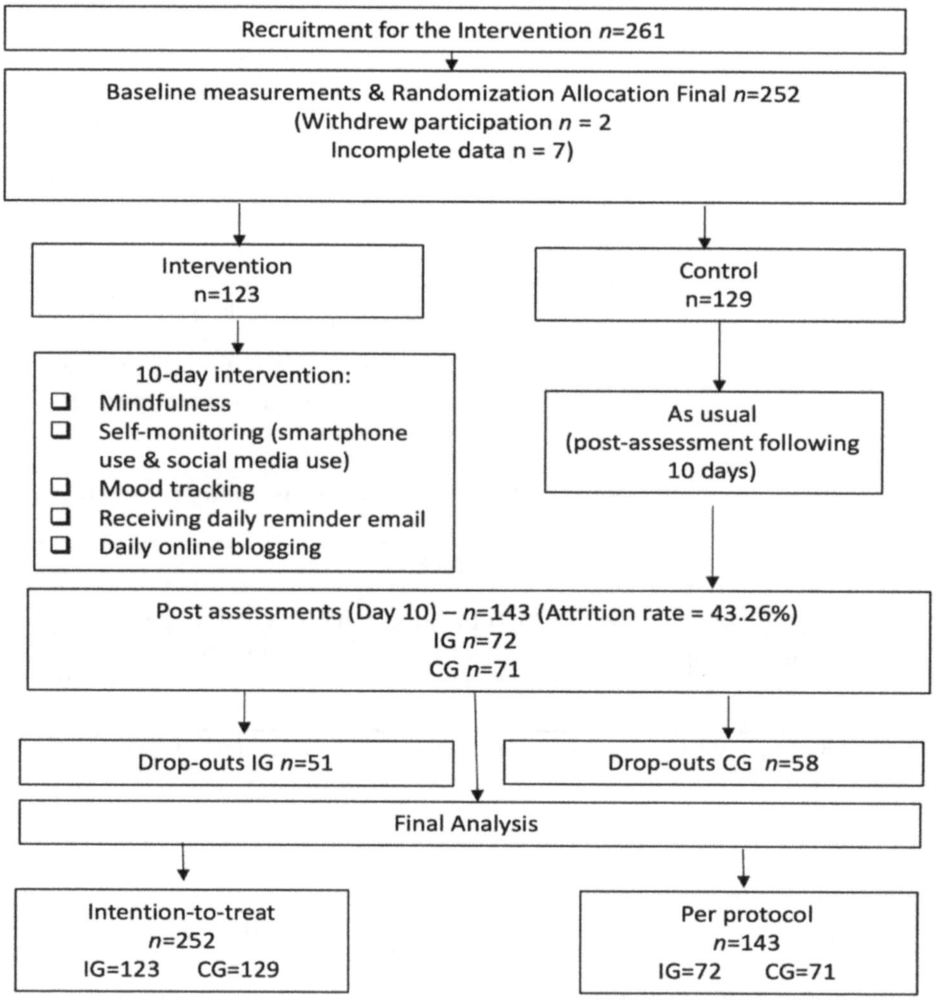


**Figure 1.** Participant flow in the intervention.

### 2.3. Materials

The survey consisted of sociodemographic and usage data (questions related specifically to smartphone and social media use [hours per day]). The demographic questions and user-related questions had open responses (i.e., "How many hours per day do you use social media?"). The following scales were used for the psychological measures of the study:

The Smartphone Distraction Scale [138] is a newly developed scale comprising of 16 Likert-type items. The scale comprises four factors: attention impulsiveness, online vigilance, emotion regulation, and multitasking. Scores range from 1 (almost never) to 5 (almost always) with higher scores representing a greater degree of distraction. Individual items on the test were summed to give composite scores. Sample items included in the scale are the following: "I get distracted by my phone notifications", and "I constantly check my phone to see who liked my recent post while doing important tasks". The scale has demonstrated good psychometric properties [138] and excellent reliability in the present study with a Cronbach's alpha of 0.90 for Time 1 (T1) and 0.88 for Time 2 (T2).

The Mindful Attention Awareness Scale (MAAS) [139] is a 15-item assessment tool that assesses the dispositional tendency of participants to be mindful in everyday life and has been validated among young people, university students and community samples [139,140]. Item statements reflect experience of mindfulness, mindlessness in general and specific daily situations and are distributed across a range of cognitive, emotional, physical, interpersonal, and general domains. Response options are based on a six-point Likert scale from 1 (almost always) to 6 (almost never). Scores were averaged across the 15 items to obtain an overall mindfulness score with higher scores reflecting higher levels of dispositional mindfulness. Sample items include "I could be experiencing some emotion and not be aware of it until sometime later" and "I find it difficult to stay focused on what's happening in the present" and exhibited a high degree of internal consistency in the present study with a Cronbach's alpha of 0.92 for T1 and 0.93 for T2.

The Emotional Self-Awareness Scale (ESAS) [92] was used to assess ESA and comprises five variables: recognition, identification, communication, contextualization, and decision making. The scale consists of 32 items (e.g., "I usually know why I feel the way I do") rated from 0 (strongly disagree) to 4 (strongly agree). The total ESA score ranged from 0 to 128, and sub-scale items are combined to produce a composite score with higher scores indicating higher ESA. The ESAS has presented reasonable internal consistency (Cronbach's alpha = 0.72, 0.69, and 0.76 for pre-test, post-test and six-week follow-up) [92]. The scale has demonstrated good validity in prior studies [92,101] and adequate internal consistency in the present study (Cronbach's alpha of 0.87 for T1 and 0.86 for T2).

The Perceived Stress Scale (PSS) [141] is one of the most widely used scales to assess perceived stress and the degree of unpredictability, uncontrollability, and burden in various situations. The scale used was the 10-item version rated from 0 (never) to 4 (very often) with sample items such as "In the last month, how often have you felt that you were unable to control the important things in your life?", and "In the last month, how often have you felt that you were on top of things?" Scores are obtained by summing the items, with the higher score indicating more perceived stress. The scale possesses good psychometric properties [142] and its internal consistency in the present study was 0.86 for T1 and 0.83 for T2.

The seven-item Generalized Anxiety Disorder Scale (GAD-7) [143] is a brief clinical measure that assesses for the presence and severity of Generalized Anxiety Disorder (GAD). The self-report scale asks how often during the last two weeks individuals experienced symptoms of GAD. Total scores range from 0–21 with cut-off scores of 5, 10, and 15 being indicative of mild, moderate, and severe anxiety, respectively. Increasing scores on the GAD-7 are strongly associated with greater functional impairment in real-world settings. Sample items are rated from 0 (not at all) to 3 (nearly every day) and sample items include: "Feeling nervous, anxious or on edge" and "Trouble relaxing". The scale has been widely used and considered a valid and reliable screening tool in previous research, presenting good reliability, factorial and concurrent validity [144,145], and demonstrated excellent internal consistency in the present study ($\alpha = 0.93$ T1 and $\alpha = 0.90$ for T2).

The Self-Report Behavioural Automaticity Index (SRBAI) [146] was used to assess habitual strength. The four-item scale was used to assess the degree of automaticity and contained items such as: "Using social media on my smartphone is something ... I do automatically" and "I start doing before I realize I'm doing it". Participants indicate their agreement with each item on a Likert scale ranging from 1 (does not apply at all) to 7 (fully applies). Scores were averaged across items to obtain an overall habit score, with higher scores indicating stronger habitual smartphone use behaviour. The scale has been reported as psychometrically sound in previous studies with good reliability, convergent and predictive validity [146,147] and demonstrated good internal consistency in the present study with a Cronbach's alpha of 0.87 (T1) and 0.89 (T2).

The Generalized Self-Efficacy Scale (GSE) [148] is a widely used psychometric instrument comprising ten items that assess perceived self-efficacy ("I can always manage to solve difficult problems if I try hard enough."). Items are rated on a four-point scale ranging from 1 (not at all true) to 4 (exactly true). The GSE has demonstrated satisfactory internal consistency and validity across studies [149,150]. Cronbach's alpha in the present study was 0.90 (T1) and 0.88 (T2).

The Online Vigilance Scale (OVS) [46] is a 12-item Likert scale which assesses a relatively new construct in the internet-related literature, referring to individuals' cognitive orientation towards online content, expressed as cognitive salience, reactivity to online cues and active monitoring of online activity. Sample items include "My thoughts often drift to online content" and "I constantly monitor what is happening online". Scale items are rated on a four-point Likert scale from 1 (does not apply at all) to 4 (fully applies). Higher mean scores indicate a higher degree of online vigilance. The scale has evidenced sound construct and nomological validity and high internal consistency [46,49,78]. The Cronbach's alpha in the present study was 0.89 (T1) and 0.87 (T2).

The eight-item Barratt Impulsiveness Scale-Alternative Version (BIS-8) [151] is a psychometrically improved abbreviated version of the 11-item BIS scale [151] presenting good construct and concurrent validity in young populations [152,153]. The scale assesses impulsive behaviour and poor self-inhibition and uses a four-point Likert scale from 1 (do not agree) to 4 (agree very much). Sample items include: "I do things without thinking" and "I act on the spur of the moment". Cronbach's alpha coefficient in the present study was 0.85 (T1) and 0.86 (T2).

The Deficient Self-Regulation Measure [154] is a seven-item scale assessing deficient self-regulation in videogame playing adapted for unregulated internet use [155]. The scale is rated on a seven-point Likert scale from 1 (almost never) to 7 (almost always) and has demonstrated sound psychometric properties [154]. The scale was adapted for smartphone use with sample items such as "I would go out of my way to satisfy my urges to use social media" and "I have to keep using social media more and more to get my thrill". The original scale and its adaptation has presented satisfactory psychometric properties [154,155]. The Cronbach's alpha coefficient in the present study was 0.89 (T1) and 0.87 (T2).

The Bergen Social Media Addiction Scale (BSMAS) [115,156–158] is a six-item self-report scale for assessing social media addiction severity based on the framework of the components model of addiction (salience, mood modification, tolerance, withdrawal, conflict, and relapse) [159]. Each item examines the experience of using social media over the past year and is rated on a five-point Likert scale from 1 (very rarely) to 5 (very often), producing a composite score ranging from 6 to 30. Higher BSMAS scores indicate greater risk of social media addiction severity. A sample question from the BSMAS is "How often during the last year have you used social media so much that it has had a negative impact on your job/studies?" A cut-off score over 19 indicates problematic social media use [160]. The BSMAS has presented sound psychometric properties [115,156–158] with high internal consistency ($\alpha = 0.82$) [161]. The Cronbach's alpha in the present study was 0.91 (T1) and 0.87 (T2).

The Fear of Missing Out Scale (FoMOS) [162] includes ten items and asks participants to evaluate the extent to which they experience symptoms of FoMO. The scale is rated on a seven-point Likert scale from 1 (not at all true) to 5 (extremely true of me). The statements include: "I fear others have more rewarding experiences than me... I get anxious when I don't know what my friends are up to...It bothers me when I miss an opportunity to meet up with friends...". A total score was calculated by averaging the scores, with higher mean scores indicating a greater level of FoMO. This instrument has demonstrated good construct validity [162,163], and good internal consistency with Cronbach's alphas of $\alpha = 0.93$ [164] and 0.87 [64] with $\alpha = 0.87$ in the present study.

The Nomophobia Questionnaire (NMP-Q) [165] comprises 20 items rated using a seven-point Likert scale from 1 (strongly disagree) to 7 (strongly agree). Total scores are calculated by summing up responses to each item, resulting in a nomophobia score ranging from 20 to 140, with higher scores corresponding to greater nomophobia severity. NMP-Q scores are interpreted in the following way: 20 = absence of nomophobia; 21–59 = mild level of nomophobia; 60–99 = moderate level of nomophobia; and 100+ = severe nomophobia. The scale has demonstrated good psychometric properties [165,166] with Cronbach's alphas of 0.94 [165] and 0.95 [167]. In the present study, internal consistency was: 0.89 for (T1) and 0.88 for (T2) respectively.

*2.4. The Intervention*

The intervention initially involved the search and identification of appropriate mobile apps (in both the Apple iTunes store and the Android Google Play store) for daily self-monitoring of social media activity for mindfulness practices and mood tracking. The apps needed to be freely available in order to be accessible by the participants. Due to time limitations, the development of an app that would encompass all three features (mindfulness of distraction, self-monitoring, and mood-tracking) was deemed adequate for the study given the ample availability of well-designed products offering these services. The following three freely available smartphone lifestyle apps were utilized: (i) Antisocial (screen time): to self-monitor screen time/social media use and for voluntary self-exclusion (block app after time limit is reached), (ii) Headspace (mindfulness): brief mindfulness sessions, (iii) Pacifica (mood tracking): the app encouraged monitoring and tracking an individual's emotional state at various times during the day to enhance awareness.

At the outset of the study, participants were directed to an information statement followed by the digital provision of informed consent before responding to the questions. At the end of the survey, they were automatically assigned through the automatic randomization procedure used by the online survey platform *Qualtrics* to either an intervention or a control group. Therefore, the intervention was double-blind (to participants and investigators). Participants assigned to the *IG* were asked to download the apps onto their smartphones and to actively engage with all three apps daily for 10 days, which was the maximum free period offered by one of these apps. Participants were encouraged to engage with mindfulness/focusing exercises to track their emotional state during the day and monitor patterns in their wellbeing as well as report daily on smartphone usage rates. Thereafter, participants received daily notifications via email for the duration of the intervention to remind them to provide online reports about their own social media usage rates, apps accessed, checking frequency, potential self-restriction from use, and satisfaction with the intervention. This process was used to motivate engagement with the apps and accountability. Efficacy was evaluated by having a CG condition where participants did not engage in any app use and only completed assessments on the first and tenth day. The target of the intervention was to induce a more mindful state, raise awareness of media and smartphone use, enhance self-regulation and therefore reduce distractions and time spent on smartphones and indirectly on social media by using these apps.

*2.5. Data Analysis*

2.5.1. Sample Size Estimation

The sample size for the RCT was determined a priori using G*Power v.3 software for the expected increased effectiveness of the intervention compared to control on the primary outcome distraction at post-assessment (T2). Empirical reviews [168] have suggested a median standardised target effect size of 0.30 (interquartile range: 0.20–0.38), with the median standardised observed effect size 0.11 (IQR 0.05–0.29). The present study was a low-threshold intervention for a non-clinical population, so a mean effect of $d = 0.30$ was expected. With a power of 1-ß = 0.8, and a significance level of $\alpha = 0.05$, the sample size was calculated to be $n = 95$ participants per group to find between- and within-group effects. To account for attrition rates in online interventions and control for both Type I and II error rates, $n = 125$ participants per group were targeted for recruitment [169].

2.5.2. Data Cleaning, Assumption Testing and Descriptive Analysis

All data were analysed through SPSS v.25 (Chicago, IL, USA). Preliminary data analyses included examining the data for data entry errors, normality testing, outliers, and missing data. Seven cases were treated with listwise deletion due to a very high percentage of incomplete data at baseline, resulting in a final sample size of 252. For the rest of the dataset, Little's Missing Completely at Random (MCAR) test showed that data were missing completely at random ($p = 0.449$). Multiple imputation was used to complete the dataset for the baseline analysis and for the non-completers from post-intervention assessment based on patterns of missingness. The data were also checked to ensure that all assumptions for the outlined statistical analyses were satisfied. The Kolmogorov-Smirnov test was used to evaluate the normal distribution of the variables, and skewness and kurtosis values were examined. For both assessments, all self-report data were normally distributed. Assumptions of *t*-tests included normality, homogeneity of variance, and independence of observations. Violations of the assumption of homogeneity of variance were tested using Levene's test of equality of variances [170]. Descriptive statistics were conducted to summarize the demographic characteristics of the sample as well as scores for the self-reported and performance-based measures of interest (i.e., stress). Pearson's correlations examined bivariate relationships between smartphone distraction and psychological variables, and frequency of smartphone and social media use (presented in Table 3).

#### 2.5.3. Randomization and Risk of Bias

While allocation randomisation aimed to reduce any differences between the groups at baseline, a series of independent sample *t*-tests for the continuous variables and chi-square tests for the categorical variables (gender, ethnicity and education and relationship status) were conducted to analyse group mean differences and compare the baseline and post-intervention outcomes for the control and intervention groups. These were also applied at post-intervention outcomes for both the control and the intervention group. A decrease from the baseline to the post-intervention assessment was hypothesised for the primary outcomes of smartphone distraction, stress, anxiety, deficient self-regulation, FoMO and NoMO and an increase was hypothesized for mindful attention, self-awareness and self-efficacy.

Following the descriptive analysis, data from the baseline and post-intervention assessments were analysed to test each of the hypotheses provided to inform the assessment of the intervention efficacy. Two approaches to analysis were adopted. First, to isolate any effect of the intervention, a per-protocol (PP) analysis was conducted to maintain the baseline equivalence of the intervention group produced by random allocation [171]. However, given the limitations to this first analysis approach and to minimise biases resulting from noncompliance, non-adherence, attrition or withdrawal [172,173], analysis was performed also on an intention-to-treat (ITT) basis [172]. However, these results were not reported in the present study.

#### 2.5.4. Analysis of Intervention Effects and Testing of Hypothesized Mechanisms

The effects of the intervention were assessed with an analysis of covariance (ANCOVA), with a minimum significance level at $p < 0.05$. ANCOVA was chosen given that it is quite robust with regard to violations of normality, with minimal effects on significance or power [174,175] with any differences between the groups at baseline, for the various assessments being used as covariates in the model and considered artefacts of the randomisation [176]. Co-varying for baseline scores supported the analysis in two ways. First, while randomisation aimed to reduce any pre-intervention differences between the groups, residual random differences may have occurred. Accounting for such differences isolated the effect of the intervention. Partial eta-squared were used as measures of strength of association [177]. To better understand the effect size of the intervention, it has been recommended to use the differences in adjusted means (standardized mean difference effect sizes) between the two groups, as standardising can easily distort judgements of the magnitude of an effect (due to changes to the sample SD but not the population SD, which may bias the estimate of the effect size measure, such as Cohen's *d*) [178]. As Cohen's *d* has been reported in other RCT and pre-post intervention studies, Cohen's *d* was estimated [179]. Finally, because the sample sizes of the two groups were unequal, Type III Sums of Squares were used for the ANCOVA.

To test the third hypothesis and the hypothesized psychological mechanisms underlying the intervention results, three different mediation analyses were performed across the chosen psychological constructs using SPSS Statistics (version 25) and PROCESS (Model 4; [180–183]), using a non-parametric resampling method bootstrap with 5000 bootstrapped samples and bias-corrected 95% confidence intervals, to probe conditional indirect effects for the variables examined. These analyses were performed on the ITT sample in post-intervention results.

## 3. Results

### 3.1. Baseline Equivalence Evaluation

The *t*-test results for the pre-test scores found no significant differences between the groups, indicating independence. The post-test scores were significantly lower in the intervention group. For the smartphone distraction scale, the mean pre-test score was 58.06 ($SD = 7.69$) for the intervention group and 59.72 ($SD = 8.08$) for the control group. The mean post-test score was 39.70 ($SD = 17.67$) for the intervention and 58.78 ($SD = 17.47$) for the control group, respectively. The pre-test score mean was not significantly different between groups ($t = -0.70$, *ns*), but the post-test score mean was significantly lower for the intervention group than for the comparison group ($t = -6.69$, $p < 0.001$). The pattern was similar in the results for the other variables except for NoMO, habitual behaviour, and social media use per day. Table 2 provides a summary of the baseline *t*-test and chi-square outcomes and internal consistency for each scale at each measurement period. All scales demonstrated good internal consistency for the sample considered.

**Table 2.** Per protocol baseline sociodemographic, usage data, psychological variables and pre-post intervention scale reliabilities.

| | Intervention ($n = 72$) | | Control ($n = 71$) | | Chi Square/ *t*-Tests | | |
|---|---|---|---|---|---|---|---|
| Socio/demographics | *n* | % | *n* | % | | - | - |
| Gender (female) | 60 | 83.33 | 62 | 87.32 | 1.83, *ns* [a] | | |
| Education (under graduates %) | 67 | 93.05 | 65 | 91.54 | 1.03, *ns* | | |
| Relationship status (% not in relation) | 40 | 55.55 | 38 | 53.52 | 1.35, *ns* | | |
| Ethnicity (White %) | 49 | 68.05 | 42 | 59.15 | 1.63, *ns* | | |
| | *M (SD)* | | *M (SD)* | | *t* Tests | Cronbach's α T1 | Cronbach's α T2 |
| Age | 20.69 (3.27) | | 20.82 (3.70) | | −0.20, *ns* | - | - |
| Smart hours/day | 4.55 (2.28) | | 5.23 (1.89) | | −0.28, *ns* | - | - |
| SM hours/day | 2.17 (1.430 | | 2.47 (1.28) | | −1.36, *ns* | - | - |
| Smart. distraction | 59.52 (7.69) | | 57.55 (8.08) | | −0.70, *ns* | 0.90 | 0.88 |
| Self-awareness | 74.71(8.20) | | 75.00 (9.38) | | −0.20, *ns* | 0.87 | 0.86 |
| Mindful Attention | 3.28 (0.52) | | 3.40 (0.56) | | −1.32, *ns* | 0.92 | 0.93 |
| Stress | 24.44 (4.72) | | 28.78 (6.05) | | −0.33, *ns* | 0.86 | 0.83 |
| Anxiety | 15.93 (5.94) | | 16.63 (4.94) | | −0.77, *ns* | 0.93 | 0.90 |
| Online vigilance | 2.43 (0.48) | | 2.38 (0.52) | | 0.63, *ns* | 0.89 | 0.87 |
| Efficacy | 28.04 (4.35) | | 28.96 (4.55) | | −2.51, *ns* | 0.90 | 0.88 |
| FoMO | 3.48 (1.36) | | 3.54 (1.34) | | −0.32, *ns* | 0.89 | 0.90 |
| NoMO | 77.17 (22.40) | | 86.32 (23.68) | | −0.49., *ns* | 0.89 | 0.88 |
| Def. self-regulation | 14.15 (5.32) | | 15.35 (5.39) | | −1.50, *ns* | 0.89 | 0.87 |
| Impulsivity | 14.74 (3.39) | | 16.27 (3.52) | | −0.264, *ns* | 0.85 | 0.86 |
| Prob. SM use | 17.15 (4.95) | | 17.18 (5.42) | | −0.035, *ns* | 0.91 | 0.89 |
| Automaticity | 5.14 (1.33) | | 5.11 (1.20) | | −0.88, *ns* | 0.87 | 0.89 |

a ns = non-significant. FoMO = Fear of Missing Out; NoMO = Nomophobia; Def. self-regulation = Deficient self-regulation; Prob. SM use = Problematic social media use.

A series of Bivariate Pearson's *r* correlation analyses was conducted to examine the results obtained amongst SDs and the secondary outcomes (Table 3). Smartphone distraction correlated significantly with problematic social media use ($r(252) = 0.63$, $p < 0.01$), anxiety ($r$ $(252) = 0.46$, $p < 0.01$), online vigilance ($r$ $(252) = 0.51$, $p < 0.01$), automaticity ($r$ $(252) = 0.57$, $p < 0.01$), impulsivity ($r(252) = 0.45$, $p < 0.01$), deficient self-regulation ($r(252) = 0.33$, $p < 0.01$), smartphone use/day ($r(252) = 0.31$, $p < 0.01$), $p < 0.01$), FoMO ($r(252) = 0.28$, $p < 0.01$) and NoMO ($r(252) = 0.51$, $p < 0.01$). However, smartphone distraction correlated negatively with two variables: mindful attention ($r(252) = -0.52$, $p < 0.01$) and self-awareness ($r(252) = -0.34$, $p < 0.01$).

**Table 3.** Bivariate Pearson's *r* correlation analyses.

| | 1 | 2 | 3 | 4 | 5 | 6 | 7 | 8 | 9 | 10 | 11 | 12 | 13 | 14 |
|---|---|---|---|---|---|---|---|---|---|---|---|---|---|---|
| 1. Distraction | 1 | | | | | | | | | | | | | |
| 2. Stress | 0.199 ** | 1 | | | | | | | | | | | | |
| 3. Pr. SM use | 0.631 ** | 0.173 ** | 1 | | | | | | | | | | | |
| 4. Mind.Att. | −0.523 ** | −0.145 * | −0.455 ** | 1 | | | | | | | | | | |
| 5. Self-Aware | −0.340 ** | 0.057 | −0.318 ** | −0.209 ** | 1 | | | | | | | | | |
| 6. Anxiety | 0.460 ** | 0.380 ** | 0.435 ** | 0.450 ** | 0.242 ** | 1 | | | | | | | | |
| 7. Onl. Vigil. | 0.507 ** | 0.280 ** | 0.620 ** | 0.380 ** | 0.223 ** | 0.283 ** | 1 | | | | | | | |
| 8. Efficacy | −0.107 | −0.343 ** | −0.149 * | −0.101 | 0.148 * | −0.399 ** | −0.056 | 1 | | | | | | |
| 9. Automat | 0.575 ** | 0.286 ** | 0.466 * | 0.324 ** | 0.194 ** | 0.304 ** | 0.348 ** | −0.179 ** | 1 | | | | | |
| 10. Impuls. | 0.455 ** | 0.006 | −0.053 | −0.037 | −0.522 | −0.026 | 0.035 | 0.086 | 0.037 | 1 | | | | |
| 11. Def. Self-reg. | 0.333 ** | 0.048 | 0.017 | 0.048 | −0.068 | 0.007 | 0.074 | 0.025 | 0.049 | 0.859 ** | 1 | | | |
| 12. Smart/day | 0.314 ** | −0.280 | 0.013 | −0.128 | −0.025 | −0.161 | 0.082 | 0.021 | −0.145 | −0.008 | −0.004 | 1 | | |
| 13. SM/day | 0.116 | 0.004 | −0.025 | −0.008 | −0.109 | 0.024 | −0.035 | −0.111 | 0.061 | 0.154 | 0.168 * | 0.423 ** | 1 | |
| 14. FoMO | 0.281 ** | 0.323 ** | 0.382 ** | 0.103 | 0.310 ** | 0.369 ** | −0.032 | −0.164 ** | 0.235 ** | 0.026 | 0.035 | 0.183 ** | 0.180 ** | 1 |
| 15. NoMO | 0.513 ** | 0.375 ** | 0.421 ** | 0.007 | 0.142 * | 0.312 ** | 0.136 * | −0.209 ** | 0.392 ** | −0.084 | −0.084 | 0.189 ** | 0.096 | 0.341 ** |

* $p < 0.05$; ** $p < 0.01$; *** $p < 0.001$. Pr. SM use: Problematic social media use; Mind. Att: Mindful attention; Onl. Vigil.: Online vigilance; FoMO: Fear of Missing Out; NoMO: Nomophobia; Def. self-regulation: Deficient self-regulation; SM/day; Social Media use/day.

### 3.2. *Intervention Efficacy Evaluation*

To test H1 and assess the effect of the intervention on smartphone distraction, two separate ANCOVAs were conducted. First, to isolate any effect of the intervention, a per-protocol analysis was conducted. As depicted in Table 4, distraction outcomes decreased significantly for the intervention group from the baseline (intervention: $M = 58.06$, $SD = 7.69$; control: $M = 59.72$, $SD = 8.08$) to the post-intervention assessment (intervention: $M = 39.70$, $SD = 17.67$; control: $M = 58.78$, $SD = 17.47$), with a non-significant difference for the control group. As confirmed by Levene's test, the outcome variances were homogenous. Confirming the homogeneity of the regression slopes, the interaction between the baseline scores and the experimental group was significant. There was a main effect of the intervention group on post-intervention distraction scores after controlling for baseline outcomes ($F(1, 140) = 46.59$, $p < 0.001$, $\eta p^2 = 0.250$). The baseline scores were not a significant predictor of post-intervention values ($F(1, 140) = 18.62$, $p = 0.117$). Post-hoc tests indicated there was a statistically significant adjusted mean difference ($M = -18.95$, $SD = 2.77$, ($p < 0.001$) in reduction between IG compared to CG (Figure 2). For the ITT analysis, a main effect on the intervention group on post-intervention SDS outcomes after controlling for the baseline values was found ($F(1, 250) = 96.88$, $p < 0.001$, $\eta p^2 = 0.28$). As indicated in Figure 2, post-hoc tests indicated there was a significant difference between IG and CG ($p < 0.001$). Comparing the estimated marginal means showed that there was an adjusted mean difference in reduction between IG ($M = 39.56$) compared to CG ($M = 58.93$). Consequently, across both analyses, this hypothesis was supported.

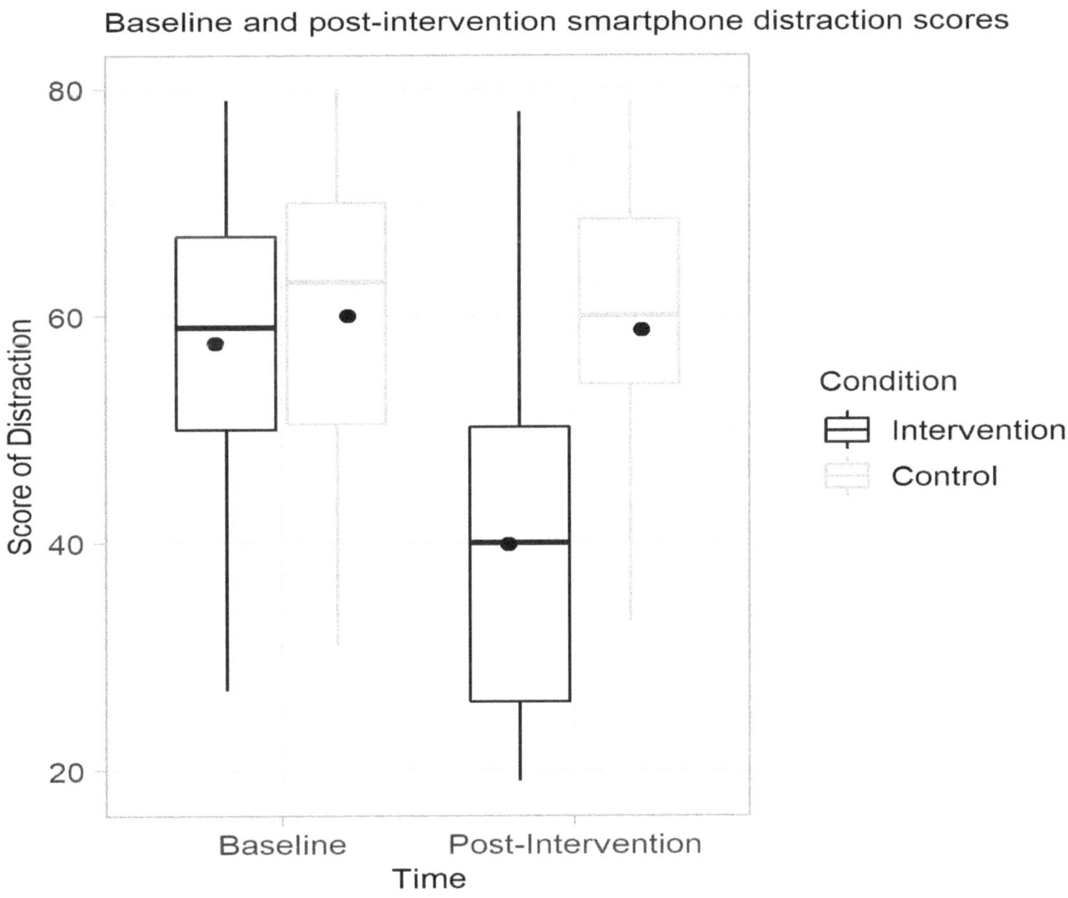


**Figure 2.** Per protocol smartphone distraction outcomes before and after the intervention.

**Table 4.** Per protocol sample ($n = 143$) primary and secondary measures, means, SDs, effect sizes and $F$-values for between-group comparisons.

| Measure | Experimental ($n = 72$) | | Control ($n = 71$) | | Effect | Effect Size | Cohen's $d$ |
|---|---|---|---|---|---|---|---|
| | Pre | Post | Pre | Post | | | |
| | M(SD) | M(SD) | M(SD) | M(SD) | $F$ | $\eta p2$ | $d$ |
| Smart.Distraction | 58.06 (7.69) | 39.70 (17.67) | 59.72 (8.08) | 58.78 (17.47) | 46.59 *** | 0.25 | 1.11 |
| Self-awareness | 74.71 (8.20) | 83.30 (9.89) | 75.00 (9.38) | 76.25 (10.25) | 18.19 *** | 0.12 | 0.69 |
| Mind.Attention | 3.28 (0.52) | 3.97 (0.69) | 3.40 (0.56) | 3.37 (0.76) | 16.24 *** | 0.22 | 0.82 |
| Stress | 24.44 (4.72) | 24.10 (4.63) | 28.78 (6.05) | 27.94 (5.24) | 23.11 *** | 0.14 | 0.77 |
| Anxiety | 15.93 (5.94) | 14.75 (4.43) | 16.63 (4.95) | 17.44 (4.42) | 12.42 *** | 0.08 | 0.60 |
| Vigilance | 2.43 (0.49) | 1.98 (0.63) | 2.38 (0.52) | 2.39 (0.52) | 18.66 *** | 0.12 | 0.70 |
| Self-efficacy | 28.04 (4.36) | 32.32 (5.08) | 28.96 (4.55) | 29.99 (5.05) | 9.40 *** | 0.06 | 0.46 |
| FoMO | 3.48 (1.36) | 2.86 (1.16) | 3.54 (1.34) | 3.32 (1.22) | 5.49 *** | 0.04 | 0.39 |
| NoMO | 77.17 (2.40) | 78.03 (2.72) | 86.32 (23.6) | 79.50 (2.74) | 7.71 | - | - |
| Def. self-reg. | 17.16 (6.70) | 14.00 (5.32) | 17.61 (6.91) | 15.32 (5.39) | 6.60 *** | 0.04 | 0.25 |
| Impulsivity | 17.32 (3.79) | 14.74 (3.41) | 17.65 (3.92) | 16.27 (3.51) | 15.91 *** | 0.10 | 0.44 |
| Probl. SM use | 17.15 (4.95) | 15.12 (4.40) | 17.18 (5.42) | 17.24 (5.11) | 6.96 *** | 0.05 | 0.44 |
| Automaticity | 5.14 (1.33) | 4.77 (1.30) | 5.11 (1.20) | 4.98 (1.59) | 0.78 | - | - |
| SM. use/day | 2.92 (1.75) | 2.17 (1.44) | 2.89 (1.52) | 2.47 (1.28) | 3.70 | - | - |
| Smart. use/day | 4.51 (2.28) | 3.51 (1.88) | 4.45 (1.89) | 4.11 (1.68) | 4.43 *** | 0.03 | 0.34 |

* $p < 0.05$; ** $p < 0.01$; *** $p < 0.001$.

ANCOVA analyses for the secondary outcomes were also tested across both PP and ITT samples. Specifically, for the PP sample, main effects of the experimental group on post-intervention outcomes after controlling for baseline scores were found for self-awareness ($F(1, 140) = 18.19$, $p < 0.001$, $\eta p^2 = 0.115$), mindful attention ($F(1, 140) = 16.24$, $p < 0.001$, $\eta p^2 = 0.22$), anxiety ($F(1, 140) = 12.42$, $p < 0.001$, $\eta p^2 = 0.08$), stress ($F(1, 140) = 23.11$, $p < 0.001$, $\eta p^2 = 0.14$), online vigilance ($F(1, 140) = 18.66$, $p < 0.001$, $\eta p^{2=}$ 0.118), FoMO ($F(1, 140) = 5.49$, $p < 0.001$, $\eta p^2 = 0.04$), deficient self-regulation ($F(1, 140) = 6.60$, $p < 0.001$, $\eta p^2 = 0.045$), self-efficacy ($F(1, 140) = 9.40$, $p < 0.001$, $\eta p^2 = 0.063$), impulsivity ($F(1, 140) = 15.91$, $p < 0.001$, $\eta p^2 = 0.10$), problematic social media use ($F(1, 140) = 6.96$, $p < 0.001$, $\eta p^2 = 0.05$), and smartphone use/day ($F(1, 140) = 4.43$, $p < 0.001$, $\eta p^2 = 0.03$). No intervention effects were found for the intervention group for the variables of social media use/day ($F(1, 140) = 3.697$, $p = 0.06$), habit strength ($F(1, 140) = 0.78$, $p = 0.78$), and NoMO ($F(1, 140) = 7.714$, $p = 0.91$). ITT analyses demonstrated similar patterns to the PP samples' outcomes.

### *3.3. Intervention Effects Based on Distraction Severity*

In order to evaluate the effects of the intervention in the intervention group based on level of distraction and to assess whether the effects were consistent in the intervention group independent of degree of distraction, participants were classed into two categories of high distractors vs. low distractors depending on perceived distraction level. A median-split analysis with high vs. low distractor levels was determined by scores above vs. below the median and these were separately analysed inside the intervention group. Therefore, a two-way mixed ANOVA with time (pre-test and post-test) as within-factor and distraction severity (high and low distraction) as between-factor was performed to investigate the impact of the intervention (time) and degree of distraction (high vs. low) as assessed at baseline on distraction levels at post-intervention. This analysis was conducted only for the dependent variable for which the interactions were found to be significant.

Results indicated there was a significant main effect of the intervention $F(1,70) = 77.17$, $p < 0.001$. There was a significant main effect of distraction $F(1,70) = 21.48$, $p < 0.001$ with high distractors ($M = 48.67$) benefiting more than the low distractors ($M = 33.54$). Additionally, there was a significant interaction between the distraction status (high vs. low) and the degree of distraction $F(1,70) = 20.10$, $p < 0.001$. No significant interactions were found for self-awareness ($F(1,70) = 1.07$, $p = 0.32$); stress ($F(1,70) = 0.17$, $p = 0.68$); online vigilance ($F(1,70) = 0.98$, $p = 0.32$), deficient self-regulation ($F(1,70) = 0.22$, $p = 0.64$), self-efficacy ($F(1,70) = 0.22$, $p = 0.64$), anxiety (F(1,70) = 1.73, $p = 0.19$), and social media use ($F(1,70) = 19.28$, $p = 0.30$). However, significant main effects were also found for self-awareness

($F(1,70) = 30.05, p < 0.001$), deficient self-regulation $F(1,70) = 20.10, p < 0.001$, stress ($F(1,70) = 47.95, p < 0.001$), online vigilance $F(1,70) = 42.07, p < 0.001$, problematic social media use $F(1,70) = 9.94, p < 0.05$; FoMO ($F(1,70) = 10.33, p < 0.001$) and smartphone use/day ($F(1,70) = 53.12, p < 0.001$).

### 3.4. Mediation Analyses

More specifically for mediation 1, the intervention group was the proposed independent variable in these analyses, mindfulness was the proposed mediator, and smartphone distraction was the outcome variable. For mediation 2, stress was the proposed independent variable in these analyses, online vigilance was the proposed mediator, and smartphone distraction was the outcome variable. For mediation 3, smartphone distraction was the predictor, social media addiction was the outcome and online vigilance was the mediator. Analysed variables included the T1 scores on the constructs examined as covariates to account for pre-intervention performance.

For mediation 1, it was hypothesized that mindful attention would mediate the relationship between the intervention and smartphone distraction (Table 5). No mediation effect was found for mindful attention on the variables. However, a main effect of the intervention on smartphone distraction (path a: $b = -0.67, t = -8.23, p < 0.001$) was found, but no main effect of mindful attention on smartphone distraction (path b; $b = 1.16, t = 0.67, ns$).

**Table 5.** Mediation effects of mindful attention and emotional self-awareness on intervention effects and smartphone distraction and of online vigilance on smartphone distraction and social media addiction ($n = 252$).

| Predictor | Outcome | Mediator | *ab* (*B*) | *a* | *b* | *c* | *c′* |
|---|---|---|---|---|---|---|---|
| Intervention | Smart.Distract. | Mindful Att. | −0.79 [−3.10, −1.59] | −0.67 [−0.84, −0.51] | 1.16 [−2.25, 4.58] | 20.75 [16.35, 25.16] | 21.55 [16.62,26.48] |
| Intervention | Smart.Distract. | Self-aware | −2.02 [−3.97, −0.35] | −6.78 [−9.15, −4.40] | 0.30 [0.07, 0.52] | 20.91 [16.59, 25.22] | 22.93 [18.38, 27.48] |
| Smart. distract. | Probl. SM use | On.vigilance | 0.02 [0.01, 0.03] | 0.01 [0.010, 0.015] | 1.66 [0.78, 2.54] | 0.11 [0.08, 0.13] | 0.089 [0.06, 0.12] |

For mediation 2, it was hypothesized that self-awareness would mediate the relationship between the intervention and smartphone distraction (Table 5). An indirect effect was found on self-awareness on the variables (a × b: $b = -2.02$, BCa CI = [−3.10, −1.59]), indicating mediation. The intervention significantly predicted self-awareness (path a; $b = -6.78, t = -4.32, p < 0.001$) and self-awareness significantly predicted lower levels of smartphone distraction (path b; $b = 0.30, t = 4.02, p < 0.001$).

For mediation 3, it was hypothesized that online vigilance would mediate the relationship between distraction and social media addiction (Table 5). An indirect effect was found on self-awareness on the variables (a × b: $b = 0.02$, BCa CI = [0.01, 0.03]), indicating mediation. The intervention significantly predicted self-awareness (path a; $b = -0.01, t = -3.32, p < 0.001$) and self-awareness significantly predicted lower levels of smartphone distraction (path b; $b = 1.66, t = 4.02, p < 0.001$).

## 4. Discussion

The present study tested the efficacy of an online intervention employing an integrative set of strategies—consisting of mindfulness, self-monitoring and mood tracking—in assisting young adults to decrease levels of smartphone distraction and improve on a variety of secondary psychological outcomes, such as mindful attention, emotional awareness, stress and anxiety, and perceived self-efficacy, as well as to reduce stress, anxiety, deficient self-regulation, problematic social media use and smartphone-related psychological outcomes (i.e., online vigilance, FoMO and NoMO). Results of the present study provided support for the online intervention effectiveness in impacting these outcomes. Findings suggested that students receiving the intervention reported a significant reduction in the primary outcome of smartphone distraction, unlike students in the control group who reported a non-significant reduction in smartphone distraction. In terms of the secondary outcomes, participants in the intervention condition experienced a significant increase in self-awareness, mindful attention, and self-efficacy, and a significant decrease in smartphone use/day, impulsivity, stress, anxiety, deficient self-regulation, FoMO, and problematic use. No significant results were found for social media use per day, habitual/automated use and NoMO.

According to the findings of the present intervention, it appears likely that practising mindfulness and monitoring mood and smartphone activity could lead to a desired behavioural change towards less distraction and less perceived stress with carry-over effects in self-awareness and self-efficacy, similar to interventions for other mental health problems [83,85,87,91,93,184,185]. These findings are consistent with the growing body of research indicating that mindfulness and self-monitoring are effective strategies to increase self-awareness and reduce stress [84–90,186]. Mindful attention could enhance awareness of individual media behaviour by: (i) raising understanding and awareness of disruptive media multitasking activities (i.e., predictors, patterns and effects), and (ii) raising awareness of different strategies for coping with digital distraction and of which strategies are most effective. Second, self-monitoring could help in developing an understanding of media habits and time spent on smartphone and social media activities and could curb perceived excess smartphone interaction, consistent with other study findings [92,101,187,188]. Therefore, strategies employing increased mindfulness practice and self-monitoring could aid attentional capacity and self-awareness, which is considered a necessary condition in the behaviour change process of risky behaviours [189,190].

Third, mood tracking could enhance awareness of triggers of negative mood and ensuing negative emotional states acting as drivers for distraction. It appears that the same technologies which may impact negatively on young people may be used to leverage smartphone use [100] and deflect psychological distress if evidence-based behaviour change strategies are applied. Intervention strategies such as mindfulness and self-monitoring may encourage increased self-awareness and thus help reduce distraction levels and increase mindful attention.

The intervention was also successful in reducing secondary outcomes, such as stress levels and FoMO, and it had a positive effect on emotion regulation and loss of control levels. Distraction appears to be associated with higher access to social media content and is mediated by online vigilance. Salience of smartphone-mediated social interactions (i.e., the salience dimension of online vigilance) has been found to be negatively related to affective wellbeing [49]. It has been reported that emotional dysregulation mediates the relationship between psychological distress and problematic smartphone use [191]. Higher self-regulation online has been identified as a moderator between need to belong and problematic social media use in young people [192] and emotion dysregulation as a mediator between insecure attachment and addiction [193]. Although distraction is an emotion regulation strategy with a protective function against emotionally distressing states [111] and dysphoric mood [194], or is used for adaptive coping [195,196], deficits in attentional control, such as distraction, may also be implicated in stress, anxiety or other affective disorders [197] and in generalized anxiety disorder with core cognitive symptoms related to excessive thoughts and deficits associated with increased perseverative worry [198]. Therefore, higher mindful attention and monitoring of mood may have influenced the reduction of distraction and the enhancement of emotional control.

Mediation analyses were also performed to understand the relationships between intervention effects on smartphone distraction via two mediators, mindful attention and self-awareness, and of online vigilance on the relationship between distraction and social media addiction. Mediation effects were significant for the relationship among intervention effects and distraction via self-awareness, and for distraction and problematic social media use via online vigilance, indicating that self-awareness could be a potential behaviour strategy to mitigate distraction levels. However, the relationship among intervention effects and distraction was not significant via mindful attention as a mediator. Therefore, in the present study it appeared that despite its statistically significant increase, mindful attention was not a mediating factor for distraction in the intervention. Mindful attention could potentially be the vehicle to increasing emotional self-awareness [93,184,199], prompting more controlled smartphone interactions. On the contrary, online vigilance was found to be a mechanism associated with smartphone distraction and problematic social media use, given the strong preoccupation with the content prompted even by the mere presence of smartphones, confirming previous findings [200].

Therefore, despite its protective function, distraction may concurrently serve as a gateway to increased smartphone engagement and time spent on devices. Time spent alone is not a defining factor and it has been argued instead that the interaction of content, context and time spent, as well as the meaning attached to these interactions, may determine the level of problematic media use [5,201]. Within smartphone use, distraction is a salient behaviour with evidence that distraction and mind-wandering are associated with online vigilance, which via reduced mindfulness may be associated with decreased wellbeing [78]. Furthermore, inattention symptoms have been implicated in risk for smartphone addiction and problematic smartphone use [202]. Therefore, handling distraction, which has neural correlates [203], may be the means to resisting cue reactivity, implicated in smartphone addiction, in reduced cognitive performance [113] or in obsessive-compulsive symptoms [204]. Further research is required to assess these cognitive and emotive dimensions of smartphone distraction and its effects on engagement in line with current trends [205]. However, it has been proposed that the construct of distraction extends beyond the debate on smartphone addiction by considering the role of the smartphone in coping with negative emotions and addressing preference for online vs. offline communications [206].

Research is still conflicted in relation to the cognitive function of distraction. Experimental smartphone research has provided initial evidence that social apps compared to non-social apps on smartphones do not capture attention despite their perceived high reward value [207,208], but other studies support a high interference effect [209]. Therefore, more research is required to elucidate the mechanisms of digital distraction and delineate how digital technologies, individual choices, and contexts affect individuals' attention spans and attentional loss, as well as mental health conditions, such as ADHD and anxiety and overall psychological wellbeing [210]. The present RCT assessed the effectiveness of the impact of the use of mindfulness, self-monitoring, and mood tracking delivered through interaction with smartphone apps in reducing distraction arising from recreational smartphone use and social media use. The findings suggest that engaging with the aforementioned practices was effective in reducing distraction levels, stress, anxiety, deficient self-regulation, impulsivity and smartphone-related psychological outcomes, and improving mindful attention and emotional self-awareness and self-efficacy.

*Limitations, Implications, and Recommendations*

Some limitations need to be taken into consideration. First, a convenience sample of university students was used, which hinders the generalizability of the findings to other groups (i.e., older adults or children). However, this population was considered of primary interest for the study because university students are digital natives liable to experience negative academic consequences due to vulnerability to problematic smartphone use [211].

The effect sizes found in this RCT were medium to large for the variables examined, exceeding the expected range for low-intensity, non-clinical interventions [212]. However, as a result of the main recruitment protocol, the intervention may have attracted participants who had an interest in the outcomes and a potential self-assessed vulnerability. Therefore, the voluntary, self-selected nature of participation could have introduced a significant degree of participant response and confirmation bias [213], resulting in the medium to high effect sizes. Additionally, the high drop-out rates, consistent with other online RCTs [214], could have significantly affected the strength of the findings [215], and the use of a passive control group might have led to an overestimation of the effects [216]. Due to the use of market-available apps, actual adherence and engagement with the intervention was not accounted for, nor were reasons for dropout [217]. Therefore, the findings should be treated with caution and replicated in future designs. Future studies should systematically address response bias and include methods in the RCT to improve the accuracy of self-reported data [218,219]. Combining self-report with behavioural data [220], ecological momentary sampling [221], psycho-informatics and digital phenotyping, the provision of a digital footprint for prognostic, diagnostic and intervention purposes [222], could enhance the ecological validity of the study. Equally, incorporating the measurement of brain activity using magnetic resonance imaging (MRI) in interventions could greatly enhance accuracy of assessment of prevention efforts and understanding of the role of neurobiology in behaviour [223,224].

The impact of the intervention on gender was not examined because this university student sample consisted mainly of female participants. Considering the gender differences reported in smartphone use [48,225] and in attention processes [226], future studies should explore its effect, which could have significant implications for the intervention and prevention of attention failures and poor student outcomes [227]. Additionally, the study design did not manage to provide a longer intervention period due to the lack of freely available apps for participants to use and did not include a second follow-up period to track maintenance of long-term effects, as is customary in RCTs, or the use of qualitative process evaluation for a critical understanding of impact of the intervention components [228]. Finally, social, economic and family conditions as well as other issues, which are critical to young people's psycho-emotional states and sense of identity, were not accounted for in the present study [229,230].

Despite these limitations, the study provides initial evidence for efficacy of strategies in curbing smartphone distraction and adds to the limited body of knowledge of cognitive-emotive processes in smartphone and social media use [205]. It also contributed to the still limited knowledge on interventions in smartphone distraction and constitutes a simple, first-step, low key intervention programme, which may be practised by individuals seeking support for attentional difficulties on a self-help basis or within a stepped-care clinical framework for prevention purposes [96]. Experiencing distraction from smartphones and social media content, interferes with high-level cognitive processes and has productivity and emotional implications (i.e., stress) in various contexts and situations [51,231–234], being further compromised by digital triggers and the structural design of smartphones prompting salience and reactivity [235].

These results have clinical implications as low-intensity interventions may prevent small scale emotional problems from developing into clinical disorders and can reduce incidences of mental health problems [236,237]. Practitioners may also find value in using mindfulness and monitoring practices as an adjunct to therapy for problematic use of smartphones. It may be of high value for academic institutions to build specific university-based programmes on maintaining balanced technology use, tackling unregulated and promoting positive smartphone use, or guiding students towards suitable methods to address attention problems more effectively [238,239]. Apps may also be utilized by schools for students that are faced with attentional/excessive use difficulties and in assisting young people to become aware of their emotions in preparation for learning more adaptive coping strategies. Distraction is an emergent phenomenon in the digital era considering that the boundaries between work and recreation are increasingly blurred with both domains arguably dependent on the use of digital media [240]. More research on attentional processes within smartphone use could aid the understanding of these processes and impacts experienced across different age groups.

## 5. Conclusions

Psychological low-cost interventions may be effective in addressing precursors of problematic behaviours and enhancing wellbeing dimensions. The aim of the present study was to assess the efficacy of an RCT combining evidence-based cognitive-behavioural strategies to reduce distraction from smartphone use, increase mindful attention, emotional self-awareness and self-efficacy and reduce stress, anxiety, deficient self-regulation and smartphone related psychological outcomes (i.e., online vigilance, FoMO and NoMO). Second, it tested the mediating effect of mindful attention and self-awareness of the intervention on distraction, and of online vigilance on the relationship between distraction and social media addiction.

Findings suggested that students receiving the intervention reported a significant reduction in the primary outcome of smartphone distraction, whereas students in the control group reported a non-significant reduction in smartphone distraction. In terms of the secondary outcomes, participants in the intervention condition experienced a significant increase in self-awareness, mindful attention and self-efficacy and a significant decrease in smartphone use/day, impulsivity, stress and anxiety levels, FoMO, deficient self-regulation and problematic social media use. No significant results were found for duration of social media use/day, habitual use and NoMO. Mediation effects of the intervention were also observed on distraction and problematic social media use via the mediators of emotional self-awareness and online vigilance in mitigating distraction levels. Mindful attention was not found to be a mediating process for reducing distraction in the intervention.

Research on digital distraction is still scarce, yet there is increasing interest in cognitive impacts within digital environments. More evidence is required to assess the nature of attention failures and difficulties occurring both in normative and excessive online use. This evidence would allow an understanding of the prevalence and the nature of these difficulties, as well as their integration in intervention media literacy and risk prevention programmes, enhancing wellbeing, productivity and academic performance.

**Author Contributions:** Conceptualization, M.A.T.; methodology, M.A.T., M.D.G., M.R., D.J.K.; formal analysis, M.A.T.; investigation, M.A.T.; data curation, M.A.T.; supervision, M.D.G., M.R., D.J.K.; writing—original draft preparation, M.A.T.; review and editing, M.A.T., M.D.G., M.R., D.J.K.; All authors have read and agreed to the published version of the manuscript.

## References

1. Ashinoff, B.K.; Abu-Akel, A. Hyperfocus: The forgotten frontier of attention. *Psychol. Res.* **2019**. [CrossRef] [PubMed]
2. Atchley, P.; Lane, S. Cognition in the attention economy. In *Psychology of Learning and Motivation*; Elsevier: Amsterdam, The Netherlands, 2014; pp. 133–177; Available online: https://linkinghub.elsevier.com/retrieve/pii/B9780128002834000046 (accessed on 11 June 2019).
3. Falkinger, J. Attention economies. *J. Econ. Theory* **2007**, *133*, 266–294. [CrossRef]
4. Lee, A.R.; Son, S.-M.; Kim, K.K. Information and communication technology overload and social networking service fatigue: A stress perspective. *Comput. Hum. Behav.* **2016**, *55*, 51–61. [CrossRef]
5. Throuvala, M.A.; Griffiths, M.D.; Rennoldson, M.; Kuss, D.J. A 'control model' of social media engagement in adolescence: A grounded theory analysis. *Int.J. Environ. Res. Public Health* **2019**, *16*, 4696. [CrossRef]
6. Rosen, C. *The Myth of Multitasking*; Center for the Study of Technology and Society: Washington, DC, USA, 2008; pp. 105–110; Available online: https://www.jstor.org/stable/43152412 (accessed on 5 April 2020).
7. Statista. Number of Smartphone Users Worldwide from 2016 to 2021. 2020. Available online: https://www.statista.com/statistics/330695/number-of-smartphone-users-worldwide/ (accessed on 20 March 2020).
8. Busch, P.A.; McCarthy, S. Antecedents and consequences of problematic smartphone use: A systematic literature review of an emerging research area. *Comput. Hum. Behav.* **2020**, 106414. [CrossRef]
9. Kuss, D.; Harkin, L.; Kanjo, E.; Billieux, J. Problematic smartphone use: Investigating contemporary experiences using a convergent design. *Int. J. Environ. Res. Public Health* **2018**, *15*, 142. [CrossRef]
10. Montag, C.; Wegmann, E.; Sariyska, R.; Demetrovics, Z.; Brand, M. How to overcome taxonomical problems in the study of Internet use disorders and what to do with "smartphone addiction"? *J. Behav. Addict.* **2019**, 1–7. [CrossRef] [PubMed]
11. Beuckels, E.; Kazakova, S.; Cauberghe, V.; Hudders, L.; De Pelsmacker, P. Freedom makes you lose control: Executive control deficits for heavy versus light media multitaskers and the implications for advertising effectiveness. *Eur. J. Mark.* **2019**, *53*, 848–870. [CrossRef]
12. Fitz, N.; Kushlev, K.; Jagannathan, R.; Lewis, T.; Paliwal, D.; Ariely, D. Batching smartphone notifications can improve well-being. *Comput. Hum. Behav.* **2019**, *101*, 84–94. [CrossRef]
13. Marsh, E.J.; Rajaram, S. The digital expansion of the mind: Implications of Internet usage for memory and cognition. *J. Appl. Res. Mem. Cogn.* **2019**, *8*, 1–14. [CrossRef]
14. Ward, A.F.; Duke, K.; Gneezy, A.; Bos, M.W. Brain drain: The mere presence of one's own smartphone reduces available cognitive capacity. *J. Assoc. Consum. Res.* **2017**, *2*, 140–154. [CrossRef]
15. Thornton, B.; Faires, A.; Robbins, M.; Rollins, E. The mere presence of a cell phone may be distracting: Implications for attention and task performance. *Soc. Psychol.* **2014**, *45*, 479–488. [CrossRef]

16. Hartanto, A.; Yang, H. Is the smartphone a smart choice? The effect of smartphone separation on executive functions. *Comput. Hum. Behav.* **2016**, *64*, 329–336. [CrossRef]
17. Wilmer, H.H.; Sherman, L.E.; Chein, J.M. Smartphones and cognition: A review of research exploring the links between mobile technology habits and cognitive functioning. *Front. Psychol.* **2017**, *8*. [CrossRef] [PubMed]
18. Canale, N.; Vieno, A.; Doro, M.; Rosa Mineo, E.; Marino, C.; Billieux, J. Emotion-related impulsivity moderates the cognitive interference effect of smartphone availability on working memory. *Sci. Rep.* **2019**, *9*, 18519. [CrossRef]
19. Hadar, A.; Hadas, I.; Lazarovits, A.; Alyagon, U.; Eliraz, D.; Zangen, A. Answering the missed call: Initial exploration of cognitive and electrophysiological changes associated with smartphone use and abuse. *PLoS ONE* **2017**, *12*, e0180094. [CrossRef] [PubMed]
20. Duke, É.; Montag, C. Smartphone addiction, daily interruptions and self-reported productivity. *Addict. Behav. Rep.* **2017**, *6*, 90–95. [CrossRef]
21. Barr, N.; Pennycook, G.; Stolz, J.A.; Fugelsang, J.A. The brain in your pocket: Evidence that smartphones are used to supplant thinking. *Comput. Hum. Behav.* **2015**, *48*, 473–480. [CrossRef]
22. Kim, I.; Kim, R.; Kim, H.; Kim, D.; Han, K.; Lee, P.H.; Mark, D.; Lee, U. Understanding smartphone usage in college classrooms: A long-term measurement study. *Comput. Educ.* **2019**, *141*, 103611. [CrossRef]
23. Rostain, A.L. Book review of the "The Distracted Mind: Ancient Brains in a High-Tech World". *J. Am. Acad. Child. Adolesc. Psychiatry* **2019**, *58*, 829–831. Available online: https://linkinghub.elsevier.com/retrieve/pii/S0890856719304125 (accessed on 3 August 2019). [CrossRef]
24. Mendoza, J.S.; Pody, B.C.; Lee, S.; Kim, M.; McDonough, I.M. The effect of cellphones on attention and learning: The influences of time, distraction, and nomophobia. *Comput. Hum. Behav.* **2018**, *86*, 52–60. [CrossRef]
25. Uncapher, M.R.K.; Thieu, M.; Wagner, A.D. Media multitasking and memory: Differences in working memory and long-term memory. *Psychon Bull. Rev.* **2016**, *23*, 483–490. [CrossRef]
26. McRae, K.; Hughes, B.; Chopra, S.; Gabrieli, J.D.E.; Gross, J.J.; Ochsner, K.N. The neural bases of distraction and reappraisal. *J. Cogn. Neurosci.* **2010**, *22*, 248–262. [CrossRef] [PubMed]
27. Nolen-Hoeksema, S.; Wisco, B.E.; Lyubomirsky, S. Rethinking rumination. *Perspect. Psychol. Sci.* **2008**, *3*, 400–424. [CrossRef] [PubMed]
28. Sheppes, G.; Scheibe, S.; Suri, G.; Gross, J.J. Emotion-regulation choice. *Psychol. Sci.* **2011**, *22*, 1391–1396. [CrossRef] [PubMed]
29. Moyal, N. Cognitive strategies to regulate emotions—current evidence and future directions. *Front. Psychol.* **2014**, *4*, 1019. [CrossRef]
30. Gross, J.J. The emerging field of emotion regulation: An integrative review. *Rev. Gen. Psychol.* **1998**. [CrossRef]
31. Gazzaley, A.; Rosen, L.D. *The Distracted Mind: Ancient Brains in a High-Tech. World*; MIT Press: Cambridge, MA, USA, 2016.
32. Rosen, L.D.; Lim, A.F.; Carrier, L.M.; Cheever, N.A. An empirical examination of the educational Impact of text message-induced task switching in the classroom: Educational implications and strategies to enhance learning. *Rev. Psicol. Educ.* **2011**, *17*, 163–177.
33. Stothart, C.; Mitchum, A.; Yehnert, C. The attentional cost of receiving a cell phone notification. *J. Exp. Psychol. Hum. Percept. Perform.* **2015**, *41*, 893–897. [CrossRef]
34. Peña-Sarrionandia, A.; Mikolajczak, M.; Gross, J.J. Integrating emotion regulation and emotional intelligence traditions: A meta-analysis. *Front. Psychol.* **2015**, *6*, 160. [CrossRef]
35. Baron, R.S. Distraction-conflict theory: Progress and problems. *Adv Exp. Soc. Psychol.* **1986**, *19*, 1–40.
36. Baron, R.S.; Moore, D.; Sanders, G.S. Distraction as a source of drive in social facilitation research. *J. Pers. Soc. Psychol.* **1978**, *36*, 816–824. [CrossRef]
37. Montagni, I.; Guichard, E.; Kurth, T. Association of screen time with self-perceived attention problems and hyperactivity levels in French students: A cross-sectional study. *BMJ Open* **2016**, *6*, e009089. [CrossRef] [PubMed]
38. Baumgartner, S.E.; van der Schuur, W.A.; Lemmens, J.S.; Te Poel, F. The relationship between media multitasking and attention problems in adolescents: Results of two longitudinal studies: Media multitasking and attention problems. *Hum. Commun. Res.* **2017**. [CrossRef]

39. Kuznekoff, J.H.; Titsworth, S. The impact of mobile phone usage on student learning. *Commun. Educ.* **2013**, *62*, 233–252. [CrossRef]
40. Giunchiglia, F.; Zeni, M.; Gobbi, E.; Bignotti, E.; Bison, I. Mobile social media usage and academic performance. *Comput. Hum. Behav.* **2018**, *82*, 177–185. [CrossRef]
41. Felisoni, D.D.; Godoi, A.S. Cell phone usage and academic performance: An experiment. *Comput. Educ.* **2018**, *117*, 175–187. [CrossRef]
42. Csibi, S.; Griffiths, M.D.; Demetrovics, Z.; Szabo, A. Analysis of problematic smartphone use across different age groups within the 'components model of addiction'. *Int. J. Ment. Health Addict.* **2019**. [CrossRef]
43. Lopez-Fernandez, O.; Kuss, D.J.; Romo, L.; Morvan, Y.; Kern, L.; Graziani, P.; Rousseau, A.; Rumpf, H.-J.; Bischof, A.; Gässler, A. Self-reported dependence on mobile phones in young adults: A European cross-cultural empirical survey. *J. Behav. Addict.* **2017**, *6*, 168–177. [CrossRef]
44. Kuss, D.J. Mobile technology and social media: The "extensions of man" in the 21st century. *Hum. Dev.* **2017**, *60*, 141–143. [CrossRef]
45. Kates, A.W.; Wu, H.; Coryn, C.L.S. The effects of mobile phone use on academic performance: A meta-analysis. *Comput. Educ.* **2018**, *127*, 107–112. [CrossRef]
46. Reinecke, L.; Klimmt, C.; Meier, A.; Reich, S.; Hefner, D.; Knop-Huelss, K.; Rieger, D.; Vorderer, P. Permanently online and permanently connected: Development and validation of the Online Vigilance Scale. *PLoS ONE* **2018**, *13*, e0205384. [CrossRef] [PubMed]
47. Oulasvirta, A.; Rattenbury, T.; Ma, L.; Raita, E. Habits make smartphone use more pervasive. *Pers. Ubiquitous Comput.* **2012**, *16*, 105–114. [CrossRef]
48. Van Deursen, A.J.A.M.; Bolle, C.L.; Hegner, S.M.; Kommers, P.A.M. Modeling habitual and addictive smartphone behavior. *Comput. Hum. Behav.* **2015**, *45*, 411–420. [CrossRef]
49. Johannes, N.; Meier, A.; Reinecke, L.; Ehlert, S.; Setiawan, D.N.; Walasek, N.; Dienlin, T.; Buijzen, M.; Veling, H. The relationship between online vigilance and affective well-being in everyday life: Combining smartphone logging with experience sampling. *PsyArXiv* **2019**. Available online: https://osf.io/t3wc2 (accessed on 4 January 2020).
50. Billieux, J.; Van der Linden, M.; d'Acremont, M.; Ceschi, G.; Zermatten, A. Does impulsivity relate to perceived dependence on and actual use of the mobile phone? *Appl. Cogn. Psychol* **2007**, *21*, 527–537. [CrossRef]
51. Wegmann, E.; Müller, S.M.; Turel, O.; Brand, M. Interactions of impulsivity, general executive functions, and specific inhibitory control explain symptoms of social-networks-use disorder: An experimental study. *Sci. Rep.* **2020**, *10*, 3866. [CrossRef]
52. Wu, E.X.W.; Liaw, G.J.; Goh, R.Z.; Chia, T.T.Y.; Chee, A.M.J.; Obana, T.; Rosenberg, M.D.; Yeo, B.T.; Asplund, C.L. Overlapping attentional networks yield divergent behavioral predictions across tasks: Neuromarkers for diffuse and focused attention? *NeuroImage* **2020**, *20*, 116535. [CrossRef]
53. Gupta, N.; Irwin, J.D. In-class distractions: The role of Facebook and the primary learning task. *Comput. Hum. Behav.* **2016**, *55*, 1165–1178. [CrossRef]
54. Unsworth, N.; McMillan, B.D. Attentional disengagements in educational contexts: A diary investigation of everyday mind-wandering and distraction. *Cogn. Res. Princ. Implic.* **2017**, *2*, 32. [CrossRef]
55. Buglass, S.L.; Binder, J.F.; Betts, L.R.; Underwood, J.D.M. Motivators of online vulnerability: The impact of social network site use and FOMO. *Comput. Hum. Behav.* **2017**, *66*, 248–255. [CrossRef]
56. Cheever, N.A.; Rosen, L.D.; Carrier, L.M.; Chavez, A. Out of sight is not out of mind: The impact of restricting wireless mobile device use on anxiety levels among low, moderate and high users. *Comput. Hum. Behav.* **2014**, *37*, 290–297. [CrossRef]
57. Clayton, R.B.; Leshner, G.; Almond, A. The extended iSelf: The impact of iPhone separation on cognition, emotion, and physiology. *J. Comput. Mediat. Commun.* **2015**, *20*, 119–135. [CrossRef]
58. Eide, T.A.; Aarestad, S.H.; Andreassen, C.S.; Bilder, R.M.; Pallesen, S. Smartphone restriction and its effect on subjective withdrawal related scores. *Front. Psychol* **2018**, *9*. [CrossRef] [PubMed]
59. Elhai, J.D.; Levine, J.C.; Dvorak, R.D.; Hall, B.J. Fear of missing out, need for touch, anxiety and depression are related to problematic smartphone use. *Comput. Hum. Behav.* **2016**, *63*, 509–516. [CrossRef]
60. Elhai, J.D.; Yang, H.; Montag, C. Fear of missing out (FOMO): Overview, theoretical underpinnings, and literature review on relations with severity of negative affectivity and problematic technology use. *Braz. J. Psychiatr.* **2020**. [CrossRef]

61. Franchina, V.; Vanden Abeele, M.; van Rooij, A.; Lo Coco, G.; De Marez, L. Fear of missing out as a predictor of problematic social media use and phubbing behavior among Flemish adolescents. *Int. J. Environ. Res. Public Health* **2018**, *15*, 2319. [CrossRef]
62. Lai, C.; Altavilla, D.; Ronconi, A.; Aceto, P. Fear of missing out (FOMO) is associated with activation of the right middle temporal gyrus during inclusion social cue. *Comput. Hum. Behav.* **2016**, *61*, 516–521. [CrossRef]
63. O'Connell, C. How FOMO (Fear of Missing Out), the smartphone, and social media may be affecting university students in the Middle East. *N. Am. J. Psychol.* **2020**, *22*, 83–102.
64. Browne, B.; Aruguete, M.S.; McCutcheon, L.E.; Medina, A.M. Social and emotional correlates of the fear of missing out. *N. Am. J. Psychol* **2018**, *20*, 341–354.
65. Vahedi, Z.; Saiphoo, A. The association between smartphone use, stress, and anxiety: A meta-analytic review. *Stress Health* **2018**, *34*, 347–358. [CrossRef] [PubMed]
66. Zhitomirsky-Geffet, M.; Blau, M. Cross-generational analysis of predictive factors of addictive behavior in smartphone usage. *Comput. Hum. Behav.* **2016**, *64*, 682–693. [CrossRef]
67. Marino, C.; Gini, G.; Angelini, F.; Vieno, A.; Spada, M.M. Social norms and e-motions in problematic social media use among adolescents. *Addict. Behav. Rep.* **2020**, *11*, 100250. [CrossRef] [PubMed]
68. Balıkçı, K.; Aydın, O.; Sönmez, İ.; Kalo, B.; Ünal-Aydın, P. The relationship between dysfunctional metacognitive beliefs and problematic social networking sites use. *Scand. J. Psychol.* **2020**. [CrossRef]
69. Kneidinger-Müller, B. When the smartphone goes offline: A factorial survey of smartphone users' experiences of mobile unavailability. *Comput. Hum. Behav.* **2019**, *98*, 1–10. [CrossRef]
70. Rozgonjuk, D.; Elhai, J.D.; Täht, K.; Vassil, K.; Levine, J.C.; Asmundson, G.J.G. Non-social smartphone use mediates the relationship between intolerance of uncertainty and problematic smartphone use: Evidence from a repeated-measures study. *Comput. Hum. Behav.* **2019**, *96*, 56–62. [CrossRef]
71. Rasmussen, E.E.; Punyanunt-Carter, N.; LaFreniere, J.R.; Norman, M.S.; Kimball, T.G. The serially mediated relationship between emerging adults' social media use and mental well-being. *Comput. Hum. Behav.* **2020**, *10*, 206–213. [CrossRef]
72. Griffiths, M.D.; Lopez-Fernandez, O.; Throuvala, M.A.; Pontes, H.; Kuss, D.J. Excessive and Problematic Use of Social Media in Adolescence: A Brief Overview. Report Submitted to the UK Parliament Science and Technology Committee (Impact of Social Media and Screen-Use on Young People's Health Inquiry). 2018. Available online: http://data.parliament.uk/writtenevidence/committeeevidence.svc/evidencedocument/science-and-technology-committee/social-media-and-mental-health/written/81105.pdf (accessed on 30 May 2018).
73. Griffiths, M.D.; Kuss, D.J.; Billieux, J.; Pontes, H.M. The evolution of Internet addiction: A global perspective. *Addict. Behav.* **2016**, *53*, 193–195. [CrossRef]
74. Kuss, D.J.; Griffiths, M.D.; Binder, J.F. Internet addiction in students: Prevalence and risk factors. *Comput. Hum. Behav.* **2013**, *29*, 959–966. [CrossRef]
75. Kelly, Y.; Zilanawala, A.; Booker, C.; Sacker, A. Social media use and adolescent mental health: Findings from the UK Millennium cohort study. *EClinicalMedicine* **2019**, *6*, 59–68. [CrossRef]
76. Ellis, D.A. Are smartphones really that bad? Improving the psychological measurement of technology-related behaviors. *Comput. Hum. Behav.* **2019**, *97*, 60–66. [CrossRef]
77. Bentley, F.; Tollmar, K. The power of mobile notifications to increase wellbeing logging behavior. In Proceedings of the SIGCHI Conference on Human Factors in Computing Systems-CHI '13; ACM Press: Paris, France, 2013; p. 1095.
78. Johannes, N.; Veling, H.; Dora, J.; Meier, A.; Reinecke, L.; Buijzen, M. Mind-wandering and mindfulness as mediators of the relation between online vigilance and well-being. *Cyberpsychol. Behav. Soc. Netw.* **2018**. [CrossRef] [PubMed]
79. Kabat-Zinn, J. Mindfulness-based interventions in context: Past, present, and future. *Clin. Psychol. Sci. Pract.* **2003**, *10*, 144–156. [CrossRef]
80. Kasson, E.M.; Wilson, A.N. Preliminary evidence on the efficacy of mindfulness combined with traditional classroom management strategies. *Behav. Anal. Pract.* **2017**, *10*, 242–251. [CrossRef]
81. Begun, A.L.; Murray, M.M. Mindfulness practices in addictive behavior prevention, treatment, and recovery. In *The Routledge Handbook of Social Work and Addictive Behaviors*; Routledge: Melbourne, Australia, 2020.
82. Broderick, P.C.; Jennings, P.A. Mindfulness for adolescents: A promising approach to supporting emotion regulation and preventing risky behavior. *New Dir. Youth Dev.* **2012**, *2012*, 111–126. [CrossRef]

83. Hölzel, B.K.; Lazar, S.W.; Gard, T.; Schuman-Olivier, Z.; Vago, D.R.; Ott, U. How does mindfulness meditation work? Proposing mechanisms of action from a conceptual and neural perspective. *Perspect. Psychol. Sci.* **2011**, *6*, 537–559. [CrossRef] [PubMed]
84. Auer, M.M.; Griffiths, M.D. The use of personalized behavioral feedback for online gamblers: An empirical study. *Front. Psychol.* **2015**, *6*, 1406. [CrossRef]
85. Bennike, I.H.; Wieghorst, A.; Kirk, U. Online-based mindfulness training reduces behavioral markers of mind wandering. *J. Cogn. Enhanc.* **2017**, *1*, 172–181. [CrossRef]
86. Bonello, M.; Griffiths, M.D. Behavioural tracking, responsible gambling tools and online voluntary self-exclusion: Implications for problem gamblers. *Casino Gambl. Int.* **2019**, *38*, 41–45.
87. Cavanagh, K.; Strauss, C.; Cicconi, F.; Griffiths, N.; Wyper, A.; Jones, F. A randomised controlled trial of a brief online mindfulness-based intervention. *Behav. Res. Ther.* **2013**, *51*, 573–578. [CrossRef]
88. Gainsbury, S.M. Review of self-exclusion from gambling venues as an intervention for problem gambling. *J. Gambl. Stud.* **2014**, *30*, 229–251. [CrossRef] [PubMed]
89. Glück, T.M.; Maercker, A. A randomized controlled pilot study of a brief web-based mindfulness training. *BMC Psychiatr.* **2011**, *11*. [CrossRef] [PubMed]
90. Ophir, E.; Nass, C.; Wagner, A.D. Cognitive control in media multitaskers. *Proc. Natl. Acad. Sci. USA* **2009**, *106*, 15583–15587. [CrossRef] [PubMed]
91. Bakosh, L.S.; Tobias Mortlock, J.M.; Querstret, D.; Morison, L. Audio-guided mindfulness training in schools and its effect on academic attainment: Contributing to theory and practice. *Learn. Instr.* **2018**, *58*, 34–41. [CrossRef]
92. Kauer, S.D.; Reid, S.C.; Crooke, A.H.D.; Khor, A.; Hearps, S.J.C.; Jorm, A.F.; Sanci, L.; Patton, G. Self-monitoring using mobile phones in the early stages of adolescent depression: Randomized controlled trial. *J. Med. Internet Res.* **2012**, *14*, e67. [CrossRef]
93. Hill, C.L.M.; Updegraff, J.A. Mindfulness and its relationship to emotional regulation. *Emotion* **2012**, *12*, 81–90. [CrossRef]
94. Gibb, B.E.; McGeary, J.E.; Beevers, C.G. Attentional biases to emotional stimuli: Key components of the RDoC constructs of sustained threat and loss. *Am. J. Med. Genet. B Neuropsychiatr. Genet.* **2016**, *171*, 65–80. [CrossRef]
95. Zhang, M.; Heng, S.; Song, G.; Fung, D.S.; Smith, H.E. Co-designing a mobile gamified attention bias modification intervention for substance use disorders: Participatory research study. *JMIR MHealth UHealth* **2019**, *7*, e15871. [CrossRef]
96. Bakker, D.; Kazantzis, N.; Rickwood, D.; Rickard, N. Mental health smartphone apps: Review and evidence-based recommendations for future developments. *JMIR Ment. Health* **2016**, *3*, e7. [CrossRef]
97. Király, O.; Potenza, M.N.; Stein, D.J.; King, D.L.; Hodgins, D.C.; Saunders, J.B.; Griffiths, M.D.; Gjoneska, B.; Billieux, J.; Brand, M.; et al. Preventing problematic internet use during the COVID-19 pandemic: Consensus guidance. *Compr. Psychiatr.* **2020**, *100*, 152180. [CrossRef]
98. Gupta, T.; Mittal, V.A. Advances in clinical staging, early intervention, and the prevention of psychosis. *F1000Research* **2019**, *8*, 2027. [CrossRef] [PubMed]
99. Linardon, J.; Cuijpers, P.; Carlbring, P.; Messer, M.; Fuller-Tyszkiewicz, M. The efficacy of app-supported smartphone interventions for mental health problems: A meta-analysis of randomized controlled trials. *World Psychiatr.* **2019**, *18*, 325–336. [CrossRef] [PubMed]
100. Bakker, D.; Kazantzis, N.; Rickwood, D.; Rickard, N. A randomized controlled trial of three smartphone apps for enhancing public mental health. *Behav. Res. Ther.* **2018**, *109*, 75–83. [CrossRef] [PubMed]
101. Bakker, D.; Rickard, N. Engagement in mobile phone app for self-monitoring of emotional wellbeing predicts changes in mental health: *MoodPrism*. *J. Affect. Disord.* **2018**, *227*, 432–442. [CrossRef] [PubMed]
102. Howells, A.; Ivtzan, I.; Eiroa-Orosa, F.J. Putting the 'app' in happiness: A randomised controlled trial of a smartphone-based mindfulness intervention to enhance wellbeing. *J. Happiness Stud.* **2016**, *17*, 163–185. [CrossRef]
103. Kummervold, P.; Chronaki, C.; Lausen, B.; Prokosch, H.-U.; Rasmussen, J.; Santana, S.; Staniszewski, A.; Wangberg, S. eHealth tends in Europe 2005-2007: A population-based survey. *J. Med. Internet Res.* **2008**, *10*, e42. [CrossRef]
104. Howarth, A.; Smith, J.G.; Perkins-Porras, L.; Ussher, M. Effects of brief mindfulness-based interventions on health-related outcomes: A systematic review. *Mindfulness* **2019**, *10*, 1957–1968. [CrossRef]

105. Melia, R.; Francis, K.; Hickey, E.; Bogue, J.; Duggan, J.; O'Sullivan, M.; Young, K. Mobile health technology interventions for suicide prevention: Systematic review. *JMIR MHealth UHealth* **2020**, *8*, e12516. [CrossRef]
106. Neary, M.; Schueller, S.M. State of the field of mental health apps. *Cogn. Behav. Pract.* **2018**, *25*, 531–537. [CrossRef]
107. Plaza, I.; Demarzo, M.M.P.; Herrera-Mercadal, P.; García-Campayo, J. Mindfulness-based mobile applications: Literature review and analysis of current features. *JMIR Mhealth Uhealth* **2013**, *1*, e24. [CrossRef]
108. Torous, J.; Powell, A.C. Current research and trends in the use of smartphone applications for mood disorders. *Internet Interv.* **2015**, *2*, 169–173. [CrossRef]
109. Sanderson, C.; Kouzoupi, N.; Hall, C.L. Technology matters: The human touch in a digital age—a blended approach in mental healthcare delivery with children and young people. *Child. Adolesc. Ment. Health* **2020**. [CrossRef] [PubMed]
110. Gainsbury, S.; Blaszczynski, A. A systematic review of Internet-based therapy for the treatment of addictions. *Clin. Psychol. Rev.* **2011**, *31*, 490–498. [CrossRef]
111. Borkovec, T.D.; Roemer, L. Perceived functions of worry among generalized anxiety disorder subjects: Distraction from more emotionally distressing topics? *J. Behav. Ther. Exp. Psychiatr.* **1995**, *26*, 25–30. [CrossRef]
112. Cho, S.; Lee, E. Distraction by smartphone use during clinical practice and opinions about smartphone restriction policies: A cross-sectional descriptive study of nursing students. *Nurse Educ. Today* **2016**, *40*, 128–133. [CrossRef]
113. Dolcos, F.; Iordan, A.D.; Kragel, J.; Stokes, J.; Campbell, R.; McCarthy, G.; Cabeza, R. Neural correlates of opposing effects of emotional distraction on working memory and episodic memory: An event-related fMRI investigation. *Front. Psychol.* **2013**, *4*, 180–195. [CrossRef] [PubMed]
114. Aagaard, J. Media multitasking, attention, and distraction: A critical discussion. *Phenomenol. Cogn. Sci.* **2015**, *14*, 885–896. [CrossRef]
115. Andreassen, C.S.; Billieux, J.; Griffiths, M.D.; Kuss, D.J.; Demetrovics, Z.; Mazzoni, E.; Pallesen, S. The relationship between addictive use of social media and video games and symptoms of psychiatric disorders: A large-scale cross-sectional study. *Psychol. Addict. Behav.* **2016**, *30*, 252–262. [CrossRef]
116. Calado, F.; Alexandre, J.; Griffiths, M.D. Gambling among adolescents and emerging adults: A cross-cultural study between Portuguese and English youth. *Int. J. Ment. Health Addict.* **2018**. [CrossRef]
117. Canale, N.; Vieno, A.; Griffiths, M.D. The extent and distribution of gambling-related harms and the prevention paradox in a British population survey. *J. Behav. Addict.* **2016**, *5*, 204–212. [CrossRef]
118. Patton, G.C.; Sawyer, S.M.; Santelli, J.S.; Ross, D.A.; Afifi, R.; Allen, N.B.; Arora, M.; Azzopardi, P.; Baldwin, W.; Bonell, C.; et al. Our future: A Lancet commission on adolescent health and wellbeing. *Lancet* **2016**, *387*, 2423–2478. [CrossRef]
119. Sohn, S.; Rees, P.; Wildridge, B.; Kalk, N.J.; Carter, B. Prevalence of problematic smartphone usage and associated mental health outcomes amongst children and young people: A systematic review, meta-analysis and GRADE of the evidence. *BMC Psychiatr.* **2019**, *19*, 356.
120. Spijkerman, M.P.J.; Pots, W.T.M.; Bohlmeijer, E.T. Effectiveness of online mindfulness-based interventions in improving mental health: A review and meta-analysis of randomised controlled trials. *Clin. Psychol. Rev.* **2016**, *45*, 102–114. [CrossRef] [PubMed]
121. Cartwright, N. Are RCTs the gold standard? *BioSocieties* **2007**, *2*, 11–20. [CrossRef]
122. Sullivan, G.M. Getting off the "gold standard": Randomized controlled trials and education research. *J. Grad. Med. Educ.* **2011**, *3*, 285–289. [CrossRef] [PubMed]
123. Deaton, A.; Cartwright, N. Understanding and misunderstanding randomized controlled trials. *Soc. Sci. Med.* **2018**, *210*, 2–21. [CrossRef]
124. Ruggeri, M.; Lasalvia, A.; Bonetto, C. A new generation of pragmatic trials of psychosocial interventions is needed. *Epidemiol. Psychiatr. Sci.* **2013**, *22*, 111–117. [CrossRef] [PubMed]
125. Campbell, M.K.; Elbourne, D.R.; Altman, D.G. CONSORT statement: Extension to cluster randomised trials. *BMJ* **2004**, *328*, 702–708. [CrossRef]
126. Schell, B.; Gillen, G. *Willard and Spackman's Cccupational Therapy*, 13th ed.; Lippincott Williams & Wilkins: Philadephia, PA, USA, 2018; 2828p.
127. Oussedik, E.; Foy, C.G.; Masicampo, E.J.; Kammrath, L.K.; Anderson, R.E.; Feldman, S.R. Accountability: A missing construct in models of adherence behavior and in clinical practice. *Patient Prefer. Adherence* **2017**, *11*, 1285–1294. [CrossRef]

128. Lanier, J.; Noyes, E.; Biederman, J. Mind wandering (internal distractibility) in ADHD: A literature review. *J. Atten. Disord.* **2019**. [CrossRef]
129. Franklin, M.S.; Mrazek, M.D.; Anderson, C.L.; Johnston, C.; Smallwood, J.; Kingstone, A.; Schooler, J. Tracking distraction: The relationship between mind-wandering, meta-awareness, and ADHD symptomatology. *J. Atten. Disord.* **2017**, *21*, 475–486. [CrossRef] [PubMed]
130. Bandura, A. Social cognitive theory of self-regulation. *Organ. Behav. Hum. Decis Process.* **1991**, *50*, 248–287. [CrossRef]
131. Tseng, V.W.-S.; Lee, M.L.; Denoue, L.; Avrahami, D. Overcoming distractions during transitions from break to work using a conversational website-blocking system. In Proceedings of the CHI 2019—2019 CHI Conference on Human Factors in Computing Systems, Glasgow, UK, 4–9 May 2019. [CrossRef]
132. Evans, C.; King, D.L.; Delfabbro, P.H. Effect of brief gaming abstinence on withdrawal in adolescent at-risk daily gamers: A randomized controlled study. *Comput. Hum. Behav.* **2018**, *88*, 70–77. [CrossRef]
133. King, D.L.; Kaptsis, D.; Delfabbro, P.H.; Gradisar, M. Effectiveness of brief abstinence for modifying problematic Internet gaming cognitions and behaviors. *J. Clin. Psychol.* **2017**, *73*, 1573–1585. [CrossRef]
134. Turel, O. Short abstinence from online social networking sites reduces perceived stress, especially in excessive users. *Psychiatr. Res.* **2018**, *270*, 947–953. [CrossRef]
135. Caldeira, C.; Chen, Y.; Chan, L.; Pham, V.; Chen, Y.; Zheng, K. Mobile apps for mood tracking: An analysis of features and user reviews. *AMIA Annu. Symp. Proc.* **2017**, *2017*, 495–504.
136. Bakker, D.; Kazantzis, N.; Rickwood, D.; Rickard, N. Development and pilot evaluation of smartphone-delivered cognitive behavior therapy strategies for mood- and anxiety-related problems: MoodMission. *Cogn. Behav. Pract.* **2018**, *25*, 496–514. [CrossRef]
137. Haug, S.; Meyer, C.; Dymalski, A.; Lippke, S.; John, U. Efficacy of a text messaging (SMS) based smoking cessation intervention for adolescents and young adults: Study protocol of a cluster randomised controlled trial. *BMC Public Health.* **2012**, *12*, 51. [CrossRef]
138. Throuvala, M.A.; Pontes, H.; Griffiths, M.D.; Rennoldson, M.; Kuss, D.J. Development and validation of the Smartphone Distraction Scale (SDS): A cognitive and emotion regulation construct. *Manuscr. Submitt. Publ.* **2020**.
139. Brown, K.W.; Ryan, R.M. The benefits of being present: Mindfulness and its role in psychological well-being. *J. Pers. Soc. Psychol.* **2003**, *84*, 822–848. [CrossRef]
140. Black, D.S.; Sussman, S.; Johnson, C.A.; Milam, J. Psychometric assessment of the Mindful Attention Awareness Scale (MAAS) among Chinese adolescents. *Assessment* **2012**, *19*, 42–52. [CrossRef]
141. Cohen, S.; Kamarck, T.; Mermelstein, R. A global measure of perceived stress. *J. Health Soc. Behav.* **1983**, *24*, 385–396. [CrossRef] [PubMed]
142. Lee, E.-H. Review of the psychometric evidence of the Perceived Stress Scale. *Asian Nurs. Res.* **2012**, *6*, 121–127. [CrossRef] [PubMed]
143. Spitzer, R.L.; Kroenke, K.; Williams, J.B.W.; Löwe, B. A brief measure for assessing generalized anxiety disorder: The GAD-7. *Arch. Intern. Med.* **2006**, *166*, 1092–1097. [CrossRef] [PubMed]
144. Donker, T.; van Straten, A.; Marks, I.; Cuijpers, P. Quick and easy self-rating of Generalized Anxiety Disorder: Validity of the Dutch web-based GAD-7, GAD-2 and GAD-SI. *Psychiatr. Res.* **2011**, *188*, 58–64. [CrossRef]
145. Sousa, T.V.; Viveiros, V.; Chai, M.V.; Vicente, F.L.; Jesus, G.; Carnot, M.J.; Gordo, A.C.; Ferreira, P. Reliability and validity of the Portuguese version of the Generalized Anxiety Disorder (GAD-7) scale. *Health Qual. Life Outcomes* **2015**, *13*, 50. [CrossRef]
146. Gardner, B.; Abraham, C.; Lally, P.; de Bruijn, G.-J. Towards parsimony in habit measurement: Testing the convergent and predictive validity of an automaticity subscale of the Self-Report Habit Index. *Int. J. Behav. Nutr. Phys. Act.* **2012**, *9*, 102. [CrossRef]
147. Marchant, G.; Chevance, G.; Boiché, J. Intention and automaticity toward physical and sedentary screen-based leisure activities in adolescents: A profile perspective. *J. Sport Health Sci.* **2018**, *7*, 481–488. [CrossRef]
148. Schwarzer, R.; Jerusalem, M. Generalized Self-Efficacy scale. In *Measures in Health Psychology: A User's Portfolio. Causal and Control Beliefs*; NFER-NELSON: Windsor, UK, 1995; pp. 35–37.
149. Schwarzer, R.; Mueller, J.; Greenglass, E. Assessment of perceived general self-efficacy on the Internet: Data collection in cyberspace. *Anxiety Stress Coping Int. J.* **1999**, *12*, 145–161. [CrossRef]
150. De las Cuevas, C.; Peñate, W. Validation of the General Self-Efficacy Scale in psychiatric outpatient care. *Psicothema* **2015**, *27*, 410–415.

151. Morean, M.E.; DeMartini, K.S.; Leeman, R.F.; Pearlson, G.D.; Anticevic, A.; Krishnan-Sarin, S.; Krystal, J.H.; O'Malley, S. Psychometrically improved, abbreviated versions of three classic measures of impulsivity and self-control. *Psychol. Assess.* **2014**, *26*, 1003–1020. [CrossRef] [PubMed]
152. Mathias, C.W.; Stanford, M.S.; Liang, Y.; Goros, M.; Charles, N.E.; Sheftall, A.H.; Mullen, J.; Hill-Kapturczak, N.; Acheson, A.; Olvera, R.L.; et al. A test of the psychometric characteristics of the BIS-Brief among three groups of youth. *Psychol. Assess.* **2018**, *30*, 847–856. [CrossRef] [PubMed]
153. Steinberg, L.; Sharp, C.; Stanford, M.S.; Tharp, A.T. New tricks for an old measure: The development of the Barratt Impulsiveness Scale–Brief (BIS-Brief). *Psychol. Assess.* **2013**, *25*, 216–226. [CrossRef]
154. Davies, J.J.; Hemingway, T.J. Guitar hero or zero?: Fantasy, self-esteem, and deficient self-regulation in rhythm-based music video games. *J. Media Psychol.* **2014**, *26*, 189–201. [CrossRef]
155. LaRose, R.; Lin, C.A.; Eastin, M.S. Unregulated Internet usage: Addiction, habit, or deficient self-regulation? *Media Psychol.* **2009**, *5*, 225–253. [CrossRef]
156. Lin, C.-Y.; Broström, A.; Nilsen, P.; Griffiths, M.D.; Pakpour, A.H. Psychometric validation of the Persian Bergen Social Media Addiction Scale using classic test theory and Rasch models. *J. Behav. Addict.* **2017**, *6*, 620–629. [CrossRef]
157. Monacis, L.; de Palo, V.; Griffiths, M.D.; Sinatra, M. Social networking addiction, attachment style, and validation of the Italian version of the Bergen Social Media Addiction Scale. *J. Behav. Addict.* **2017**, *6*, 178–186. [CrossRef]
158. Pontes, H.M.; Andreassen, C.S.; Griffiths, M.D. Portuguese validation of the Bergen Facebook Addiction Scale: An empirical study. *Int. J. Ment. Health Addict.* **2016**, *14*, 1062–1073. [CrossRef]
159. Griffiths, M.D. A 'components' model of addiction within a biopsychosocial framework. *J. Subst Use* **2005**, *10*, 191–197. [CrossRef]
160. Bányai, F.; Zsila, Á.; Király, O.; Maraz, A.; Elekes, Z.; Griffiths, M.D.; Andreassen, C.S.; Demetrovics, Z. Problematic social media use: Results from a large-scale nationally representative adolescent sample. *PLoS ONE* **2017**, *12*, e0169839. [CrossRef]
161. Yam, C.-W.; Pakpour, A.H.; Griffiths, M.D.; Yau, W.-Y.; Lo, C.-L.M.; Ng, J.M.T.; Lin, C.-Y.; Leung, H. Psychometric testing of three Chinese online-related addictive behavior instruments among Hong Kong University students. *Psychiatr. Q.* **2019**, *90*, 117–128. [CrossRef]
162. Przybylski, A.K.; Murayama, K.; DeHaan, C.R.; Gladwell, V. Motivational, emotional, and behavioral correlates of fear of missing out. *Comput. Hum. Behav.* **2013**, *29*, 1841–1848. [CrossRef]
163. Can, G.; Satici, S.A. Adaptation of fear of missing out scale (FoMOs): Turkish version validity and reliability study. *Psicol. Reflex E Crítica* **2019**, *32*, 3. [CrossRef] [PubMed]
164. Perrone, M.A. #FoMO: Establishing Validity of the Fear of Missing Out Scale with an Adolescent Population 2016. Available online: https://aura.alfred.edu/handle/10829/7399 (accessed on 30 May 2020).
165. Yildirim, C.; Correia, A.-P. Exploring the dimensions of nomophobia: Development and validation of a self-reported questionnaire. *Comput. Hum. Behav.* **2015**, *49*, 130–137. [CrossRef]
166. Lee, S.; Kim, M.; Mendoza, J.S.; McDonough, I.M. Addicted to cellphones: Exploring the psychometric properties between the nomophobia questionnaire and obsessiveness in college students. *Heliyon* **2018**, *4*, e00895. [CrossRef] [PubMed]
167. Tams, S.; Legoux, R.; Leger, P.-M. Smartphone withdrawal creates stress: A moderated mediation model of nomophobia, social threat, and phone withdrawal context. *Comput. Hum. Behav.* **2018**, *81*, 1–9. [CrossRef]
168. Rothwell, J.C.; Julious, S.A.; Cooper, C.L. A study of target effect sizes in randomised controlled trials. *Trials* **2018**, *19*, 544. [CrossRef]
169. Bhide, A.; Shah, P.S.; Acharya, G. A simplified guide to randomized controlled trials. *Acta Obstet. Gynecol. Scand.* **2018**, *97*, 380–387. [CrossRef]
170. Grimm, L.G.; Yarnold, P.R. *Reading and Understanding Multivariate Statistics*; Reading and Understanding Multivariate Statistics; American Psychological Association: Washington, DC, USA, 1995; 373p.
171. Gupta, S.K. Intention-to-treat concept: A review. *Perspect. Clin. Res.* **2011**, *2*, 109–112. [CrossRef]
172. Montori, V.M.; Guyatt, G.H. Intention-to-treat principle. *CMAJ Can. Med. Assoc. J.* **2001**, *165*, 1339–1341.
173. Altman, D.G.; Doré, C.J. Randomisation and baseline comparisons in clinical trials. *Lancet* **1990**, *335*, 149–153. [CrossRef]
174. Anderson, S.R.; Auquier, A.; Hauck, W.W.; Oakes, D.; Vandaele, W.; Weisberg, H.I. *Statistical Methods for Comparative Studies: Techniques for Bias Reduction*; John Wiley & Sons: Hoboken, NJ, USA, 2009; 310p.

175. Olejnik, S.F.; Algina, J. Parametric ANCOVA and the rank transform ANCOVA when the data are conditionally non-normal and heteroscedastic. *J. Educ. Stat.* **1984**, *9*, 129–149. [CrossRef]
176. Keppel, G.; Wickens, T.D. *Design and Analysis: A Researcher's Handbook*, 4th ed.; Prentice Hall: Upper Saddle River, NJ, USA, 2004.
177. Pierce, C.A.; Block, R.A.; Aguinis, H. Cautionary note on reporting eta-squared values from multifactor ANOVA designs. *Educ. Psychol. Meas* **2004**, *64*, 916–924. [CrossRef]
178. Olejnik, S.; Algina, J. Measures of effect size for comparative studies: Applications, interpretations, and limitations. *Contemp. Educ. Psychol* **2000**, *25*, 241–286. [CrossRef]
179. Cohen, J. A power primer. *Psychol. Bull.* **1992**, *112*, 155–159. [CrossRef] [PubMed]
180. Hayes, A.F.; Montoya, A.K.; Rockwood, N.J. The analysis of mechanisms and their contingencies: PROCESS versus structural equation modeling. *Australas Mark. J. AMJ* **2017**, *25*, 76–81. [CrossRef]
181. Hayes, A.F.; Rockwood, N.J. Regression-based statistical mediation and moderation analysis in clinical research: Observations, recommendations, and implementation. *Behav. Res. Ther.* **2017**, *98*, 39–57. [CrossRef]
182. Hayes, A.F.; Preacher, K.J. Statistical mediation analysis with a multicategorical independent variable. *Br. J. Math. Stat. Psychol.* **2014**, *67*, 451–470. [CrossRef]
183. Hayes, A.F. PROCESS: A Versatile Computational Tool for Observed Variable Mediation, Moderation, and Conditional Process Modelling; White Paper; 2012. Available online: http://www.afhayes.com/public/process2012.pdf (accessed on 12 June 2018).
184. Gámez-Guadix, M.; Calvete, E. Assessing the relationship between mindful awareness and problematic internet use among adolescents. *Mindfulness* **2016**, *7*, 1281–1288. [CrossRef]
185. Mrazek, M.D.; Franklin, M.S.; Phillips, D.T.; Baird, B.; Schooler, J.W. Mindfulness training improves working memory capacity and GRE performance while reducing mind wandering. *Psychol. Sci* **2013**, *24*, 776–781. [CrossRef]
186. Calvete, E.; Gámez-Guadix, M.; Cortazar, N. Mindfulness facets and problematic Internet use: A six-month longitudinal study. *Addict. Behav* **2017**, *72*, 57–63. [CrossRef] [PubMed]
187. Biddle, S.J.; Edwardson, C.L.; Wilmot, E.G.; Yates, T.; Gorely, T.; Bodicoat, D.H.; Ashra, N.; Khunti, K.; Nimmo, M.A.; Davies, M. A randomised controlled trial to reduce sedentary time in young adults at risk of Type 2 Diabetes Mellitus: Project STAND (sedentary time and diabetes). *PLoS ONE* **2015**, *10*, e0143398. [CrossRef] [PubMed]
188. Kazdin, A.E. Reactive self-monitoring: The effects of response desirability, goal setting, and feedback. *J. Consult. Clin. Psychol* **1974**, *42*, 704–716. [CrossRef] [PubMed]
189. Prochaska, J.O.; Velicer, W.F. The transtheoretical model of health behavior change. *Am. J. Health Promot. AJHP* **1997**, *12*, 38–48. [CrossRef] [PubMed]
190. Prochaska, J.O.; DiClemente, C.C.; Norcross, J.C. In search of how people change. Applications to addictive behaviors. *Am. Psychol.* **1992**, *47*, 1102–1114. [CrossRef] [PubMed]
191. Squires, L.R.; Hollett, K.B.; Hesson, J.; Harris, N. Psychological distress, emotion dysregulation, and coping behaviour: A theoretical perspective of problematic smartphone use. Advance online publication. *Int. J. Ment. Health Addict.* **2020**. [CrossRef]
192. Ostendorf, S.; Wegmann, E.; Brand, M. Problematic social networks use in German children and adolescents—The interaction of need to belong, online self-regulative competences, and age. *Int. J. Environ. Res. Public Health* **2020**, *17*, 2518. [CrossRef]
193. Liese, B.S.; Kim, H.S.; Hodgins, D.C. Insecure attachment and addiction: Testing the mediating role of emotion dysregulation in four potentially addictive behaviors. *Addict. Behav.* **2020**, 106432. [CrossRef]
194. Kuehner, C.; Huffziger, S.; Liebsch, K. Rumination, distraction and mindful self-focus: Effects on mood, dysfunctional attitudes and cortisol stress response. *Psychol. Med.* **2009**, *39*, 219–228. [CrossRef]
195. Colder Carras, M.; Kalbarczyk, A.; Wells, K.; Banks, J.; Kowert, R.; Gillespie, C.; Latkin, C. Connection, meaning, and distraction: A qualitative study of video game play and mental health recovery in veterans treated for mental and/or behavioral health problems. *Soc. Sci. Med.* **2018**, *216*, 124–132. [CrossRef]
196. Huffziger, S.; Reinhard, I.; Kuehner, C. A longitudinal study of rumination and distraction in formerly depressed inpatients and community controls. *J. Abnorm. Psychol.* **2009**, *118*, 746–756. [CrossRef] [PubMed]
197. Denkova, E.; Wong, G.; Dolcos, S.; Sung, K.; Wang, L.; Coupland, N.; Dolcos, F. The impact of anxiety-inducing distraction on cognitive performance: A combined brain imaging and personality investigation. *PLoS ONE* **2010**, *5*, e14150. [CrossRef]

198. Armstrong, T.; Zald, D.H.; Olatunji, B.O. Attentional control in OCD and GAD: Specificity and associations with core cognitive symptoms. *Behav. Res. Ther.* **2011**, *49*, 756–762. [CrossRef] [PubMed]
199. Mrazek, M.D.; Smallwood, J.; Schooler, J.W. Mindfulness and mind-wandering: Finding convergence through opposing constructs. *Emotion* **2012**, *12*, 442–448. [CrossRef]
200. Johannes, N.; Veling, H.; Verwijmeren, T.; Buijzen, M. Hard to resist? The effect of smartphone visibility and notifications on response inhibition. *J. Media Psychol. Theor Methods Appl.* **2019**, *31*, 214–225. [CrossRef]
201. Griffiths, M.D.; Szabo, A. Is excessive online usage a function of medium or activity? *Empirical Pilot Study. J. Behav. Addict.* **2014**, *3*, 74–77. [CrossRef]
202. Panagiotidi, M.; Overton, P. Attention deficit hyperactivity symptoms predict problematic mobile phone use. *Curr. Psychol.* **2020**. [CrossRef]
203. Schmitgen, M.M.; Horvath, J.; Mundinger, C.; Wolf, N.D.; Sambataro, F.; Hirjak, D.; Kubera, K.; Koenig, J.; Christian Wolf, R. Neural correlates of cue reactivity in individuals with smartphone addiction. *Addict. Behav.* **2020**, *108*, 106422. [CrossRef]
204. Kempf, C.A.; Ehrhard, K.A.; Stoner, S.C. Evaluation of obsessive-compulsive symptoms in relation to smartphone use. *Ment. Health Clin.* **2020**, *10*, 44–48. [CrossRef]
205. Wegmann, E.; Brand, M. Cognitive correlates in gaming disorder and social networks use disorder: A comparison. *Curr. Addict. Rep.* **2020**. [CrossRef]
206. Pancani, L.; Preti, E.; Riva, P. The psychology of smartphone: The development of the Smartphone Impact Scale (SIS). *Assessment* **2019**. [CrossRef]
207. Johannes, N.; Dora, J.; Rusz, D. Social smartphone apps do not capture attention despite their perceived high reward value. *Collabra Psychol.* **2019**, *5*, 14. [CrossRef]
208. Levine, L.E.; Waite, B.M.; Bowman, L.L. Use of instant messaging predicts self-report but not performance measures of inattention, impulsiveness, and distractibility. *Cyberpsychology Behav. Soc. Netw* **2013**, *16*, 898–903. [CrossRef] [PubMed]
209. Boer, M.; Stevens, G.; Finkenauer, C.; Eijnden, R. Attention deficit hyperactivity disorder-symptoms, social media use intensity, and social media use problems in adolescents: Investigating directionality. *Child. Dev.* **2019**. [CrossRef] [PubMed]
210. Kushlev, K.; Proulx, J.; Dunn, E.W. 'Silence Your Phones': Smartphone notifications increase inattention and hyperactivity symptoms. In Proceedings of the 2016 CHI Conference on Human Factors in Computing Systems-CHI '16; ACM Press: Santa Clara, CA, USA, 2016; pp. 1011–1020. Available online: http://dl.acm.org/citation.cfm?doi:d=2858036.2858359 (accessed on 17 July 2019).
211. Rozgonjuk, D.; Elhai, J.D.; Ryan, T.; Scott, G.G. Fear of missing out is associated with disrupted activities from receiving smartphone notifications and surface learning in college students. *Comput. Educ.* **2019**, *140*, 103590. [CrossRef]
212. Richards, D.; Farrand, P.; Christensen, H.; Griffiths, K.; Kavanagh, D.; Klein, B.; Lau, M.A.; Proudfoot, J. *Oxford Guide to Low Intensity CBT Interventions*, 1st ed.; Bennett-Levy, J., Ed.; Oxford University Press: Oxford, UK, 2010; 628p.
213. Althubaiti, A. Information bias in health research: Definition, pitfalls, and adjustment methods. *J. Multidiscip. Healthc.* **2016**, *9*, 211–217. [CrossRef]
214. Melville, K.M.; Casey, L.; Kavanagh, D.J. Dropout from Internet-based treatment for psychological disorders. *Br. J. Clin. Psychol.* **2009**, *49*, 455–471. [CrossRef]
215. Dumville, J.C.; Torgerson, D.J.; Hewitt, C.E. Reporting attrition in randomised controlled trials. *BMJ* **2006**, *332*, 969–971. [CrossRef]
216. Furukawa, T.A.; Noma, H.; Caldwell, D.M.; Honyashiki, M.; Shinohara, K.; Imai, H.; Chen, P.; Hunot, V.; Churchill, R. Waiting list may be a nocebo condition in psychotherapy trials: A contribution from network meta-analysis. *Acta Psychiatr. Scand.* **2014**, *130*, 181–192. [CrossRef]
217. Christensen, H.; Griffiths, K.M.; Farrer, L. Adherence in Internet interventions for anxiety and depression: Systematic review. *J. Med. Internet Res.* **2009**, *11*, e13. [CrossRef]
218. Andrews, S.; Ellis, D.A.; Shaw, H.; Piwek, L. Beyond self-report: Tools to compare estimated and real-world smartphone use. Pietschnig, J.; editor. *PLoS ONE* **2015**, *10*, e0139004. [CrossRef]
219. Lin, Y.-H.; Lin, Y.-C.; Lee, Y.-H.; Lin, P.-H.; Lin, S.-H.; Chang, L.-R.; Tseng, H.-W.; Yen, L.-Y.; Yang, C.C.H.; Kuo, T.B.J. Time distortion associated with smartphone addiction: Identifying smartphone addiction via a mobile application (App). *J. Psychiatr. Res.* **2015**, *65*, 139–145. [CrossRef] [PubMed]

220. Bauman, A.E.; Petersen, C.B.; Blond, K.; Rangul, V.; Hardy, L.L. The descriptive epidemiology of sedentary behaviour. In *Sedentary Behaviour Epidemiology*; Springer Series on Epidemiology and Public Health; Leitzmann, M.F., Jochem, C., Schmid, D., Eds.; Springer International: New York, NY, USA, 2018; pp. 73–106.
221. Davis, K.; Charmaraman, L.; Weinstein, E. Introduction to Special Issue: Adolescent and Emerging Adult Development in an Age of Social Media. *J. Adolesc. Res.* **2019**. [CrossRef]
222. Baumeister, H.; Montag, C. Digital phenotyping and mobile sensing: Rapidly evolving interdisciplinary research endeavor. In *Digital Phenotyping and Mobile Sensing: New Developments in Psychoinformatics*; Springer: Cham, Switzerland, 2019.
223. Garrison, K.A.; Potenza, M.N. Neuroimaging and biomarkers in addiction treatment. *Curr. Psychiatr. Rep.* **2014**, *16*, 513. [CrossRef]
224. Suckling, J.; Nestor, L.J. The neurobiology of addiction: The perspective from magnetic resonance imaging present and future. *Addict. Abingdon Engl.* **2017**, *112*, 360–369. [CrossRef] [PubMed]
225. Andone, I.; Błaszkiewicz, K.; Eibes, M.; Trendafilov, B.; Montag, C.; Markowetz, A. How age and gender affect smartphone usage. In *Proceedings of the 2016 ACM International JoInt. Conference on Pervasive and Ubiquitous Computing*; ACM: Heidelberg, Germany, 2016; pp. 9–12. [CrossRef]
226. Feng, Q.; Zheng, Y.; Zhang, X.; Song, Y.; Luo, Y.-J.; Li, Y.; Talhelm, T. Gender differences in visual reflexive attention shifting: Evidence from an ERP study. *Brain Res.* **2011**, *1401*, 59–65. [CrossRef]
227. Wu, J.-Y.; Cheng, T. Who is better adapted in learning online within the personal learning environment? Relating gender differences in cognitive attention networks to digital distraction. *Comput. Educ.* **2018**, *128*, 312–329. [CrossRef]
228. Albright, K.; Gechter, K.; Kempe, A. Importance of mixed methods in pragmatic trials and dissemination and implementation research. *Acad. Pediatr.* **2013**, *13*, 400–407. [CrossRef]
229. Alegría, M.; NeMoyer, A.; Falgas, I.; Wang, Y.; Alvarez, K. Social determinants of mental health: Where we are and where we need to go. *Curr. Psychiatr. Rep.* **2018**, *20*, 95. [CrossRef]
230. Macintyre, A.; Ferris, D.; Gonçalves, B.; Quinn, N. What has economics got to do with it? The impact of socioeconomic factors on mental health and the case for collective action. *Palgrave Commun.* **2018**, *4*, 10. [CrossRef]
231. Posner, M.I. Orienting of attention. *Q. J. Exp. Psychol.* **1980**, *32*, 3–25. [CrossRef] [PubMed]
232. Risko, E.F. Examining the implications of Internet usage for memory and cognition: Prospects and promise. *J. Appl. Res. Mem. Cogn* **2019**, *8*, 36–39. [CrossRef]
233. Russell, D.M. Commentary on the paper: "The digital expansion of the mind: Implications of Internet usage for memory and cognition". *J. Appl. Res. Mem. Cogn.* **2019**, *8*, 33–35. [CrossRef]
234. Garland, E.L.; Farb, N.A.; Goldin, P.R.; Fredrickson, B.L. Mindfulness broadens awareness and builds eudaimonic meaning: A process model of mindful positive emotion regulation. *Psychol. Inq.* **2015**, *26*, 293–314. [CrossRef] [PubMed]
235. Wegmann, E.; Oberst, U.; Stodt, B.; Brand, M. Online-specific fear of missing out and Internet-use expectancies contribute to symptoms of Internet-communication disorder. *Addict. Behav. Rep.* **2017**, *5*, 33–42. [CrossRef] [PubMed]
236. Boehm, J.K.; Vie, L.L.; Kubzansky, L.D. The promise of well-being interventions for improving health risk behaviors. *Curr. Cardiovasc. Risk Rep.* **2012**, *6*, 511–519. [CrossRef]
237. Trudel-Fitzgerald, C.; Millstein, R.A.; von Hippel, C.; Howe, C.J.; Tomasso, L.P.; Wagner, G.R.; VanderWeele, T. Psychological well-being as part of the public health debate? Insight into dimensions, interventions, and policy. *BMC Public Health* **2019**, *19*, 1712. [CrossRef]
238. Stellefson, M.; Hanik, B.; Chaney, B.; Chaney, D.; Tennant, B.; Chavarria, E.A. eHealth literacy among college students: A systematicreview with implications for eHealth education. *J. Med. Internet Res.* **2011**, *13*, e102. [CrossRef]
239. Van der Heide, I.; Snoeijs, S.; Boerma, W.G.W.; Schellevis, F.G.; Rijken, M.P. How to Strengthen Patient-Centredness in Caring for People with Multimorbidity in Europe? Policy Brief 22 ICARE4EU Consortium. 2017; p. 32. Available online: https://www.ncbi.nlm.nih.gov/books/NBK464537/pdf/Bookshelf_NBK464537.pdf (accessed on 26 April 2020).
240. Chen, L.; Nath, R.; Tang, Z. Understanding the determinants of digital distraction: An automatic thinking behavior perspective. *Comput. Hum. Behav.* **2020**, *104*, 106195. [CrossRef]

# 4

# Problematic Relationships with Smartphones of Spanish and Colombian University Students

**Verónica Marín-Díaz *, Juan Manuel Muñoz-González and Begoña-Esther Sampedro-Requena**

Education department, University of Cordoba, 14071 Córdoba, Spain; juan.manuel@uco.es (J.M.M.-G.); bsampedro@uco.es (B.-E.S.-R.)

* Correspondence: vmarin@uco.es

**Abstract:** The presence of smartphones in the lives of the population in general, and of youth in particular, is evident, and is derived from elements such as the diversity of prices as well as the ease of access of all the resources that can be reached through the internet. With the use of a descriptive approach using a quantitative poll, the objective of the present study was to discover the opinions of university students in Spain and Colombia about smartphone use, as well as the consequences of its use, and if this use could derive into so-called problematic smartphone use (PSU). For gathering the information, the *Mobile Phone Problematic Use Scale* (MPPUSA) was utilized, with a sample size $n = 4009$. The main result reached was that the model obtained is structured around six factors that determined the elements in light of PSU. The initial conclusion found was that the model applied can be utilized with Colombian students, with young Spanish women and students in the macro area of Social Sciences, the ones who had problematic behavior with the devices, as compared to the Health Sciences students who did not have it.

**Keywords:** problematic smartphone use; university student; internet; MPPUSA

---

## 1. Introduction

It is a known fact that the present society is digital and that the so-called Information and Communication Technologies (from here on ICT) coexist with us systematically, allowing for the interactions with fellow humans to occur at anytime and anywhere [1]. All of this is thanks to the universalization of the internet in general, and the tools which we can use through it, as these tools provide abundant means for socializing with others, perform consultations of any kind, search for knowledge, entertain ourselves, etc. [1–3].

The IWS [4] points out that in 2019, there were more than 4 billion people connected in the world, and in the specific case of Spain [5] this figure was the non-negligible amount of 42.4 million users and in Colombia more than 31 million people from a population of more than 49 million [4,6]. In both countries, 96% and 63% of users accessed the internet through their smartphones, respectively.

Nowadays, independently of the country where we live, the smartphone is one of the key technologies for the population at large. The diversity of the possible functions of these devices, apart from the use for which they were originally conceived [7], has made them become a key feature in the processes of socialization and learning of children, adolescents and young adults. As indicated by many studies [8–12], these devices allow accessing a great variety of content presented in different formats, messaging services and social networks, allowing for the development of different skills and competencies beyond the digital, allowing access to other technological resources, etc., which makes them even more attractive.

Related to this, diverse studies [13,14] have shown that Spanish university students, most of whom are younger than 35 years old, use smartphones from a social, academic and personal point of view. Likewise, for Colombian university students [15], smartphone use has different aims, such as navigating on the internet, or checking e-mail. It is unquestionable that the use of this device has increased around the world in the last few years, especially in the population within this age range (university students younger than 35). This has extended its use to the area of education, where some studies [16] have shown the student's habits within and outside university spaces, where in the first scenario it is commonly used in transportation and outdoors; while in the second scenario the classrooms, the hallways and the libraries are the most exploited places. It is precisely the attractiveness they possess that has resulted on their use increasing exponentially, with some authors [3,17–19] already speaking about the problematic use of smartphones.

Before continuing, it should be mentioned that within the scientific community, there is no clear definition of this behavioral disorder, as we have found authors who discuss the problematic use of the device [3,17–19], while others prefer to talk about addiction [1,2,20–22]. However, the purpose of this study is not to delve into this debate, as the starting position of this work is that only a problematic relationship exists [17,18], detailed on the fifth version of the *Diagnostic and Statistical Manual of Mental Disorders* [23] which points to this relationship not having an addiction factor, given that this publication only mentions addiction in cases of pathological gambling and a behavioral disorders. Thus, it is understood that only a problematic use of the device exists, indicating that a medical condition recognized by the entire community does not exist [11].

On the other hand, some authors [17,24–27] point to factors such as the lack of sleep, hyperactivity, insecurity when driving, anxiety, depression, personality disorders, etc., associated to harmful behaviors such as in the use drugs including heroin, alcohol, cannabis, speed, etc., that although not linked to technologies, have been observed in the population who have a problematic use of mobile phones. Nevertheless, some research studies [28] suggest that there is a common factor among the addictive behaviors in the use of substances and the internet, the impulsivity which is manifested, among other aspects, by low academic performance or low levels of concentration, however, this cannot be extrapolated to an addictive use of the smartphone.

At the same time, it should be pointed out that as [11] indicate, the population, who along with adolescents, are the main population at risk of having a problematic use of the devices, are the university students, given that they consider the device as part of them [11,24]. On the other hand, the fear of being left out of relationships and developing the so-called FOMO syndrome [29], makes this population group more susceptible to developing a behavioral disorder, which is translated into the problematic use of the phone.

Mobile phones, as previously indicated [1–3,30], provide their users with numerous gratifications which begs the question of what type of relationship we as individuals have developed towards them or with them. Some research studies have determined that a variable that determines the presence of problematic use is the amount of time spent utilizing the devices [11,30,31], while others indicate that the variable gender is the one that defines this relationship, with women showing a greater relationship with them. Thus, works such as [32] point out that younger people aged 18–29 years old have a high dependency on their mobile phones, which can lead to the individuals developing an emotional support relationship [18]. These aspects, in the education sphere for example, have resulted in some education centers prohibiting their presence in the centers [8].

As a result and given the high number of connections produced with smartphones in Spain and in Colombia [4–6], it is necessary to clarify the attitude of university students towards these devices. In this sense, the main objective of the present research, which will be described below, is to discover the opinions of the university students in Spain and Colombia on the use of smartphones, as well as the consequences of this use. Studies conducted among Spanish and Colombian university students [8,12,17,18] have brought to light that this scale fits the smartphone user profile, as well as the needs of the context.

The main conclusions found are: on the one hand, that younger students show a problematic use of smartphones [18,32], and in general, women more frequently display this behavioral disorder [11,30,31], without differences also found as a function of the country of origin.

The main objective of the research was to analyze the behavior of the six MPPUSA factors according to sex, age, country, macro area and self-perception in the problematic use of the smartphones by university students from Spain and Colombia. This general objective, at the same time, is concretized in the following specific objectives:

- To discover the existence of a problematic use of the mobile phone in Spanish and Colombian university students.
- To analyze if there are differences between the students objects of the study with respect to the problematic use of the mobile phone as a function of their age and sex, as well as their country of origin and macro area.
- To verify if there are relationships between the different dimensions of the questionnaire
- To explain which factors have an influence on the perceptions of the students of the problematic use of mobile phones, as well as its consideration as a function of the country, of their age and sex.

## 2. Materials and Methods

The design of the study utilized a descriptive approach with a cross-sectional, quantitative survey, due to the numerical and reliable nature of the data collected, and the use of a deductive and structured research strategy.

### 2.1. Sample

To select the sample, non-probabilistic, convenience sampling [33] was utilized, given that the questionnaire was provided to the students whom the study researchers had access to during 2017–2018 academic year.

The sample was comprised by a total of 4009 students, of which 60.1% were female and 39.9% male, distributed in the following manner: 2965 were enrolled in the National Open and Distance University (UNAD), Colombia (74.0%) and 1044 from the University of Cordoba, Spain (26%). As for the student profiles, the macro area of enrollment was considered, addressing the five university macro areas established in both countries, which were: Social and Judicial Sciences (S and JS, $n$ = 1911, 47.7%), Health Sciences (HS, $n$ = 726, 18.1%), Arts and Humanities (A and H, $n$ = 164, 4.1%), Experimental Sciences (ES, $n$ = 168, 4.2%), and Engineering and Architecture (E and A, $n$ = 1039, 25.9%), as well as age, as shown in Table 1.

**Table 1.** Profile of the students as a function of the macro area, age and country.

| | | | | Macro Area | | | | | | |
|---|---|---|---|---|---|---|---|---|---|---|
| | | | | SJS | HS | AH | ES | EA | TOTAL | TOTAL Country |
| Country | Colombia | Age | From 18 to 20 y.o. | 3.5% | 4.5% | 1.5% | 1.0% | 6.5% | 16.9% | 74.0% |
| | | | From 21 to 23 y.o. | 3.2% | 3.1% | 0.8% | 0.5% | 5.0% | 12.6% | |
| | | | From 24 to 26 y.o. | 3.6% | 2.4% | 0.4% | 0.7% | 4.4% | 11.5% | |
| | | | Older than 26 | 11.4% | 8.1% | 1.4% | 2.0% | 10.1% | 33.0% | |
| | Spain | Age | From 18 to 20 y.o. | 13.9% | 0.0% | 0.0% | 0.0% | 0.0% | 13.9% | 26.0% |
| | | | From 21 to 23 y.o. | 8.9% | 0.0% | 0.0% | 0.0% | 0.0% | 8.9% | |
| | | | From 24 to 26 y.o. | 2.1% | 0.0% | 0.0% | 0.0% | 0.0% | 2.1% | |
| | | | Older than 26 | 1.1% | 0.0% | 0.0% | 0.0% | 0.0% | 1.1% | |
| | | | TOTAL | 47.7% | 18.1% | 4.1% | 4.2% | 25.9% | 100% | |

Notes: SJS = Social and Judicial Sciences; HS = Health Sciences; AH = Arts and Humanities; ES = Experimental Sciences; EA = Engineering and Architecture.

### 2.2. Instrument

The data collection instrument utilized in this research was based on the Mobile Phone Problematic Use Scale for Adolescent (MPPUSA) [34], it is contextualized to the Spanish-speaking population.

This questionnaire is anonymous, with closed-ended questions and polythematic, with a Likert-type response scale, ranging from complete disagreement (1) to complete agreement (5). The factorial structure was determined through an Exploratory Factorial Analysis (EFA), using the principal components method for extracting the factors, with the following indices of adjustment: KMO = 0.98, Bartlett's sphericity test with $p < 0.001$, and a total explained variance of 56.83%. The classification of the MPPUSA items by [35] was used as a reference providing the following structure with six dimensions as a result:

- Tolerance (Cronbach's alpha = 0.904): this dimension alludes to aspects related with the usage time of the smartphone and the impossibility of decreasing it. It encompasses a total of three items.
- Escape route (Cronbach's alpha = 0.907): comprised by three items, it alludes to the device as a resource for evading specific problems. It encompasses elements such as the increase in the feeling of well-being, its use when feeling lonely, as well as its prioritization against urgent matters or tasks.
- Disconnection (Cronbach's alpha = 0.912): this dimension covers aspects such as the appearance of worry if the subject cannot answer a call, the inability of disconnecting the mobile phone or the appearance of the feeling of disorientation in the case of not having the device available.
- Anxiety (Cronbach's alpha = 0.919): composed by three items that allude to the inability of the subjects to reduce the smartphone usage time, the appearance of nervousness in the case of not being able to read messages or answer calls, as well as the anger when they have the obligation of turning the device off.
- Negative consequences (Cronbach's alpha = 0.935): it constitutes the broadest dimension of the questionnaire, as it encompasses a total of 12 items that refer to the prioritization of the use of the smartphone against other tasks, the reduction of hours of sleep of the subjects, the making of economic investments beyond their means, the appearance of tardiness, the appearance of inconveniences from its use or the decrease in academic and/or professional performance, among other aspects.
- Social motivations (Cronbach's alpha = 0.901): this dimension alludes to aspects such as the impossibility of maintaining communication with one's peers in the case of not having the device, as well as the perception of anger by them in the case that the terminal is not connected; it encompasses two items.

As for reliability, it was measured through the internal consistency approach, obtaining a Cronbach's alpha value of > 0.90, for the dimensions as a set, as well as individually, demonstrating the high reliability of the instrument.

Lastly, an item with a dichotomous answer (yes/no) was included about the self-perception they considered they had about the problematic use of Smartphones (explaining it according to [19], as a persistent deterioration or anguish), formulated in the following terms: «I believe I have a problematic use of the Smartphone», as well as a series of independent variables from the academic area (macro area) and sociodemographic areas (age, gender and country).

Lastly, the instrument had a total of 26 items written as statements and structured into the six dimensions previously mentioned,

*2.3. Procedure*

The filling of the questionnaire was done in person and anonymously, with the study researchers present in the classroom to help answer any possible doubts of the students in the understanding of the items in the instrument. In the case of the Colombian students, a videoconference system was established, which allowed for the resolution of problems in real time during the completion of the instrument.

### 2.4. Analysis Conducted

In this study, the following analysis were utilized to reach the objectives set:

First, a descriptive analysis of the 26 variables of the questionnaire was performed, through the measurements of central tendency (mean) and dispersion (standard deviation). And the variable of the self-perception of the problematic use of the Smartphone.

In second place, a descriptive analysis was performed of the six dimensions of the questionnaire, which was similar to the analysis described above. In third place, an analysis of variance was conducted to verify the existence or not of differences in each of the dimensions of the questionnaire as a function of the independent variables (country, gender, age and macro area), through Student's $t$-test and ANOVA (both with n.s = 0.05). Afterwards, the relationship between the dimensions that comprised the questionnaire were verified through bivariate correlations.

Lastly, binary logistic regressions were utilized with a forward selection Wald's test and considering the goodness-of-fit of Hosmer-Lemeshow and the Confidence Interval (CI) for exp(B), to explain the influence of the six factors studied on the self-perception of the problematic use of the smartphone and the influence of the country.

All of these analyses were performed with the SPSS statistical package, version 23 (IBM Corp., Armonk, NY).

## 3. Results

### 3.1. Descriptive Study

In first place, the descriptive results (mean and standard deviation) of the 26 items that compose the *MPPUSA Questionnaire* used in this research study are listed (see Table 2).

**Table 2.** Frequency distribution of the items from the MPPUSA Questionnaire.

| MPPUSA Items | $n$ | M | SD |
|---|---|---|---|
| I can never spend enough time on my mobile phone | 4009 | 2.61 | 1.279 |
| I have used my mobile phone to make myself feel better when I was feeling down | 4009 | 2.83 | 1.423 |
| I find myself occupied on my mobile phone when I should be doing other things, and it causes problems | 4009 | 2.82 | 1.413 |
| I have tried to hide from others how much time I spend on my mobile phone | 4009 | 1.77 | 1.209 |
| I lose sleep due to the time I spend on my mobile phone | 4009 | 3.06 | 1.457 |
| I have spent with the mobile phone more than I should have | 4009 | 2.36 | 1.421 |
| When out of range for some time, I become worried about the thought of missing a call | 4009 | 2.81 | 1.442 |
| Sometimes, when I am on my mobile phone and I am doing other things, I get carried away with the conversation and I don't pay attention to what I am doing | 4009 | 2.78 | 1.368 |
| The time I spend on my mobile phone has increased over the last 12 months | 4009 | 3.54 | 1.269 |
| I have used my mobile phone to talk to others when I was feeling isolated | 4009 | 3.76 | 1.301 |
| I have attempted to spend less time on my mobile phone but am unable to | 4009 | 2.23 | 1.343 |
| I find it difficult to switch off/switch to silent my mobile phone | 4009 | 2.67 | 1.518 |
| I feel anxious if I have not checked for messages or switched on my mobile phone for some time | 4009 | 2.37 | 1.391 |
| I have frequent dreams about my mobile phone | 4009 | 1.39 | .973 |
| My friends and family complain about my use of the mobile phone | 4009 | 2.45 | 1.406 |
| If I don't have a mobile phone, my friends would find it hard to get in touch with me | 4009 | 3.62 | 1.287 |
| My academic performance has decreased as a direct result of the time I spend on my mobile phone | 4009 | 2.15 | 1.333 |
| I have aches and pains that are associated with my mobile phone use | 4009 | 2.08 | 1.336 |
| I find myself using on my mobile phone for longer periods of time than intended | 4009 | 2.86 | 1.406 |
| There are times when I would rather use my mobile phone than deal with other more urgent matters | 4009 | 2.11 | 1.364 |
| I am often late for appointments because I'm talking on my mobile phone when I shouldn't be | 4009 | 1.80 | 1.245 |
| I become irritable if I have to switch off/to silent my mobile phone for classes, meals, or at the cinema | 4009 | 1.56 | 1.086 |
| I have been told that I spend too much time on my mobile phone | 4009 | 2.69 | 1.445 |
| More than once I have been in trouble because my mobile phone has gone off during a class, at the cinema, or in a theatre | 4009 | 2.37 | 1.438 |
| My friends don't like it when my mobile phone is switched off/to silent | 4009 | 2.84 | 1.410 |
| I feel lost without my mobile phone | 4009 | 2.43 | 1.420 |

Notes: M = mean; SD= standard deviation. Source: Author created.

It can be observed that the items 5, 9, 10 and 16 point to being more in agreement with the statements as compared with items 4, 14, 21 and 22, which point to being more in disagreement.

Likewise, the results obtained in the self-perception on the problematic use of the Smartphone, point that 79.9% ($n = 3205$) considered that they did not have a problematic use, as compared to 20.1% ($n = 804$) who did.

#### 3.1.1. Tolerance

The results obtained highlight that the students were indifferent as for the tolerance in the use of the smartphone (M = 3.00, SD = 0.87).

With respect to the comparison of means related with country and gender, the Student's $t$-test for independent samples showed statistically significant differences in the first case, as $t = 6.167$, $p < 0.050$, with the Colombian students being the ones who obtained a greater score in this dimension (M = 3.04 vs. M = 2.87).

Lastly, for age and the macro area, the analysis of variance (ANOVA) only pointed to the existence of statistically significant differences in the second case, as [F (4, 4003) = 5.373; $p < 0.050$]. The post hoc multiple comparisons using the Games-Howell test showed within which macro area the differences in means were found. These macro areas were Experimental Sciences along with Engineering and Architecture, with respect to Social and Judicial Sciences, which had the greatest score ($\mu = 3.13$ and y $\mu = 3.05$ vs. $\mu = 2.93$).

#### 3.1.2. Escape Route

Once the analysis was performed, the results pointed out that the students were partially in disagreement as for the use of the smartphone as an escape route (M = 2.90, SD = 0.94).

As for the comparison of means, the Student's $t$-test for independent samples provided evidence of the existence of statistically significant differences for the country, exclusively ($t = 2.262$, $p < 0.050$), with the mean for the Colombian subjects being higher than the Spanish ones (2.91 vs. 2.85).

Lastly, for age and macro area, the analysis of variance (ANOVA), showed statistically significant differences in the first case [F (3, 4005) = 20.038; $p < 0.050$], with the difference of means found in students older than 26 with respect to those aged 18 to 20, 21 to 23, 24 to 26, respectively ($\mu = 2.74$ vs. $\mu = 3.01$, $\mu = 2.97$ and $\mu = 2.89$).

#### 3.1.3. Disconnection

The results obtained showed that the students were partially in disagreement with respect to the disconnection of the mobile phone (M = 2.63, SD = 1.09).

The Student's $t$-test for independent samples, performed to detect possible differences with respect to the country and gender, highlighted statistically significant differences in both cases. In the first ($t = -3.577$, $p < 0.050$), the Spanish students obtained a greater score with respect to the Colombian students (M = 2.73 vs. M = 2.60). As for gender ($t = -3.456$, $p = 0.001$), women were the ones who obtained a greater score with respect to the men (M = 2.68 vs. M = 2.56).

On the other hand, the analysis of variance (ANOVA) utilized to find statistically significant differences between age and the macro area, showed statistically significant differences in both cases, with the students older than 26 obtaining the lowest score [F (3, 4005) = 6.778; $p = 0.000$], as compared to those aged 18–20, 21 to 23 and 24 to 26, respectively ($\mu = 2.54$ vs. $\mu = 2.71$, $\mu = 2.70$ and $\mu = 2.58$). On the other hand, as for the macro area [F (4, 4003) = 2.634; $p < 0.050$], differences were found in the area of Social Sciences with respect to Health Sciences, with this last obtaining the lowest score ($\mu = 2.54$ vs. $\mu = 2.68$).

#### 3.1.4. Anxiety

The results obtained highlight that the students had an opinion that was partially in disagreement for the anxiety dimension of the use of the smartphone (M = 2.19, SD = 1.04).

With respect to the comparison of means related with country and gender, Student's *t*-test for independent samples showed statistically significant differences only in the second case, as $t = -2.225$, $p = 0.020$, with the women receiving a higher score in this dimension (M = 2.22 vs. M = 2.14).

Lastly, for age and the macro area, the analysis of variance (ANOVA) only pointed to the existence of statistically significant differences in the first case (age), as [F (3, 4005) = 7.180; $p = 0.000$]. The multiple post-hoc comparisons with the Games-Howell test allowed us to find exactly in what age range were these differences in means found, with those older than 26 being the ones who had a lower score with respect to students with ages between 18 and 20, and 21 and 23, respectively $\mu = 2.09$ vs. $\mu = 2.28$ and $\mu = 2.21$)

#### 3.1.5. Negative Consequences

Once the analysis was performed, the results showed that the students were partially in disagreement about the negative consequences derived from the use of the smartphone (M = 2.31, SD = 0.84).

For the comparison of means, Student's *t*-test for independent samples showed the existence of statistically significant differences for country, exclusively ($t = 8.891$, $p = 0.000$), with the means for the Colombian students being higher than for the Spanish ones (2.36 vs. 2.14).

Lastly, for the age and the macro area, the analysis of variance (ANOVA) indicated statistically significant differences in both cases. In the first case [F (3, 4005) = 13.181; $p = 0.000$], finding the differences in means of the students aged between 18 and 20, with respect to the rest ($\mu = 2.42$ vs. $\mu = 2.30$, $\mu = 2.29$ and $\mu = 2.21$), and in the second [F (4, 4003) = 9.024; $p = 0.000$], the differences in means were found in the students belonging to the macro area of Social and Judicial Sciences with respect to those in Arts and Humanities and Engineering and Architecture, respectively ($\mu = 2.23$ vs. $\mu = 2.48$, $\mu = 2.39$).

#### 3.1.6. Social Motivations

The results obtained showed that the students were partially in disagreement with respect to the social motivations derived from the use of the mobile phone (M = 3.22, SD = 1.03).

Student's *t*-test for independent samples, performed to detect possible differences with respect to country and gender, highlighted statistically significant differences only in the first case, $t = 5.079$, $p = 0.000$, with the Colombian students the ones who had the highest scores as compared to the Spanish ones (M = 3.27 vs. M = 3.09).

Also, the ANOVA performed to verify statistically significant differences between age and macro area, showed that there were no statistically significant differences in any of the cases.

### *3.2. Correlational Analysis*

This section addresses the correlational study between the six dimensions of the questionnaire. The data obtained, after the use of a Spearman's correlation test to observe the relationship between the six dimensions of the scale, can be observed below (see Table 3):

**Table 3.** Results of the bivariate correlations of the items from the 6 dimensions of the questionnaire.

| | | T | E | D | A | C | M |
|---|---|---|---|---|---|---|---|
| T | r | 1.000 | 0.443 ** | 0.466 ** | 0.444 ** | 0.592 ** | 0.307 ** |
| | *p* | | 0.000 | 0.000 | 0.000 | 0.000 | 0.000 |
| E | r | | 1.000 | 0.473 ** | 0.495 ** | 0.598 ** | 0.328 ** |
| | *p* | | | 0.000 | 0.000 | 0.000 | 0.000 |
| D | r | | | 1.000 | 0.754 ** | 0.589 ** | 0.354 ** |
| | *p* | | | | 0.000 | 0.000 | 0.000 |
| A | r | | | | 1.000 | 0.678 ** | 0.314 ** |
| | *p* | | | | | 0.000 | 0.000 |
| C | r | | | | | 1.000 | 0.334 ** |
| | *p* | | | | | | 0.000 |
| M | r | | | | | | 1.000 |
| | *p* | | | | | | |

Note: T = Tolerance; E = Escape; D = Disconnection; A = Anxiety; C = Consequences; M = Motivations.
** The correlation is significant at 0.01 (2-tailed).

As a function of the data obtained, it is observed that all the dimensions were correlated amongst themselves, with these correlations being high and moderate [36], using as a reference the value of their respective coefficients. In this sense, the following had a high correlation: the dimension Disconnection with the dimension Anxiety, as Rho = 0.754 and $p = 0.000$; as well as this last with the dimension Negative consequences (Rho = 0.678 and $p = 0.000$). As for moderate correlations (as defined by the authors cited previously), these were observed in the rest of the dimensions, as they obtained values between 0.300 and 0.600.

### *3.3. Binary Logistic Regression Analysis*

The best fitting model with respect to the self-perception shown by the university students from Spain and Colombia on the problematic use they display, was produced through a binary logistic regression. As this independent dependent variable is dichotomous in nature, with Yes/No values, the forward selection Wald test was utilized [37]. This model had a high specificity (98.8%) and high sensitivity (95%), with an overall percentage of 98% for the cut-off value of 50%, which indicates that the model classifies equally well those who consider themselves to have a self-perception on the problematic use of the Smartphone as well as those who do not.

The results shown from the analysis point out, for a sample of 4009 subjects, where 3205 answered No (79.9%) and 804 Yes (20.1%), that the goodness-of-fit of the best fitting model shows: a -2log of likelihood = 354.509, a Cox and Snell $R^2 = 0.599$; and an $R^2$ of Nagelkerke = 94.6% (0.946); aside from the value of the Hosmer and Lemeshow test which shows a good fit, as its significance is 0.988 ($\geq$0.05 according to [38]). Likewise, the values obtained in the Chi-square test for step ($\chi^2 = 3663.81$, gl = 6 and $p < 0.05$); block ($\chi^2 = 3663.81$, gl = 6 and $p < 0.05$); and model ($\chi^2 = 3663.81$, gl = 6 and $p < 0.05$), shows that the fitted model is significantly differentiated from the initial or base model.

As shown in Table 4, it can be observed how all the factors that appear in the MPPUSA intervene in the explanation in a significant manner. From them and tending to their relevance according to the value of B, these would be ordered as Consequences; Tolerance; Disconnection; Escape; Motivations and Anxiety.

Thus, the logistic equation would be:

$$\begin{aligned} \text{Y (self-perception in the problematic use)} = -89.07 + 1.13\text{Tolerance} + 1.11\text{Escape} + \\ 1.12\text{Disconnection} + 0.54\text{Anxiety} + 1.18\text{Consequences} + 0.99\text{Motivations} \end{aligned} \quad (1)$$

Thus, it can be observed that all the factors resulting from the MPPUSA positively and significantly influence the self-perception of considering that a problem with the use of the smartphone exists (reference category).

**Table 4.** Binary logistic regression of the self-perception on the problematic smartphone use [a] of Spanish and Colombian university students with respect to the MPPUSA.

| | B | E.T. | Wald | gl | Sig. | Exp (B) | C.I. 95% for EXP(B) | |
|---|---|---|---|---|---|---|---|---|
| | | | | | | | Lower | Upper |
| Tolerance | 1.129 | 0.122 | 86.236 | 1 | 0.000 | 3.093 | 2.437 | 3.926 |
| Escape | 1.105 | 0.107 | 106.641 | 1 | 0.000 | 3.020 | 2.448 | 3.724 |
| Disconnection | 1.115 | 0.106 | 110.914 | 1 | 0.000 | 3.051 | 2.479 | 3.755 |
| Anxiety | 0.540 | 0.077 | 49.069 | 1 | 0.000 | 1.715 | 1.475 | 1.995 |
| Consequences | 1.179 | 0.091 | 166.350 | 1 | 0.000 | 3.252 | 2.718 | 3.890 |
| Motivations | 0.987 | 0.112 | 77.352 | 1 | 0.000 | 2.683 | 2.153 | 3.343 |
| Constant | −89.073 | 6.691 | 177.220 | 1 | 0.000 | 0.000 | | |

Note. [a] = Dependent variable: Self-perception of having a problematic use of the smartphone Yes and No.

When analyzing the explanatory model of the self-perception of the problematic Smartphone use, having in mind the country of origin as the selection variable, it is observed, for 2965 Colombian students, of which 2266 answered No (76.4%) and 699 Yes (23.6%), that the goodness-of-fit had the following values: a -2log of likelihood = 290.826; a Cox and Snell $R^2 = 0.630$; and a, $R^2$ from Nagelkerke = 94.8% (0.948); with the Hosmer and Lemeshow value = 0.999, which demonstrates a good fit, as its significance is ≥0.05 [38]. Also, it has a high specificity (98.5) and a high sensitivity (95%), with an overall percentage of 97.7% for the cut-off value of 50%, which indicates that the model classifies those who consider themselves to have a self-perception on the problematic use of the Smartphone as well as those who do not equally well.

Table 5 shows how all the factors obtained from the MPPUSA significantly intervene in the explanation, as it occurred in the general model, in the same order according to their relevance (B value).

**Table 5.** Binary logistic regression of the self-perception of the problematic smartphone use [a] of Colombian university students with respect to the MPPUSA.

| | B | E.T. | Wald | gl | Sig. | Exp (B) | C.I. 95% for EXP(B) | |
|---|---|---|---|---|---|---|---|---|
| | | | | | | | Lower | Lower |
| Tolerance | 1.124 | 0.131 | 73.716 | 1 | 0.000 | 3.077 | 2.381 | 3.977 |
| Escape | 1.062 | 0.113 | 87.622 | 1 | 0.000 | 2.892 | 2.315 | 3.612 |
| Disconnection | 1.089 | 0.114 | 91.520 | 1 | 0.000 | 2.970 | 2.376 | 3.712 |
| Anxiety | 0.495 | 0.080 | 37.976 | 1 | 0.000 | 1.640 | 1.401 | 1.919 |
| Consequences | 1.191 | 0.103 | 133.351 | 1 | 0.000 | 3.291 | 2.688 | 4.028 |
| Motivations | 0.952 | 0.121 | 61.350 | 1 | 0.000 | 2.590 | 2.041 | 3.286 |
| Constant | −88.133 | 7.340 | 144.163 | 1 | 0.000 | 0.000 | | |

Note. [a] = Dependent variable: Self-perception of having a problematic use of the Smartphone Yes and No.

In this occasion, the logistical equation is the following:

$$\text{Y (self-perception on the problematic use of Colombian students)} = -88.13 + 1.12\text{Tolerance} + 1.06\text{Escape} + 1.09\text{Disconnection} + 0.50\text{Anxiety} + 1.19\text{Consequences} + 0.95\text{Motivations} \quad (2)$$

As a result, the self-perception of the Colombian students when considering if they have a problematic smartphone use (reference category), all the factors from the MPPUSA have a positive and significant influence.

Lastly, Table 6 shows the results of the explanatory model of the self-perception on the problematic use of the smartphone of Spanish university students (selection variable). Of the 1044 students, 939 who answered No (89.9%) and 105 Yes (10.1%). The goodness-of-fit of the best fitting model obtained the following values: a -2log of likelihood= 54.446; a Cox and Snell $R^2 = 0.451$; and a Nagelkerke $R^2 = 94.2\%$ (0.942); with the Hosmer and Lemeshow test obtaining a value of 1.0, which demonstrates a good fit, as its significance is ≥0.05 [38]. The specificity is high (99.4%), as well as its sensitivity (94.3%), with an overall percentage of 98.9%) for the cut-off value of 50%), which indicates that the model classifies those who consider themselves to have a self-perception on the problematic use of the Smartphone as well as those who do not equally well.

**Table 6.** Binary logistic regression of the self-perception on the problematic smartphone use [a] of Spanish university students with respect to the MPPUSA.

| | B | E.T. | Wald | gl | Sig. | Exp (B) | C.I. 95% for EXP(B) | |
|---|---|---|---|---|---|---|---|---|
| | | | | | | | Lower | Lower |
| Tolerance | 1.461 | 0.399 | 13.394 | 1 | 0.000 | 4.309 | 1.971 | 9.422 |
| Escape | 1.475 | 0.354 | 17.312 | 1 | 0.000 | 4.369 | 2.181 | 8.751 |
| Disconnection | 1.084 | 0.306 | 12.516 | 1 | 0.000 | 2.957 | 1.622 | 5.392 |
| Anxiety | 1.247 | 0.347 | 12.923 | 1 | 0.000 | 3.478 | 1.763 | 6.863 |
| Consequences | 1.266 | 0.232 | 29.758 | 1 | 0.000 | 3.548 | 2.251 | 5.593 |
| Motivations | 1.461 | 0.367 | 15.821 | 1 | 0.000 | 4.312 | 2.099 | 8.859 |
| Constant | −108.940 | 19.958 | 29.795 | 1 | 0.000 | 0.000 | | |

Note. [a] = Dependent variable: Self-perception of having a problematic use of the smartphone Yes and No.

Thus, the equation is:

$$\text{Y (self-perception of the problematic use of the smartphone of Spanish university students)} = -108.94 + 1.46\text{Tolerance} + 1.48\text{Escape} + 1.08\text{Disconnection} + 1.25\text{Anxiety} + 1.27\text{Consequences} + 1.46\text{Motivations}. \quad (3)$$

On Table 6, it is observed that the factors that appear in the MPPUSA significantly intervene in the explanation; however, when taking into account their relevance (B value), it is observed that the order is different from the general model and the order found for the Colombian students, being: Escape; Motivations; Tolerance; Consequences; Anxiety; Disconnection.

In summary, for the self-perception of the Spanish students who consider if they have a problem with the use of smartphones (reference category), all the factors found from the MPPUSA have a positive and significant influence.

When comparing the Spanish students with the Colombian ones, it is observed that although all the factors contribute to the best fitting models, in Spain the factor Escape had more weight than in Colombia, with Consequences being more significant for the latter.

The analysis of the explanatory model of the self-perception on the problematic Smartphone use, with sex as the selection variable, shows that for 1601 male students, of which 1270 answered No (79.3%) and 331 Yes (20.7%), the goodness-of-fit had the following values: a -2log of likelihood = 134.565; a Cox and Snell $R^2 = 0.607$; and a $R^2$ from Nagelkerke = 95% (0.950); with a Hosmer and Lemeshow value = 0.994. This demonstrates a good fit, as its significance is ≥0.05 [38]. Also, it had a high specificity (98.8%) and a high sensitivity (94.3%), with an overall percentage of 97.9% for the cut-off value of 50%, indicating that the model classifies both of those who consider themselves to have a self-perception on the problematic use of the smartphone as well as those who do not, equally well.

Table 7 shows that all the factors obtained from the MPPUSA significantly intervened in the explanation, as in the general model, in the same order according to their relevance (B value).

**Table 7.** Binary logistic regression of the self-perception of the problematic Smartphone use [a] of male university students with respect to the MPPUSA.

| | B | E.T. | Wald | gl | Sig. | Exp (B) | C.I. 95% for EXP(B) | |
|---|---|---|---|---|---|---|---|---|
| | | | | | | | Inferior | Superior |
| Tolerance | 1.258 | 0.210 | 35.838 | 1 | 0.000 | 3.517 | 2.330 | 5.308 |
| Escape | 1.223 | 0.175 | 48.813 | 1 | 0.000 | 3.397 | 2.411 | 4.787 |
| Disconnection | 1.164 | 0.179 | 42.275 | 1 | 0.000 | 3.204 | 2.256 | 4.552 |
| Anxiety | 0.598 | 0.121 | 24.422 | 1 | 0.000 | 1.819 | 1.435 | 2.307 |
| Consequences | 1.216 | 0.153 | 63.448 | 1 | 0.000 | 3.373 | 2.501 | 4.550 |
| Motivations | 0.899 | 0.174 | 26.843 | 1 | 0.000 | 2.457 | 1.749 | 3.453 |
| Constant | −93.506 | 11.329 | 68.122 | 1 | 0.000 | 0.000 | | |

Note. [a] = Dependent variable: Self-perception of having a problematic use of the smartphone Yes and No.

On this occasion, the logistical equation is the following:

$$\text{Y (self-perception on the problematic use of male students)} = -93.51 + 1.26\text{Tolerance} + 1.22\text{Escape} + 1.16\text{Disconnection} + 0.60\text{Anxiety} + 1.22\text{Consequences} + 0.90\text{Motivations} \quad (4)$$

As a result, all the factors from the MPPUSA have a positive and significant influence on the self-perception of the male students when considering if they have a problematic use of the smartphone (reference category).

Table 8 shows the results of the explanatory model for female university students (selection variable). Of these 2408 students, 1935 answered No (80.4%) and 473 Yes (19.6%). The goodness-of-fit of the best fitting model had the following values: a -2log of likelihood = 215.28; a Cox and Snell $R^2 = 0.594$; and a Nagelkerke $R^2 = 94.5\%$ (0.945); with the Hosmer and Lemeshow test obtaining a value of 0.897, which demonstrates a good fit, as its significance was ≥0.05 [38]. The specificity and the sensitivity were high (98.7% and 94.3%, respectively), with an overall percentage of 97.8% for the cut-off value of 50%, indicating that the model classifies both of those who consider themselves to have a self-perception on the problematic use of the Smartphone as well as those who do not, equally well.

**Table 8.** Binary logistic regression of the self-perception on the problematic smartphone use [a] of female university students with respect to the MPPUSA.

| | B | E.T. | Wald | gl | Sig. | Exp (B) | C.I. 95% for EXP(B) | |
|---|---|---|---|---|---|---|---|---|
| | | | | | | | Lower | Lower |
| Tolerance | 1.086 | 0.154 | 49.572 | 1 | 0.000 | 2.963 | 2.190 | 4.010 |
| Escape | 1.029 | 0.140 | 54.110 | 1 | 0.000 | 2.799 | 2.127 | 3.682 |
| Disconnection | 1.113 | 0.138 | 64.931 | 1 | 0.000 | 3.045 | 2.323 | 3.992 |
| Anxiety | 0.483 | 0.103 | 21.964 | 1 | 0.000 | 1.621 | 1.324 | 1.983 |
| Consequences | 1.194 | 0.120 | 98.472 | 1 | 0.000 | 3.301 | 2.607 | 4.179 |
| Motivations | 1.081 | 0.152 | 50.779 | 1 | 0.000 | 2.947 | 2.189 | 3.967 |
| Constant | −88.400 | 8.595 | 105.794 | 1 | 0.000 | 0.000 | | |

Note. [a] = Dependent variable: Self-perception of having a problematic use of the smartphone Yes and No.

Thus, the equation is

$$\text{Y (self-perception of the problematic use of the smartphone of female university students)} = -88.4 + 1.09\text{Tolerance} + 1.03\text{Escape} + 1.11\text{Disconnection} + 0.48\text{Anxiety} + 1.19\text{Consequences} + 1.08\text{Motivations}. \quad (5)$$

In Table 8, it is observed that the factors from the MPPUSA significantly intervened in the explanation; however, when taking into account their relevance (B value), it was observed that the order was different from both the general model and the one for the male students. Thus, for females, the order was: Consequences; Disconnection; Tolerance; Motivations; Escape; Anxiety.

Having in mind age as the selection variable, the explanatory model for 1237 university students aged from 18 to 20 years old, of whom 979 answered No (79.1%) and 258 Yes (20.9%), had the following goodness-of-fit values: a -2log of likelihood = 146.052; a Cox and Snell $R^2 = 0.596$; and a $R^2$ from Nagelkerke = 93% (0.930); with the Hosmer and Lemeshow value = 0.993, which demonstrates a good fit, as its significance was ≥0.05 [38]. Also, it had a high specificity (98.1%) and a high sensitivity (93.8%), with an overall percentage of 97.2% for the cut-off value of 50%, which indicates that the model classifies those who considered themselves to have a self-perception on the problematic use of the Smartphone as well as those who do not, equally well.

Table 9 shows how all the factors obtained from the MPPUSA significantly intervene in the explanation, as it occurred in the general model, in the same order according to their relevance (B value).

**Table 9.** Binary logistic regression of the self-perception of the problematic smartphones use [a] of university students aged between 18 and 20 years old with respect to the MPPUSA.

| | B | E.T. | Wald | gl | Sig. | Exp (B) | C.I. 95% for EXP(B) | |
|---|---|---|---|---|---|---|---|---|
| | | | | | | | Inferior | Superior |
| Tolerance | 0.875 | 0.179 | 23.795 | 1 | 0.000 | 2.399 | 1.688 | 3.410 |
| Escape | 0.951 | 0.159 | 36.032 | 1 | 0.000 | 2.590 | 1.898 | 3.533 |
| Disconnection | 0.988 | 0.153 | 41.600 | 1 | 0.000 | 2.686 | 1.989 | 3.627 |
| Anxiety | 0.490 | 0.117 | 17.473 | 1 | 0.000 | 1.632 | 1.297 | 2.054 |
| Consequences | 1.034 | 0.129 | 64.056 | 1 | 0.000 | 2.813 | 2.184 | 3.625 |
| Motivations | 0.829 | 0.168 | 24.417 | 1 | 0.000 | 2.292 | 1.649 | 3.185 |
| Constant | −76.999 | 9.391 | 67.220 | 1 | 0.000 | 0.000 | | |

Note. [a] = Dependent variable: Self-perception of having a problematic use of the smartphone Yes and No.

On this occasion, the logistical equation is the following:

$$\text{Y (self-perception on the problematic use of smartphone of students between 18 and 20 years)} = -76.99 + 0.88\text{Tolerance} + 0.95\text{Escape} + 0.99\text{Disconnection} + 0.49\text{Anxiety} + 1.03\text{Consequences} + 0.83\text{Motivations} \quad (6)$$

As a result, all the factors of the MPPUSA have a positive and significant influence on the self-perception of university students aged between 18 and 20 years old when considering whether they have a problematic use of smartphones (reference category).

Table 10 shows the results of the explanatory model of students aged from 21 to 23 years old (age selection variable). Of these 860 students, 696 answered No (80.9%) and 164 Yes (19.1%). The goodness-of-fit of the best fitting model obtained the following values: a -2log of likelihood= 45.820; a Cox and Snell $R^2 = 0.602$; and a Nagelkerke $R^2 = 96.7\%$ (0.967); with the Hosmer and Lemeshow test obtaining a value of 0.995, which demonstrates a good fit, as its significance is ≥0.05 [38]. Both the specificity and sensitivity were high (99.1% and 97%, respectively), with an overall percentage of 98.7% for the cut-off value of 50%, which indicates that the model classifies those who consider themselves to have a self-perception on the problematic use of the smartphone as well as those who do not equally well.

**Table 10.** Binary logistic regression of the self-perception on the problematic smartphone use [a] of university students between 21 to 23 years of age with respect to the MPPUSA.

| | B | E.T. | Wald | gl | Sig. | Exp (B) | C.I. 95% for EXP(B) | |
|---|---|---|---|---|---|---|---|---|
| | | | | | | | Lower | Lower |
| Tolerance | 1.323 | 0.382 | 12.004 | 1 | 0.001 | 3.753 | 1.776 | 7.931 |
| Escape | 1.339 | 0.338 | 15.669 | 1 | 0.000 | 3.816 | 1.966 | 7.406 |
| Disconnection | 1.594 | 0.362 | 19.439 | 1 | 0.000 | 4.924 | 2.424 | 10.003 |
| Anxiety | 0.770 | 0.226 | 11.617 | 1 | 0.001 | 2.159 | 1.387 | 3.361 |
| Consequences | 1.952 | 0.446 | 19.174 | 1 | 0.000 | 7.044 | 2.940 | 16.876 |
| Motivations | 1.939 | 0.560 | 12.001 | 1 | 0.001 | 6.952 | 2.321 | 20.821 |
| Constant | −134.749 | 29.206 | 21.286 | 1 | 0.000 | 0.000 | | |

Note. [a] = Dependent variable: Self-perception of having a problematic use of the smartphone Yes and No.

Thus, the equation is:

$$Y \text{ (self-perception on the problematic use of smartphone of students between 21 and 23 years)} = -134.75 + 1.32\text{Tolerance} + 1.34\text{Escape} + 1.59\text{Disconnection} + 0.77\text{Anxiety} + 1.95\text{Consequences} + 1.94\text{Motivations}. \quad (7)$$

For university students between the ages of 24 and 26, the results of the explanatory self-perception model had the following aspects (see Table 11): of the 546 students, 442 answered No (81%) and 104 Yes (19%). The goodness-of-fit of the best fitting model obtained the following values: a -2log of likelihood = 56.168; a Cox and Snell $R^2 = 0.581$; and a Nagelkerke $R^2 = 93.4\%$ (0.934); with the Hosmer and Lemeshow test obtaining a value of 0.876, which demonstrates a good fit, as its significance is ≥0.05 [38]. The specificity and sensitivity were high (99.1% and 94.2%, respectively), with an overall percentage of 98.2% for the cut-off value of 50%, indicating that the model classifies those who consider themselves to have a self-perception on the problematic use of the smartphone as well as those who do not, equally well.

**Table 11.** Binary logistic regression of the self-perception on the problematic smartphone use [a] of university students between 24 to 26 years of age with respect to the MPPUSA.

| | B | E.T. | Wald | gl | Sig. | Exp (B) | C.I. 95% for EXP(B) | |
|---|---|---|---|---|---|---|---|---|
| | | | | | | | Lower | Lower |
| Tolerance | 1.058 | 0.257 | 16.939 | 1 | 0.000 | 2.882 | 1.741 | 4.771 |
| Escape | 0.922 | 0.247 | 13.943 | 1 | 0.000 | 2.514 | 1.550 | 4.078 |
| Disconnection | 0.790 | 0.246 | 10.282 | 1 | 0.001 | 2.203 | 1.359 | 3.569 |
| Anxiety | 0.472 | 0.191 | 6.071 | 1 | 0.014 | 1.603 | 1.101 | 2.332 |
| Consequences | 1.060 | 0.203 | 27.378 | 1 | 0.000 | 2.885 | 1.940 | 4.291 |
| Motivations | 0.829 | 0.295 | 7.875 | 1 | 0.005 | 2.291 | 1.284 | 4.088 |
| Constant | −77.268 | 14.469 | 28.517 | 1 | 0.000 | 0.000 | | |

Note. [a] = Dependent variable: Self-perception of having a problematic use of the smartphone Yes and No.

Thus, the equation is:

$$Y \text{ (self-perception on the problematic use of smartphone of students between 24 and 26 years)} = -77.27 + 1.06\text{Tolerance} + 0.92\text{Escape} + 0.79\text{Disconnection} + 0.47\text{Anxiety} + 1.06\text{Consequences} + 0.83\text{Motivations}. \quad (8)$$

Table 12 shows the results of the explanatory model of students older than 26 (age selection variable). Of the 1366 students, 1088 answered No (79.6%) and 278 Yes (20.4%). The goodness-of-fit of the best fitting model obtained the following values: a -2log of likelihood = 86.276; a Cox and Snell $R^2 = 0.612$; and a Nagelkerke $R^2 = 96.3\%$ (0.963); with the Hosmer and Lemeshow test obtaining a value of 0.987, which demonstrates a good fit, as its significance is ≥0.05 [38]. Both the specificity and its sensitivity were high (99.2% and 96.4%, respectively), with an overall percentage of 98.6% for the cut-off value of 50%, which indicates that the model classifies those who consider themselves to have a self-perception on the problematic use of the Smartphone as well as those who do not, equally well.

**Table 12.** Binary logistic regression of the self-perception on the problematic smartphone use [a] of students older than 26 years old with respect to the MPPUSA.

| | B | E.T. | Wald | gl | Sig. | Exp (B) | C.I. 95% for EXP(B) | |
|---|---|---|---|---|---|---|---|---|
| | | | | | | | Lower | Lower |
| Tolerance | 1.721 | 0.346 | 24.689 | 1 | 0.000 | 5.591 | 2.836 | 11.024 |
| Escape | 1.562 | 0.285 | 30.009 | 1 | 0.000 | 4.768 | 2.727 | 8.337 |
| Disconnection | 1.486 | 0.275 | 29.122 | 1 | 0.000 | 4.418 | 2.576 | 7.579 |
| Anxiety | 0.747 | 0.193 | 14.941 | 1 | 0.000 | 2.111 | 1.445 | 3.083 |
| Consequences | 1.476 | 0.241 | 37.435 | 1 | 0.000 | 4.375 | 2.727 | 7.019 |
| Motivations | 1.222 | 0.229 | 28.590 | 1 | 0.000 | 3.394 | 2.169 | 5.312 |
| Constant | −117.614 | 18.738 | 39.397 | 1 | 0.000 | 0.000 | | |

Note. [a] = Dependent variable: Self-perception of having a problematic use of the smartphone Yes and No.

Thus, the equation is:

$$\begin{aligned} &\text{Y (self-perception on the problematic use of smartphone of students older than 26 years)} \\ &= -117.61 + 1.72\text{Tolerance} + 1.56\text{Escape} + 1.49\text{Disconnection} + 0.75\text{Anxiety} + \\ &\quad 1.48\text{Consequences} + 1.22\text{Motivations} \end{aligned} \tag{9}$$

On Table 12, it is observed that the factors that appeared in the MPPUSA significantly intervened on the explanation; However, having in mind its relevance (B value), it was observed that the order was different from the general model and the order found for different ages, being Tolerance; Escape; Disconnection; Consequences; Motivations; Anxiety for those over 26 years old.

## 4. Discussion

We are in agreement with [39] in that the technologies themselves are not elements that can provoke a problematic behavior in its use, but it is the individuals who develop this behavior, which may or may not be problematic [9].

In this sense, after utilizing the MPPUSA, the results obtained provided us with a profile of a young Spanish and Colombian university student who has a problematic behavior with the mobile device as a function of 6 factors relative to the tolerance towards the time spent using the device, its regard as a means of escape or the disconnection to the world that surrounds them, linked to the anxiety that could be caused if they do not use it, just as the results reached by [17], who showed that the university students with whom the same instrument was utilized, felt better when they utilized the smartphone to evade or avoid situations they found themselves in. The results also showed that the participating students felt that not having the device available gave them anxiety and stress, the negative consequences its use could have due to their using it most of their time in different ways, and lastly, the social motivations related to its use of not, in line with data from [12,17,18,34]. It is meaningful that these results coincide with those from [40], who reached similar results after the use of an instrument called Questionnaire of Experiences Related to the Mobile Phone (Spanish acronym: CERM) with university students, although its short length (10 items) did not analyze in detail aspects such as feelings of avoidance or FOMO.

Taking into account the objectives established, it was verified that the students self-perceived not having a problematic use of the device. This result should be pondered, given that the study by [13] pointed that the university students have control over the addiction to the Internet (85.17%), and in our case, the perception of not having a problematic use was 79.9%. This shows that the university students younger than 35 years old do not consider a problematic or addictive use of the Smartphone or the Internet.

As opposed to results reached by [17,18,21], after the use of the same instrument along the same line, and also as opposed from results reached by [41], who reported an increasing trend of cell phone use after the use of MMPUS. Nevertheless, it is significant that in general, the Colombian students were more aware of the negative consequences that its use could imply, pointing out that this is linked to the time they spend connected or using it in a generalized manner or having to hide this usage time from family and friends, data that coincides with those from [42], who after the application of the HUTL, pointed out the same aspects for this study population. They are also more aware that their state of rest and their academic performance will the affected due to the excessive use of the Smartphone [18,43], with this aspect being common to all the research studies performed with other instruments such as MMPUS, CERM or HUTL [17,40–43]. Nevertheless, these behaviors that are detrimental, in one way or another, to daily life, are also observed in the use of substances o addiction to the Internet, where the study by [44] points that the altered behaviors related to the Internet, taking into account the sex of the students, could be due to the use or contents consumed. Therefore, we should ask ourselves if the devices are understood as mere devices or associated to the consumption of contents they enjoy.

They also indicated that when they are bored, sad or alone, they use the mobile phone. On other hand, they also commented that if they did not have a device such as this, it would be difficult for their friends to locate them and that they did not like it when the turned their phones off, and this is where the importance a smartphone has in their social relations is derived from just as the results found after the use of the MMPUS [42]. On the other hand, the Spanish students have features of the FOMO syndrome, manifesting that they are worried about not having the device with them, and they would miss calls or messages, and that it is difficult for them to turn the phone off [12,18,29,43].

If we center our attention to the age of the participants, it is verified, as in the work by [12], that the younger students from both countries had a PSU as compared to those who were older, as opposed to the results from [45], given that significant differences were found in the factors found that referred to the use of the mobile phone as a means of escape, to disconnect, anxiety and the negative consequences due to its use.

Gender could be pointed out as an element that determines the attitude towards the mobile phone [32,43] an aspect that coincides with other tests applied [40–42]. As opposed to the work by [12,41–43], it was the women, and more specifically Spanish women, the ones who had a problematic attitude with the device, such as the shown in the results from works by [18,20,46–49], as the participating sample expressed feeling anxiety and disconnection with their surroundings if they did not have a working phone [47–50].

On the other hand, if attention is placed on the macro area of study, as referred to the awareness of the consequences, the Arts and Humanities students, as well as the Engineering and Architecture ones, as compared to the other macro areas, such in the case of Social Sciences, are ones who had features of the so-called FOMO [10,29,45]. As for the elements that comprise the factor Tolerance, it was verified that the students from the macro areas of Experimental Sciences, Engineering and Architecture, were more aware of having less tolerance (being in a bad mood, using the device due to boredom or for feeling alone, and to make superfluous calls) [46,50]. It should be highlighted that the students from the area of Health Sciences did not have any prevalence of problematic behavior.

With respect to the factors reached in this study, it can be confirmed that the previous works [30,34,49,50] have shown the existence of 6 factors, and that the grouping of the items, aside from the correlations between themselves, determine the elements that define a problematic behavior towards smartphones, and about which work models should be developed to be able to perform an intervention.

Lastly, it was verified that the model of 6 factors created in line with the one from [35], follows the trail of the data from [17,30,49,50], and points to the Colombian students being closer to this model as compared to the Spanish students, as it describes the factor Consequences as being more significant in the model, as compared to Escape from the Spanish group. On the other hand, age and sex do not exactly follow the general model.

The section should not end without indicating the limitations of this international study, where the Latin American context, as well as the geography of the terrain, could define uses, trends, and views. One of these limitations could language used. Although in this case the language used was Spanish, it should be point out that just as with other languages, it has local variations depending on the country we find ourselves in. Therefore, the initial instrument developed in the Spanish utilized in Spain had to be adapted to Colombian Spanish, resulting in a delay of the research study.

On the other hand, although the sample was large, the Spanish representation should be increased, not only for the generalization of the data, but also for the performing a comparison that is not catalogued as cross-sectional, and that contributes a PSU analysis model for the entire Latin American context, which entails the intention of widening the study to other countries in the American continent.

## 5. Conclusions

Based on the above, it can be concluded that on the one hand, women in general, and in particular the Spanish women who studied within the macro area of Social Sciences, were the ones who had a problematic use of the mobile phone as compared to the men in both countries, showing the same factors as a pharmacological addiction. On the other hand, the students who resided in Colombia utilized the smartphone as a means of escape from boredom. These same students are aware of the consequences of the excessive use of the device on their personal and academic life. Also, the younger Spanish students had symptomatic signs of the FOMO syndrome. Along this line, in both countries, the students who showed these signs were enrolled in the area of Social Sciences. With respect to the Experimental Sciences and Engineering and Architecture students, these recognized spending too many hours being preoccupied with the phone. It should be pointed out that in the macro areas of Arts and Humanities, and Engineering and Architecture, their students were aware of the negative consequences of its use on their personal and academic lives.

Ultimately, it should be indicated, specifically for the differences found according to age and the country of origin, that the younger students, independently of the country, had a problematic use of smartphones and that Colombian students were closer to the general model, while for the Spanish ones, the order of relevance of each of the factors varied, while the general model does not fit the age or sex of the students.

**Author Contributions:** Conceptualización, V.M.-D.; curación de datos, J.M.M.-G. and B.-E.S. R.; investigación, J.M.M.-G. and B.-E.S.-R.; metodología, J.M.M.-G. and B.-E.S.-R.; administración de proyecto, V.M.-D.; supervisión, V.M.-D. and B.-E.S.-R.; redacción-borrador original, V.M.-D. All authors have read and agreed to the published version of the manuscript.

## References

1. Babakr, Z.H.; Majeed, K.; Soran, P.M.; Kakamad, K. Internet addiction in kurdistan university students: Prevalence and association with self-control. *Euro. J. Edu. Res.* **2019**, *8*, 867–873. [CrossRef]
2. Longstreet, P.; Brooks, S.; Gonzalez, E.S. Internet addiction: When the positive emotions are not so positive. *Tech. Soc.* **2019**, *57*, 76–85. [CrossRef]
3. Mendes, I.; Silvia, I. Uso problemático da internet em adultos: Que relação com sintomas clínicos? *Revista De Estudios E Investigación En Psicología Y Educación* **2017**, *13*, 129–133. [CrossRef]
4. Internet World Stast. Usage and Population Statistics. 2020. Available online: https://www.internetworldstats.com/top20.htm (accessed on 10 April 2020).
5. DITRENDIA. Informe Ditrendia: Mobile en España y en el mundo 2019. 2019. Available online: https://ditrendia.es/informe-mobile-espana-mundo-2019/ (accessed on 15 April 2020).
6. DANE. Indicadores básicos de TIC en Hogares. 2019. Available online: https://www.dane.gov.co/index.php/estadisticas-por-tema/tecnologia-e-innovacion/tecnologias-de-la-informacion-y-las-comunicaciones-tic/indicadores-basicos-de-tic-en-hogares (accessed on 10 April 2020).

7. Fernández-Castillo, E.; Choliz, M.; Martínez, A.C.; Rodríguez, Y.C.; Monteagudo, P. Evaluación de las propiedades psicométricas del Test de dependencia al Teléfono Móvil en estudiantes universitarios cubanos. *Katharsis Rev. de Cienc. Soc.* **2019**, *27*, 73–85.
8. Besolí, G.; Palomas, N.; Chamorro, A. Uso del móvil en padres, niños y adolescentes: Creencias a cerca de sus riesgos y beneficios. *Aloma* **2018**, *36*, 29–39.
9. Fombona, J.; Roza Martin, P. Uso de los dispositivos móviles en educación infantil. *Edmetic* **2016**, *5*, 158–181. [CrossRef]
10. Kumcagiz, H.; Gunduz, Y. Relationship between psychological well-being and smartphone addiction of university students. *Int. J. High. Edu.* **2016**, *5*, 144–156. [CrossRef]
11. Panova, T.; Carbonell, J. Smartphone addiction really addiction? *J. Behav. Addic.* **2018**, *7*, 250–259. [CrossRef]
12. Romero, J.M.; Aznar, I. Análisis de la adicción al smartphone en estudiantes universitarios. *Revista de Educación a Distancia* **2019**, 19. [CrossRef]
13. Sánchez Vega, E.; Cantero-Téllez, R.; Rodríguez-Martínez, M.C. Adicción a internet en futuros profesores. Un estudio de caso con alumnado universitario. *Int. J. Technol. Educ. Innov.* **2016**, *2*, 46–53. [CrossRef]
14. Cabrera, Y. Hábitos de uso y consumo de la generación millennial en sus teléfonos móviles. adComunica. *Sci. J. Stra. Tren. Inn. Comm.* **2019**, *18*, 21–40. [CrossRef]
15. Rodríguez, H.; Restrepo, L.; García, G. Habilidades digitales y uso de teléfonos inteligentes (smartphones) en el aprendizaje en la educación superior. *Virt. J. Uni. Cat. Nor.* **2017**, *50*, 126–142.
16. Vázquez-Cano, E.; Sevillano García, L. El smartphone en la educación superior. Un estudio comparativo del uso educativo, social y ubicuo en universidades españolas e hispanoamericanas. *Signo y Pensamiento* **2015**, *34*, 132–149. [CrossRef]
17. Marín, V.; Vega, E.; Sampedro, E. Uso problemático del smartphone en estudiantes universitarios. *Rev. Revista Española De Drogodependencias* **2018**, *43*, 62–76.
18. Olivencia-Carrión, M.A.; Ramírez-Uctes, I.; Holgado-Tello, P.; López-Torrecillas, F. Validation of a Spanish questionnaire on mobile phone abuse. *Fron. Psych.* **2018**, *9*, 824. [CrossRef]
19. Elhai, J.D.; Dvorak, R.D.; Levine, J.C.; Hall, B.J. Problematic smartphone use: A conceptual overview and systematic review of relations with anxiety and depression psychopathology. *J. Affec. Disor.* **2017**, *207*, 251–259. [CrossRef]
20. Roberts, J.A.; Yaya, L.H.; Manolis, C. The invisible addiction: Cell-phone activities and addiction among male and female college students. *J. Behav. Addic.* **2014**, *3*, 254–265. [CrossRef] [PubMed]
21. Roberts, J.A.; Pulling, C.; Manolis, C. I need my smartphone a hierarchical model of personality and cell-phone addiction. *Perso. Indi. Diff.* **2015**, *79*, 13–19. [CrossRef]
22. Sigerson, L.; Li, A.Y.-L.; Cheung, M.W.-L.; Cheng, C. Examining common information technology addictions and their relationships with non-technology-related addictions. *Comp. Hum. Behav.* **2017**, *75*, 520–526. [CrossRef]
23. American Psychiatric Association (APA). *Diagnostic and Statistical Manual of Mental Disorders*; American Psychiatric Association: Arlington, VA, USA, 2013.
24. Biglu, M.H.; Ghavami, M. Factors influencing dependence on mobile phone. *J. Anal. Res. Clin. Med.* **2016**, *4*, 158–162. [CrossRef]
25. Bunyalug, M.; Kanchanakhan, N. Effect of using smartphone before bed on sleep quality among undergraduate students at Chulalongkorn University. *Thai. J. Health Res.* **2017**, *31* (Suppl. 2), S225–S231. [CrossRef]
26. Echeburúa, E.; del Corral, P. Adicción a las nuevas tecnologías y a las redes sociales en jóvenes: Un nuevo reto. *Adicciones* **2010**, *22*, 91–96. [CrossRef]
27. Rozgonjuk, D.; Levine, J.C.; Hall, B.J.; Elhai, J.D. The association between problematic smartphone use, depression and anxiety symptom severity, and objectively measured smartphone use over one week. *Comp. Hum. Behav.* **2018**, *87*, 10–17. [CrossRef]
28. Zsidó, A.N.; Darnai, G.; Inhóf, O.; Perlaki, G.; Orsi, G.; Nagy, S.; Lábadi, B.; Lénárd, K.; Kovács, N.; Dóczi, T.; et al. Differentiation between young adult Internet addicts, smokers, and healthy controls by the interaction between impulsivity and temporal lobe thickness. *J. Behav. Addict.* **2019**, *8*, 35–47. [CrossRef] [PubMed]
29. Przybylski, A.K.; Murayama, K.; DeHaan, C.R.; Gladwell, V. Motivational, emotional, and behavioral correlates of fear of missing out. *Comp. Hum. Behav.* **2013**, *29*, 1841–1848. [CrossRef]

30. Ruíz, C. Perfil de uso del teléfono móvil e internet en una muestra de universitarios españoles: ¿usan o abusan? *Bordón* **2016**, *68*, 131–145. [CrossRef]
31. Polo, M.I.; Mendo, S.; León, B.; Felipe, E. Abuso del móvil en estudiantes universitarios y perfiles de victimización y agresión. *Adicciones* **2017**, *29*, 245–255. [CrossRef] [PubMed]
32. Smith, A. US smartphone use in 2015. 2015. Available online: https://www.pewresearch.org/internet/2015/04/01/us-smartphone-use-in-2015/ (accessed on 18 April 2020).
33. Otzen, T.; Manterola, C. Técnicas de muestreo sobre una población a estudio. *Mor. Int. J.* **2017**, *35*, 227–232. [CrossRef]
34. López-Fernández, O.; Honrubia-Serrano, L.; Freixa-Blanxart, M. Adaptación española del "mobile phone problem use scale" para población adolescente. *Adicciones* **2012**, *24*, 123–130. [CrossRef]
35. López-Fernández, O.; Honrubia-Serrano, L.; Freixa-Blanxart, M.; Gibson, W. Prevalence of problematic mobile phone use in British Adolescents. *Cyberpsych. Behav. Soc. Netw.* **2014**, *17*, 1–8. [CrossRef]
36. Pérez, R.; García, J.L.; Gil, J.A.; Galán, A. *Estadística Aplicada A La Educación*; Pearson Prentice Hall: Madrid, Spain, 2009.
37. Berlanga-Silvente, V.; Vilà-Baños, R. Cómo obtener un modelo de regresión logística binaria con SPSS. *REIRE. Rev.* **2014**, *7*, 105–118. [CrossRef]
38. López-Roldán, P.; Fachelli, S. *Metodología De La Investigación Social Cuantitativa*; UAB: Barcelona, Spain, 2015.
39. García-Oliva, C.; Piqueras, J.A.; Marzo, J.C. Uso problemático de internet, el móvil y los videojuegos en una muestra de adolescentes alicantinos. *Heal. Addic.* **2017**, *17*, 189–200. [CrossRef]
40. Beranuy, M.; Chamarro, A.; Graner, C.; Carbonell, X. Validación de dos escalas breves para evaluar la adicción a Internet y el abuso de móvil. *Psicothema* **2009**, *21*, 480–485.
41. Medrano, J.L.; Rosales, F.L.; Loving, R.D. Conducta adictiva a las redes sociales y su relación con el uso problemático del móvil. *Acta De Investigación Psicológica* **2017**, *7*, 2832–2838. [CrossRef]
42. Olivencia-Carrión, M.A.; Pérez-Marfil, M.N.; Ramos-Revelles, M.B.; López-Torrecillas, F. Personalidad y su relación con el uso versus abuso del teléfono móvil. *Acción Psicológica* **2016**, *13*, 109–118. [CrossRef]
43. Ruiz-Palmero, J.; Sánchez-Rivas, E.; Gómez-García, M.; Sánchez, E. Future Teachers' Smartphone Uses and Dependence. *Educ. Sci.* **2019**, *9*, 194. [CrossRef]
44. Inhóf, O.; Zsidó, A.N.; Perlaki, G.; Orsi, G.; Lábadi, B.; Kovács, N.; Szente, A.; Dóczi, T.; Janszky, J.; Darnai, G. Internet addiction associated with right pars opercularis in females. *J. Behav. Addict.* **2019**, *8*, 162–168. [CrossRef]
45. González, N.; Estévez, A. El apoyo social percibido moderador entre el uso problemático de Internet y la sintomatología depresiva en jóvenes adultos. *Heal. Addic.* **2017**, *17*, 53–62. [CrossRef]
46. Carbonell, X.; Chamarro, A.; Griffiths, M.; Oberst, U.; Cladellas, R.; Talarn, A. Problematic Internet and cell phone use in Spanish teenagers and young students. *Anales De psicología* **2012**, *28*, 789–796. [CrossRef]
47. Loconi, C.; Alvitres, V.; Ortega, B.; Zapirain, I. Uso del Smartphone en estudiantes de 2° año escuela administración de empresas de universidad particular de chiclayo. *Manglar* **2017**, *12*, 63–70. [CrossRef]
48. Demirhan, E.; Randler, C.; Horzum, M.B. Is problematic mobile phone use explained by chronotype and personality? *Chronob. Int.* **2016**, *33*, 821–831. [CrossRef] [PubMed]
49. de la Villa, M.; Suárez, C. Factores de riesgo en el uso problemático de Internet y del teléfono móvil en adolescentes españoles. *Revista Iberoamericana De Psicología Y Salud* **2016**, *7*, 69–78. [CrossRef]
50. Aljomaa, S.S.; Al.Qudah, M.F.; Albursan, I.S.; Bakhiet, S.F.; Abduljabbar, S.F. Smartphone addiction among university students in the light of some variables. *Comp. H. Behav.* **2016**, *61*, 155–164. [CrossRef]

# 5

# Internet Gaming Disorder Clustering Based on Personality Traits in Adolescents and its Relation with Comorbid Psychological Symptoms

**Vega González-Bueso [1,*,†], Juan José Santamaría [1,*,†], Ignasi Oliveras [2], Daniel Fernández [3,4,5], Elena Montero [2], Marta Baño [1], Susana Jiménez-Murcia [6,7,8], Amparo del Pino-Gutiérrez [6,9] and Joan Ribas [1]**

1 Atención e Investigación en Socioadicciones (AIS), Mental Health and Addictions Network, Generalitat de Catalunya (XHUB), 08014 Barcelona, Spain; mbano@ais-info.org (M.B.); 38039jrs@comb.cat (J.R.)
2 Department of Psychiatry & Forensic Medicine, Institute of Neurosciences, Universitat Autònoma de Barcelona, Bellaterra, 08193 Barcelona, Spain; ignasi.oliveras@uab.cat (I.O.); emontero@ais-info.org (E.M.)
3 Research and Development Unit, Parc Sanitari Sant Joan de Déu, Fundació Sant Joan de Déu, Sant Boi de Llobregat, 08830 Barcelona, Spain; df.martinez@pssjd.org
4 Department of Statistics and Operations Research, Polytechnic University of Catalonia-BarcelonaTech, 08028 Barcelona, Spain
5 Centro de Investigación Biomédica en Red de Salud Mental (CIBERSAM), Instituto de Salud Carlos III, 28029 Madrid, Spain
6 Pathological Gambling Unit, Department of Psychiatry, Bellvitge University Hospital-IDIBELL, 08907 Barcelona, Spain; sjimenez@bellvitgehospital.cat (S.J.-M.); adelpino@ub.edu (A.d.P.-G.)
7 Ciber Fisiopatología Obesidad y Nutrición (CIBERObn), Instituto de Salud Carlos III, 28029 Madrid, Spain
8 Department of Clinical Sciences, School of Medicine and Health Sciences, University of Barcelona, 08907 Barcelona, Spain
9 Nursing Department of Mental Health, Public Health, Maternal and Child Health, Nursing School of the University of Barcelona, 08907 Barcelona, Spain
* Correspondence: vgonzalez@ais-info.org (V.G.-B.); jsantamaria@ais-info.org (J.J.S.)
† These authors contributed equally to this work and share first authorship.

**Abstract:** In recent years, the evidence regarding Internet Gaming Disorder (IGD) suggests that some personality traits are important risk factors for developing this problem. The heterogeneity involved in problematic online gaming and differences found in the literature regarding the comorbid psychopathology associated with the problem could be explained through different types of gamers. Clustering analysis can allow organization of a collection of personality traits into clusters based on similarity. The objectives of this study were: (1) to obtain an empirical classification of IGD patients according to personality variables and (2) to describe the resultant groups in terms of clinical and sociodemographic variables. The sample included 66 IGD adolescent patients who were consecutive referrals at a mental health center in Barcelona, Spain. A Gaussian mixture model cluster analysis was used in order to classify the subjects based on their personality. Two clusters based on personality traits were detected: type I "higher comorbid symptoms" ($n$ = 24), and type II "lower comorbid symptoms" ($n$ = 42). The type I included higher scores in introversive, inhibited, doleful, unruly, forceful, oppositional, self-demeaning and borderline tendency traits, and lower scores in histrionic, egotistic and conforming traits. The type I obtained higher scores on all the Symptom Check List-90 items-Revised, all the State-Trait Anxiety Index scales, and on the DSM-5 IGD criteria. Differences in personality can be useful in determining clusters with different types of dysfunctionality.

**Keywords:** internet gaming disorder; cluster analysis; video game; video game addiction; personality; comorbidity

## 1. Introduction

According to the ICD-11 (International Classification of Diseases) [1], Internet Gaming Disorder (IGD) is defined as "a pattern of persistent or recurrent gaming behavior ('digital gaming' or 'video-gaming'), which may be online (i.e., over the Internet) or offline, manifested by: (1) impaired control over gaming (e.g., onset, frequency, intensity, duration, termination, context); (2) increasing priority given to gaming to the extent that gaming takes precedence over other life interests and daily activities; and (3) continuation or escalation of gaming despite the occurrence of negative consequences. The behavior pattern is of sufficient severity to result in significant impairment in personal, family, social, educational, occupational or other important areas of functioning. The pattern of gaming behavior may be either continuous or, on the other hand, episodic and recurrent. The gaming behavior and other features are normally evident over a period of at least 12 months for a diagnosis to be assigned, although the required duration may be shortened if all diagnostic requirements are met and symptoms are severe".

Nowadays, behavioral addictions, including IGD, are increasingly being documented worldwide [2]. The current versions of the official diagnostic classification manuals have included addictions without substances in the behavioral addictions category. At the moment, only Gambling Disorder has been included in this category, and although IGD seems to share many factors with this disorder such as the negative reinforcement as a maintaining variable in the long-term maintenance of the behavior, or the use of positive reinforcement as a developing mechanism at the beginning of the problem [3,4], the DSM-5 work group decided to include IGD in Section III of the diagnostic manual DSM-5 [5] as a condition that requires further study.

In recent years, numerous factors involved in the etiology of problematic online gaming and of IGD have been identified. Although more research is needed, the evidence suggests that some personality traits are important risk factors for developing this problem [6,7]. Personality traits are different across individuals, influence their behavior, reflect people's characteristic patterns of thoughts, attitudes, emotions, and behaviors [8], and they have relatively high stability over a lifetime, even though some authors have found changes after cognitive behavioral therapies [9]. Specifically, researchers have linked patients with IGD to personality traits common in other addictive disorders.

Regarding the Big Five Model of personality, some of the factors of the model seem to have relevance in the addiction process [10]. Among them, high neuroticism is the most commonly present in IGD, and has been interpreted as a way to use online gaming to overcome negative life effects [11] or to modify negative emotions [12,13]. The results regarding the other traits of the model and male gamers are various, with low agreeableness [14], low conscientiousness and low extraversion [15] being the most consistent findings. These domains reflect an impaired offline social cooperation with their peers, low self-discipline, and low motivation to maintain positive interpersonal relations.

Taking other personality models as a reference, some authors have found that low sociability [16], low openness to experience [17], and the combination of low self-directedness and cooperativeness [18] were correlated with problematic gaming and IGD. Finally, low self-directness [14] has been found as a predictor of IGD. This trait reflects the lack of regulation and adaptation of one's own behavior in order to achieve personally chosen goals and values, and the tendency to be laid back.

All these traits combined can predispose people to avoid social interactions and new activities. This diminished social participation in the "real world" and the need to establish some kind of social interactions with others could lead gamers to find online relationships, which are commonly more distant and superficial, with people with similar interests. Thus, they expand their social network [19] and find themselves in a safe environment when they are in the online world.

Clustering can be defined as the statistical methods that allow us to organize a collection of data points into clusters based on similarity [20]. These methods are part of what we call unsupervised learning and they are used in a wide range of research fields such as psychology, biology and market research [21–23]. Clustering methods have been used to classify individuals based upon behavioral patterns [24], personality traits [25] and severity of mental disorder [26].

Several studies have focused on classifying the personality traits of patients with behavioral addictions using clusters, and their relationships with psychiatric comorbidity and sociodemographic characteristics. The study of personality profiles for gambling disorder [25,27,28] and compulsive buying [29] shows that there is a heterogeneity in the personality patterns of the affected people, and these different profiles are associated with differences in the number and severity of other psychological comorbid symptoms. These results suggest that the experience with problematic behavior varies between patients, and that the processing of the negative consequences derived from it may affect them in different ways.

Focusing on the use of videogames, Billieux et al. [30] classified a group of 1057 general population online gamers, playing a massive multiplayer online roleplaying-game, into five reliable clusters (three problematic and two non-problematic clusters) according to several psychological risk factors (impulsivity, motives to play, self-esteem) and potential consequences of playing (addiction symptoms, positive and negative affect). Members of the two non-problematic clusters were defined by low impulsivity and high and low levels of self-esteem, respectively. The motivations to play of these two clusters vary between non-fundamental, to motivations related to social exchange and roleplaying.

With respect to the three problematic clusters, the first one was composed of gamers with poor self-esteem and high impulsivity (but low sensation seeking), and by low achievement and high escapism motives. The second problematic cluster included high self-esteem, high impulsivity, and motivations regarding achievements in the game. The last cluster comprise gamers with high self-esteem, high impulsivity, and motives related to roleplaying, achievements and escapism. This study demonstrated the existence of distinct subtypes of problematic online gamers, emphasizing the high heterogeneity and the wide range of psychological factors involved in the problem.

Therefore, it could be possible that, similar to what happens in other behavioral addictions, the different personality types of the gamers have a role not only in the development or perpetuation of the problem, but also in the comorbid psychopathology associated to the disorder. In that sense, several authors have analyzed the different personality and psychopathological features among IGD patients [31,32], finding fewer functional personality traits and higher psychopathological scores compared with a normative population.

Nevertheless, the relationship between personality and psychopathology in IGD remains unclear, and the associations between comorbidity and IGD in adolescents and young adults have shown inconsistent results with depression, anxiety, ADHD or hyperactivity, social phobia/anxiety, and obsessive-compulsive disorder, finding among different authors full, partial and no associations with these symptoms [33]. It is possible that these inconsistencies could be related to the analysis as a whole of different personality types among video game players.

In other words, cluster analyses can help in the conceptualization of patients consulting for IGD, and these profiles of similarities and differences among individuals can contribute to clarifying some of the results found in previous research regarding clinical profiles, and can help to improve the clinical treatments. Considering this, the objectives of this study are as follows: (1) to obtain an empirical classification of IGD patients according to personality variables and (2) to describe the resultant groups in terms of clinical and sociodemographic variables.

## 2. Materials and Methods

### 2.1. Participants

The sample included 66 IGD patients who were consecutive referrals for assessment and outpatient treatment at the Behavioral Addiction Unit in the mental health center AIS-PRO JUVENTUD (Care and Research in Behavioral Addiction) (AIS), located in Barcelona, Spain.

The required sample size was calculated based on the standard deviations of the questionnaire Millon Adolescent Personality Inventory (MACI). Thus, by setting an alpha risk of 0.05 and a beta risk of 0.20 in a two-sided test with a 10% estimated dropout rate, we required a sample size of 59 individuals to detect a minimum expected difference between groups of 6 units. We therefore decided to recruit 66 patients.

The exclusion criteria for being included in the analyses were: (1) had neurological disorders or primary psychiatric conditions that could affect cognitive function (assessed through semi-structured, face-to-face, clinical interview, (2) had a head injury with loss of consciousness for more than 2 min or a learning disorder, (3) used psychostimulants or drugs that could interfere with the assessment, (4) were older than 21 years or younger than 12. No potential participants were excluded based on exclusion criteria 1, 2, or 3.

This study was carried out according to the latest version of the Declaration of Helsinki. The Ethics Committee of CEIC Fundació Unió Catalana d'Hospitals (CEIC14/71) approved the study, and informed consent (signed document) was obtained from parents of adolescents under the age of 18 years and adolescents over the age of 18 years (and assent in adolescents under the age of 18 years).

The characteristics of the sample were as follows: all patients were Caucasian and male. All the adolescents included have as their main and problematic videogame an online videogame, with a mean age of 15.80 (SD 2.18) years. Most patients had elementary education (92.4%). Regarding their main problem, all the patients included played online videogames, and the mean duration of the problem was 2.2 (SD 1.7) years. There was no consumption of alcohol or drugs and only a 3.0% of the sample were smokers.

### 2.2. *Instruments*

#### 2.2.1. Millon Adolescent Personality Inventory (MACI)

This personality test [34] has 160 items and is self-administered. It measures thirty-one scales: twelve Personality Patterns scales (Axis II), eight Expressed Concerns Scales, seven Clinical Syndrome Scales, three Modifying Indices (particular response styles), and a Validity scale. The instrument has been translated and validated into a Spanish population with a good internal consistency of 0.82 (mean Cronbach's alpha) [35]. The MACI is one of the most widely used personality assessment tests for adolescents [36–40]. The MACI is constructed using an underlying theory of personality and psychopathology, and can identify and assess a wide range of psychological difficulties in adolescents. Studies have examined the potential utility of the MACI for assessing substance use disorders [41], reporting support for MACI as a screening instrument. We used this instrument in order to facilitate current and future comparisons in other studies regarding IGD or other psychological problems.

#### 2.2.2. Symptom CheckList-90 Items-Revised (SCL-90-R)

This questionnaire [42] evaluates psychological problems and psychopathological symptoms. It contains ninety items and measures nine primary symptom dimensions: somatization, obsession-compulsion, interpersonal sensitivity, depression, anxiety, hostility, phobic anxiety, paranoid ideation, and psychoticism. It also includes three global indices, such as a global severity index (GSI), that measures overall psychological distress, a positive symptom distress index (PSDI), to measure the intensity of symptoms; and a positive symptom total (PST). This scale has been translated to Spanish and validated in a Spanish population [43], and presents a good internal consistency (mean Cronbach's alpha = 0.75).

#### 2.2.3. State-Trait Anxiety Index (STAI)

This questionnaire [44] includes forty items on a 4-point rating scale and is self-reported, measuring state anxiety (twenty items) and trait anxiety (twenty items). The minimum score is 20 and the maximum is 80 points. The state anxiety uses items that measure subjective feelings of apprehension, tension, nervousness, worry, and activation/arousal of the autonomic nervous system and evaluates the current state of anxiety. The trait anxiety scale includes general states of calmness, confidence, and security and evaluates relatively stable aspects of "anxiety proneness". The STAI has been translated to Spanish and validated in the Spanish population with a mean Cronbach's alpha coefficient of 0.92 [45].

#### 2.2.4. DSM-5 IGD Criteria

This instrument is a questionnaire evaluating the criteria for IGD proposed in the DSM-5 [5]. The diagnostic criteria of IGD are composed of 9 items: preoccupation, withdrawal, tolerance, unsuccessful attempts to control, loss of other interests, continued excessive use despite psychosocial problems, deceiving regarding online gaming, escape, and functional impairment. Five or more DSM-5 criteria of IGD indicates Internet gaming problems. The criteria were asked in a questionnaire form using a "yes" or "no" response.

#### 2.2.5. Sociodemographical Variables

Additional demographic, clinical, and social/family variables related to internet gaming were measured using a semi-structured face-to-face clinical interview, including age, sex, duration of the problem, and education level.

### 2.3. *Procedure*

First, at intake, a face-to-face specific clinical interview and a functional analysis of IGD was carried by experienced psychologists (more than 5 years of clinical experience in behavioral addictions) using the semi-structured clinical interview SCID-I [46]. The questions included in this interview were about tolerance, preoccupation, withdrawal, loss of control, playing for long periods, escaping from adverse mental states, risking or losing relationships or opportunities because of the behavior, deception/covering up, giving up other activities, persistence of the behavior despite problems, and functional impairment (e.g., functional impairment in familial relationships, other social relationships, and academic achievement), and questions regarding demographic data.

During a second session (with an average duration of 90 min) before starting the treatment, were administered the above-mentioned questionnaires.

With regard to meeting the diagnostic criteria for IGD, the results obtained through the DSM-5 diagnostic criteria questionnaire were compared post hoc with the results obtained through the face-to-face clinical interview, and only patients who met the DSM-5 criteria for IGD were included in our analysis.

### 2.4. *Statistical Analysis*

Statistical analysis was carried out using the statistical software R version 3.5.3 (R Core Team, Vienna, Austria) and, in particular, its R packages mclust [47] and factoextra [48].

We obtained clusters based on the scores of the 12 sub-scales of the personality patterns scale of the MACI (Introversive, Inhibited, Doleful, Submissive, Histrionic, Egotistic, Unruly, Forceful, Conforming, Oppositional, Self-Demeaning, and Borderline Tendency) conducting a Gaussian Mixture Model (GMM) cluster analysis. Model-fitting is performed using the expectation-maximization (EM) algorithm [49,50], which later is used to initialize a hierarchical model-based agglomerative clustering [51,52]. The optimal number of clusters was selected based on the Bayesian Information Criterion (BIC), where the lowest values indicate better fit. Each individual was allocated to one class only according to their highest probability of membership.

Chi-square tests ($\chi^2$) for categorical variables and *t*-test (2 groups) for quantitative measures were computed to assess differences between clusters. When the normality assumption was not accomplished according to Shapiro–Wilk test, the equivalent non-parametric Mann–Whitney U test was performed. A two-sided $p$-value $< 0.05$ was considered statistically significant. Cohen's $d$ was used to measure the effect size for power analysis purposes. The effect size was classified as high ($d$ = 0.8), medium ($d$ = 0.5) or low ($d$ = 0.2) according to Cohen [53].

## 3. Results

### 3.1. Cluster Composition: Description for the Cluster Indicators

In the MACI scale ($n$ = 66 men, age: 15.80 ± 2.18) there are 12 sub-scales: Introversive, Inhibited, Doleful, Submissive, Histrionic, Egotistic, Unruly, Forceful, Conforming, Oppositional, Self-Demeaning, and Borderline Tendency. The descriptive statistics of the sample are presented in Table 1.

**Table 1.** Descriptive statistics of the personality traits of the Millon Adolescent Personality Inventory (MACI) scale ($n$ = 66).

| Personality Traits | Mean | SD | Median | IQR | Min | Max |
|---|---|---|---|---|---|---|
| Introversive | 25.20 | 11.61 | 23 | 17.80 | 9 | 52 |
| Inhibited | 20.86 | 10.82 | 18.50 | 25.50 | 4 | 48 |
| Doleful | 11.47 | 9.92 | 8 | 14 | 0 | 41 |
| Submissive | 43.85 | 10.00 | 45.50 | 13 | 21 | 69 |
| Histrionic | 36.55 | 9.97 | 37 | 14.30 | 12 | 54 |
| Egotistic | 33.47 | 10.85 | 35 | 15 | 3 | 51 |
| Unruly | 30.23 | 9.39 | 29.50 | 11.80 | 10 | 52 |
| Forceful | 10.59 | 6.81 | 9 | 7.6 | 0 | 34 |
| Conforming | 45.41 | 9.05 | 46 | 13.30 | 18 | 62 |
| Oppositional | 20.30 | 9.86 | 20 | 12.80 | 4 | 44 |
| Self-Demeaning | 19.42 | 13.84 | 16 | 20 | 0 | 55 |
| Borderline Tendency | 11.70 | 7.72 | 11 | 12.50 | 0 | 30 |

SD = Standard Deviation, IQR = Interquartile range.

We conducted a Gaussian finite mixture model cluster analysis. The results, for the personality patterns scale, showed that a 2 cluster (VEE: ellipsoidal, equal shape and orientation) was the optimal solution. The cluster classification for each subject is shown in Figure 1. The first cluster has 24 subjects and the second cluster has 42 subjects.

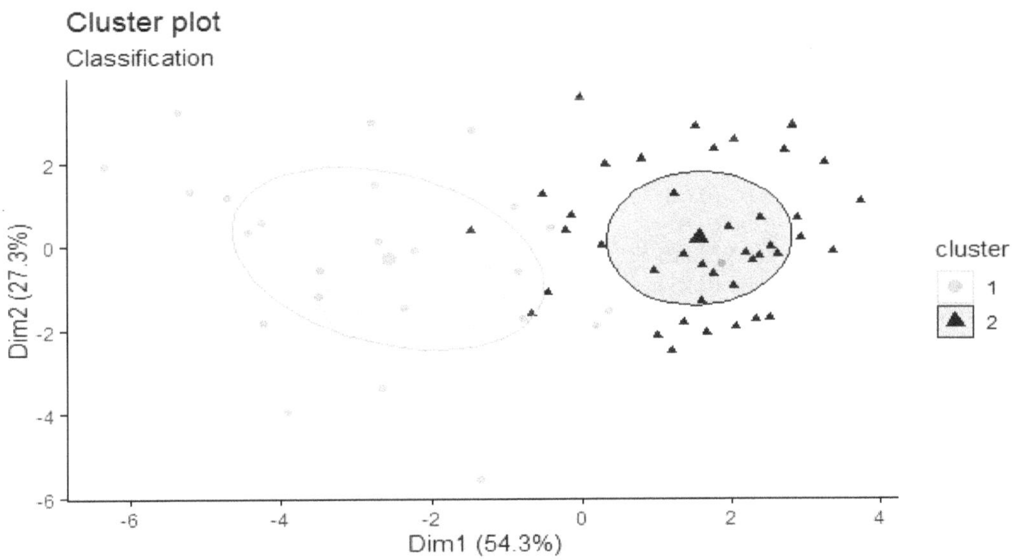


**Figure 1.** Classification of subjects for each cluster.

The results of the $t$-test and the Mann–Whitney U test comparing the two clusters created by the model-based clustering algorithm show that there are significant differences in all the sub-scales, except in the Submissive. The first cluster has higher values in the following sub-scales: introversive, inhibited, doleful, unruly, forceful, oppositional, self-demeaning and borderline tendency, while in the histrionic, egotistic and conforming sub-scales the first cluster has lower values (see Tables 2 and 3).

The results of the Cohen's d show that the effect size was high in all scales apart from the Submissive and Unruly scales (*d*-values < 0.8; Tables 2 and 3).

**Table 2.** T-test comparison between clusters of the personality traits of the MACI and the State-Trait Anxiety Index (STAI) scales (cluster 1 $n = 24$, cluster 2 $n = 42$).

| Independent Samples Test | | | | | | |
|---|---|---|---|---|---|---|
| | CLUSTER 1 | CLUSTER 2 | | | | |
| | Mean (SD) | Mean (SD) | t | df | Sig. (2 tailed) | Cohen's d |
| MACI | | | | | | |
| Submissive | 46.48 (11.86) | 42.24 (8.42) | 1.69 | 64 | 0.126 | 0.43 |
| Egotistic | 27.80 (3.03) | 36.93 (7.33) | −3.16 | 33.15 | 0.003 | **−0.92** |
| Unruly | 34.12 (9.70) | 27.85 (8.45) | 2.76 | 64 | 0.010 | 0.70 |
| Conforming | 39.44 (8.19) | 49.04 (7.49) | −4.86 | 64 | 0.000 | **−1.23** |
| Oppositional | 28.76 (8.58) | 15.14 (6.46) | 7.32 | 64 | 0.000 | **1.86** |
| STAI | | | | | | |
| Anxiety State | 18.72 (8.35) | 11.38 (7.52) | 3.67 | 63 | 0.000 | **0.94** |
| Anxiety Trait | 23.48 (8.11) | 12.64 (7.00) | 5.75 | 64 | 0.000 | **1.46** |

SD = Standard Deviation; df = degrees of freedom (Cohen's d > 0.80 in bold).

**Table 3.** Mann–Whitney U-test for the MACI, Symptom CheckList-90 items-Revised (SCL-90-R), and DSM 5 criteria mean scores (cluster 1 $n = 24$, cluster 2 $n = 42$).

| Mann–Whitney U Test | | | | | |
|---|---|---|---|---|---|
| | CLUSTER 1 | CLUSTER 2 | | | |
| | Mean (SD) | Mean (SD) | U | Sig. (2 tailed) | Cohen's d |
| MACI | | | | | |
| Introversive | 35.76 (9.27) | 18.76 (7.44) | 948.50 | 0.000 | **2.08** |
| Inhibited | 29.88 (11.04) | 15.37 (5.94) | 883 | 0.000 | **1.76** |
| Doleful | 20.44 (9.42) | 6.00 (5.07) | 941 | 0.000 | **2.05** |
| Histrionic | 29.88 (10.95) | 40.61 (6.70) | 223.50 | 0.000 | **−1.26** |
| Forceful | 14.56 (7.49) | 8.17 (5.07) | 781 | 0.000 | **1.05** |
| Self-Demeaning | 32.96 (11.51) | 11.17 (6.97) | 974 | 0.000 | **2.45** |
| Borderline Tend. | 19.44 (5.34) | 6.97 (4.39) | 998.5 | 0.000 | **2.61** |
| SCL-90-R | | | | | |
| Somatization | 0.55 (0.54) | 0.26 (0.27) | 718 | 0.006 | 0.75 |
| Obsessive-comp | 1.03 (0.60) | 0.61 (0.51) | 719 | 0.006 | 0.76 |
| Interp. sens. | 1.00 (0.81) | 0.38 (0.39) | 781 | 0.000 | **1.04** |
| Depression | 0.93 (0.72) | 0.28 (0.30) | 840.50 | 0.000 | **1.28** |
| Anxiety | 0.69 (0.81) | 0.21 (0.22) | 700 | 0.012 | **0.90** |
| Hostility | 1.10 (0.91) | 0.56 (0.45) | 708 | 0.009 | **0.81** |
| Phobia | 0.40 (0.57) | 0.10 (0.19) | 782.50 | 0.000 | 0.77 |
| Paranoid ideation | 1.03 (0.82) | 0.38 (0.43) | 773 | 0.000 | **1.06** |
| Psychoticism | 0.56 (0.50) | 0.14 (0.20) | 845 | 0.000 | **1.18** |
| Global severity | 0.80(0.56) | 0.33(0.25) | 833 | 0.000 | **1.20** |
| DSM 5 criteria | 5.84 (1.82) | 4.95 (1.55) | 684 | 0.019 | 0.54 |

SD = Standard Deviation; df = degrees of freedom (Cohen's d > 0.80 in bold).

### *3.2. Comparison between the Clusters in Sociodemographic and Clinical Variables*

After that, we compared the two clusters regarding a series of sociodemographic variables, i.e., age, age of onset of the disorder, disorder duration, and education level. The results of the *t*-tests showed that there were no significant differences between clusters regarding age, age of onset, and years with IGD. Besides, the Fisher exact test, to elucidate whether the education level was related to the cluster classification, was also non-significant.

In order to investigate if there were other significant psychopathological differences between clusters, we conducted Student's *t*-tests and Mann–Whitney U-tests to compare the clusters in the Symptom Check List-90 items-Revised scores, in the DSM 5 diagnostic criteria scores and the STAI. The SCL-R has nine dimensions: somatization, obsessive-compulsive, interpersonal sensitivity, depression, anxiety, hostility, phobic anxiety, paranoid ideation and psychoticism. The results of the analyses showed that the first cluster had significantly increased scores in all dimensions of the SCL-R, except for the somatization. Regarding the diagnostic criteria, the analysis comparing the cluster regarding the DSM scores yielded a significant result ($U = 684$, $p < 0.05$) indicating that the subjects in the first cluster had higher scores. Regarding Cohen's d values, we observed high effect sizes except for the three dimensions of the SCL-90-R (Somatization, Obsessive-Compulsive and Phobia), and for the DSM-5 scores, the effect size was moderate.

In a similar manner, we conducted the same analyses for the anxiety-trait and anxiety-state of the STAI and all the comparisons were statistically significant (all $t = 5.54$; $p < 0.001$ for anxiety trait and $t = 3.58$; $p < 0.001$ for anxiety state), indicating that the first cluster of each scale had higher anxiety levels than the members of the second cluster.

## 4. Discussion

This work explores the existence of empirical clusters for IGD starting from the patients' personality trait scores, using a person-centered methodology.

Two clusters were detected: type I "higher comorbid symptoms" and type II "lower comorbid symptoms". The main differences in the clustering variables between both clusters were the mean scores in the personality traits introversive, inhibited, doleful, unruly, forceful, oppositional, self-demeaning and borderline tendency (higher scores for the type I), histrionic, egotistic and conforming (lower scores for the type I). It should be noted the similarity between this cluster I and the IGD dimensional personality profile found in other studies.

In line with our results, literature about personality traits and IGD suggests that high scores in neuroticism [54], impulsivity [55] and introversion [15,18], and lower levels in agreeableness [14,15], cooperativeness [18] and self-regulation [56], are risk factors for this disorder. Furthermore, some authors have found that low levels of self- directedness uniquely predicted video game abuse in an adult population with Gambling Disorder [14], and others have identified lower responsibility as a risk factor associated with this IGD [57]. Summarizing the conclusions of this previous research, this combination of personality traits could lead the affected people to use online gaming as a maladaptive mood modifier and/or a strategy to overcome negative life events, to having higher tendency toward competition, lower life satisfaction, lower expectations of self-efficacy, less face-to-face social support, and increased feelings of anger.

Analyzing the comorbidity level of both clusters, the type I has the higher comorbidity, obtaining higher scores on all SCL-90R scales (i.e., somatization, obsessive-compulsive, sensitivity, depression, anxiety, hostility, phobia, paranoid ideation and psychoticism) all STAI scales (anxiety trait and state), and on the IGD diagnostic criteria, being the obsessive-compulsive, sensitivity, depression, anxiety, hostility, paranoid ideation, psychoticism and anxiety trait above general population scoring. Despite the literature regarding comorbid psychopathology in adolescents and young adults with IGD having found full associations with anxiety [55], depression [58], ADHD or hyperactivity symptoms [59], and social phobia/anxiety [60], other authors have found partial associations [61,62] and no associations [63] with these same symptoms. These contradictory results and a possible publication bias [33] makes it difficult to detect the directionality and the relationship of these associations and shows the existing complexity of the relationship between IGD, personality and psychopathology.

Some authors have found relationships between personality factors and psychopathology in adolescents. According to the results found by Castellanos-Ryan [64], general psychopathology was related to high disinhibition/impulsivity, low agreeableness, high neuroticism and hopelessness, high delay-discounting and poor response inhibition. Of all of this, high neuroticism is the Big Five trait most strongly associated with several psychopathological symptoms, especially with anxiety and mood disorders and their comorbidity [65]. It has been hypothesized that the negative emotionality related with this trait could mediate this association [66]. Other personality trait predictors of psychopathology in adolescents are low conscientiousness, low extraversion [67], hopelessness and high impulsivity [68]. Regarding the Egotistic personality scale, where cluster 2 scored higher, adolescents who score high in the Egotistic Personality subscale have a passive-independent pattern, are perceived as conceited, have strong self-esteem, may take others for granted, and may fantasize about future success and power [69]. Some authors showed that certain narcissistic features are adaptive when paired with high levels of self-esteem [70]. Taking these results into account, the differences between the Type I and Type II personality traits could suggest that the higher negative affect, the lower positive affect, the difficulties in establishing social support, and the poor general behavioral control involved in the Type I personality profiles may be characterizing the chances of developing comorbid psychopathology, and could partially explain the inconsistent results regarding IGD and psychopathology.

When interpreting the results of this study, the effects of maturity and personality development in adolescence must be taken into account. Recent research has shown a spontaneous recovery of video game addiction [71,72] and it must be noted that personality traits may change during individual development [73]. Therefore, it is possible that the dysfunctional personality traits found will change or disappear in the future, and with them the influence they are having on the development or maintenance of IGD and the associated comorbidity.

In addition, our results show that there is a group of patients with IGD whose comorbid mental health symptoms are non-existent, or similar to the non-psychiatric population. Since there are no differences in the age at which the disorder begins or in the duration of the disorder between both cluster groups, it seems that in at least some individuals, IGD presents itself as a solitary condition or as an originating condition.

Regardless of the debate about the diagnosis and comorbidity [74], across the years the prevalence of the disordered gaming and the incidence of patients seeking treatment for IGD has remained stable [75]. This study is focused on the heterogeneity of the disorder and in the existence of different subgroups of IGD patients, based on personality, with differences in the seriousness of their psychological comorbidity. Our results suggest that these variables appear to be useful in determining clusters which represent different clinical subtypes with different degrees of severity. Such differences among online gamers imply that the experience of playing may vary in patients and the general population. Therefore, in order to succeed in developing instruments, planning efficient prevention programs for general population and targeting at-risk gamers, these dependent effects should be considered. Furthermore, the data regarding standard therapy for IGD are limited, with cognitive-behavioral therapy, family therapy and pharmacological intervention showing some significant results [76,77]. In order to develop more specific and accurate treatment interventions, the existence of IGD clusters should be considered.

Concerning limitations, the results of this study are based on a small sample, but considering that the sample is formed by a clinical sample, evaluated in a controlled setting, there may be a reason to anticipate that our findings may be of value for similar profile patients. Second, the measures used are based on self-administered questionnaires, although a trained psychologist supervised the entire process. Third, the cross-sectional design does not allow us to determine causality of the variables assessed. Fourth, the severity of IGD has not been reflected in this paper, as the objective of this work was to describe the different types of IGD-diagnosed adolescents with respect to personality traits and to analyze the comorbidity of each cluster groups.

Future research could complement these results using longitudinal designs addressing the potential mediating role of personality in the etiological factors and clinical course of IGD, in order to try to develop a predictive model of problematic video games use and its comorbidity.

## 5. Conclusions

Problematic use of online videogames is a growing clinical issue in developed countries. There is ongoing debate about the suitability of the current proposed definition and diagnostic criteria and about its related dysfunctional consequences and clinical correlates. The current literature shows that IGD is a complex problem where neurobiological systems, personality, and socioeconomic and environmental variables are involved. The objective of this study was to explore the heterogeneity of the affected people and the existence of differentiated subgroups based on different personality traits.

The results suggest that differences in personality can be useful in determining clusters with different levels of comorbidity. These differences imply that the experience of playing online videogames may affect different players, and clinicians and researchers should consider them in order to develop treatment options or assessment instruments. Future research should include more heterogeneous samples in relation to age and sex, and consider treatment outcome as a variable to analyze.

**Author Contributions:** D.F., V.G.-B. and J.J.S. conceived and planned this article. V.G.-B. and J.J.S. carried out the search and revision of the literature. D.F. and I.O. analyzed the data. V.G.-B. and J.J.S. drafted the study. All authors (V.G.-B., J.J.S., D.F., I.O., E.M., M.B., S.J.-M., A.d.P.-G. and J.R.) revised the article critically for important intellectual content. All authors (V.G.-B., J.J.S., D.F., I.O., E.M., M.B., S.J.-M., A.d.P.-G. and J.R.) commented on and approved the final manuscript and are accountable for all aspects of the work. All authors have read and agreed to the published version of the manuscript.

## References


1. World Health Organization. *International Classification of Diseases for Mortality and Morbidity Statistics 11th Revision*; World Health Organization: Geneva, Switzerland, 2018.
2. Poli, R. Internet addiction update: Diagnostic criteria, assessment and prevalence. *Neuropsychiatry* **2017**, *07*, 4–8. [CrossRef]
3. Fauth-Bühler, M.; Mann, K. Neurobiological correlates of internet gaming disorder: Similarities to pathological gambling. *Addict. Behav.* **2017**, *64*, 349–356. [CrossRef] [PubMed]
4. Kaptsis, D.; King, D.; Delfabbro, P.; Gradisar, M. Withdrawal symptoms in internet gaming disorder: A systematic review. *Clin. Psychol. Rev.* **2016**, *43*, 58–66. [CrossRef] [PubMed]
5. APA. *Diagnostic and Statistical Manual of Mental Disorders*, 5th ed.; (DSM-5); American Psychiatric Association, Ed.; APA: Washington, DC, USA, 2013.
6. Gervasi, A.M.; La Marca, L.; Costanzo, A.; Pace, U.; Guglielmucci, F.; Schimmenti, A. Personality and Internet Gaming Disorder: A Systematic Review of Recent Literature. *Curr. Addict. Rep.* **2017**, *4*, 293–307. [CrossRef]
7. Şalvarlı, Ş.İ.; Griffiths, M.D. Internet Gaming Disorder and Its Associated Personality Traits: A Systematic Review Using PRISMA Guidelines. *Int. J. Ment. Health Addict.* **2019**. [CrossRef]
8. Matthews, G.; Deary, I.J.; Whiteman, M.C. *Personality Traits*, 3rd ed.; Cambridge University Press: Cambridge, UK, 2009; ISBN 9780511812743.
9. Agüera, Z.; Krug, I.; Sánchez, I.; Granero, R.; Penelo, E.; Peñas-Lledó, E.; Jiménez-Murcia, S.; Menchón, J.M.; Fernández-Aranda, F. Personality Changes in Bulimia Nervosa after a Cognitive Behaviour Therapy. *Eur. Eat. Disord. Rev.* **2012**, *20*, 379–385. [CrossRef]
10. Kim, E.J.; Namkoong, K.; Ku, T.; Kim, S.J. The relationship between online game addiction and aggression, self-control and narcissistic personality traits. *Eur. Psychiatry* **2008**, *23*, 212–218. [CrossRef]
11. Kardefelt-Winther, D. The moderating role of psychosocial well-being on the relationship between escapism and excessive online gaming. *Comput. Hum. Behav.* **2014**, *38*, 68–74. [CrossRef]
12. Mehroof, M.; Griffiths, M.D. Online gaming addiction: The role of sensation seeking, self-control, neuroticism, aggression, state anxiety, and trait anxiety. *Cyberpsychol. Behav. Soc. Netw.* **2010**, *13*, 313–316. [CrossRef]
13. Khazaal, Y.; Chatton, A.; Rothen, S.; Achab, S.; Thorens, G.; Zullino, D.; Gmel, G. Psychometric properties of the 7-item game addiction scale among french and German speaking adults. *BMC Psychiatry* **2016**, *16*, 132. [CrossRef]
14. Jiménez-Murcia, S.; Fernández-Aranda, F.; Granero, R.; Chóliz, M.; La Verde, M.; Aguglia, E.; Signorelli, M.S.; Sá, G.M.; Aymamí, N.; Gómez-Peña, M.; et al. Video game addiction in gambling disorder: Clinical, psychopathological, and personality correlates. *BioMed Res. Int.* **2014**, *7*, 105–110. [CrossRef]

15. Müller, K.W.; Beutel, M.E.; Egloff, B.; Wölfling, K. Investigating risk factors for Internet gaming disorder: A comparison of patients with addictive gaming, pathological gamblers and healthy controls regarding the big five personality traits. *Eur. Addict. Res.* **2014**, *20*, 129–136. [CrossRef]
16. Festl, R.; Scharkow, M.; Quandt, T. Problematic computer game use among adolescents, younger and older adults. *Addiction* **2013**, *108*, 592–599. [CrossRef] [PubMed]
17. Wang, C.W.; Ho, R.T.H.; Chan, C.L.W.; Tse, S. Exploring personality characteristics of Chinese adolescents with internet-related addictive behaviors: Trait differences for gaming addiction and social networking addiction. *Addict. Behav.* **2015**, *42*, 32–35. [CrossRef] [PubMed]
18. Montag, C.; Flierl, M.; Markett, S.; Walter, N.; Jurkiewicz, M.; Reuter, M. Internet addiction and personality in first-person-shooter video gamers. *J. Media Psychol.* **2011**, *23*, 163–173. [CrossRef]
19. Goby, V.P. Personality and Online/Offline Choices: MBTI Profiles and Favored Communication Modes in a Singapore Study. *CyberPsychol. Behav.* **2006**, *9*, 5–13. [CrossRef] [PubMed]
20. Jain, A.K.; Jain, A.K.; Murty, M.N.; Flynn, P.J. Data Clustering: A Review. *ACM Comput. Surv.* **1999**, *31*, 264–323. [CrossRef]
21. Noori, H.R.; Helinski, S.; Spanagel, R. Cluster and meta-analyses on factors influencing stress-induced alcohol drinking and relapse in rodents. *Addict. Biol.* **2014**, *19*, 225–232. [CrossRef]
22. Alikhanian, H.; Crawford, J.D.; DeSouza, J.F.X.; Cheyne, D.O.; Blohm, G. Adaptive cluster analysis approach for functional localization using magnetoencephalography. *Front. Neurosci.* **2013**. [CrossRef]
23. Henry, D.; Dymnicki, A.B.; Mohatt, N.; Allen, J.; Kelly, J.G. Clustering Methods with Qualitative Data: A Mixed-Methods Approach for Prevention Research with Small Samples. *Prev. Sci.* **2015**, *16*, 1007–1016. [CrossRef]
24. Gamito, P.S.; Morais, D.G.; Oliveira, J.G.; Brito, R.; Rosa, P.J.; Gaspar De Matos, M. Frequency is not enough: Patterns of use associated with risk of Internet addiction in Portuguese adolescents. *Comput. Hum. Behav.* **2016**, *58*, 471–478. [CrossRef]
25. Álvarez-Moya, E.M.; Jiménez-Murcia, S.; Aymamí, M.N.; Gómez-Peña, M.; Granero, R.; Santamaría, J.; Menchón, J.M.; Fernández-Aranda, F. Subtyping study of a pathological gamblers sample. *Can. J. Psychiatry* **2010**, *55*, 498–506. [CrossRef] [PubMed]
26. de la Fuente-Tomas, L.; Arranz, B.; Safont, G.; Sierra, P.; Sanchez-Autet, M.; Garcia-Blanco, A.; Garcia-Portilla, M.P. Classification of patients with bipolar disorder using k-means clustering. *PLoS ONE* **2019**, *14*. [CrossRef] [PubMed]
27. Vachon, D.D.; Bagby, R.M. Pathological Gambling Subtypes. *Psychol. Assess.* **2009**, *21*, 608–615. [CrossRef]
28. Suomi, A.; Dowling, N.A.; Jackson, A.C. Problem gambling subtypes based on psychological distress, alcohol abuse and impulsivity. *Addict. Behav.* **2014**, *39*, 1741–1745. [CrossRef]
29. Granero, R.; Fernandez-Aranda, F.; Mestre-Bach, G.; Steward, T.; Bano, M.; Agvera, Z.; Mallorqui-Bague, N.; Aymami, N.; Gomez-Pena, M.; Sancho, M.; et al. Cognitive behavioral therapy for compulsive buying behavior: Predictors of treatment outcome. *Eur. Psychiatry* **2017**, *39*. [CrossRef]
30. Billieux, J.; Thorens, G.; Khazaal, Y.; Zullino, D.; Achab, S.; Van der Linden, M. Problematic involvement in online games: A cluster analytic approach. *Comput. Hum. Behav.* **2015**, *43*, 242–250. [CrossRef]
31. Torres-Rodríguez, A.; Griffiths, M.D.; Carbonell, X.; Oberst, U. Internet gaming disorder in adolescence: Psychological characteristics of a clinical sample. *J. Behav. Addict.* **2018**, *7*, 707–718. [CrossRef]
32. Mallorquí-Bagué, N.; Fernández-Aranda, F.; Lozano-Madrid, M.; Granero, R.; Mestre-Bach, G.; Baño, M.; Pino-Gutiérrez, A.D.; Gómez-Peña, M.; Aymamí, N.; Menchón, J.M.; et al. Internet gaming disorder and online gambling disorder: Clinical and personality correlates. *J. Behav. Addict.* **2017**, *6*, 669–677. [CrossRef]
33. González-Bueso, V.; Santamaría, J.; Fernández, D.; Merino, L.; Montero, E.; Ribas, J. Association between Internet Gaming Disorder or Pathological Video-Game Use and Comorbid Psychopathology: A Comprehensive Review. *Int. J. Environ. Res. Public Health.* **2018**, *15*, 668. [CrossRef]
34. Millon, T. *Manual of Millon Adolescent Clinical Inventory*; National Computer Systems: Minneapolis, MN, USA, 1993.
35. Aguirre, G. *Adaptación Español del MACI*; TEA: Madrid, Spain, 2004.
36. Murrie, D.C.; Cornell, D.G. Psychopathy screening of incarcerated juveniles: A comparison of measures. *Psychol. Assess.* **2002**, *14*, 390–396. [CrossRef] [PubMed]
37. Salekin, R.T.; Larrea, M.A.; Ziegler, T. Relationships between the MACI and the BASC in the assessment of child and adolescent offenders. *J. Forensic Psychol. Pract.* **2002**, *2*, 35–50. [CrossRef]

38. Velting, D.M.; Rathus, J.H.; Miller, A.L. MACI personality scale profiles of depressed adolescent suicide attempters: A pilot study. *J. Clin. Psychol.* **2000**, *56*, 1381–1385. [CrossRef]
39. Burton, D.L.; Duty, K.J.; Leibowitz, G.S. Differences between sexually victimized and nonsexually victimized male adolescent sexual abusers: Developmental antecedents and behavioral comparisons. *J. Child Sex. Abus.* **2011**, *20*, 77–93. [CrossRef] [PubMed]
40. Ferrer, L.; Kirchner, T. Suicidal tendency among adolescents with adjustment disorder: Risk and protective personality factors. *Crisis* **2015**, *36*, 202–210. [CrossRef] [PubMed]
41. Grilo, C.M.; Fehon, D.C.; Walker, M.; Martino, S. A comparison of adolescent inpatients with and without wubstance abuse using the Millon Adolescent Clinical Inventory. *J. Youth Adolesc.* **1996**, *25*, 379–388. [CrossRef]
42. Derogatis, L.R. *SCL-90-R. Administration, Scoring and Procedures Manual*; Clinical Psychometric: Baltimore, MD, USA, 1990.
43. Derogatis, L.R. *SCL-90-R. Cuestionario de 90 Síntomas-Manual. [Questionnaire of the 90 Symptoms-Manual]*; TEA Ediciones: Madrid, Spain, 2002.
44. Spielberger, C.; Gorsuch, R.L.; Lushene, R.E. *Manual for the State/Trait Anxiety Inventory*; Consulting Psychologists Press: Palo Alto, CA, USA, 1970.
45. Guillén-Riquelme, A.; Buela-Casal, G. Psychometric revision and differential item functioning in the State Trait Anxiety Inventory (STAI). *Psicothema* **2011**, *23*, 510–515.
46. First, M.; Gibbon, M.; Spitzer, R.; Williams, J. *Users Guide for the Structured Clinical Interview for DSM IV Axis I Disorders—Research Version (SCID-I, Version 2.0)*; New York State Psychiatric Institute: New York, NY, USA, 1996.
47. Scrucca, L.; Raftery, A.E. Clustvarsel: A package implementing variable selection for Gaussian model-based clustering in R. *J. Stat. Softw.* **2018**, *84*. [CrossRef]
48. Kassambara, A.; Mundt, F. Factoextra: Extract and Visualize the Results of Multivariate Data Analyses. *R Package Version* **2017**, *1*, 1–74.
49. Dempster, A.P.; Laird, N.M.; Rubin, D.B. Maximum Likelihood from Incomplete Data via the EM Algorithm. *J. R. Stat. Soc. B* **1977**, *39*, 1–22.
50. McLachlan, G.J.; Krishnan, T. *(Thriyambakam) The EM Algorithm and Extensions*; Wiley-Interscience: New York, NY, USA, 2008; ISBN 9780471201700.
51. Fraley, C.; Raftery, A.E. Model-based methods of classification: Using the mclust software in chemometrics. *J. Stat. Softw.* **2007**, *18*, 1–13. [CrossRef]
52. Mclachlan, G.J.; Lee, S.X.; Rathnayake, S.I. Annual Review of Statistics and Its Application Finite Mixture Models. *Annu. Rev. Stat.* **2019**. [CrossRef]
53. Cohen, J. *Statistical Power Analysis for the Behavioral Sciences*, 2nd ed.; L. Erlbaum Associates: Hillsdale, NJ, USA, 1988; ISBN 9780805802832.
54. Lehenbauer-Baum, M.; Klaps, A.; Kovacovsky, Z.; Witzmann, K.; Zahlbruckner, R.; Stetina, B.U. Addiction and Engagement: An Explorative Study Toward Classification Criteria for Internet Gaming Disorder. *Cyberpsychology. Behav. Soc. Netw.* **2015**, *18*, 343–349. [CrossRef] [PubMed]
55. Gentile, D.A.; Choo, H.; Liau, A.; Sim, T.; Li, D.; Fung, D.; Khoo, A. Pathological video game use among youths: A two-year longitudinal study. *Pediatrics* **2011**, *127*, e319–e329. [CrossRef] [PubMed]
56. Seay, A.F.; Kraut, R.E. Project Massive: Self-Regulation and Problematic Use of Online Gaming. In Proceedings of the Conference on Human Factors in Computing Systems, San Jose, CA, USA, 24–28 April 2007; pp. 829–838.
57. Müller, K.W.; Koch, A.; Dickenhorst, U.; Beutel, M.E.; Duven, E.; Wölfling, K. Addressing the Question of Disorder-Specific Risk Factors of Internet Addiction: A Comparison of Personality Traits in Patients with Addictive Behaviors and Comorbid Internet Addiction. *Biomed Res. Int.* **2013**. [CrossRef]
58. Van Rooij, A.J.; Schoenmakers, T.M.; Vermulst, A.A.; Van Den Eijnden, R.J.J.M.; Van De Mheen, D. Online video game addiction: Identification of addicted adolescent gamers. *Addiction* **2011**, *106*, 205–212. [CrossRef]
59. Baer, S.; Bogusz, E.; Green, D.A. Stuck on screens: Patterns of computer and gaming station use in youth seen in a psychiatric clinic. *J. Can. Acad. Child Adolesc. Psychiatry* **2011**, *20*, 86–94.
60. Cole, S.H.; Hooley, J.M. Clinical and Personality Correlates of MMO Gaming. *Soc. Sci. Comput. Rev.* **2013**, *31*, 424–436. [CrossRef]

61. Starcevic, V.; Berle, D.; Porter, G.; Fenech, P. Problem Video Game Use and Dimensions of Psychopathology. *Int. J. Ment. Health Addict.* **2011**, *9*, 248–256. [CrossRef]
62. Stetina, B.U.; Kothgassner, O.D.; Lehenbauer, M.; Kryspin-Exner, I. Beyond the fascination of online-games: Probing addictive behavior and depression in the world of online-gaming. *Comput. Hum. Behav.* **2011**, *27*, 473–479. [CrossRef]
63. King, D.L.; Delfabbro, P.H.; Zwaans, T.; Kaptsis, D. Clinical features and axis I comorbidity of Australian adolescent pathological Internet and video game users. *Aust. N. Zeal. J. Psychiatry* **2013**, *47*, 1058–1067. [CrossRef] [PubMed]
64. Castellanos-Ryan, N.; Briere, F.N.; O'Leary-Barrett, M.; Banaschewski, T.; Bokde, A.; Bromberg, U.; Biichel, C.; Flor, H.; Frouin, V.; Gallinat, J.; et al. The IMAGEN Consortium The structure of psychopathology in adolescence and its common personality and cognitive correlates. *J. Abnorm. Psychol.* **2016**, *125*, 1039–1052. [CrossRef] [PubMed]
65. Kotov, R.; Gamez, W.; Schmidt, F.; Watson, D. Linking "Big" personality traits to anxiety, depressive, and substance use disorders: A meta-analysis. *Psychol. Bull.* **2010**, *136*, 768–821. [CrossRef] [PubMed]
66. Tackett, J.L.; Kushner, S.C.; De Fruyt, F.; Mervielde, I. Delineating Personality Traits in Childhood and Adolescence: Associations Across Measures, Temperament, and Behavioral Problems. *Assessment* **2013**, *20*, 738–751. [CrossRef] [PubMed]
67. Malouff, J.M.; Thorsteinsson, E.B.; Schutte, N.S. The relationship between the five-factor model of personality and symptoms of clinical disorders: A meta-analysis. *J. Psychopathol. Behav. Assess.* **2005**, *27*, 101–114. [CrossRef]
68. Carragher, N.; Teesson, M.; Sunderland, M.; Newton, N.C.; Krueger, R.F.; Conrod, P.J.; Barrett, E.L.; Champion, K.E.; Nair, N.K.; Slade, T. The structure of adolescent psychopathology: A symptom-level analysis. *Psychol. Med.* **2016**, *46*, 981–994. [CrossRef]
69. McCann, J.T. The MACI: Composition and Clinical Applications. In *The Millon Inventories: Clinical and Personality Assessment*; Millon, T., Ed.; The Guilford Press: New York, NY, USA, 1997; pp. 363–388.
70. Barry, C.T.; Frick, P.J.; Killian, A.L. The relation of narcissism and self-esteem to conduct problems in children: A preliminary investigation. *J. Clin. Child Adolesc. Psychol.* **2003**, *32*, 139–152. [CrossRef]
71. Przybylski, A.K.; Weinstein, N.; Murayama, K. Internet gaming disorder: Investigating the clinical relevance of a new phenomenon. *Am. J. Psychiatry* **2017**, *174*, 230–235. [CrossRef]
72. Rothmund, T.; Klimmt, C.; Gollwitzer, M. Low Temporal Stability of Excessive Video Game Use in German Adolescents. *J. Media Psychol.* **2018**, *30*, 53–65. [CrossRef]
73. Soto, C.J.; John, O.P.; Gosling, S.D.; Potter, J. Age Differences in Personality Traits From 10 to 65: Big Five Domains and Facets in a Large Cross-Sectional Sample. *J. Pers. Soc. Psychol.* **2011**, *100*, 330–348. [CrossRef]
74. Bean, A.M.; Nielsen, R.K.L.; van Rooij, A.J.; Ferguson, C.J. Video game addiction: The push to pathologize video games. *Prof. Psychol. Res. Pract.* **2017**, *48*, 378–389. [CrossRef]
75. Feng, W.; Ramo, D.E.; Steven, R.C.; Bourgeois, J.A. Internet gaming disorder: Trends in prevalence 1998–2016. *Addict. Behav.* **2017**, *75*, 17–24. [CrossRef] [PubMed]
76. Han, D.H.; Kim, S.M.; Lee, Y.S.; Renshaw, P.F. The effect of family therapy on the changes in the severity of on-line game play and brain activity in adolescents with on-line game addiction. *Psychiatry Res. Neuroimaging* **2012**, *202*, 126–131. [CrossRef] [PubMed]
77. Kim, S.M.; Han, D.H.; Lee, Y.S.; Renshaw, P.F. Combined cognitive behavioral therapy and bupropion for the treatment of problematic on-line game play in adolescents with major depressive disorder. *Comput. Hum. Behav.* **2012**, *28*, 1954–1959. [CrossRef]

6

# Investigating the Effect of Personality, Internet Literacy and Use Expectancies in Internet-Use Disorder: A Comparative Study between China and Germany

**Benjamin Stodt [1], Matthias Brand [1,2], Cornelia Sindermann [3], Elisa Wegmann [1], Mei Li [4], Min Zhou [5], Peng Sha [6] and Christian Montag [3,7,*]**

1 General Psychology: Cognition and Center for Behavioral Addiction Research (CeBAR), University of Duisburg-Essen, 47057 Duisburg, Germany; benjamin.stodt@uni-due.de (B.S.); matthias.brand@uni-due.de (M.B.); elisa.wegmann@uni-due.de (E.W.)

2 Erwin L. Hahn Institute for Magnetic Resonance Imaging, 45141 Essen, Germany

3 Department of Molecular Psychology, Institute of Psychology and Education, Ulm University, 89081 Ulm, Germany; cornelia.sindermann@uni-ulm.de

4 Student Counselling Centre, Beijing University of Civil Engineering and Architecture, Beijing 100037, China; amorelm415@gmail.com

5 Institute of Medical Statistics, Informatics and Epidemiology, University of Cologne, 50923 Cologne, Germany; min.zhou@hotmail.de

6 School of Journalism and Communication, Southwest University, Chongqing 400716, China; a2352893@gmail.com

7 Key Laboratory for NeuroInformation/Center for Information in Medicine, School of Life Science and Technology, University of Electronic Science and Technology of China, Chengdu 611731, China

* Correspondence: christian.montag@uni-ulm.de

**Abstract:** Research on Internet-use Disorder (IUD) has increased rapidly, indicating its clinical and global importance. Past studies suggested cultural diversity regarding the prevalence of an IUD, e.g., between Asian and European countries. Additionally, it was found that personality factors, Internet-related cognitions and specific competences seem to influence IUD tendencies, but research lacks in cultural comparative studies regarding these mechanisms. This study focuses on differences between Germany and China regarding the above-mentioned characteristics. German ($n$ = 411; $M$ = 20.70 years, $SD$ = 3.34 years) and Chinese participants ($n$ = 410; $M$ = 20.72 years, $SD$ = 2.65 years) answered the short Internet Addiction Test, Big Five Inventories, the Internet-use Expectancies Scale, as well as the Internet Literacy Questionnaire. The results revealed higher occurrence of IUD symptoms in China. Furthermore, Chinese participants scored significantly higher on neuroticism and agreeableness, whereas German participants scored higher on extraversion and openness. Compared to German participants, Chinese showed higher expectancies to avoid negative feelings online and to be positively reinforced. Regarding Internet literacy, German participants indicated higher skills concerning the reflection and critical analysis of online content, whereas Chinese showed higher expertise in producing and interacting online. Further, simple slope analyses indicated that certain Internet literacy domains were related differentially to IUD symptoms in Germany and China. While Chinese participants with higher reflective skills indicated highest IUD symptoms, reflective skills revealed no effect in Germany. Additionally, higher self-regulative skills correlated with lower IUD symptoms in the German, but not in the Chinese sample. The results give a hint to potential cultural differences regarding IUD, especially on the predictive and protective role of Internet literacy domains.

**Keywords:** Internet addiction; Internet-use disorder; Internet literacy; expectancies; personality; cultural differences

## 1. Introduction

Since the late 90s, the phenomenon of Internet addiction or Internet-use disorder (IUD) is focused more and more in the scientific literature (based on the term Internet-gaming disorder, the term Internet-use disorder is used in the following as a synonym for Internet addiction or pathological Internet use). Further, the number of theoretical assumptions about its classification as well as empirical studies, which give insights into the underlying mechanisms of its development, increase constantly [1–3]. Past research differentiates between unspecific and specific IUDs [4]. While an unspecific IUD goes along with an excessive and uncontrolled use of different Internet applications and websites without a clear preference [1], a specific IUD describes the addictive use of one specific application or certain type of website, such as games, shopping sites, or Internet communication applications (for an overview, see [2]). Not just since Internet-gaming disorder has been added to section III of the DSM-5 [5], there is an undisputable clinical relevance of IUDs. Nevertheless, further research is needed to conduct and clarify potential diagnostic criteria for an unspecified IUD or further specific forms, such as Internet-pornography-use disorder or Internet-communication disorder (ICD).

### *1.1. Prevalence of an IUD*

According to a meta-analysis by Cheng and Li [6], who reviewed studies from 31 nations across seven world regions, the global occurrence of an IUD is estimated at 6%, illustrating it as a global phenomenon and universal issue. Past research on the epidemiology and cultural diversity of an IUD showed that prevalence rates strongly differ between different countries and cultures [7]. Cheng and Li [6] reported an occurrence of IUD symptoms in 2.6% of European individuals, which confirms the results by Spada [8], who identified 1 to 9% of the European population showing symptoms of a pathological Internet use. In a German representative population sample, a prevalence rate of 1% was estimated [9]. While prevalence rates in the Middle East range between 1% and 12%, highest prevalence rates up to 38% are reported for Asian countries [7,8,10]. Confirming the quality of real life hypothesis, Cheng and Li [6] identified several environmental characteristics associated with a higher occurrence of an IUD, like perception of less life satisfaction, greater traffic commute time consumption, as well as lower national income. Other reasons for cultural differences, such as Hofstede's [11] assumptions on power-distance, collectivism, and individualism, have also been discussed [12]. Besides, the broad range of reported prevalence rates can also be due to the absence of standardized diagnostic tools. Former studies used various questionnaires to measure symptoms of an IUD, which are grounded on different diagnostic criteria and cut-off scores [7]. Consequently, cross-cultural differences in the prevalence of an IUD found in previous studies still require a cautious interpretation.

### *1.2. Cultural Issues of an IUD: Results from Germany and China*

Along with research on the occurrence of an IUD, former studies already focused on specific psychological aspects which are associated with an excessive and addictive use of the Internet in different nations and cultures [7,13,14]. However, there are just a few studies concentrating on cultural issues regarding the occurrence of an IUD as well as the effect of personality traits and Internet-related state variables on its development. In order to better understand the development and maintenance of an IUD within different national backgrounds, cross-cultural studies are important [13]. Besides, Ko and Yao [15] emphasized that cultures psychologically differ in a variety of individual characteristics, such as personality, emotions, and cognitions. Therefore, nationally differing effects of personal characteristics on the development of an IUD can be expected.

Within the scope of cultural-comparative studies, Asian and Western samples have been compared most frequently regarding specific individual characteristics as well as economic and infrastructural background [15]. Regarding digitization and Internet penetration rates, Germany and China display two key nations of their continents [16,17]. In Germany, 89.6% of the population is online (which are 72.3 million people) [16]. This corresponds to 11.1% of all European Internet users and is the second highest rate after Russia (16.6%). Nevertheless, only 76.4% of the Russian population is online [16]. In China, the Internet penetration rate is at 54.6% (772 million users), which displays the highest amount of Internet users in Asia with 38.1% in terms of total user numbers [16]. The highest Internet penetration rate for Asian nations is found in Japan (93.3%) [16]. However, this rate corresponds to just 5.9% of the Asian population. Due to these facts, we chose Germany and China as two representatives for well-digitized European and Asian nations.

Within Germany, IUD displays a serious health problem. In a representative study, 1% of the German population has been identified as pathological Internet users [9]. Higher prevalence rates were observed within the age of 14 to 24 (2.4%) and 14 to 16 years (4%) [9]. Another German study reported a prevalence rate of 2.1%, where the group of people suffering from IUD reported significant psychosocial and health consequences due to their excessive Internet use [18]. Further, male gender and social factors were significantly associated with IUD symptoms [18]. Further studies from Germany highlighted significant correlations of tendencies towards an unspecific and specific IUD with psychopathological symptoms (e.g., depression and interpersonal sensitivity [19–21]), higher impulsivity [19], younger age [22] and male gender [18,19].

Even if IUD is a growing topic of research in Germany, IUD has been studied more frequently in China. There, IUD has been recognized as a nationwide health problem with prevalence rates ranging from 2.4 to 6.4% [23,24]. Within China, Internet addicted individuals have been characterized with higher impulsivity [25], lower prosocial behaviors [23], higher depressive symptoms [24,26], shyness [27], lower self-esteem [26], younger age [24,28], and male gender [28].

In the following, results on the effect of specific personality traits and Internet-related state variables on IUD symptoms are summarized. Here, we focus on investigations carried out in Germany and China, supplemented by results from Western and Asian countries.

*1.3. Predictors of an IUD: Trait Variables*

Beyond epidemiological studies, many studies focus on individual factors influencing the development and maintenance of IUDs. Here it has to be distinguished between personal predispositions [29,30], which persist over a long period of time (traits), and factors which are situation-dependent, such as expectancies or actual mood (states) [31,32]. Regarding trait variables, depression, attention-deficit/hyperactivity disorder (ADHD), as well as social anxiety disorders have been verified as three main comorbid personal predispositions of IUDs [32–34]. Next to these predispositions, further person's core characteristics could play an important role in the addiction process. One popular concept of one person's core personality is the Big Five personality model, including the personality traits of neuroticism, extraversion, openness to experience, conscientiousness, and agreeableness [35,36]. In their theoretical model, called I-PACE, Brand et al. [2] describe different stages of the addiction process of specific Internet-use disorders, including the interaction of state and trait variables as well as different mediation effects. In this model and their previous literature review, the authors highlighted the relevance of the Big Five personality traits, especially low conscientiousness, low extraversion, and high neuroticism, as predispositions in persons who are vulnerable to use specific Internet applications excessively and uncontrolled [2].

According to cross-cultural studies, differences regarding the Big Five personality traits between East Asian and Western cultures exist. A meta-analysis revealed that especially East Asian countries score significant lower on the traits of extraversion, agreeableness, conscientiousness, and openness, but higher on neuroticism than other countries and cultures [37]. Moreover, mainly higher neuroticism and lower extraversion were found as main correlates of an IUD across different countries [38–40]. However, openness, conscientiousness and agreeableness also indicated significant relations to IUD symptoms within a sample of Chinese adolescents [28]. Despite these general cultural differences concerning Big Five personality traits and the correlations with IUD symptoms found within country-specific samples, it remains under-uninvestigated whether the strength of impact regarding these traits on the development and maintenance of an IUD significantly differs between different countries and cultures.

### *1.4. Predictors of an IUD: State Variables*

Next to personal predispositions and traits, researchers focused on state variables, which are considered as situation-dependent factors, influencing and triggering human behavior [31]. In the context of an IUD, such factors are especially motivational factors, coping strategies, and cognitive biases [2,3]. It is assumed that these factors interact with trait variables and core characteristics in the developmental process of an IUD and in turn reinforce and stabilize cognitive and affective responses [2]. In the following, Internet-use expectancies and specific Internet literacy domains are discussed as two exemplary predictors of an IUD.

#### 1.4.1. Internet-Use Expectancies

According to Lee et al. [41], person's expectancies towards the use of the Internet affect his or her attitudes regarding specific online applications. Furthermore, Internet users' expectancies (e.g., to gratify a certain need) lead to the decision to use the Internet or a specific application to experience gratification, as shown in the I-PACE model by Brand et al. [2] (also see their article for a more comprehensive overview of this decision-making process). One step further, symptoms of an IUD increase, when positive expectancies and metacognitions towards the Internet exist [42,43]. Brand et al. [44] already showed that Internet-use expectancies for positive reinforcement as well as avoidance expectancies are correlated with psychopathological symptoms and further personality aspects within a German sample. In turn, certain use expectancies and dysfunctional coping mechanisms are correlated with symptoms of an unspecified IUD. Also within a German sample, Wegmann et al. [21] could replicate these findings, as they found associations between psychopathological symptoms, Internet-use expectancies, self-regulation abilities, and symptoms of an excessive use of Internet-communication applications. According to a Taiwanese study by Lee et al. [41], Internet-use expectancies positively predicted students' attitudes towards and the use of specific Internet applications. In another Taiwanese study, Wu et al. [45] found that having expectancies that the use of the Internet helps to relieve negative emotions increases the probability of IUD symptoms in persons with borderline personality disorder. The authors stated that it is important to teach individuals to develop alternative coping strategies and not to use the Internet for escaping from negative feelings.

#### 1.4.2. Internet Literacy

As an additional state variable, specific skills and competences in using the Internet and its applications could also play a key role in the development and maintenance of IUDs [22]. Today, there is still no common term summarizing such skills, whereas researchers stated that more empirical research in this area is required [46]. Some of these concepts are termed e.g., digital literacy [47], new media literacy [48,49], information literacy [50], or Internet literacy [22,51]. Fraillon et al. [52] defined digital literacy as "an individual's ability to use computers to investigate, create, and communicate in order to participate effectively at home, at school, in the workplace, and in society" (p. 18). Stodt, Wegmann, and Brand [22] recently published a four-dimensional concept of Internet literacy which they had also operationalized with a self-assessment questionnaire. Beyond the pure technical expertise in handling Internet applications and relevant software, the concept of Internet literacy by Stodt et al. [22] specifically focuses on a rather deliberate, conscious and reflective use of the Internet and certain applications (see also [51]). Besides that, the increasing possibilities through interactive participation brought by social media cause that Internet users need to critically evaluate online content and information. This is also crucial to become an inherent part of online social networks as an active producer of content [53,54]. As a last skill, it is necessary for individuals to control and self-regulate their own online behavior [55].

Some empirical studies found that specific domains of an Internet literacy could be both positively and negatively related to symptoms of an IUD or ICD in Asian as well as European samples, e.g., [22,51]. More detailed, the high impact of self-regulative skills in IUD and ICD was already highlighted in Western cultures, e.g., [21,56]. Here, the authors assumed that people with less self-regulative skills are more vulnerable to develop an IUD, also due to reduced cognitive control. Stodt et al. [22] demonstrated that higher technical and productive skills increase the risk to suffer from IUD symptoms, whereas higher reflective and self-regulative skills were negatively correlated with IUD symptoms within a German sample. Therefore, the latter domains of an Internet literacy can be seen as preventive factors, which are not stable but learnable. Nevertheless, the preventive values of specific Internet literacy domains and their mediating or moderating role in the addiction process is an important topic of research. In another German study, Wegmann et al. [21] showed that both Internet-use expectancies and self-regulation as one domain of Internet literacy mediate the effect between psychopathological predispositions and ICD symptoms and especially productive and self-regulative skills are correlated with expectancies towards the Internet. More detailed, higher productive and interactive skills as well as lower self-regulation abilities go along with higher expectancies regarding positive reinforcement and the avoidance of negative feelings.

### *1.5. Aims and Hypotheses*

Recent German studies declared IUD as a nationwide problem, e.g., [9]. Its symptoms are correlated with lower extraversion and higher neuroticism as well as the expectancies someone has towards using the Internet, and certain Internet literacy dimensions [20–22,44,57]. Besides this, most epidemiological studies revealed high prevalence rates in China and adjacent nations, e.g., [6,10]. Addressing personality, also higher neuroticism and lower extraversion are mostly reported as significant predictors of an IUD in China, even if some studies indicated correlations with all traits of the Big Five [28]. Regarding Internet literacy, just a few findings have been reported for Chinese samples [51], while from our knowledge no research has been done on Internet-related specific cognitions.

The first aim of our study was to investigate whether previous findings regarding the relationship of personality, Internet-use expectancies, different Internet literacy domains and IUD symptoms could be replicated across different nations and cultures. We expect that (i) primarily lower extraversion and higher neuroticism should be linked to higher tendencies towards IUD, (ii) higher Internet use expectancies should be accompanied with IUD symptoms and (iii) primarily higher productive and interactive as well as lower self-regulative skills should be correlated with higher tendencies towards an IUD. Secondly, we wanted to have a closer look at potential differences and interaction effects between the above-mentioned factors among two countries which differ in their cultural background and most likely in their Internet-use behavior.

## 2. Materials and Methods

### *2.1. Participants*

Overall, 821 participants (334 female, 487 male) from Germany and China took part in a multi-parted data acquisition. The mean age of the whole sample was $M = 20.71$ years ($SD = 3.01$) with a range from 16 to 30.

The German convenience subsample consisted of 411 participants (179 female, 232 male; age: $M = 20.70$, $SD = 3.34$, range: 16–29 years). German participants were recruited from all over Germany by advertisements in university, e-mail lists, announcements on social networking sites, as well as word-of-mouth recommendation. Most of the German participants were university students (33.5%), of which 72.3% named the Abitur (German's secondary school leaving diploma) and 13.1% the

Fachabitur (vocational baccalaureate diploma) to be their highest school educational level. Additionally, 10.2% of the university students already received their bachelor's degree and 2.2% received their master's degree or a comparable graduation. Further, 25.2% of the German sample were pupils, 22.2% trainees, 10.3% were employees (of which 50.1% had a university degree), and 8.8% of the subsample practiced other professions.

The Chinese convenience subsample consisted of 410 participants (155 female, 255 male; age: $M = 20.72$, $SD = 2.65$, range: 16–30 years). Chinese participants were recruited via announcements and postings in university as well as advertisements in university online forums. Overall, 202 Chinese participants took part in a data collection carried out in Beijing. Further 151 participants took part in the *Chengdu Gene Brain Behavior Project (CGBBP)* and have been recruited in Chengdu. An additional subsample of 57 participants took part in another data acquisition in Chengdu. The data collection was performed in these two Chinese cities due to location-dependent reasons (e.g., the studies were carried out in laboratories in these cities' universities). Within all surveys, most of the Chinese participants were undergraduate students (74.6%), followed by graduate students (23.4%) and high school graduates (2.0%). The corresponding local ethics committees approved the study.

### 2.2. Measures

Online surveys were used to gather participants' information of the below mentioned measurements in Germany and China. The short Internet Addiction Test, the Internet-use Expectancies Scale, and the Internet Literacy Questionnaire were already available in German language and professionally translated into Chinese. Due to methodological issues, which are described later, two different personality questionnaires were used in the two countries. In the German subsample, the 10-Item Big Five Inventory (BFI-10) was used to assess the Big Five personality traits, whereas the NEO Five-Factor Inventory was used in the Chinese subsample. Both questionnaires were already available in the respective languages. In former studies, all of the used questionnaires showed good psychometric properties and validity. In this study's sample, all questionnaires and its subscales revealed a good internal consistency with Cronbach's $\alpha > 0.700$, except for the subscale *openness* and *agreeableness* of the Chinese NEO Five-Factor Inventory, which however were still in the acceptable range. All reliabilities (Cronbach's $\alpha$) of the used questionnaires are presented in Table 1. Cronbach's $\alpha$ reliabilities of the BFI-10 are not reported because this measure is not appropriate for calculating Cronbach's $\alpha$ as only two items are building each scale [58].

**Table 1.** Overview on reliabilities (Cronbach's $\alpha$) of the NEO Five-Factor Inventory (NEO-FFI) *, Internet-use Expectancies Scale (IUES), Internet Literacy Questionnaire (ILQ), short Internet Addiction Test (s-IAT) and their subscales in the German and Chinese samples.

| | **Germany** | **China** |
|---|---|---|
| NEO-FFI—*Neuroticism* | - | 0.820 |
| NEO-FFI—*Extraversion* | - | 0.732 |
| NEO-FFI—*Openness* | - | 0.602 |
| NEO-FFI—*Conscientiousness* | - | 0.747 |
| NEO-FFI—*Agreeableness* | - | 0.698 |
| IUES—*Positive reinforcement* | 0.855 | 0.775 |
| IUES—*Avoidance expectancies* | 0.784 | 0.810 |
| s-IAT—*Total score* | 0.869 | 0.919 |
| s-IAT—*Loss of control/time management* | 0.819 | 0.862 |
| s-IAT—*Craving/social problems* | 0.809 | 0.870 |
| ILQ—*Technical expertise* | 0.805 | 0.775 |
| ILQ—*Production and interaction* | 0.759 | 0.834 |
| ILQ—*Reflection and critical analysis* | 0.707 | 0.723 |
| ILQ—*Self-regulation* | 0.772 | 0.810 |

* Note that in the German sample the BFI-10 was used, where no reliabilities can be presented.

We further compared the factorial structure of the short Internet Addiction Test, the Internet-use Expectancies Scale, and Internet Literacy Questionnaire using mean structure analyses with nation as grouping variable. Here, the model fits revealed no good fit with the data indicating that the factorial structure of the scales seem to be different between the nations. Nevertheless, all items scored significantly on their respective factor/latent dimension with acceptable to good factor loadings in both nations (weakest factor loading = 0.350, highest factor loading = 0.896). This issue will be further discussed in the limitations section.

### 2.2.1. Short Internet Addiction Test (s-IAT)

To measure symptoms of unspecified IUD, the short Internet Addiction Test (s-IAT; [19]) was used. It is a 12-item short version of Young's original Internet Addiction Test (IAT; [59]), an internationally esteemed questionnaire to cover IUD symptoms. The s-IAT has already been validated and frequently used in past research. Within this questionnaire, participants have to evaluate their subjective complaints and experienced negative consequences due to excessive online activities in everyday life. Besides the total sum score, the questionnaire consists of the two subscales *loss of control/time management* and *craving/social problems*, each consisting of six items. Items were rated on a 5-point Likert scale from 1 (*never*) to 5 (*very often*). The total sum score ranges from 12 to 60, in which a higher sum score of the s-IAT indicates higher symptoms of an IUD. To evaluate the strength of IUD symptoms, the cut-off for the total score was >30 to indicate a problematic Internet use and >37 to indicate a pathological Internet use [19]. The questionnaire in English, German, and Chinese language is reported in Table A1.

### 2.2.2. Big Five Inventory-10 and NEO Five-Factor Inventory

Because of methodological issues, we used two different questionnaires to measure the Big Five personality traits. These two questionnaires represent reliable and valid instruments for the measurement of the above-mentioned traits in the respective country. For the German data collection, we preferred to use the Big Five Inventory-10 (BFI-10; [60]), which (despite its shortness) represents a well-evaluated and valid instrument in Western countries. While the validity of the BFI-10 in Chinese language still has to be further tested [61], we decided to use the 60-item version of the NEO Five-Factor Inventory (NEO-FFI; [62]), which has been used in several Asian studies before and revealed a good validity, e.g., [63]. Both questionnaires were used to measure the participants' level of *neuroticism*, *extraversion*, *openness*, *conscientiousness*, and *agreeableness*. In both questionnaires, higher mean scores reveal a higher level of the respective characteristic.

The BFI-10 consists of 10 items with two items on each trait. All of the items were rated on a 5-point Likert scale ranging from 1 (*strongly disagree*) to 5 (*strongly agree*).

The NEO-FFI comprises overall 60 statements, which have to be evaluated on a 5-point Likert scale from 1 (*strongly disagree*) to 5 (*strongly agree*).

### 2.2.3. Internet-Use Expectancies Scale

To measure expectancies and motivating factors for using the Internet in general, the Internet-use Expectancies Scale (IUES; [44]) was used. The scale consists of the two dimensions *positive reinforcement* and *avoidance expectancies* (each having four items). The dimension positive expectancies measures positive feelings, which are accompanied by using the Internet, whereas the dimension avoidance expectancies indicated whether the Internet is used to avoid negative feelings. Every item was answered on a 6-point Likert scale with a range from 1 (*completely disagree*) to 6 (*completely agree*). Mean scores for each subscale have been calculated. Although the IUES is a relatively new developed questionnaire, it has already been used in several studies [20,21,44] and has also been adapted for specific Internet-use patterns, like Internet-communication, e.g., [57]. The questionnaire in English, German, and Chinese language is shown in Table A2.

#### 2.2.4. Internet Literacy Questionnaire

The Internet Literacy Questionnaire (ILQ; [22]) was applied to measure the individuals' competent and adequate dealing with the Internet on the following four dimensions: *technical expertise, reflection and critical analysis, production and interaction*, and *self-regulation*. Depending on a new calculated exploratory factor analysis, a more economical version of the ILQ was used. The shortened version includes 18 items on the four above-mentioned dimensions, compared to the original 24-item version. According to Stodt et al. [22], the first dimension *technical expertise* measures "the individual's expertise in handling computer hard- and software as well as Internet applications" ([22], p. 31) on four items. The dimension *production and interaction* covers five items measuring "how and why an individual uses the Internet to create own content and to interact with others" ([22], p. 31). The third dimension *reflection and critical analysis* covers "the individual's ability to evaluate the credibility of online content and the behavior of others as well as critically reflecting one's own activities on the Internet" ([22], p. 31) on four items. The dimension *self-regulation* consists of five items covering "the individuals' ability to regulate their own Internet use to prevent negative consequences for daily life" ([22], p. 31). Every item had to be answered on a 6-point Likert scale ranging from 0 (*strongly disagree*) to 5 (*strongly agree*). Mean scores were calculated for each dimension.

Due to translation problems, item number 8 from the Chinese version of the ILQ had to be removed. Therefore, the subscale *reflection and critical analysis* consists of 3 items in the Chinese version. The subscales' internal consistency was still in a good range (Cronbach's $\alpha$ = 0.723). Nevertheless, we provide readers with the complete questionnaire in English, German, and Chinese language as presented in Table A3, including a revised version of item number 8.

### 2.3. *Statistical Analysis Section*

Aside from the presentation of descriptive statistics, inferential statistics are provided in the following result section with respect to both the German and Chinese sample. *t*-Tests were used to examine differences between both nations regarding the manifold Internet variables, whereas Pearson's correlations were used to provide insights into correlation patterns between Internet variables in both countries. In addition, moderated regression analyses were used to consider possible interaction effects between nationality and Internet literacy within the development and maintenance of an IUD. The statistical analyses were performed by using IBM SPSS 24. MPlus version 6.12 (IBM, Armonk, NY, USA) was used to carry out the mean structure analyses. Reported effect sizes are in accordance with Cohen's $d$ (small effect: $d = 0.30$; medium effect: $d = 0.50$; large effect: $d = 0.80$) for $t$-tests and $r$ (small effect: $r = 0.10$; medium effect: $r = 0.30$; large effect: $r = 0.50$) for Pearson correlations [64].

## 3. Results

### 3.1. *Descriptive Results*

Table 2 contains the whole sample's (German and Chinese collapsed) descriptive statistics of the different questionnaires including average scores, standard deviations, and range.

**Table 2.** Descriptive statistics of the s-IAT, IUES, ILQ, BFI-10, and NEO-FFI.

| Domain/Variable | *M* | *SD* | *Min–Max* [1] |
|---|---|---|---|
| **Internet-use disorder (s-IAT)** | | | |
| Total score | 27.76 | 9.23 | 12.00–60.00 |
| Loss of control/time management | 15.62 | 4.98 | 6.00–30.00 |
| Craving/social problems | 12.14 | 4.97 | 6.00–30.00 |
| **Internet-use expectancies (IUES)** | | | |
| Positive reinforcement | 4.00 | 1.11 | 1.00–6.00 |
| Avoidance expectancies | 2.93 | 1.23 | 1.00–6.00 |

**Table 2.** *Cont.*

| Domain/Variable | *M* | *SD* | *Min–Max* [1] |
|---|---|---|---|
| **Internet literacy (ILQ)** | | | |
| Technical expertise | 2.99 | 1.16 | 0.00–5.00 |
| Production and interaction | 2.52 | 1.72 | 0.00–5.00 |
| Reflection and critical analysis | 3.11 | 0.96 | 0.00–5.00 |
| Self-regulation | 3.00 | 1.00 | 0.00–5.00 |
| **Big Five personality (BFI-10)** [2] | | | |
| Neuroticism | 2.66 | 0.95 | 1.00–5.00 |
| Extraversion | 3.53 | 0.96 | 1.00–5.00 |
| Openness | 3.46 | 1.08 | 1.00–5.00 |
| Conscientiousness | 3.30 | 0.90 | 1.00–5.00 |
| Agreeableness | 3.03 | 0.81 | 1.00–5.00 |
| **Big Five personality (NEO-FFI)** [3] | | | |
| Neuroticism | 2.84 | 0.58 | 1.00–4.50 |
| Extraversion | 3.20 | 0.47 | 1.50–4.67 |
| Openness | 3.28 | 0.43 | 2.17–4.58 |
| Conscientiousness | 3.34 | 0.45 | 2.25–5.00 |
| Agreeableness | 3.38 | 0.46 | 2.00–4.83 |

[1] Actual range of each scale, including the lowest and highest values measured in both subsamples. [2] Used in the German subsample ($n$ = 411). [3] Used in the Chinese subsample ($n$ = 410).

### 3.1.1. Occurrence of IUD

Based on the suggested cut-off scores of the s-IAT by Pawlikowski et al. [19], 55 participants of the German sample indicated a problematic use and 25 participants reported symptoms of a pathological use of the Internet. In China, 115 of the participants reported a problematic, 95 a pathological use. Figure 1 illustrates the percentage distribution of IUD tendencies in both countries.

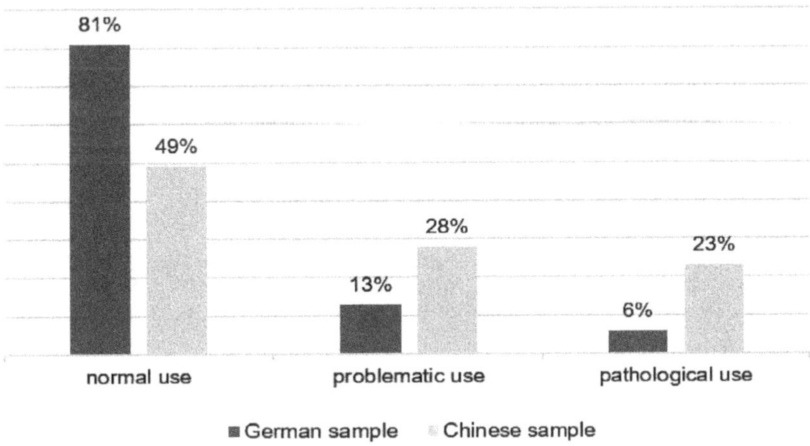


**Figure 1.** Internet-use disorder symptoms in the German and Chinese sample.

## 3.2. *Inferential Statistical Analyses*

### 3.2.1. Testing Both the Chinese and German Sample for Differences in Age and Gender Ratios

Both samples did not differ with respect to age ($t$ = 0.12, $p$ = 0.901) and gender ratios ($\chi^2$ = 2.81, df = 1, $p$ = 0.094). However, since both subsamples were tried to be parallelized as good as possible regarding sample size and age, no age differences were expected. In terms of gender ratios, both samples show merely slight descriptive differences. We further tested for significant age and gender differences in tendencies towards IUD, Internet-use expectancies, Internet literacy, and personality in both samples. Here, age was significantly associated with IUD in the Chinese ($r = 0.142$, $p = 0.004$), but not in the German sample ($r = -0.072$, $p = 0.145$). Regarding gender effects, male participants in the German sample indicated higher scores in the s-IAT compared with females ($t = 1.98$, $p = 0.049$; $M = 24.81$, $SD = 7.48$ versus $M = 23.35$, $SD = 7.38$). No significant gender differences in the Chinese sample could be observed ($t = 0.46$, $p = 0.644$; $M = 31.53$, $SD = 8.89$ versus $M = 31.08$, $SD = 10.30$). While investigating the hypothesized cultural differences, we additionally controlled for the variables of age and gender. Calculated ANCOVAs revealed that the significant cultural effects on the observed variables reported below are not caused by age and gender effects. Nevertheless, some significant effects of age and gender on the measured Internet and personality variables in both countries could be observed. For an overview please see Tables S1 and S2 in the Supplementary Materials.

### 3.2.2. Comparative Analyses

In a first step, *t*-tests for independent samples including effect sizes by Cohen [64] were calculated to compare the different scores of the s-IAT, ILQ, IUES, and the personality questionnaires of both countries. The analyses revealed significant differences between Germany and China regarding the s-IAT total score and both subscores with medium to high effect sizes, in which the Chinese sample indicated higher scores. Concerning Internet-use expectancies, also the Chinese sample showed higher scores regarding the *positive reinforcement* and *avoidance expectancies* with medium to high effect sizes. Regarding the self-evaluated Internet literacy, Chinese participants indicated significant higher scores in the dimension *production and interaction* (medium effect size), whereas the German sample scored higher on the dimension *reflection and critical analysis* (small effect size). No significant differences were found regarding the dimensions *technical expertise* and *self-regulation*. With regard to personality differences, the Chinese sample reported significantly higher scores of *neuroticism* and *agreeableness* than the German sample (small effect size). For *extraversion* and *openness*, German participants indicated higher scores (small to medium effect sizes). No significant differences were found regarding the trait *conscientiousness* (see Table 3).

**Table 3.** Differences between the German and Chinese samples regarding the s-IAT, IUES, ILQ, and Big Five personality traits.

| Domain/Variable | Germany | | China | | *t* | *df* | *p* | *d* |
|---|---|---|---|---|---|---|---|---|
| | *M* | *SD* | *M* | *SD* | | | | |
| **Internet-use disorder (s-IAT)** | | | | | | | | |
| Total score | 24.17 | 7.46 | 31.36 | 9.44 | −12.10 | 776.84 | <0.001 | 0.85 |
| Loss of control/time management | 14.14 | 4.56 | 17.10 | 4.96 | −8.89 | 819.00 | <0.001 | 0.62 |
| Craving/social problems | 10.03 | 3.81 | 14.26 | 5.10 | −13.47 | 757.47 | <0.001 | 0.94 |
| **Internet-use expectancies (IUES)** | | | | | | | | |
| Positive reinforcement | 3.70 | 1.20 | 4.31 | 0.92 | −8.27 | 765.55 | <0.001 | 0.57 |
| Avoidance expectancies | 2.47 | 1.14 | 3.40 | 1.13 | −11.77 | 819.00 | <0.001 | 0.82 |
| **Internet literacy (ILQ)** | | | | | | | | |
| Technical expertise | 2.94 | 1.23 | 3.03 | 1.10 | −1.06 | 808.87 | 0.291 | 0.08 |
| Production and interaction | 2.12 | 1.11 | 2.93 | 1.08 | −10.59 | 819.00 | <0.001 | 0.74 |
| Reflection and critical analysis [1] | 3.18 | 0.88 | 3.03 | 1.09 | 2.29 | 798.88 | 0.022 | 0.15 |
| Self-regulation | 3.06 | 1.02 | 2.94 | 0.99 | 1.73 | 819.00 | 0.085 | 0.12 |
| **Big Five personality [2]** | | | | | | | | |
| Neuroticism | 2.66 | 0.95 | 2.84 | 0.58 | −3.22 | 679.50 | 0.001 | 0.23 |
| Extraversion | 3.53 | 0.96 | 3.20 | 0.47 | 6.34 | 595.08 | <0.001 | 0.44 |
| Openness | 3.46 | 1.08 | 3.28 | 0.43 | 3.10 | 536.97 | 0.002 | 0.22 |
| Conscientiousness | 3.30 | 0.90 | 3.34 | 0.45 | −0.93 | 607.75 | 0.354 | 0.06 |
| Agreeableness | 3.03 | 0.81 | 3.38 | 0.46 | 7.57 | 650.46 | <0.001 | 0.53 |

[1] As already mentioned in the method section, the mean score of this dimension was calculated by using three instead of four items in the Chinese subsample. [2] German sample ($n = 411$): measured with BFI-10; Chinese sample ($n = 410$): measured with NEO-FFI.

### 3.2.3. Correlations

Table 4 shows bivariate correlations between the s-IAT and the Big Five personality traits, divided by country. In the German sample, *neuroticism* (positive), *extraversion*, and *conscientiousness* (both negative) indicated a significant relationship to the s-IAT with low effects. For the Chinese sample, all personality traits of the Big Five showed significant relations with the s-IAT. *Neuroticism*, *conscientiousness*, and *agreeableness* indicated the highest effect sizes. Except for *neuroticism*, all scores of the Big Five were negatively related to the scores of the s-IAT. According to Fisher's $z$ comparisons, the correlations between *neuroticism*, *extraversion*, *conscientiousness*, *agreeableness*, and the s-IAT were significantly different between both countries (see Table 4).

**Table 4.** Correlations between s-IAT and Big Five personality traits [1] (Pearson correlations) including Fisher's $z$ comparison.

| Domain/Variable [2] | Germany | | | China | | | Fisher's $z$ | | |
|---|---|---|---|---|---|---|---|---|---|
| | s-IAT Total Score | s-IAT LoC/TM [3] | s-IAT C/SP [3] | s-IAT Total Score | s-IAT LoC/TM [3] | s-IAT C/SP [3] | s-IAT Total Score | s-IAT LoC/TM [3] | s-IAT C/SP [3] |
| N | 0.219 ** | 0.180 ** | 0.213 ** | 0.502 ** | 0.438 ** | 0.504 ** | −4.70 ** | −4.11 ** | −4.83 ** |
| E | −0.242 ** | −0.183 ** | −0.254 ** | −0.186 ** | −0.155 ** | −0.195 ** | −0.84 | −0.41 | −0.89 |
| O | −0.012 | −0.056 | 0.043 | −0.160 ** | −0.105 * | −0.193 ** | 2.13 * | 0.70 | 3.40 ** |
| C | −0.192 ** | −0.204 ** | −0.131 ** | −0.365 ** | −0.377 ** | −0.308 ** | 2.69 ** | 2.71 ** | 2.66 ** |
| A | −0.030 | 0.023 | −0.085 | −0.386 ** | −0.275 ** | −0.447 ** | 5.38 ** | 4.36 ** | 5.65 ** |

[1] German sample ($n$ = 411): measured with BFI-10; Chinese sample ($n$ = 410): measured with NEO-FFI. [2] N = neuroticism, E = extraversion, O = openness, C = conscientiousness, A = agreeableness. [3] LoC/TM = Loss of control/time management, C/SP = Craving/social problems. * $p \leq 0.05$, ** $p \leq 0.01$.

Table 5 includes the bivariate correlations between the s-IAT, ILQ and IUES scores, divided by country. For both countries, Internet-use expectancies correlated positively with the s-IAT total score and both subscores with medium to high effect sizes. The ILQ dimension *technical expertise* showed small significant correlations with the s-IAT scores in both samples. Here, the correlation between *technical expertise* and the s-IAT subscore *craving/social problems* differs significantly between Germany and China. The ILQ dimension *production and interaction* correlated positively with symptoms of an IUD in both countries. Regarding the domain *reflection and critical analysis*, the correlations just revealed significant positive and small effects with the s-IAT total score and the subscore *craving/social problems* in the Chinese sample. Here, Fisher's $z$ revealed significant differences between the countries. Lastly, the ILQ score for *self-regulation* showed significant negative correlations with IUD symptoms in the German but not in the Chinese sample (except for one s-IAT subdimension), resulting in a significant Fisher's $z$ comparison.

**Table 5.** Correlations between s-IAT and Internet literacy as well as Internet-use expectancies (Pearson correlations) including Fisher's $z$ comparison.

| Domain/Variable [1] | Germany | | | China | | | Fisher's $z$ | | |
|---|---|---|---|---|---|---|---|---|---|
| | s-IAT Total Score | s-IAT LoC/TM [2] | s-IAT C/SP [2] | s-IAT Total Score | s-IAT LoC/TM [2] | s-IAT C/SP [2] | s-IAT Total Score | s-IAT LoC/TM [2] | s-IAT C/SP [2] |
| **Internet-use expectancies** | | | | | | | | | |
| PR | 0.390 ** | 0.352 ** | 0.344 ** | 0.369 ** | 0.338 ** | 0.356 ** | 0.35 | 0.23 | −0.20 |
| AE | 0.567 ** | 0.507 ** | 0.505 ** | 0.556 ** | 0.480 ** | 0.564 ** | 0.23 | 0.51 | −1.18 |
| **Internet literacy** | | | | | | | | | |
| TE | 0.105 * | 0.120 * | 0.062 | 0.153 * | 0.069 | 0.215 ** | −0.70 | 0.74 | −2.23 * |
| PI | 0.317 ** | 0.236 ** | 0.339 ** | 0.346 ** | 0.298 ** | 0.350 ** | −0.47 | −0.95 | −0.18 |
| RCA | −0.074 | −0.064 | −0.068 | 0.165 ** | 0.086 | 0.221 ** | −3.44 ** | −2.15 * | −4.18 ** |
| SR | −0.516 ** | −0.531 ** | −0.375 ** | −0.088 | −0.185 ** | 0.018 | −6.89 ** | −5.77 ** | −5.88 ** |

[1] PR = positive reinforcement, AE = avoidance expectancies, TE = technical expertise, PI = production and interaction, RCA = reflection and critical analysis, SR = self-regulation. [2] LoC/TM = Loss of control/time management, C/SP = Craving/social problems. * $p \leq 0.05$, ** $p \leq 0.01$.

#### 3.2.4. Analyses of Interaction Effects

Based on the relationships found between certain Internet literacy domains and IUD symptoms as well as the different correlation effects between both samples, we calculated further moderated regression analyses to consider possible interaction effects between Internet literacy and the participants' cultural background explaining the level of IUD symptoms. Because particularly the two domains *reflection and critical analysis* as well as *self-regulation* revealed high cross-cultural differences regarding their association with IUD symptoms, we used these two domains as the predictors in the upcoming analyses.

In the first analysis, the ILQ score for *reflection and critical analysis* explained no significant amount of variance in the s-IAT total score ($R^2 = 0.001$, $F(1, 819) = 0.83$, $p = 0.361$). Nevertheless, the country ($\Delta R^2 = 0.155$, $\Delta F(1, 818) = 149.94$, $p < 0.001$) and the interaction term of both variables explained a significant part of variance ($\Delta R^2 = 0.012$, $\Delta F(1, 817) = 11.75$, $p = 0.001$). The whole moderation model explained 16.8% of the s-IAT score's variance ($R^2 = 0.168$, $F(3, 817) = 54.89$, $p < 0.001$; see Table 6, model 1 for beta-coefficients).

For further illustration of this interaction effect, we calculated simple slope analysis (see Figure 2). The slope illustrating the Chinese sample was significantly different from zero ($t = 3.73$, $p < 0.001$). The slope for Germany was not significant ($t = 1.32$, $p = 0.187$). These results indicate that there was an effect of reflective skills on the level of IUD symptoms in the Chinese sample. More detailed, Chinese participants with higher reflective skills tend to indicate higher s-IAT total scores in contrast to participants with lower skills. In the German sample the domain of *reflection and critical analysis* revealed no significant effect on IUD symptoms.

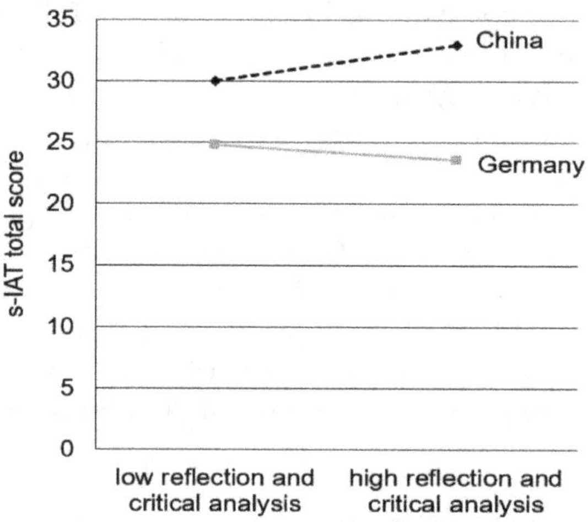


**Figure 2.** Simple slopes to illustrate the interaction effect between reflection and critical analysis and country on the s-IAT total score.

Secondly, we calculated a moderated regression analysis where we added the ILQ domain *self-regulation* as the predictor. Here, the score for *self-regulation* ($R^2 = 0.078$, $F(1, 819) = 68.83$, $p < 0.001$), the country ($\Delta R^2 = 0.140$, $\Delta F(1, 818) = 145.76$, $p < 0.001$), and the interaction term of both variables explained a significant part of variance ($\Delta R^2 = 0.026$, $\Delta F(1, 817) = 27.90$, $p < 0.001$). All variables explained 24.3% of the s-IAT score's variance ($R^2 = 0.243$, $F(3, 817) = 87.37$, $p < 0.001$; see Table 6, model 2 for beta-coefficients).

Simple slope analysis revealed significant slopes for the Chinese ($t = 2.08$, $p = 0.038$) and the German sample ($t = 9.69$, $p < 0.001$). However, while the effect of self-regulating skills is relatively low in the Chinese sample, in the German sample higher self-regulative skills reduce the score for IUD symptoms considerably in contrast to the Chinese sample (see Figure 3).

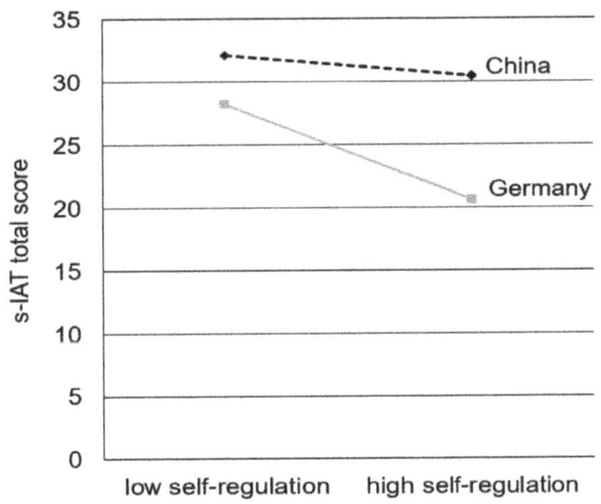


**Figure 3.** Simple slopes to illustrate the interaction effect between self-regulation and country on the s-IAT total score.

**Table 6.** Regression coefficients of the moderated regression analyses with the s-IAT total score as dependent variable.

| | *B* | *SE (B)* | *β* | *t* | *p* |
|---|---|---|---|---|---|
| **Model 1** | | | | | |
| Reflection and critical analysis | 0.44 | 0.31 | 0.046 | 1.42 | 0.156 |
| Country | 7.26 | 0.59 | 0.393 | 12.28 | <0.001 |
| Interaction | 2.14 | 0.63 | 0.111 | 3.42 | 0.001 |
| **Model 2** | | | | | |
| Self-regulation | −2.32 | 0.28 | −0.252 | −8.27 | <0.001 |
| Country | −6.91 | 0.56 | −0.374 | −12.278 | <0.001 |
| Interaction | −2.96 | 0.56 | −0.161 | −5.28 | <0.001 |

## 4. Discussion

This study is the first one investigating a cultural comparison of the relationship between personal core characteristics, specific Internet-related cognitions and skills, as well as symptoms of an IUD. The present study's first aim was to verify whether previous findings on the effect of personality traits as well as state variables like Internet-use expectancies and Internet literacy on the development and maintenance of an IUD are stable across different cultures and nations. Another purpose was to point out potential differences in the relationship of these variables between two countries from different cultural areas.

### *4.1. IUD Symptoms*

By using the same questionnaire across both countries, we found significant higher IUD symptoms in the Chinese sample, where the average total score of the s-IAT was almost at the cut-off score for a problematic Internet use. The significant cultural difference is reflected by the prevalence rates found in both countries: Whereas 6% of the German sample indicated a pathological Internet use, which value is in line with former epidemiological studies [7,65], 23% of the Chinese sample indicated an excessive and pathological use of the Internet. This rate is much higher than the prevalence reported for China in recent studies, where the rates range between 8 and 15 percent [66–68]. A different age range as well as different locations of recruitment in this study may explain the higher prevalence compared to previous investigations. Further, the year of publication could explain varying IUD frequencies, since prevalence rates could have been grown in the recent five years. Higher prevalence rates of IUD in Asian countries with respect to Western cultures have also been reported in the past [7,14]. However, because of the missing clinical evidence and differentiating diagnostic criteria of the methods used, reported prevalence rates generally have to be compared with caution.

### 4.2. Theoretical Integration of the Results

In the following, we want to integrate the results of this study into a recently published theoretical framework, called the I-PACE model (I-PACE stands for Interaction of Person-Affect-Cognition-Execution). In this empirically based model, Brand et al. [2] illustrate different stages of the addiction process of specific Internet-use disorders. The model illustrates the interaction of person's core characteristics, such as personality traits, social cognitions, and psychopathological symptoms (P-component) and possible mediating or moderating state variables like coping styles, Internet-related cognitive biases, as well as affective and cognitive responses (A/C-component). According to the authors, the interaction of these variables lead to the decision to use a certain application (E-component). The later experienced gratification could positively reinforce such mediating and moderating effects, resulting in an addictive use.

#### 4.2.1. Personality

In accordance with the addiction process described in the I-PACE model, we start to discuss our findings regarding the Big Five personality traits. The found cultural differences in the traits extraversion, openness, and neuroticism are in line with a worldwide comparative study, where East Asian countries indicated the lowest scores of extraversion and openness as well as the highest scores in neuroticism [37]. The results on conscientiousness (no significant difference) and agreeableness (higher scores in China), are in line with typical national stereotypes. Both German and Chinese citizens are described as working hard to reach their goals and having a strong will power [69–72]. This cultural commonality might be reflected by a comparable score in the conscientiousness scale of both samples. In addition, China is considered as a nation tending to hierarchical structures and following social norms [69]. This could be reflected by higher levels of agreeableness of the Chinese sample compared to the German sample. However, the agreeableness finding speaks against observations, where Chinese samples scored significantly lower on agreeableness compared to a German sample [63,73]. It remains difficult to interpret and ascribe the found personality differences solely to cultural differences. Therefore, the results of this study have to be interpreted cautiously. Previous German and Chinese studies on the association between personality, general Internet use and IUDs revealed controversial results, but most consistent relations have been found between IUDs, low conscientiousness and high neuroticism [2,19,74–76]. Following this, we could show similar findings by indicating significant correlations between high neuroticism, low conscientiousness and IUD symptoms in both countries. Both traits revealed higher effect sizes in the Chinese sample, meaning that higher levels of neuroticism and lower levels of conscientiousness are more strongly associated with IUD symptoms in China than in Germany. Our results also demonstrate negative correlations between openness, agreeableness, and IUD symptoms in the Chinese sample. Regarding extraversion, significant relationships in both countries were found, which do not significantly differ. While interpreting these results, it must be considered that some personality factors have not been extracted consistently over several cultural regions [37]. Furthermore, the Big Five personality model mostly displays typical traits of people living in Western individualistic cultures but not of citizens in Asian cultures, which are more collectivistic [37]. This could lead to the different effects of some of the Big Five personality traits on IUD symptoms in both samples.

#### 4.2.2. Internet-Related Cognitions and Skills

The next level of the I-PACE model comprises mediating and moderating state variables between the P-component and the decision to use a certain application. In this study, this component is represented by Internet-use expectancies and Internet literacy. Regarding Internet use expectancies, we found that Chinese participants indicated higher expectancies towards the Internet as a useful tool to reduce stress or to feel confident compared with the German sample. This is in line with Li and Kirkup [13], who found cultural differences between British and Chinese students regarding Internet experiences and attitudes. Although higher use expectancies were accompanied with higher IUD scores in both countries, no significant cultural differences regarding the strength of this relationship were found. There are already some empirical German studies underlining Internet-use expectancies as mediating variables, reinforcing the effect between personal predispositions and IUD symptoms [20,21,44,57]. Our study's results suggest similar effects in China, but further research with mean structure analyses is needed to investigate the role of Internet-use expectancies in the addiction process in a cross-cultural comparison.

Even though Internet literacy covers no inherent part in the I-PACE model, previous studies already indicated that Internet-related skills play an important role in the addiction process, e.g., [21,22,51]. Further, the dimensions of Internet literacy postulated by Stodt et al. [22] share similarities with Internet-related cognitive biases, as productive and interactive skills are a result of the subjective awareness of today's technological possibilities. In addition, the possession of self-regulative skills is theoretically accompanied with addiction-related concepts like cue-reactivity and craving as well as coping mechanisms. This study indicates less productive and interactive skills as well as higher reflective and analyzing skills of the German compared to the Chinese sample. Besides that, our analyses revealed two further interesting findings on the interaction between Internet literacy and IUD symptoms across both countries. Firstly, reflective and analytical skills seem to play no role in the development and maintenance of an IUD in German individuals. In contrast, we found a positive relationship between reflective skills and IUD symptoms in the Chinese sample. Simple slope analyses illustrated that Chinese participants show higher symptoms of an IUD compared to the German sample, but surprisingly indicate the highest symptomatology, when reflective skills are well-marked. At first site, this result appears to be counterintuitive, since reflective skills have been emphasized as preventive factors in past studies, e.g., [22]. However, it can be assumed that culture affects in what way an effect of reflective skills on IUD symptoms can occur. People living in collectivistic cultures like China are described as being more concerned about the effect of one's own behavior on others [11]. It can be assumed that the possession of reflective skills is necessary to evaluate this effect. In fact that in online environments such as games or social networks the interaction with others displays an essential feature, it could be that especially collectivistic thinking people with high reflective skills tend to use such applications more frequently and intense while neglecting personal needs and duties, leading to higher IUD symptoms. Past studies already investigated that people living in collectivistic countries are associated with a preference for online social interaction and appreciate their online social network [77,78].

Secondly, the ability to self-regulate one's own Internet use had just a low negative effect on the level of IUD symptoms among Chinese participants. On the other hand, the effect of self-regulation was much higher in the German sample, where individuals who cannot self-regulate their Internet-use behavior showed higher IUD symptoms compared to the people who have good self-regulation skills. The latter finding is in line with former research, where people with symptoms of an IUD reported problems in regulating and controlling their own Internet-use [21,22]. Regarding Cloninger [79], higher self-regulation abilities (in the offline context) are associated with higher self-directedness. Furthermore, people scoring high on self-directedness indicate high levels of self-esteem, will-power, and are self-satisfied with their own personality and problem-solving. As a result the authors emphasized self-directedness as an important personality dimension affecting personality disorders. Further, less self-directed people indicate higher symptoms of an IUD [29,30,80–83]. In a cross-cultural study by Sariyska et al. [30], however, the relation between self-directedness and IUD was slightly different across countries. Here, the effect sizes in two Chinese samples were lower than in the German sample. Our study found that even though online-focused self-regulation is not different across both investigated countries, it has no significant impact on IUD in China. Putting it together with previous research, these findings suggest the existence of heterogeneous mechanisms and effects regarding the interaction of online-focused self-regulation skills, self-directedness, and IUD symptoms in different countries and cultures.

### 4.3. Further Theoretical Integration

In the following, further reasons regarding the described cultural differences are discussed. The continuum of collectivism and individualism represents a frequently studied dimension of cultural variability, showing high differences such as between European and Asian countries, e.g., [12,84,85]. While European population indicates a higher degree of individualism, resulting from being more concerned about consequences of one's own behavior, needs, and goals, Asian population displays higher degrees of collectivism, represented by being more concerned of one's own behavior on others, collective needs, and group goals [11,12]. Further, individuals living in collectivistic societies show greater levels of a need to belong, while members of individualistic cultures show a greater need for self-presentation [11,84,86]. Also comparing a German and a Chinese sample, a recent study by Montag et al. [12] pointed out that low acceptance of power distance as a predictive factor for IUD symptoms, especially in males and Chinese individuals. The authors assume that an individual's greater acceptance of power distance and the higher exerted power on themselves leads to the desire to find a way and place to relieve from stress, which could be the Internet.

Furthermore, China displays the world's fastest growing Internet population [87] with an increasing online gaming industry [88]. Especially in today's social, mobile, or online role-playing games, it is necessary for users to play together with others to reach certain group goals. It can be assumed that the collectivistic orientation within the Chinese society contribute to a high involvement in online gaming as well as social networking due to its collaborative features. Further, the competitive character of online games as well as further social factors (e.g., socializing, giving support, teamwork) display important motivational factors for playing online games [89,90], which could be more distinct in collectivistic cultures. Specific using motives have been assumed as significant predictors of an addictive behavior [2]. Further studies should examine potential effects of collectivism/individualism in different countries and its impact on (excessive) Internet use.

### 4.4. Practical Implications for Both Countries

Although both investigated samples are not representative for its respective population, we think that this study's results could give a contribution to prevention and intervention programs in both nations, which are mentioned in the following.

#### 4.4.1. Practical Implications for Germany

The results of the current study point IUD out as a significant problem within the investigated German sample, where especially two Internet literacy domains are related to higher symptoms: higher productive/interactive as well as lower self-regulative skills. Besides, no considerable effect of technical and reflective skills on tendencies towards an IUD have been found. These correlations strengthen the findings by Stodt et al. [22], who stated that pure technical skills do not counteract a dysfunctional Internet use. As demonstrated in the I-PACE model and relying on empirical investigations, Internet-related cognitions and skills play a key role in the process of developing a specific Internet-use disorder [2,20,21]. Such state factors could be addressed in specific training programs and probably diminish the effect of dysfunctional personality factors and psychopathological symptoms on the development of an IUD. Currently, the improvement of self-regulative skills (without disregarding technical knowledge) still does not find its way into today's curricula of media and/or Internet literacy in Germany. Based on the current findings, we recommend to include the improvement of self-regulative skills in current curricula of media competence in Germany.

#### 4.4.2. Practical Implications for China

Statistics revealed high occurrence of a pathological use of the Internet as well as a high number of people who indicated a problematic use in the investigated sample, mostly consisting of university students. Taking the pathological and the problematic groups together, more than half of the Chinese sample indicated at least a problematic Internet use, pointing towards a serious health problem in these Chinese students. Previous studies from China showed that especially university freshmen suffer from higher IUD symptoms, often associated with psychopathological symptoms, such as depressive symptoms, social anxiety, or higher levels of loneliness [24]. These findings emphasize the importance of prevention and intervention programs not only in middle school, but also in university. Such programs should screen for high-risk Internet users and focus on the improvement of Internet-related cognitions and skills that are related to IUD symptoms, as the current study shows. More detailed, Chinese participants indicated to have high expectancies towards the use of the Internet. Those people who think that the Internet is helpful to avoid negative feelings, like stress and loneliness, or to gain positive emotions to a high degree tend to use the Internet more excessively. That is why prevention and intervention programs in China should focus on the outcomes people expect by using certain Internet applications and should demonstrate alternative coping strategies. Besides that, self-regulation skills are not correlated with the s-IAT total score in the Chinese students, which is different from the German sample. Nevertheless, based on the results of the current study that specific skills play a significant role in the development and maintenance of an IUD, we propose to include such skills in current prevention programs. Future studies should address how these skills could be systematically integrated in upcoming prevention programs.

### *4.5. Limitations*

Some limitations of this study need to be addressed in the following. First, the use of two different questionnaires for measuring the Big Five personality traits, the BFI-10, which was used in the German sample, and the NEO-FFI, which was used in the Chinese sample, could be a reason for the different results regarding the personality traits and their impact on IUD symptoms in both samples. Nevertheless, the use of these two questionnaires was carefully considered during planning the study. In previous studies, the BFI-10 displayed a valid and reliable instrument with good psychometric properties in German samples. Further, its 10-item version is very efficient and advantageous for the use in online studies, where time is limited. For the best of our knowledge, there is no valid and evaluated short version of a Big Five questionnaire in Chinese language (to be more precise: please see that the BFI-10 has been published in Mandarin, recently, but a problem concerning one introversion/extraversion item is discussed in Lachmann et al. [61]). That is why we decided to use the 60-item version of the NEO-FFI, which has been used in several Asian studies before and therefore displays a well-evaluated instrument. Although, the NEO-FFI is also evaluated sufficiently in Germany and other Western countries, we used the BFI-10 in the German data collection due to practical reasons and its above mentioned advantages.

One further limitation is the removal of one item out of the subscale *reflection and critical analysis* of the ILQ in the Chinese sample. We had to remove this item directly after data collection because of a problematic translation, which could lead to different possible understandings by the participants. Additionally, the removal should ensure the subscale's content validity. Regarding the subscale's internal consistency, Cronbach's $\alpha$ was still in the acceptable range. With the removal of one item, we do not expect different results because the remaining items substantially represent the same theoretical facet. For the German sample, we additionally calculated all analyses including the subscale *reflection and critical analysis* again with the same three items as used in the Chinese sample. The results did not differ between the three- and four-item solutions.

As a further limitation, the different factorial structures of the s-IAT, IUES, and ILQ in both nations, which are based on weak model fits in mean structure analyses, have to be mentioned. Even if the analyses revealed non-acceptable model fits, we had a closer look on the factor loadings within both nations. Here, every item loaded significantly on its theoretically suggested and empirically approved factor with just slightly varying effects between both nations. Therefore, we assume that the results of the current study are quite comparable. Further, former studies already demonstrated the applicability of the s-IAT and the IUES in a cross-cultural setting, e.g., [57]. However, further studies are needed to test if these questionnaires are suitable for investigating cross-cultural issues.

Furthermore, limitations regarding the representativeness of both investigated samples exist. First, in China and Germany data was collected from convenience samples. Whereas German participants came from all over Germany and were not recruited in a specific region, Chinese data was collected in two certain cities exclusively due to location-dependent reasons, which may have led to region-based effects. Second, the Chinese sample almost consisted of university students, whereas the German sample also contains participants who are employed. Strictly speaking, these facts reduce the level of generalizability and interpretation of the findings in terms of underlying cultural differences. Nevertheless, the German sample was predominately well educated with a high number of participants holding a university degree. Furthermore, both samples did not differ in age and gender. At this point, we want to clarify that this study did not have the intention to examine cultural differences with two nationally representative samples. Notwithstanding, although several limitations exist that have to be beared in mind, this study indicated several similarities between both nations (e.g., level of Internet-use expectancies and personality correlations) which are theoretically grounded and indicate global effects. On the other hand, the differences found between both nations (influence of reflective and regulative skills) have to be interpreted with caution. Here, further replications are necessary to check the meaningfulness of these results. Hence, this study's findings provide evidence that cultural differences between Germany and China regarding symptoms of an IUD and influencing trait and state variables could exist. However, these differences need to be replicated and further investigated in upcoming research explicitly.

### 4.6. Future Directions

This study suggests some directions for upcoming research. Future studies should address possible mediating and moderating effects between personality traits, Internet-related cognitions and skills, as well as IUD symptoms across different countries such as by using structural equation modelling and mean structure analyses. Based on the findings of this study, examining certain parts and interaction effects of the I-PACE model with representative samples from different countries would be helpful promoting a better understanding of cultural differences in IUD. Additionally, further empirical studies should focus on the role of one person's knowledge and skills, which could represent additional mediating or moderating factors in the addiction process but have not been a part of previous theoretical models. Furthermore, there are just a few longitudinal studies covering IUD.

The investigation of long-term effects in different countries and cultures would be helpful to shed light onto the reinforcing or protective value of Internet literacy and further Internet-related cognitive biases on the development and maintenance of an IUD and respective cultural differences. Especially, longitudinal designs would be helpful to develop specific prevention and intervention programs.

## 5. Conclusions

The present study strengthens previous findings on the effect of personality traits as well as state variables such as Internet-use expectancies and Internet literacy domains on the development and maintenance of an IUD within two samples from different countries and cultural areas. In addition, some interesting country-specific differences regarding these variables and their relationship to symptoms of an IUD were pointed out. Next to a higher occurrence of IUD symptoms in the Chinese sample compared to the German sample, Chinese participants scored significantly higher on the Big Five personality traits of neuroticism and agreeableness, whereas German participants scored higher on the traits of extraversion and openness. However, please note that different inventories to measure the Big Five personality traits were applied in each country. Furthermore, Chinese individuals showed higher Internet-use expectancies to avoid negative feelings or to be positively reinforced. Further analyses indicated that Chinese participants with higher reflective skills regarding their Internet behavior indicated highest IUD symptoms, whereas such skills indicated no effect within the German sample. Moreover, higher skills in self-regulating one's own Internet use were accompanied with lower IUD symptoms in the German, but not in the Chinese sample. Despite the missing representativeness of both samples and some limitations of the current study, several theoretically grounded findings have to be underlined, strengthening the global applicability of this study and providing evidence that cultural differences between Germany and China regarding IUD symptoms and influencing trait and state variables could exist. Because Internet literacy domains seem to play a significant role in the development and maintenance of an IUD, we propose to encourage skills such as reflective and self-regulating skills in current or future IUD prevention programs, which should be individually matched to each countries conditions. Upcoming research should address the replication of this study's results to check its meaningfulness.

**Acknowledgments:** The position of Christian Montag is funded by a Heisenberg grant awarded to him by the German Research Foundation (DFG, MO 2363/3-2). Cornelia Sindermann is a stipend of the German Academic Scholarship Foundation (Studienstiftung des deutschen Volkes). Moreover, the study has been funded by a grant to study Internet-gaming disorder and Internet addiction by the German Research Foundation (DFG, MO 2363/2-1).

**Author Contributions:** Christian Montag and Matthias Brand designed the present study. Benjamin Stodt wrote the manuscript and carried out the statistical analysis. Elisa Wegmann, Matthias Brand and Benjamin Stodt collected the German data. Cornelia Sindermann, Christian Montag and Mei Li collected the Chinese data. Min Zhou and Peng Sha were responsible for the translation process of the inventories into the Chinese language. All authors critically revised the manuscript and approved the final version.

# Appendix A

**Table A1.** Short Internet Addiction Test (s-IAT) in English, German, and Chinese language.

| | English | German | Chinese |
|---|---|---|---|
| 1. | How often do you find that you stay online longer than you intended? | Wie oft stellen Sie fest, dass Sie länger als beabsichtigt im Internet waren? | 你经常会发现自己在网上呆的时间比你预期的要长么? |
| 2. | How often do you neglect household chores to spend more time online? | Wie oft vernachlässigen Sie alltägliche Pflichten, um mehr Zeit online zu verbringen? | 你经常会为了在网上多呆一会儿而忽略家务琐事么? |
| 3. | How often do your grades or school work suffer because of the amount of time you spend online? | Wie häufig leidet Ihre schulische, Ihre universitäre oder Ihre berufliche Arbeit darunter, dass Sie so viel Zeit online verbringen? | 你经常会因为上网用了很多时间而耽误了成绩或者大学的功课么? |
| 4. | How often do you become defensive or secretive when anyone asks you what you do online? | Wie häufig reagieren Sie ausweichend oder verteidigend, wenn Sie jemand fragt, was Sie online tun? | 你经常会在别人问起你在网上做什么的时候变得防御或者遮遮掩掩么? |
| 5. | How often do you snap, yell, or act annoyed if someone bothers you while you are online? | Wie oft reagieren Sie patzig, schimpfen oder sind genervt, wenn Sie jemand stört, während Sie online sind? | 你经常会因为别人打扰你上网而呵斥、大叫或者作出生气的行为么? |
| 6. | How often do you lose sleep due to being online late at night? | Wie oft fehlt Ihnen Schlaf, weil Sie spät nachts noch online sind? | 你经常会因为上网到半夜而失眠么? |
| 7. | How often do you feel preoccupied with the Internet when offline, or fantasize about being online? | Wie oft denken Sie ans Internet, wenn Sie offline sind oder stellen sich vor, online zu sein? | 你经常会在线下的时候总想着上网的事情或者想象着在网络上么? |
| 8. | How often do you find yourself saying "just a few more minutes" when online? | Wie oft ertappen Sie sich dabei zu sagen: "Nur noch ein paar Minuten", während Sie online sind? | 你经常会发现在上网时你对自己说"再多几分钟"么? |
| 9. | How often do you try to cut down the amount of time you spend online and fail? | Wie häufig versuchen Sie weniger Zeit im Internet zu verbringen und schaffen es nicht? | 你经常试图减少上网的时间但是却以失败告终么? |
| 10. | How often do you try to hide how long you've been online? | Wie häufig versuchen Sie zu verbergen, wie lange Sie online waren? | 你经常会尝试隐瞒实际在网上呆的时间么? |
| 11. | How often do you choose to spend more time online over going out with others? | Wie oft kommt es vor, dass Sie lieber mehr Zeit online verbringen als mit Anderen etwas zu unternehmen? | 你经常会在网络上花费的时间比与他人一起外出的时间更多么? |
| 12. | How often do you feel depressed, moody, or nervous when you are offline, which goes away once you are back online? | Wie oft fühlen Sie sich deprimiert, verstimmt oder nervös, wenn Sie offline sind – was sich ändert, wenn Sie wieder online sind? | 你经常会因为下线而感到郁闷、不高兴或焦虑，而一旦上网这些感受就烟消云散了么? |

Items must be answered on a 5-point Likert scale with the following response levels: 1 = never/nie/从不, 2 = rarely/selten/很少, 3 = sometimes/manchmal/有时, 4 = often/oft/经常, 5 = very often/sehr oft/非常常见. Scoring of the s-IAT scales: *Total score* is based on the sum score of all 12 items; *Loss of control/time management* is based on the sum score of the following items: 1, 2, 3, 6, 8, 9; *Craving/social problems* is based on the sum score of the following items: 4, 5, 7, 10, 11, 12.

**Table A2.** Internet-Use Expectancies Scale (IUES) in English, German, and Chinese language.

| | English | German | Chinese |
|---|---|---|---|
| | I use the Internet because it makes possible/facilitates ... | Ich nutze das Internet, weil es mir ermöglicht/erleichtert ... | 我使用网络是因为它在如下方面创造了可能性／便利性: |
| 1. | to experience pleasure. | Freude zu erleben. | 为了体验快乐。 |
| 2. | to distract from problems. | Problemen aus dem Weg zu gehen. | 为了从问题（麻烦）中转移注意力。 |
| 3. | to have fun. | Spaß zu haben. | 为了玩得愉快。 |
| 4. | to avoid loneliness. | Gefühle der Einsamkeit zu vermeiden. | 为了避免孤独。 |
| 5. | to feel good. | mich gut zu fühlen. | 为了感觉好。 |
| 6. | to escape from reality. | vor der Realität zu flüchten. | 为了逃避现实。 |
| 7. | to gain positive emotions. | positive Gefühle zu erreichen. | 为了获得正性情感。 |
| 8. | to avoid annoying duties. | lästige Aufgaben zu vermeiden. | 为了回避恼人的责任。 |

Items must be answered on a 6-point Likert scale with the following response levels: 1 = completely disagree/stimme gar nicht zu/完全不同意, 2 = disagree/stimme nicht zu/不同意, 3 = rather disagree/stimme eher nicht zu/有一点不同意, 4 = rather agree/stimme eher zu/有点同意, 5 = agree/stimme zu/同意, 6 = completely agree/stimme voll und ganz zu/完全同意. Scoring of the IUES scales: *Positive reinforcement* is based on the mean score of the following items: 1, 3, 5, 7; *Avoidance expectancies* is based on the mean score of the following items: 2, 4, 6, 8.

**Table A3.** Internet Literacy Questionnaire (ILQ) in English, German, and Chinese language.

| | English | German | Chinese |
|---|---|---|---|
| 1. | I can quickly familiarize myself with new sites on the Internet or applications I have not used before. | Ich kann mich schnell mit neuen Internetseiten oder -anwendungen vertraut machen, die ich zuvor noch nicht benutzt habe. | 我能够很快熟悉那些我从未使用过的网站和应用。 |
| 2. | It is easy for me to limit my Internet use when I notice that it has a negative effect on my private life. | Es fällt mir leicht, meinen Internetkonsum einzuschränken, wenn ich merke, dass er sich negativ auf mein Privatleben auswirkt. | 当我察觉网络使用已经对我的个人生活产生负面影响时，我可以很容易地控制自己使用网络。 |
| 3. | It is easier to maintain social contacts on the Internet than offline. | Es ist einfacher im Internet soziale Kontakte zu pflegen als offline. | 在网络中保持社交接触比线下更容易。 |
| 4. | I make sure to use the Internet to an extent that is appropriate for me. | Ich achte darauf, das Internet in einem für mich angemessenen Umfang zu nutzen. | 我确保在一个对我适度的范围内使用网络。 |
| 5. | I can easily assess the credibility of information on websites even when I am not familiar with the topic. | Ich kann Informationen auf Internetseiten mühelos hinsichtlich ihrer Glaubwürdigkeit einschätzen, auch wenn mir das Thema nicht vertraut ist. | 即便在不熟悉的领域里，我也可以比较容易地确定网站上的信息的可信程度。 |

**Table A3.** *Cont.*

| | English | German | Chinese |
|---|---|---|---|
| 6. | I inform myself regularly about developments regarding the Internet. | Ich informiere mich regelmäßig über Entwicklungen im Bereich des Internets. | 我经常关注互联网发展方面的信息。 |
| 7. | When I am online, I make sure that my Internet use does not negatively affect my private life. | Wenn ich online bin, achte ich darauf, dass sich meine Internetnutzung nicht negativ auf mein Privatleben auswirkt. | 当我在线的时候，我会注意我的网络使用情况不会对我的个人生活造成负面的影响。 |
| 8. | I notice very quickly when my counterpart on the Internet is pretending. | Ich merke sehr schnell, wenn sich mein Gegenüber im Internet verstellt. | 当对方在网络上假意的时候，我很快可以注意到。 |
| 9. | Friends and acquaintances ask me for advice when they have problems with Internet applications. | Freunde und Bekannte fragen mich nach Rat, wenn sie Probleme mit Internetanwendungen haben. | 当朋友们或熟人们遇到网络运用方面的问题时会请教我。 |
| 10. | Causally exchanging views with other people on the Internet is easier than offline. | Im Internet kann man sich zwangloser mit anderen Personen austauschen als offline. | 在线上和他人随意地交换观点要比在线下更加容易。 |
| 11. | It is easier for me to make casual contact with another person online than offline. | Es fällt mir online leichter, unverbindlichen Kontakt mit einer anderen Person zu knüpfen als offline. | 对我来说，与别人建立一般的联系在线上要比在线下更容易。 |
| 12. | I can easily assess what others on the Internet want to achieve with their behavior. | Ich kann gut einschätzen, was Andere im Internet mit ihrem Verhalten bezwecken wollen. | 在网络中　我能比较容易地从他人的行为中推断出他们想要达到的目的。 |
| 13. | I can tell the difference between credible and untrustworthy content on the Internet. | Ich kann zwischen glaubwürdigen und unglaubwürdigen Inhalten im Internet unterscheiden. | 我能在网络中分辨清楚可信和不可信的内容。 |
| 14. | It is easier for me to be creative online than offline. | Es fällt mir online leichter kreativ zu sein als offline. | 对我来说，在线上比线下更容易有创造力。 |
| 15. | I go offline when I feel I have done or found everything on the Internet that is relevant at the time. | Ich gehe offline, wenn ich das Gefühl habe, alles gerade Relevante im Internet erledigt oder gefunden zu haben. | 当我认为已经找到相关的信息或处理完相关的事情后，我就会下线。 |
| 16. | When I am on the Internet, I make sure not to be online longer than planned. | Wenn ich im Internet bin, achte ich darauf, dass ich nicht länger als beabsichtigt online bin. | 当我使用网络时，我会确保不要超过计划的时间。 |
| 17. | I can deal with errors in computer software and apps and can fix them myself. | Ich kann mit auftretenden Fehlern in Computerprogrammen/Apps umgehen und sie eigenständig beheben. | 我会自己处理和修理电脑软件和应用软件里的错误。 |
| 18. | I can more easily express myself on a topic on the Internet than offline. | Im Internet kann ich mich leichter zu einem Thema äußern als offline. | 与线下相比，在网络上我更容易针对某一个话题发表自己的观点。 |

Items must be answered on a Likert scale of six response levels from 0 (=strongly disagree/stimme überhaupt nicht zu/非常不同意) to 5 (=strongly agree/stimme vollkommen zu/非常同意). Scoring of the ILQ scales: *Technical expertise* is based on the mean score of the following items: 1, 6, 9, 17; *Production & interaction* is based on the mean score of the following items: 3, 10, 11, 14, 18; *Reflection & critical analysis* is based on the mean score of the following items: 5, 8, 12, 13; *Self-regulation* is based on the mean score of the following items: 2, 4, 7, 15, 16.

## References


1. Davis, R.A. A cognitive-behavioral model of pathological Internet use. *Comput. Hum. Behav.* **2001**, *17*, 187–195. [CrossRef]
2. Brand, M.; Young, K.; Laier, C.; Wölfling, K.; Potenza, M. Integrating psychological and neurobiological considerations regarding the development and maintenance of specific Internet-use disorders: An Interaction of Person-Affect-Cognition-Execution (I-PACE) model. *Neurosci. Biobehav. Rev.* **2016**, *71*, 252–266. [CrossRef] [PubMed]
3. Brand, M.; Young, K.S.; Laier, C. Prefrontal control and Internet addiction: A theoretical model and review of neuropsychological and neuroimaging findings. *Front. Hum. Neurosci.* **2014**, *8*, 375. [CrossRef] [PubMed]
4. Montag, C.; Bey, K.; Sha, P.; Li, M.; Chen, Y.-F.; Liu, W.-Y.; Zhu, Y.-K.; Li, C.-B.; Markett, S.; Keiper, J.; et al. Is it meaningful to distinguish between generalized and specific Internet addiction? Evidence from a cross-cultural study from Germany, Sweden, Taiwan and China. *Asia Pac. Psychiatry* **2015**, *7*, 20–26. [CrossRef] [PubMed]
5. American Psychiatric Association. *Diagnostic and Statistical Manual of Mental Disorders*, 5th ed.; American Psychiatric Publishing: Washington, DC, USA, 2013; ISBN 8123923791.
6. Cheng, C.; Li, A.Y.-L. Internet addiction prevalence and quality of (real) life: A meta-analysis of 31 nations across seven world regions. *Cyberpsychol. Behav. Soc. Netw.* **2014**, *17*, 755–760. [CrossRef] [PubMed]
7. Kuss, D.J.; Griffiths, M.; Karila, M.; Billieux, J. Internet addiction: A systematic review of epidemiological research for the last decade. *Curr. Pharm. Des.* **2014**, *20*, 4026–4052. [CrossRef] [PubMed]
8. Spada, M.M. An overview of problematic Internet use. *Addict. Behav.* **2014**, *39*, 3–6. [CrossRef] [PubMed]
9. Rumpf, H.-J.; Meyer, C.; Kreuzer, A.; John, U. Prävalenz der Internetabhängigkeit (PINTA). Bericht an das Bundesministerium für Gesundheit (Prevalence of Internet addiction (PINTA). Report to the Federal Ministry of Health). Available online: https://www.bundesgesundheitsministerium.de/fileadmin/Dateien/5_Publikationen/Drogen_und_Sucht/Berichte/Forschungsbericht/Studie_Praevalenz_der_Internetabhaengigkeit__PINTA_.pdf (accessed on 18 January 2018).
10. Ko, C.H.; Yen, J.Y.; Yen, C.F.; Chen, C.S.; Chen, C.C. The association between Internet addiction and psychiatric disorder: A review of the literature. *Eur. Psychiatry* **2012**, *27*, 1–8. [CrossRef] [PubMed]
11. Hofstede, G. *Culture's Consequences: International Differences in Work-related Values*; Sage Publications: Newbury Park, CA, USA, 1984; ISBN 0803913060.
12. Montag, C.; Duke, E.; Sha, P.; Zhou, M.; Sindermann, C.; Li, M. Does acceptance of power distance influence propensities for problematic Internet use? Evidence from a cross-cultural study. *Asia Pac. Psychiatry* **2016**, *8*, 296–301. [CrossRef] [PubMed]
13. Li, N.; Kirkup, G. Gender and cultural differences in Internet use: A study of China and the UK. *Comput. Educ.* **2007**, *48*, 301–317. [CrossRef]
14. Zhang, L.; Amos, C.; Mcdowell, W.C. A comparative study of Internet addiction between the United States and China. *Cyberpsychol. Behav.* **2008**, *11*, 727–729. [CrossRef] [PubMed]
15. Ko, D.; Yao, M. Internet addiction: An cross-cultural perspective. In *The Psychology of Social Networking Vol. 2: Identity and Relationships in Online Communities*; Riva, G., Wiederhold, B.K., Cipresso, P., Eds.; De Gruyter: Warsaw, Poland; Berlin, Germany, 2016; pp. 141–158, ISBN 3110473844.
16. Internet World Stats. World Internet Users and 2017 Population Stats. Available online: http://www.internetworldstats.com/stats.htm (accessed on 26 January 2018).
17. Internet Live Stats. Internet Users by Country. Available online: http://www.internetlivestats.com/internet-users-by-country/ (accessed on 26 January 2018).
18. Müller, K.W.; Glaesmer, H.; Brähler, E.; Wölfling, K.; Beutel, M.E. Prevalence of Internet addiction in the general population: Results from a German population-based survey. *Behav. Inf. Technol.* **2014**, *33*, 757–766. [CrossRef]
19. Pawlikowski, M.; Altstötter-Gleich, C.; Brand, M. Validation and psychometric properties of a short version of Young's Internet Addiction Test. *Comput. Human Behav.* **2013**, *29*, 1212–1223. [CrossRef]
20. Wegmann, E.; Brand, M. Internet-communication disorder: It's a matter of social aspects, coping, and Internet-use expectancies. *Front. Psychol.* **2016**, *7*, 1747. [CrossRef] [PubMed]

21. Wegmann, E.; Stodt, B.; Brand, M. Addictive use of social networking sites can be explained by the interaction of Internet use expectancies, Internet literacy, and psychopathological symptoms. *J. Behav. Addict.* **2015**, *4*, 155–162. [CrossRef] [PubMed]
22. Stodt, B.; Wegmann, E.; Brand, M. Predicting dysfunctional Internet use: The role of age, conscientiousness, and Internet literacy in Internet addiction and cyberbullying. *IJCBPL* **2016**, *6*, 28–43. [CrossRef]
23. Cao, F.; Su, L. Internet addiction among Chinese adolescents: Prevalence and psychological features. *Child Care Health Dev.* **2006**, *33*, 275–282. [CrossRef] [PubMed]
24. Ni, X.; Yan, H.; Chen, S.; Liu, Z. Factors influencing Internet addiction in a sample of freshmen university students in China. *Cyberpsychol. Behav.* **2009**, *12*, 327–330. [CrossRef] [PubMed]
25. Cao, F.; Su, L.; Liu, T.; Gao, X. The relationship between impulsivity and Internet addiction in a sample of Chinese adolescents. *Eur. Psychiatry* **2007**, *22*, 466–471. [CrossRef] [PubMed]
26. Nie, J.; Zhang, W.; Liu, Y. Exploring depression, self-esteem and verbal fluency with different degrees of Internet addiction among Chinese college students. *Compr. Psychiatry* **2017**, *72*, 114–120. [CrossRef] [PubMed]
27. Chak, K.; Leung, L. Shyness and locus of control as predictors of Internet addiction and Internet use. *Cyberpsychol. Behav.* **2004**, *7*, 559–570. [CrossRef] [PubMed]
28. Zhou, Y.; Li, D.; Li, X.; Wang, Y.; Zhao, L. Big five personality and adolescent Internet addiction: The mediating role of coping style. *Addict. Behav.* **2017**, *64*, 42–48. [CrossRef] [PubMed]
29. Montag, C.; Jurkiewicz, M.; Reuter, M. Low self-directedness is a better predictor for problematic Internet use than high neuroticism. *Comput. Hum. Behav.* **2010**, *26*, 1531–1535. [CrossRef]
30. Sariyska, R.; Reuter, M.; Bey, K.; Sha, P.; Li, M.; Chen, Y.F.; Liu, W.Y.; Zhu, Y.K.; Li, C.B.; Suárez-Rivillas, A.; et al. Self-esteem, personality and Internet addiction: A cross-cultural comparison study. *Pers. Individ. Differ.* **2014**, *61–62*, 28–33. [CrossRef]
31. Chaplin, W.F.; John, O.P.; Goldberg, L.R. Conceptions of states and traits: Dimensional attributes with ideals as prototypes. *J. Pers. Soc. Psychol.* **1988**, *54*, 541–557. [CrossRef] [PubMed]
32. Steyer, R.; Mayer, A.; Geiser, C.; Cole, D.A. A theory of states and traits - revised. *Annu. Rev. Clin. Psychol.* **2015**, *11*, 71–98. [CrossRef] [PubMed]
33. Sariyska, R.; Reuter, M.; Lachmann, B.; Montag, C. Attention deficit/hyperactivity disorder is a better predictor for problematic Internet use than depression: Evidence from Germany. *J. Addict. Res. Ther.* **2015**, *6*, 1–6. [CrossRef]
34. Prizant-Passal, S.; Shechner, T.; Aderka, I.M. Social anxiety and Internet use—A meta-analysis: What do we know? What are we missing? *Comput. Hum. Behav.* **2016**, *62*, 221–229. [CrossRef]
35. Goldberg, L.R. An alternative "description of personality": The Big-Five factor structure. *J. Pers. Soc. Psychol.* **1990**, *59*, 1216–1229. [CrossRef] [PubMed]
36. Soto, C.J.; John, O.P.; Gosling, S.D.; Potter, J. Age differences in personality traits from 10 to 65: Big Five domains and facets in a large cross-sectional sample. *J. Pers. Soc. Psychol.* **2011**, *100*, 330–348. [CrossRef] [PubMed]
37. Schmitt, D.P.; McCrae, R.R.; Bennett, K.L.; Grammer, K. The geographic distribution of Big Five personality traits—Patterns and profiles of human self-description across 56 nations. *J. Cross Cult. Psychol.* **2007**, *38*, 173–212. [CrossRef]
38. Hardie, E.; Tee, M.Y. Excessive Internet use: The role of personality, loneliness, and social support networks in Internet addiction. *AJETS* **2007**, *5*, 34–47.
39. Tsai, H.F.; Cheng, S.H.; Yeh, T.L.; Shih, C.-C.; Chen, K.C.; Yang, Y.C.; Yang, Y.K. The risk factors of Internet addiction—A survey of university freshmen. *Psychiatry Res.* **2009**, *167*, 294–299. [CrossRef] [PubMed]
40. Montag, C.; Reuter, M. Molecular genetics, personality and Internet addiction. In *Internet Addiction: Neuroscientific Approaches and Therapeutical Interventions*; Springer International Publishing: Heidelberg, Germany, 2015; pp. 93–109, ISBN 9781611226164.
41. Lee, Y.H.; Ko, C.H.; Chou, C. Re-visiting Internet addiction among Taiwanese students: A cross-sectional comparison of students' expectations, online gaming, and online social interaction. *J. Abnorm. Child Psychol.* **2015**, *43*, 589–599. [CrossRef] [PubMed]
42. Lin, M.-P.; Ko, H.-C.; Wu, J.Y.-W. The role of positive/negative outcome expectancy and refusal self-efficacy of Internet use on Internet addiction among college students in Taiwan. *Cyberpsychol. Behav.* **2008**, *11*, 451–457. [CrossRef] [PubMed]

43. Casale, S.; Caplan, S.E.; Fioravanti, G. Positive metacognitions about Internet use: The mediating role in the relationship between emotional dysregulation and problematic use. *Addict. Behav.* **2016**, *59*, 84–88. [CrossRef] [PubMed]
44. Brand, M.; Laier, C.; Young, K.S. Internet addiction: Coping styles, expectancies, and treatment implications. *Front. Psychol.* **2014**, *5*, 1256. [CrossRef] [PubMed]
45. Wu, J.Y.W.; Ko, H.C.; Tung, Y.Y.; Li, C.C. Internet use expectancy for tension reduction and disinhibition mediates the relationship between borderline personality disorder features and Internet addiction among college students—One-year follow-up. *Comput. Hum. Behav.* **2016**, *55*, 851–855. [CrossRef]
46. Iordache, C.; Mariën, I.; Baelden, D. Developing digital skills and competences: A quick-scan analysis of 13 digital literacy models. *IJSE* **2017**, *9*, 6–30. [CrossRef]
47. Martin, A.; Madigan, D. *Digital Literacies for Learning*; Facet: London, UK, 2006; ISBN 1856045633.
48. Jenkins, H. *Confronting the Challenges of Participatory Culture: Media Education for the 21st Century*; MIT Press: Cambridge, MA, USA, 2009; ISBN 978-0-262-51362-3.
49. Lin, T.-B.; Jen-Yi, L.; Deng, F.; Lee, L. Understanding new media literacy: An explorative theoretical framework. *J. Educ. Technol. Soc.* **2013**, *16*, 160–170.
50. Katz, I.R.; Elliot, N. Information literacy in digital environments: Construct mediation, construct modeling, and validation processes. In *Information Literacy: Research and Collaboration across Disciplines*; D'Angelo, B.J., Jamieson, S., Maid, B., Walker, J.R., Eds.; The WAC Clearinghouse: Fort Collins, CO, USA, 2016; pp. 97–116.
51. Leung, L.; Lee, P.S.N. The influences of information literacy, Internet addiction and parenting styles on Internet risks. *New Media Soc.* **2011**, *14*, 117–136. [CrossRef]
52. Fraillon, J.; Schulz, W.; Ainley, J. *International Computer and Information Literacy Study: Assessment Framework*; International Association for the Evaluation of Educational Achievement (IEA): Amsterdam, The Netherlands, 2013.
53. Johnson, G.M. Functional Internet literacy: Required cognitive skills with implications for instruction. *E-Learn. Digit. Media* **2007**, *4*, 433–441. [CrossRef]
54. Livingstone, S.; Helsper, E. Balancing opportunities and risks in teenagers' use of the Internet: The role of online skills and Internet self-efficacy. *New Media Soc.* **2009**, *12*, 309–329. [CrossRef]
55. LaRose, R.; Lin, C.A.; Eastin, M.S. Unregulated Internet usage: Addiction, habit, or deficient self-regulation? *Media Psychol.* **2003**, *5*, 225–253. [CrossRef]
56. Hahn, E.; Reuter, M.; Spinath, F.M.; Montag, C. Internet addiction and its facets: The role of genetics and the relation to self-directedness. *Addict. Behav.* **2017**, *65*, 137–146. [CrossRef] [PubMed]
57. Wegmann, E.; Oberst, U.; Stodt, B.; Brand, M. Online-specific fear of missing out and Internet-use expectancies contribute to symptoms of Internet-communication disorder. *Addict. Behav. Rep.* **2017**, *5*, 33–42. [CrossRef] [PubMed]
58. Eisinga, R.; Te Grotenhuis, M.; Pelzer, B. The reliability of a two-item scale: Pearson, Cronbach, or Spearman-Brown? *Int. J. Public Health* **2013**, *58*, 637–642. [CrossRef] [PubMed]
59. Young, K.S. *Caught in the Net: How to Recognize the Signs of Internet Addiction—And a Winning Strategy for Recovery*; John Wiley & Sons: New York, NY, USA, 1998; ISBN 0471191590.
60. Rammstedt, B.; John, O.P. Measuring personality in one minute or less: A 10-item short version of the Big Five Inventory in English and German. *J. Res. Pers.* **2007**, *41*, 203–212. [CrossRef]
61. Lachmann, B.; Sariyska, R.; Kannen, C.; Błaszkiewicz, K.; Trendafilov, B.; Andone, I.; Eibes, M.; Markowetz, A.; Li, M.; Kendrick, K.M.; et al. Contributing to overall life satisfaction: Personality traits versus life satisfaction variables revisited—Is replication impossible? *Behav. Sci.* **2018**, *8*, 1. [CrossRef] [PubMed]
62. Costa, P.T.; McCrae, R.R. *NEO Five-Factor Inventory (NEO-FFI): Professional Manual*; Psychological Assessment Resources: Odessa, FL, USA, 1989.
63. Melchers, M.C.; Li, M.; Haas, B.W.; Reuter, M.; Bischoff, L.; Montag, C. Similar personality patterns are associated with empathy in four different countries. *Front. Psychol.* **2016**, *7*, 290. [CrossRef] [PubMed]
64. Cohen, J. *Statistical Power Analysis for the Behavioral Sciences*; Lawrence Earlbaum Associates: Hillsdale, NJ, USA, 1988.
65. Durkee, T.; Kaess, M.; Carli, V.; Parzer, P.; Wasserman, C.; Floderus, B.; Apter, A.; Balazs, J.; Barzilay, S.; Bobes, J.; et al. Prevalence of pathological Internet use among adolescents in Europe: Demographic and social factors. *Addiction* **2012**, *107*, 2210–2222. [CrossRef] [PubMed]

66. Cao, H.; Sun, Y.; Wan, Y.; Hao, J.; Tao, F. Problematic Internet use in Chinese adolescents and its relation to psychosomatic symptoms and life satisfaction. *BMC Public Health* **2011**, *11*, 802. [CrossRef] [PubMed]
67. Liu, Q.-X.; Fang, X.-Y.; Deng, L.-Y.; Zhang, J.-T. Parent–adolescent communication, parental Internet use and Internet-specific norms and pathological Internet use among Chinese adolescents. *Comput. Hum. Behav.* **2012**, *28*, 1269–1275. [CrossRef]
68. Chi, X.; Lin, L.; Zhang, P. Internet addiction among college students in China: Prevalence and psychosocial correlates. *Cyberpsychol. Behav. Soc. Netw.* **2016**, *19*, 567–573. [CrossRef] [PubMed]
69. Bond, M.H. *The Oxford Handbook of Chinese Psychology*; Oxford Library of Psychology: Oxford, NY, USA, 2010; ISBN 019954185X.
70. Noesselt, N.; Schüller, M.; Schüler-Zhou, Y. Deutschland und China—Wahrnehmung und Realität—Die Huawei-Studie 2014 (Germany and China—Perception and Reality—The Huawei Study 2014). Available online: www.huawei-studie.de/downloads/Huawei-Studie-2014-DE.pdf (accessed on 24 January 2018).
71. Noesselt, N.; Schüller, M.; Schüler-Zhou, Y. Deutschland und China—Wahrnehmung und Realität—Die Huawei-Studie 2016 (Germany and China—Perception and Reality—The Huawei Study 2016). Available online: http://www.huawei-studie.de/downloads/Huawei-Studie-2016-DE.pdf (accessed on 24 January 2018).
72. Schroll-Machl, S. *Doing Business with Germans: Their Perception, Our Perception*; Vandenhoeck & Ruprecht: Göttingen, Germany, 2008; ISBN 3525461674.
73. Sindermann, C.; Luo, R.; Zhao, Z.; Li, M.; Kendrick, K.; Becker, B.; Panksepp, J.; Montag, C. High ANGER and low agreeableness predict vengefulness in German and Chinese participants. *Pers. Individ. Differ.* **2018**, *121*, 184–192. [CrossRef]
74. Müller, K.W.; Beutel, M.E.; Egloff, B.; Wölfling, K. Investigating risk factors for Internet gaming disorder: A comparison of patients with addictive gaming, pathological gamblers and healthy controls regarding the Big Five personality traits. *Eur. Addict. Res.* **2014**, *20*, 129–136. [CrossRef] [PubMed]
75. Hong, F.-Y.; Huang, D.-H.; Lin, H.-Y.; Chiu, S.-L. Analysis of the psychological traits, Facebook usage, and Facebook addiction model of Taiwanese university students. *Telemat. Inform.* **2014**, *31*, 597–606. [CrossRef]
76. Wang, C.-W.; Ho, R.T.H.; Chan, C.L.W.; Tse, S. Exploring personality characteristics of Chinese adolescents with Internet-related addictive behaviors: Trait differences for gaming addiction and social networking addiction. *Addict. Behav.* **2015**, *42*, 32–35. [CrossRef] [PubMed]
77. La Ferle, C.; Kim, H.-J. Cultural influences on Internet motivations and communication styles: A comparison of Korean and US consumers. *IJIMA* **2006**, *3*, 142–157. [CrossRef]
78. Xu-Priour, D.-L.; Truong, Y.; Klink, R.R. The effects of collectivism and polychronic time orientation on online social interaction and shopping behavior: A comparative study between China and France. *Technol. Forecast. Soc. Chang.* **2014**, *88*, 265–275. [CrossRef]
79. Cloninger, C.R.; Svrakic, D.M.; Przybeck, T.R. A psychobiological model of temperament and character. *Arch. Gen. Psychiatry* **1993**, *50*, 975–990. [CrossRef] [PubMed]
80. Ha, J.H.; Kim, S.Y.; Bae, S.C.; Bae, S.; Kim, H.; Sim, M.; Lyoo, I.K.; Cho, S.C. Depression and Internet addiction in adolescents. *Psychopathology* **2007**, *40*, 424–430. [CrossRef] [PubMed]
81. June, K.J.; Sohn, S.Y.; So, A.Y.; Yi, G.M.; Park, S.H. A study of factors that influence Internet addiction, smoking, and drinking in high school students. *J. Korean Acad. Nurs.* **2007**, *37*, 872–882. [CrossRef]
82. Stieger, S.; Burger, C. Implicit and explicit self-esteem in the context of Internet addiction. *Cyberpsychol. Behav. Soc. Netw.* **2010**, *13*, 681–688. [CrossRef] [PubMed]
83. Montag, C.; Flierl, M.; Markett, S.; Walter, N.; Jurkiewicz, M.; Reuter, M. Internet addiction and personality in first-person-shooter video gamers. *J. Media Psychol.* **2011**, *23*, 163–173. [CrossRef]
84. Triandis, H.C. The self and social behavior in differing cultural contexts. *Psychol. Rev.* **1989**, *96*, 506–520. [CrossRef]
85. Wheeler, L.; Reis, H.T.; Bond, M.H. Collectivism-individualism in everyday social life: The middle kingdom and the melting pot. *J. Pers. Soc. Psychol.* **1989**, *57*, 79–86. [CrossRef]
86. Nadkarni, A.; Hofmann, S.G. Why do people use Facebook? *Pers. Individ. Differ.* **2012**, *52*, 243–249. [CrossRef] [PubMed]
87. Weber, I.; Jia, L. Internet and self-regulation in China: The cultural logic of controlled commodification. *Media Cult. Soc.* **2007**, *29*, 772–789. [CrossRef]

88. Kshetri, N. The evolution of the Chinese online gaming industry. *JTMC* **2009**, *4*, 158–179. [CrossRef]
89. Yee, N. Motivations for play in online games. *Cyberpsychol. Behav.* **2006**, *9*, 772–775. [CrossRef] [PubMed]
90. Demetrovics, Z.; Urbán, R.; Nagygyörgy, K.; Farkas, J.; Zilahy, D.; Mervó, B.; Reindl, A.; Ágoston, C.; Kertész, A.; Harmath, E. Why do you play? The development of the motives for online gaming questionnaire (MOGQ). *Behav. Res. Methods* **2011**, *43*, 814–825. [CrossRef] [PubMed]

# Pathological Traits Associated to Facebook and Twitter among French Users

**Élodie Verseillié, Stéphanie Laconi * and Henri Chabrol**

Centre d'Etudes et de Recherches en Psychopathologie et Psychologie de la Santé (CERPPS) EA7411, Université de Toulouse, 5, Allées Antonio Machado, 31058 Toulouse Cedex, France; elodie.verseillie@univ-tlse2.fr (É.V.); henri.chabrol@univ-tlse2.fr (H.C.)

* Correspondence: stephanielaconi.b@gmail.com

**Abstract:** Background: With a growing number of users, social networking sites have been the subject of numerous recent studies, but little investigation has been given to their problematic use. Objectives: Our main objective was to study the relationship between psychopathological variables (i.e., personality traits, depressive and anxiety symptoms, and stress) and problematic Facebook and Twitter use. Participants and method: A sample of 1068 Internet users (Mage = 26.64; SD = 9.5) has been recruited online. Participants completed scales exploring problematic Facebook and Twitter use, and psychopathological variables. Results: Problematic Facebook and Twitter use were predicted by different pathological personality traits, regrouped in clusters in our study. Depressive and anxiety symptoms were also predictive of problematic Facebook and Twitter use but only stress explained problematic Facebook use. Gender differences have been observed. Discussion: This study highlights the relationship between depression, anxiety, stress, pathological personality traits, and problematic Facebook and Twitter use. Significant differences have been retrieved between these two uses and their relationship to psychopathology. Future research should also explore the causal relationship between social networking sites use and psychopathology and consider gender.

**Keywords:** problematic use; addiction; Twitter; Facebook; psychopathology; personality

## 1. Introduction

Facebook and Twitter are among the most popular Social Networking Sites (SNS) worldwide [1]. All SNS facilitate social interactions, even if they do not have the same finalities. Twitter is more about sharing information and opinions [2] than about developing social interactions like Facebook [3]. Besides, Twitter restores anonymity sought initially through SNS [3] and seems more focused on what users say than on what they are or look like.

Several researches highlight the existence of addictive-like symptoms related to SNS use [4,5]. In recent years, the use of some SNS has been described as pathological, problematic, or even addictive. In this paper, the term of problematic use will be preferred because of the lack of consensual definition and designation [6]. Moreover, this term allows us to avoid the unreasonable pathologization of every SNS use. Problematic Facebook Use (PFU) has been defined as a "problematic behavior that is likely to be characterized by addictive-like symptoms and/or self-regulation difficulties leading to negative consequences in personal and social life" [5] (p. 263). Given the risks associated to SNS use, a growing interest has been put on PFU [7,8] while few studies focused on Problematic Twitter Use (PTU) [9–11]. Some authors [10] found patterns of addiction in PTU through withdrawal symptoms, salience, and desire to control the use.

As for Problematic Internet Use (PIU) or Internet addiction, problematic SNS uses seem to be more frequent among adolescents and young adults. However, a prevalence of these problematic use is complicated to establish given methodological differences which are partially related to the lack of standardized definitions and assessment tools [12]. In occidental Europe, prevalence estimates of PFU are approximately ranged from 4.5% to 10% [13–15]. Regarding Twitter use, one French study revealed that 3.1% of participants (n = 822; Mage = 21.6; SD = 2.8; Sex Ratio = 0.59) have PTU [14].

Few studies focused on the relationship between PFU and psychological disorders. A French researcher [16] showed that among French Internet users with a PFU, 69% had anxiety symptoms and 48% had depressive symptoms. Depression has been frequently linked to PFU [16–19]. As for anxiety, mood disorders would have a causal relationship with PIU, as risk factors and consequences [20]. Besides, some studies highlighted the significant relationships between several pathological personality traits and PIU [21–25], yet no study focused on their relationships with SNS addictions, except for particular pathological traits. For example, borderline personality traits have been shown to be a risk factor for PFU [17], such as narcissistic personality traits, which also appeared to be related to Facebook and Twitter use [26,27].

In order to complete a lack of empirical data on PFU and PTU, particularly on French samples, our main objective was to explore the relationship between psychopathological variables (i.e., personality traits, depressive and anxiety symptoms, and stress) and problematic Facebook and Twitter use. Another aim of this research was to look at gender differences.

## 2. Materials and Methods

### 2.1. Participants

The sample consisted of 1068 participants aged from 18 to 64 years old (M = 26.64; SD = 9.5). There were 37% (n = 398) of men for 63% (n = 670) of women. The majority of participants were students (56%; n = 598). More detailed results are presented in Table 1.

**Table 1.** General characteristics of the study subjects.

| Samples | Total | | Facebook Users (n = 679) | | Twitter Users (n = 389) | |
|---|---|---|---|---|---|---|
| Variables | n | % | n | % | n | % |
| Gender | | | | | | |
| Women | 670 | 62.7 | 462 | 68 | 208 | 53.5 |
| Men | 398 | 37.3 | 217 | 32 | 181 | 46.5 |
| Working status | | | | | | |
| Students | 598 | 56 | 383 | 56.4 | 215 | 55.3 |
| Workers | 397 | 37.2 | 255 | 37.6 | 142 | 36.5 |
| Unemployed | 73 | 6.8 | 41 | 6 | 32 | 8.2 |
| Marital status | | | | | | |
| Single | 608 | 57 | 381 | 56 | 227 | 58.4 |
| In relationship | 460 | 43 | 298 | 44 | 162 | 41.6 |
| Academic level | | | | | | |
| School certificate | 47 | 4.4 | 27 | 4 | 20 | 5.1 |
| High school degree | 164 | 15.4 | 92 | 13.5 | 72 | 18.5 |
| Bachelor degree | 496 | 46.4 | 327 | 48.2 | 169 | 43.4 |
| Master | 309 | 28.9 | 198 | 29.2 | 111 | 28.5 |
| Doctoral degree | 52 | 4.9 | 35 | 5.2 | 17 | 4.4 |
| Number of visits per day | | | | | | |
| Less than once a day | - | - | 34 | 5 | 27 | 6.9 |
| Between 1 and 5 times a day | - | - | 289 | 42.6 | 148 | 38 |
| Between 6 and 10 times a day | - | - | 164 | 24.2 | 106 | 27.2 |
| More than 10 times a day | - | - | 192 | 28.3 | 108 | 27.8 |
| Time per connection | | | | | | |
| Less than 10 min | - | - | 329 | 48.5 | 218 | 56 |
| Between 10 and 30 min | - | - | 236 | 34.8 | 125 | 32.1 |
| Between 31 and 60 min | - | - | 58 | 8.5 | 22 | 5.7 |
| More than an hour | - | - | 56 | 8.2 | 24 | 6.2 |

**Table 1.** *Cont.*

| Samples | Total | | Facebook Users (n = 679) | | Twitter Users (n = 389) | |
|---|---|---|---|---|---|---|
| Hours per day | | | | | | |
| One hour or less | - | - | 346 | 51 | 216 | 55.5 |
| Two hours | - | - | 180 | 26.5 | 93 | 23.9 |
| Three hours | - | - | 68 | 10 | 44 | 11.3 |
| Four hours | - | - | 46 | 6.8 | 17 | 4.4 |
| Five hours or more | - | - | 39 | 5.6 | 19 | 5 |

We spread our survey online with Survey Monkey through Facebook groups. These groups were randomly selected and covered a variety of topics (education, online games, sports, etc.) to reach the widest possible range of French users. For Twitter, the link of our survey has been shared with the most popular hashtags at different time periods. Participants were informed of the anonymity and confidentiality of their responses and gave their free and informed consent. Our study follows the ethical principles of the Declaration of Helsinki. Inclusion criteria were being at least 18 years old, understanding and speaking French, and having an account on Facebook and/or Twitter.

### 2.2. Measures

The Bergen Facebook Addiction Scale (BFAS) [28] has been used to assess PFU. Given there was no French validation, we used a previous translated version [14]. The BFAS had six items rated on a 5-point scale ranged from 1 "Very rarely" to 5 "Very often" (e.g., How often have you used Facebook in order to forget about personal problems?). Scores varied from 5 to 30, and high scores suggest a plausible PFU. The internal consistency was $\alpha = 0.83$ [28], $\alpha = 0.81$ [14], and $\alpha = 0.78$ in our study.

Given the lack of scale to measure PTU, we chose to use an adapted version of the BFAS [28] by replacing the term "Facebook" by "Twitter" (BFAS-T), similar to a previous study [14]. The Cronbach coefficient for the BFAS-T was $\alpha = 0.90$ [14]. In this study, it was $\alpha = 0.87$.

The Depression Anxiety and Stress Scale (DASS 12) [29] has been used to assess depressive and anxiety symptoms, and stress. This scale is composed of 12 items rated on a 4-point scale from 0 "Rarely or never" to 3 "Most of the time or always". Scores are ranged from 0 to 36. Cut off scores suggesting a severe symptomatology were respectively of 4, 4, and 6. Cronbach' alphas were ranged between $\alpha = 0.72$ and $\alpha = 0.76$ [29], and between $\alpha = 0.67$ and $\alpha = 0.78$ in the present study.

The Personality Diagnostic Questionnaire 4+ (PDQ4+) [30,31] measures the ten pathological personality traits of the DSM-IV with 99 items on a dichotomous scale. For this study, we used a Likert scale from 1 "Not typical to me" to 5 "very typical to me" as in previous studies [32,33]. Cronbach' alphas for each subscale were ranged between $\alpha = 0.47$ and $\alpha = 0.83$ [32,33]. In our study, it varied from $\alpha = 0.38$ to $\alpha = 0.94$. Given this, we decided to use clusters of pathological personalities as classified in the DSM for statistical analyses. According to the DSM, Cluster A is composed of eccentric personalities (paranoid, schizoid, schizotypal), Cluster B regroups dramatic personalities (antisocial, borderline, histrionic, narcissistic), and Cluster C anxious personalities (avoidant, dependent, obsessive-compulsive). Cronbach' alphas were $\alpha = 0.85$ for Cluster A and $\alpha = 0.87$ for Clusters B and C [28]. In our study, it was $\alpha = 0.78$ for Cluster A, $\alpha = 0.79$ for Cluster B, and $\alpha = 0.84$ for Cluster C.

### 2.3. Statistical Analyses

Descriptive analyses were conducted in the entire sample, and among Facebook and Twitter users. Pearson correlation analyses have been performed to assess the relationship between Facebook and Twitter use (including problematic use) and psychopathological variables (i.e., personality traits, depression, anxiety, stress). Multiple linear regressions helped to assess the influence of these last on Facebook and Twitter use. These analyses have also been performed separately for men and women.

### 3. Results

Among participants, 679 (64%) had a Facebook account only and 389 (36%) also had a Twitter account. No participant had only a Twitter account. As show in Table 1, the majority of participants (41%; n = 437) go to Facebook between one and five time a day and do not stay connected for long: Less than 10 min by connection (51%; n = 547). For Twitter, people connect once a day (50%; n = 193) and stay connected also less than 10 min by connection (67%; n = 262).

Results of correlation analyses between independent variables (depression, anxiety, stress, and cluster A, B, and C of personality) are presented in Table 2 for Facebook users only and in Table 3 for Facebook and Twitter users. There is a poor but significant correlation between dependent variables PFU and PTU ($r = 0.11$; $p < 0.05$).

**Table 2.** Bivariate Pearson correlations between variables among users with an account on Facebook (n = 679).

| Variables | 1 | 2 | 3 | 4 | 5 | 6 |
|---|---|---|---|---|---|---|
| Depression (1) | - | 0.61 | 0.51 | 0.40 | 0.34 | 0.50 |
| Anxiety (2) | | - | 0.59 | 0.36 | 0.32 | 0.47 |
| Stress (3) | | | - | 0.29 | 0.35 | 0.39 |
| Cluster A (4) | | | | - | 0.59 | 0.60 |
| Cluster B (5) | | | | | - | 0.53 |
| Cluster C (6) | | | | | | - |

Note. All correlations were significant at $p < 0.01$.

**Table 3.** Bivariate Pearson correlations between variables among users of an account on Facebook and on Twitter (n = 389).

| Variables | 1 | 2 | 3 | 4 | 5 | 6 |
|---|---|---|---|---|---|---|
| Depression (1) | - | 0.63 ** | 0.56 ** | 0.54 ** | 0.41 ** | 0.67 ** |
| Anxiety (2) | | - | 0.65 ** | 0.43 ** | 0.43 ** | 0.59 ** |
| Stress (3) | | | - | 0.43 ** | 0.46 ** | 0.51 ** |
| Cluster A (4) | | | | - | 0.60 ** | 0.69 ** |
| Cluster B (5) | | | | | - | 0.57 ** |
| Cluster C (6) | | | | | | - |

Note. * = $p < 0.05$; ** = $p < 0.01$.

Regression model assumptions were checked by examining the plot of predicted values of the dependent variable against residuals. It showed that assumptions were sufficiently met. Thus, among Facebook users only (n = 679), PFU has been explained by depressive symptoms ($\beta = 0.14$; $p < 0.01$), anxiety ($\beta = 0.12$; $p < 0.05$) and stress ($\beta = 0.14$; $p < 0.01$). Among Twitter users (n = 389), PTU has been explained by depressive symptoms ($\beta = 0.17$; $p < 0.01$) and anxiety ($\beta = 0.19$; $p < 0.01$).

For personality, PFU has been explained by cluster B personality traits ($\beta = 0.17$; $p < 0.001$) and cluster C personality traits ($\beta = 0.26$; $p < 0.001$) contrary to Twitter, which has been explained by cluster A personality traits ($\beta = 0.16$; $p < 0.05$).

Correlation performed separately for men and women revealed few significant differences (see Table 4). Among women there was no significant correlation between PFU and PTU ($r = 0.05$; $p = 0.50$) compared to men ($r = 0.22$; $p < 0.01$).

Regression analysis performed separately for men and women revealed significant differences for psychopathological variables. Among women, PFU was explained by depressive symptoms ($\beta = 0.15$; $p < 0.05$) whereas PTU was explained by anxiety ($\beta = 0.24$; $p < 0.05$). However, among men, no significant result has been retrieved for PFU and PTU, and psychopathological variables. Regarding personality, PFU was explained by cluster B and cluster C personality traits among women ($\beta = 0.11$; $p < 0.05$ and $\beta = 0.15$; $p < 0.05$) and men ($\beta = 0.22$; $p < 0.01$ and $\beta = 0.21$; $p < 0.05$), whereas PTU has been explained by cluster A personality traits ($\beta = 0.23$; $p < 0.05$) for women. PTU have not been explained by personality variables among men.

**Table 4.** Bivariate Pearson correlations between variables among users of an account on Facebook and on Twitter (n = 389) regarding gender.

| Variables | 1 | 2 | 3 | 4 | 5 | 6 |
|---|---|---|---|---|---|---|
| Depression (1) | - | 0.67 ** | 0.56 ** | 0.55 ** | 0.51 ** | 0.70 ** |
| Anxiety (2) | 0.58 ** | - | 0.64 ** | 0.46 ** | 0.48 ** | 0.60 ** |
| Stress (3) | 0.55 ** | 0.66* | - | 0.39 ** | 0.47 ** | 0.48 ** |
| Cluster A (4) | 0.52 ** | 0.39 ** | 0.47 ** | - | 0.65 ** | 0.73 ** |
| Cluster B (5) | 0.32 ** | 0.40 ** | 0.47 ** | 0.55 ** | - | 0.65 ** |
| Cluster C (6) | 0.64 ** | 0.55 ** | 0.52 ** | 0.64 ** | 0.52 ** | - |

Note. Grey = Men; * = $p < 0.05$; ** = $p < 0.01$.

## 4. Discussion

### 4.1. Relationships with Depressive and Anxiety Symptoms

Our results are similar to those retrieved in previous studies in PFU regarding the relationship with depressive and anxiety symptoms [16–19,34,35] and PIU [36,37]. These results are not surprising and it is still necessary to fill the lack of studies on the causal relationship between these variables. The cognitive and behavioral model of problematic Internet use [20] suggests that depressive or socially anxious individuals are more prone to use Internet in order to relieve negative feelings. Young adults also experience a lot of stress in their lives due to their academic responsibilities, uncertainty about professional life or financial difficulty, which can lead to anxiety and depressive symptoms increasing the risk of PFU [34]. Using SNS in particular could induce more depressive and anxiety symptoms [38].

As expected, PTU was also significantly correlated to psychopathology in our study, but with a lower coefficient with stress than with PFU, among men and women. This should be explored and confirmed in other studies.

### 4.2. Relationships with Pathological Personality Traits

Our results showed that pathological traits of Clusters B and C predicted PFU, with no significant differences among gender, as it has already been shown [34,39]. Previous works highlighted the relationship between PFU and Cluster B symptomatology such as borderline [35,40] and narcissism traits [41–43]. This is similar with results found with PIU for Cluster B [21,23,25,28] and Cluster C [21,25]. Borderline and antisocial traits have been frequently associated to addictive disorders, with impulsivity in common, which could be a supplementary evidence of the high similarity between PFU and other addictive disorders [44]. Besides, we can assume that borderline personalities spend a lot of time on Facebook, especially adding/searching new friends to avoid true or imagined abandonment, while narcissistic and histrionic personalities used their time on posting content hoping to receive the expected attention and compliments. Antisocial personalities might use SNS to fulfill a lack of harmonious relationships in real life with less close individuals, but also to find a satisfaction by watching others' profiles. Cluster C traits, such as the social anxiety and the fear of being criticized or rejected in social situations, may lead to a preference for SNS with a strong control on one's public image. The relationship between PFU and social anxiety has already been shown [45]. PFU has an effect on social anxiety and depression that decrease the level of life satisfaction [46]. Other studies showed links between PFU and obsessive-compulsive traits [38,40]. Users seems to experience craving—the urge desire to check Facebook (assimilated to compulsions), which can be explain by the fear of missing out [38]. We can suppose that dependent personality spent a lot of time on Facebook with an important Facebook involvement to maintain social relationships because of their fear of the separation and their need to be reassured. Avoidant personality traits can be easily related to PFU; avoidant individuals might feel more prone to look for online communication rather than face-to-face interaction [47]. However, similarly to what we have found, other studies found a significant relationship between PIU and Clusters B and C personalities [25,47]. Facebook appears as more similar to Internet than Twitter, which can explain some similarities.

Contrarily to PFU, PTU was predicted by Cluster A traits. This is not surprising given that Twitter restores anonymity, compared to Facebook [48]. People with Cluster A' traits are more detached from social relationships and intimacy, and present more social anxiety and suspiciousness. Anonymity appears as initially looked for in SNS use [3] but the reduction of the social pressure and paranoid fears induced by anonymity can be the reason why Twitter use is preferred by individuals with Cluster A personality traits. Future researches should continue to study these relationships to try to confirm these results.

### *4.3. Gender Differences*

An interesting result is the lack of significant relationship between PTU and PFU among women, which highlights the specificity of these problematic SNS use as those found in gender. It could be interesting to explore if women are indeed more prone to have PFU or PTU than both as men. This result should also be interpreted given the association between other variables, such as personality traits.

Correlation analyses revealed small differences between men and women. Among men, the correlation between Cluster B and PTU was lower than among women. PFU was also more highly related to Cluster B and C in women than men. This could suggest that problematic SNS use, in women, was related to a higher level of pathological personality traits. This is confirmed by the results of regression where no psychopathological variables explained PFU or PTU among men. Their use of SNS seems to be less related to psychopathology than for women.

Our regression analyses suggested that the relationship between PTU and cluster A is only significant among women, and that among them, PTU was explained by anxiety (and PFU by depressive symptoms). Cluster A personalities experienced more stress than other personality and it is known that women are also more at risk for anxiety symptoms [49]. Therefore, this could explain the significant relationship between PTU and cluster A, particularly among women.

### *4.4. Implications*

Even if SNS received increasing attention worldwide, the lack of data on problematic SNS use or their relationship with psychopathological variables makes this research particularly relevant. Given the increasing number of SNS users, it seems necessary to better understand SNS use and the characteristics of their users. Prevention campaign adapted for specific audience (different for Twitter and Facebook users, and probably for users of other SNS) as early detection would have a positive impact on the health of youth and could prevent people to develop a problematic use but also depressive and anxiety symptoms, as a constant pathological personality even if there is no study on the causality of these relationships. This could improve the care of these specific problematic users, with a different orientation and different therapeutic objectives according to the SNS use, its characteristics, and the presence of psychopathological symptoms and traits.

### *4.5. Limits*

Some methodological bias might have an influence on our results, such as sampling method and online recruitment. However, it seems that the use of Internet recruitment compared to the paper-and-pencil methodology has little influence on the consistency of the results [50]. Given the significant number of Facebook users, it was impossible to create a sample with only Twitter users which can make it difficult to read our results and can have an influence on them. The BFAS, which evaluates the PFU, does not have a cut off score. Thus, we have been unable to distinguish those with PFU and/or PTU from those without which did not give us the opportunity to make more precise statistics. Therefore, our assessment tools seem to be a limitation for the interpretation of our results, especially in the absence of diagnostic value. Besides, there are no consensual diagnostic criteria or definition of problematic SNS use, therefore our study lacks of a validated and diagnostic assessment tool to confirm the diagnosis of PFU and PTU such as in any study focused on this topic. Consistent in most studies, the criteria used to assess problematic SNS use are based on those of PIU even if many differences have been observed between specific and generalized Internet use [33]. This lack of specific evaluation increases the need for a unified definition and well-established and validated tools in the field of problematic SNS use. Besides, the lack of similar studies impedes our interpretation.

## 5. Conclusions

Our objectives were to explore the relationship between PFU, PTU, and psychopathological variables. This study confirmed the relationship between PFU and psychopathological variables but also brings new data about PTU. More importantly, pathological personality traits of cluster A were related to Twitter use and PTU whereas those of cluster B and C were related to Facebook use and PFU. In light of a lack of data in this area, another aim of this research was to look at gender differences in the context of PFU and PTU. Depressive and anxiety symptoms were related to PFU, whereas stress was related to PTU in both gender but with a lower intensity. Women have more anxiety symptoms and PTU than men. As a result, women seem now at a higher risk of developing a problematic SNS use. This research is one of the first to explore problematic Facebook and Twitter use and pathological personality traits. It would deserve to be replicated and deepened.

**Author Contributions:** Conceptualization, É.V. and S.L.; methodology, É.V. and S.L.; formal analysis, É.V. and S.L.; investigation, É.V.; * writing—original draft preparation, É.V.; writing—review and editing, É.V., S.L. and H.C.; supervision, H.C. All authors have read and agreed to the published version of the manuscript.

## References

1. Blog du Modérateur. Available online: http://www.blogdumoderateur.com/50-chiffres-medias-sociaux-2020/ (accessed on 23 February 2020).
2. Kwak, H.; Lee, C.; Park, H.; Moon, S. What is Twitter, a social network or a news media? In Proceedings of the 19th International Conference on World Wide Web, Raleigh, NC, USA, 26-30 April 2010.
3. Huberman, B.A.; Romero, D.M.; Wu, F. Social networks that matter: Twitter under the micro-scope. *First Monday* **2009**, *14*, 1–9.
4. Kuss, D.J.; Griffiths, M.D. Online social networking and addiction—A review of the psychological literature. *Int. J. Environ. Res. Public Health* **2011**, *8*, 3528–3552. [CrossRef] [PubMed]
5. Marino, C.; Gini, G.; Vieno, A.; Spada, M.M. A comprehensive meta-analysis on Problematic Facebook Use. *Comput. Hum. Behav.* **2018**, *83*, 262–277. [CrossRef]
6. Caci, B.; Cardaci, M.; Scrima, F.; Tabacchi, M.E. The Dimensions of Facebook Addiction as Measured by Facebook Addiction Italian Questionnaire and Their Relationships with Individual Differences. *Cyberpsychol. Behav. Soc. Netw.* **2017**, *20*, 251–258. [CrossRef]
7. Marino, C.; Finos, L.; Vieno, A.; Lenzi, M.; Spada, M.M. Objective Facebook behaviour: Differences between problematic and non-problematic users. *Comput. Hum. Behav.* **2017**, *73*, 541–546. [CrossRef]
8. Moretta, T.; Buodo, G. Modeling Problematic Facebook Use: Highlighting the role of mood regulation and preference for online social interaction. *Addict. Behav.* **2018**, *87*, 214–221. [CrossRef]
9. Kircaburun, K. Self-Esteem, Daily Internet Use and Social Media Addiction as Predictors of Depression among Turkish Adolescents. *J. Educ. Pract.* **2016**, *7*, 64–72.
10. Miles, P.C.; Zhang, L.G. China turns to Tweeting: Exploring the problematic use of Tweeting in China. *Int. J. Bus. Soc. Sci.* **2012**, *3*, 91–94.
11. Saaid, S.A.; Al-Rashid, N.A.A.; Abdullah, Z. The impact of addiction to Twitter among university students. In *Future Information Technology*; Springer: Berlin/Heidelberg, Germany, 2014; pp. 231–236.
12. Griffiths, M.D.; Kuss, D.J.; Demetrovics, Z. Social networking addiction: An overview of preliminary findings. In *Behavioral Addictions: Criteria, Evidence and Treatment*, 1st ed.; Rosenberg, K., Feder, L., Eds.; Elsevier: New York, NY, USA, 2014; pp. 119–141.

13. Brailovskaia, J.; Margraf, J. Facebook addiction disorder (FAD) among German students—A longitudinal approach. *PLoS ONE* **2017**, *12*, e0189719. [CrossRef]
14. Laconi, S.; Verseillié, E.; Chabrol, H. Exploration of the Problematic Twitter, Facebook Uses and Their Relationships with Psychopathological Symptoms among Facebook Users. *Int. J. High Risk Behav.* **2018**, *7*, e61775. [CrossRef]
15. Walburg, V.; Mialhes, A.; Moncla, D. Does school-related burnout influence problematic Facebook use? *Child. Youth Serv. Rev.* **2016**, *61*, 327–331. [CrossRef]
16. Couderc, E. Search for an addiction to social networks and study of the concerned user profile [Recherche d'une addiction aux réseaux sociaux et étude du profil d'utilisateur concerné]. Ph.D. Thesis, Université de Limoge, Limoges, France, 2012.
17. Delfour, M.; Moreau, A.; Laconi, S.; Goutaudier, N.; Chabrol, H. Problematic Facebook use in adolescents and young adultsProblematic Facebook use in adolescents and young adults [Utilisation problématique de Facebook à l'adolescence et au jeune âge adulte]. *Neuropsychiatrie de L'enfance de et L'adolescence* **2014**, *63*, 244–249. [CrossRef]
18. Herrera-Harfuch, M.F.; Pacheco Murguia, M.P.; Lever, J.P.; Andrade, D.Z. La adiccion a Facebook relacionada con la baja autoestima, la depression y la falta de habilitades sociales. *Psicol. Iberoam.* **2010**, *18*, 6–18.
19. Hong, F.Y.; Huang, D.H.; Lin, H.Y.; Chiu, S.L. Analysis of the psychological traits, Facebook usage, and Facebook addiction model of Taiwanese University students. *Telemat. Inform.* **2014**, *31*, 597–606. [CrossRef]
20. Caplan, S.E. Theory and measurement of generalized problematic Internet use: A two-step approach. *Comput. Hum. Behav.* **2010**, *26*, 1089–1097. [CrossRef]
21. Bernardi, S.; Pallanti, S. Internet addiction: A descriptive clinical study focusing on comorbidities and dissociative symptoms. *Compr. Psychiatry* **2009**, *50*, 510–516. [CrossRef]
22. Laconi, S.; Andreoletti, A.; Chauchard, E.; Rodgers, R.; Chabrol, H. Problematic Internet Use, time spent online and personality traits [Utilisation problématique d'Internet, temps passé en ligne et traits de personnalité]. *Encéphale* **2016**, *42*, 214–218. [CrossRef]
23. Leménager, T.; Hoffmann, S.; Dieter, J.; Reinhard, I.; Mann, K.; Kiefer, F. The links between healthy, problematic, and addicted Internet use regarding comorbidities and self-concept-related characteristics. *J. Behav. Addict.* **2018**, *7*, 31–43. [CrossRef]
24. Sepehrian, F.; Lotf, J.J. Study of the relationship between Internet addiction with anxiety and personality types A and B. *Aust. J. Basic Appl. Sci.* **2011**, *5*, 928–934.
25. Zadra, S.; Bischof, G.; Besser, B.; Bischof, A.; Meyer, C.; John, U.; Rumpf, H.J. The association between Internet addiction and personality disorders in a general population-based sample. *J. Behav. Addict.* **2016**, *5*, 691–699. [CrossRef]
26. Davenport, S.W.; Bergman, S.M.; Bergman, J.Z.; Fearington, M.E. Twitter versus Facebook: Exploring the role of narcissism in the motives and usage of different social media platforms. *Comput. Hum. Behav.* **2014**, *32*, 212–220. [CrossRef]
27. Walters, N.T.; Horton, R. A diary of the influence of Facebook use on narcissism among male college students. *Comput. Hum. Behav.* **2015**, *52*, 326–330. [CrossRef]
28. Andreassen, C.S.; Torsheim, T.; Brunborg, G.C.; Pallesen, S. Development of Facebook addiction scale. *Psychol. Rep.* **2012**, *110*, 501–517. [CrossRef] [PubMed]
29. Yussof, M.S.B. Psychometric properties of the Depression Anxiety Stress Scale in a sample of medical degree applicants. *Int. Med. J.* **2013**, *20*, 295–300.
30. Bouvard, M. *Questionnaires et Echelles D'évaluation de la Personnalité*, 3rd ed.; Masson: Paris, France, 2002.
31. Hyler, S.E. *Personality Diagnostic Questionnaire (PDQ-4 Plus)*; New York State Psychiatric Institute: New York, NY, USA, 1994.
32. Chabrol, H.; van Leeuwen, N.; Rodgers, R.; Séjourné, N. Contributions of psychopathic, narcissistic, Machiavellian, and sadistic personality traits to juvenile delinquency. *Personal. Individ. Differ.* **2009**, *47*, 734–739. [CrossRef]
33. Laconi, S.; Tricard, N.; Chabrol, H. Differences between specific and generalized problematic Internet uses according to gender, age, time spent online and psychopathological symptoms. *Comput. Hum. Behav.* **2015**, *48*, 236–244. [CrossRef]
34. Koc, M.; Gulyagci, S. Facebook Addiction among Turkish college students: The role of psychological health, demographic, and usage characteristics. *Cyberpsychol. Behav. Soc. Netw.* **2013**, *16*, 279–284. [CrossRef]

35. Moreau, A.; Laconi, S.; Delfour, M.; Chabrol, H. Psychopathological profiles of adolescent and young adult problematic Facebook users. *Comput. Hum. Behav.* **2015**, *44*, 64–69. [CrossRef]
36. Ostovar, S.; Allahyar, N.; Aminpoor, H.; Moafian, F.; Nor, M.B.M.; Griffiths, M.D. Internet addiction and its psychosocial risks (depression, anxiety, stress and loneliness) among Iranian adolescents and young adults: A structural equation model in a cross-sectional study. *Int. J. Ment. Health Addict.* **2016**, *14*, 257–267. [CrossRef]
37. Stavropoulos, V.; Gomez, R.; Steen, E.; Beard, C.; Liew, L.; Griffiths, M.D. The longitudinal association between anxiety and Internet addiction in adolescence: The moderating effect of classroom extraversion. *J. Behav. Addict.* **2017**, *6*, 237–247. [CrossRef]
38. Andreassen, C.S.; Billieux, J.; Griffiths, M.D.; Kuss, D.J.; Demetrovics, Z.; Mazzoni, E.; Pallesen, S. The relationship between addictive use of social media and video games and symptoms of psychiatric disorders: A large-scale cross-sectional study. *Psychol. Addict. Behav.* **2016**, *30*, 252–262. [CrossRef] [PubMed]
39. Beyens, I.; Frison, E.; Eggermont, S. "I don't want to miss a thing": Adolescents' fear of missing out and its relationship to adolescents' social needs, Facebook use, and Facebook related stress. *Comput. Hum. Behav.* **2016**, *64*, 1–8. [CrossRef]
40. Chabrol, H.; Laconi, S.; Delfour, M.; Moreau, A. Contributions of psychopathological and interpersonal variables to problematic Facebook use in adolescents and young adults. *Int. J. High Risk Behav. Addict.* **2017**, *6*, e32773. [CrossRef]
41. Atroszko, P.A.; Balcerowska, J.M.; Bereznowski, P.; Biernatowska, A.; Pallesen, S.; Andreassen, C.S. Facebook addiction among Polish undergraduate students: Validity of measurement and relationship with personality and well-being. *Comput. Hum. Behav.* **2018**, *85*, 329–338. [CrossRef]
42. Błachnio, A.; Przepiórka, A. Facebook intrusion, fear of missing out, narcissism, and life satisfaction: A cross-sectional study. *Psychiatry Res.* **2018**, *259*, 514–519. [CrossRef] [PubMed]
43. Casale, S.; Fioravanti, G. Why narcissists are at risk for developing Facebook addiction: The need to be admired and the need to belong. *Addict. Behav.* **2018**, *76*, 312–318. [CrossRef]
44. Echeburua, E. Addiction to new technologies and to online social networking in young people: A new challenge. *Adicciones* **2010**, *22*, 91–95.
45. Lee-Won, R.J.; Herzog, L.; Park, S.G. Hooked on Facebook: The role of social anxiety and need for social assurance in problematic use of Facebook. *Cyberpsychol. Behav. Soc. Netw.* **2015**, *18*, 567–574. [CrossRef]
46. Foroughi, B.; Iranmanesh, M.; Nikbin, D.; Hyun, S.S. Are depression and social anxiety the missing link between Facebook addiction and life satisfaction? The interactive effect of needs and self-regulation. *Telemat. Inform.* **2019**, *43*, e101247. [CrossRef]
47. Laconi, S.; Vigouroux, M.; Lafuente, C.; Chabrol, H. Problematic Internet Use, Psychopathology, Personality, Defense and Coping. *Comput. Hum. Behav.* **2017**, *73*, 47–54. [CrossRef]
48. Petrocchi, N.; Asnaani, A.; Martinez, A.P.; Nadkarni, A.; Hofmann, S.G. Differences between people who use only Facebook and those who use Facebook plus Twitter. *Int. J. Hum. Comput. Interact.* **2015**, *31*, 157–165. [CrossRef] [PubMed]
49. Donner, N.C.; Lowry, C.A. Sex differences in anxiety and emotional behavior. *Pflügers Arch. Eur. J. Physiol.* **2013**, *465*, 601–626. [CrossRef] [PubMed]
50. Brock, R.L.; Barry, R.A.; Lawrence, E.; Dey, J.; Rolffs, J. Internet administration of paper-and-pencil questionnaires used in couple research: Assessing psychometric equivalence. *Assessment* **2012**, *19*, 226–242. [CrossRef] [PubMed]

8

# Stakeholders' Consensus on Strategies for Self- and Other-Regulation of Video Game Play: A Mixed Methods Study

**Michelle Colder Carras [1,*], Matthew Carras [2] and Alain B. Labrique [3]**

1 Department of International Health, Johns Hopkins Bloomberg School of Public Health, 615 N. Wolfe St. W5501, Baltimore, MD 21205, USA
2 Carras Consulting, 1407 Scanlan Drive, Glen Burnie, MD 21205, USA; matthew.carras@gmail.com
3 Departments of International Health, Epidemiology, and Health Policy and Management, Johns Hopkins Bloomberg School of Public Health, 615 N. Wolfe St. W5501, Baltimore, MD 21205, USA; alabriq1@jhu.edu
* Correspondence: mcarras@jhu.edu

**Abstract:** *Background:* Little is known about strategies or mechanics to improve self-regulation of video game play that could be developed into novel interventions. This study used a participatory approach with the gaming community to uncover insider knowledge about techniques to promote healthy play and prevent gaming disorder. *Methods:* We used a pragmatic approach to conduct a convergent-design mixed-methods study with participants attending a science fiction and education convention. Six participants answered questions about gaming engagement and self- or game-based regulation of gaming which were then categorized into pre-determined (a priori) themes by the presenters during the presentation. The categorized themes and examples from participant responses were presented back to participants for review and discussion. Seven participants ranked their top choices of themes for each question. The rankings were analyzed using a nonparametric approach to show consensus around specific themes. *Results:* Participants suggested several novel potential targets for preventive interventions including specific types of social (e.g., play with others in a group) or self-regulation processes (e.g., set timers or alarms). Suggestions for game mechanics that could help included clear break points and short missions, but loot boxes were not mentioned. *Conclusions:* Our consensus development approach produced many specific suggestions that could be implemented by game developers or tested as public health interventions, such as encouraging breaks through game mechanics, alarms or other limit setting; encouraging group gaming; and discussing and supporting setting appropriate time or activity goals around gaming (e.g., three quests, one hour). As some suggestions here have not been addressed previously as potential interventions, this suggests the importance of including gamers as stakeholders in research on the prevention of gaming disorder and the promotion of healthy gaming. A large-scale, online approach using these methods with multiple stakeholder groups could make effective use of players' in-depth knowledge and help speed discovery and translation of possible preventive interventions into practice and policy.

**Keywords:** gaming disorder; prevention; video games; mixed methods research; stakeholder engagement; consensus development

## 1. Introduction

Research on problems with video game play has led to a proposed diagnosis of Internet gaming disorder (IGD) in the Diagnostic and Statistical Manual 5 [1] and inclusion of gaming disorder in ICD-11 [2]. Representative surveys usually show that only a small percentage of the general population has clinical problems related to excessive gaming [3]. Systematic reviews link gaming disorder to correlates such as impulsivity, male gender, impaired mental health and low psychosocial well-being [3–5]. However, the Goldilocks hypothesis (based on the fairytale character Goldilocks, who struggles to find sizes of chair, porridge and bed that are "just right) suggests that engaging with technology in a moderate way is not harmful [6]. The WHO notes that most people are able to play video games without problems [7]. As this suggests that moderate video game play is a reasonable public health goal, investigating how people can play in a healthy way is vital to support the public health objective of preventing gaming disorder.

While many studies examine motivations to play, less is known about how gamers self-regulate their gaming. One qualitative study in children uncovered several reasons for engaging (e.g., motives, habit, and contextual factors) or disengaging (e.g., self-regulation, parental intervention, or disruption/frustration of gaming outcomes or psychological needs; [8]). Contextual factors of games or the environment also contribute to the length of gaming sessions: gaming sessions may be prolonged through losing track of time [9], achievement, winning or game mechanics, including gambling-like mechanisms such as loot boxes [8,10]. Disengaging from play may also be easier with support from real-life friends [11] or when using strategies like setting an alarm, taking regular breaks, or setting goals in the game [9]. The above findings show a range of individual, game and contextual factors that can promote healthy gaming and prevent disorder.

However, policy responses have focused largely on limiting time gaming [12] or regulating loot boxes as gambling [13]. Commentaries suggest that existing tools for self-regulation of gambling, such as self-exclusion, mandatory breaks, or pop-up messaging, might be useful for gaming [14]. A few technology platforms have already implemented feedback mechanisms to alert players about time or allow them to limit their time [15,16]. Games also provide such mechanisms in the form of parental controls. Some also remind players to take breaks, but forcing shutdown or exclusion periods as a preventive mechanism has so far been limited [12]. The current focus on a few limited policy aspects also neglects the need to take into account cultural factors, individual player factors, and how games change over time [12].

With the recent inclusion of gaming disorder in ICD-11, calls for collaboration with industry stakeholders have increased. Many researchers have suggested that the game industry has a responsibility to protect the health of gamers [14,17,18]. Fewer researchers support including gamers as partners in research and policy efforts to understand or prevent gaming disorder [19,20].

Participatory and multi-stakeholder approaches in health research allow for better translation of research into practice [21,22]. Stakeholders are members of diverse groups, including experts and the general public, who can provide unique perspectives on an issue. In the case of gaming disorder, this could mean not just clinicians, researchers, and policy makers, but also gamers, their families, and people who create games. Stakeholder-engaged research that involves group deliberation and decision-making promotes the type of co-learning that allows researchers to better examine all aspects of a problem or question, encourages decision-makers to consider multiple perspectives, and makes science more transparent [23,24]. Using systematic methods that integrate perspectives of those in the know—in this case video game players and developers—with research and theory will be vital to allow research on problematic gaming to address insider perspectives and cultural differences and keep up with changing technologies.

This approach has been used with gamers to explore their unique insights into what it means to be "addicted" [19]. As an illustration of the usefulness of this approach, we discovered that a small sample of gamers at a gaming fan convention were not only interested in discussing game "addiction", their ideas overlapped only partially with criteria for IGD. In fact, their suggestions leaned toward less strict criteria for social impairment and they suggested appointment mechanics (a game feature promoting engagement) as a primary contributor to loss of control. These findings suggest that including gamers in discussions of research into gaming disorder may improve research.

However, a systematic, perspective-integrating approach that examines factors associated with gaming self-regulation would better contribute to intervention development.

To address this gap and provide clinicians, decision-makers, the game industry and the general public with additional insights about gaming self-regulation, we conducted participatory, mixed-methods, convergent-design research with gamers to discuss the challenges of regulating video game play. This research builds on our prior study regarding gamers' insights on game "addiction" [19]. The qualitative objectives of our study were to elicit a wide variety of knowledge from the video gaming stakeholder community about why gamers play, why they stop playing, and how they self-regulate gaming time and to map these to known themes in the literature. The quantitative goal was to numerically rank the consensus on importance of themes. The overall mixed methods goal was to demonstrate a rapid and transparent consensus-development approach that can be used with multiple stakeholders. Such an approach would foster knowledge development and research co-creation in order to develop and prioritize research and prevention interventions for problematic video game play.

## 2. Materials and Methods

### 2.1. Overview

Mixed methods research combines qualitative and quantitative data to answer research questions that require a deep understanding of multiple perspectives, contexts, and/or communities/cultures [25]. We used a convergent mixed methods design, i.e., we combined qualitative and quantitative data simultaneously, to develop a rapid consensus on the relative importance of themes related to video gaming engagement and self-regulation. We used a pragmatic approach toward study design and analysis, as these allow researchers to combine diverse approaches to best answer the research question and place equal value on both objective and subjective knowledge [26]. In our previous study [19], for example, we used an emic, free-listing approach, working with our gamer audience at a panel to generate categories and themes for free-listed responses. As this proved difficult within the one-hour time frame of a panel at a convention, we opted to combine deductive (pre-determined themes from the literature) and inductive (free-listing) approaches in the qualitative part of our study design here.

As qualitative research benefits from researchers' self-reflection, we describe our relevant background here. All authors are researchers with experience in conducting mixed methods research in technology and health, particularly in video games. We have conducted a similar study in another setting to address gamers' insights into game "addiction" [19]. The first two authors, who conducted the panel, also identify as members of the gaming community, regularly attend gaming fan conventions, and have personal experience with regulating their gaming time. They use this personal experience to connect with stakeholders and facilitate meaningful discussion of healthy and unhealthy video game play. Author MCC is a researcher specializing in video game play, technology use and mental health; author MC is an information technology specialist with game industry experience; and author AL is a professor specializing in digital health.

To address our mixed method goal of demonstrating a rapid and transparent consensus-development technique, we first used a deductive approach among authors to identify prominent themes around self-regulation and gaming from the literature (Section 2.2). We then used an emic, inductive, free-listing approach to gather data about self- and other-regulation of video game play from audience members at a presentation (Section 2.4). We then facilitated a group decision-making procedure (Delphi process) with the audience to brainstorm, discuss/debate, and finally quantitatively rank concepts related to gaming self-regulation and steps the gaming industry could take to facilitate healthy play. We present the qualitative, quantitative and mixed methods results to better understand self-regulation as gamers see it. Our presentation here was guided by American Psychological Association standards for mixed methods and qualitative research reporting [27,28].

### 2.2. Selection of Themes for Framework

Prior to the presentation, the authors first briefly reviewed relevant literature on game engagement [8,9,29] and design [29–32]. We extracted themes and frameworks from these into tables and bulleted notes and discussed and combined results to condense themes surrounding game engagement and self-regulation. This deductive approach was not meant to be exhaustive but to present the most salient themes for discussion; other themes could be incorporated during data collection if necessary. This condensed list of themes (Table 1) was used to facilitate rapid thematic analysis during presentation and discussion with audience stakeholders. Themes were transcribed to index cards placed on the table in front of the presenters and used in a deductive, top-down theoretical thematic analysis approach [33] to rapidly classify participant responses during the presentations.

**Table 1.** Prepared themes and examples used in thematic analysis.

| Theme | Example Theme/Concept from Literature [8,9,29–32] |
|---|---|
| Achievement | Non-competitive. Also includes general success in completing objectives Achievement, challenge, Advancement, Mechanics, Being stronger, Rare items, Meta-game rewards |
| Behavioral game mechanics | Game-driven regulation, Alerts, Behavioral tracking, Exit points, Timed rewards, Fast loading times |
| Environmental | Forces outside the scope of the game's design Content-driven, family/parent driven, outside needs & responsibilities |
| Habit | Habit |
| Immersion | The feeling of being one with the game Narrative, Look and feel, Interface, Autonomy, Customization, Role-playing, Discovery, Fantasy |
| Mood regulation | Arousal/enjoyment, seeking diversion or distraction, escapism |
| Novelty | New or interesting aspects of the game |
| Self-regulation | Self-regulation |
| Social | Social interaction, relationships, teamwork |

### 2.3. Participants

A panel was presented at a science fiction and education convention, Escape Velocity, held in Washington, D.C. in 2017. The convention featured topics and events relevant to science and technology, STEAM education, video games, and pop culture. The conference is sponsored by the Museum of Science Fiction and science organizations like NASA, nonprofit organizations and industry groups, and in its first year was attended by over 2000 people [34].

Participants were recruited passively through panel descriptions in the convention schedule and through posters on the door to the panel room. Our panel on Day 1 was entitled "Insights Needed: Video Gaming and the Goldilocks Principle" and our panel on Day 2 was entitled "Insights Needed Wrap-Up: Give Us Your Feedback on Video Games and Engagement Preliminary Analysis." The authors had no prior relationship with the research participants. Each session began with the reading of a consent document where participants were offered the opportunity to leave if they did not want to participate; no audience members left. Participants did not receive compensation for participation. As the pragmatic study design was dependent on the setting of a panel at a convention, we did not identify a needed number of participants ahead of time and our sample was one of convenience. One participant arrived late and two participants did not complete all portions of the questionnaire.

Six respondents completed at least some demographic information and percentages are reported out of those who answered the question. Age ranged from 27 to 49 (Mean = 35, SD 7.9) and one participant was female. Most respondents (66.7%) were white, one identified as mixed race, and one declined to answer. Half had a graduate degree and another 33.3% had graduated from college. All respondents identified as members of the gamer stakeholder group, but also identified with other groups such as family/friend of a gamer (n = 3), researcher (n = 3), educator (n = 1), and industry (n = 1). In response to the question "Do you see yourself as a gamer", all responded either Yes or "Kind of (intermediate/casual)" but one participant also answered "No" to the question "Do you play video games, including mobile games (e.g., Candy Crush, Pokémon GO)?". (This participant identified primarily as a member of the game industry.) All worked full time and the majority (80%) earned over $40,000/year. The group played on average 3.13 h a day (SD 1.31) and 5.33 days per week (SD 1.15). Half played about 1–2 h per session while the other half played 2–3 h per session.

### *2.4. Data Collection and Study Procedure*

Questionnaire responses, sticky notes used in free listing, and field notes made up the qualitative and quantitative data as described here. This approach described is a combination of nominal group technique and Delphi approach that the authors used in a previous study [19]. Prior to data collection the authors printed out questionnaires with questions about demographics, stakeholder group membership, gaming experience and ranking of themes and added a number to each questionnaire. We then created a set of sticky notes with matching participant numbers. Each set of sticky notes contained five sticky notes for each of our four questions. Each note was labeled with a participant number and Q1, Q2, Q3, or Q4.

Data were collected over the course of an hour at a panel discussion. At the beginning of the panel, the presenters (the first two authors) introduced themselves as researchers and gamers and described the presentation as a study using group decision-making techniques to help answer questions about how to achieve just the right amount of engagement with video games. We then asked participants to list ideas for promoting healthy gaming by asking four open-ended questions (Table 2) about gaming engagement and regulation strategies. Participants recorded answers on sticky notes, then completed paper questionnaires asking about demographics and gaming experience. We allowed 10 min for data collection. Participants were asked not to complete the questions about ranking the importance of themes until told to do so.

**Table 2.** Themes and examples presented for ranking.

| Theme | Example 1 | Example 2 | Example 3 |
|---|---|---|---|
| Q1 What features of games make you want to play them or keep playing? | | | |
| Competition | *Winning* | | |
| Game type | *Arcade games* | | |
| Immersion | *Known intellectual property that you like* | *Customizing* | |
| Mood regulation | *Repeatable enjoyment* | | |
| Achievement | *Well-balanced gameplay* | *Rewards* | |
| Q2 What features of games make you want to stop playing? | | | |
| Social | Playing online with terrible people | *Losing* | |
| Environmental | *Out of time* | | |
| Immersion | *Broken games* | *Games that crash* | *Unclear control of avatar* |
| Achievement | *Games that are not balanced* | *Hard learning curve* | |
| Mood regulation | *Not fun anymore* | | |
| Novelty | *Repetition/grinding* | | |
| Q3 What are some strategies people can use to regulate the amount of time they game? | | | |
| Self-regulation | *Set an alarm* | *Set goals for gameplay* | |
| Social | *Play with others to limit time* | | |
| Analyze moves | *Slower-move analytically* | | |
| Q4 What are some things the game industry could do to make it easier to regulate the amount that people play games? | | | |
| Game mechanics | *Game-breaking pop-ups* | *Provide break points* | *On screen clock* |
| Environmental | *Integrate health tips* | | |
| Social | *Local multiplayer only* | | |
| Novelty | *Local multiplayer—AR fun with new tech* | | |

As data on sticky notes was collected, responses were categorized by the presenters by placing each sticky note under a pre-determined theme's index card. Disagreements about how to categorize responses were resolved through discussion between presenters. Once all responses were categorized (about 10 min after all responses were received) they were transcribed into the slideshow and displayed to all participants. We asked for clarifications of some responses and, as a participant check, discussed whether we had categorized responses for each question appropriately based on our own understanding as gamers and researchers. Field notes were incorporated into the response examples at times for further clarification. Participants elaborated on some responses, disagreed with one another or provided additional explanation, and a robust discussion of specific responses and themes ensued. The authors' goal was to ensure clarity of themes and their examples; this was accomplished with about three minutes of discussion for each question.

Participants were then asked to rank the top three themes they felt best answered each question by listing their choices for most important themes in order on the last page of the questionnaire, e.g., Question 1: #1 = immersion, #2 = game type, #3 = achievement. The numeric ranking participants gave to themes for a particular question constituted the quantitative data. Participants were invited to return in two days for the results. After the panel, one author transcribed questions, responses, and themes into an Excel spreadsheet to record qualitative data and the results of thematic analysis. Another author entered rankings and questionnaire responses directly into a Stata do-file to create and analyze a quantitative analysis database. To validate data quality, data entry was double-checked and analyses re-run prior to manuscript revision.

At a second panel two days later, we discussed the study's organizing frameworks and procedures and presented the results of the ranking. We again asked for clarifications of some responses and further discussed difficult-to-categorize responses. Finally, we presented the limitations and strengths we felt the process provided and invited participants to provide additional feedback. Data are available as Supplementary Materials.

### 2.5. *Qualitative and Quantitative Analysis*

#### 2.5.1. Categorization of Responses

We categorized responses as the unit of analysis during the presentation using a deductive approach based on the a priori themes. We chose theory-based thematic analysis as a practical way to facilitate rapid categorization in keeping with our pragmatic approach. Initial thematic analysis was performed at the panel and final categorizations and themes for each question were arrived at after discussion with participants; we used participant checks to facilitate categorization of some responses. Themes and examples (Table 2) were then projected onscreen to allow participants to rank them.

#### 2.5.2. Calculation of Ranks

We used an observational design to gather participants' perspectives on the importance of themes for each question. Ranked themes were assigned a numerical value from one to eleven to represent the eleven total themes (the nine a priori themes from Table 1 and two themes emerging during group discussion). We validated data entry against collected data by listing database results for each question in a table and checking against each participant's questionnaire.

For each question, we transformed a participant's ranked themes into coded rankings by replacing a placeholder variable for each theme with the numeral 1, 2, or 3 if a participant ranked it among their top three choices. This resulted in a unique subset of themes as the domain for each question. If a respondent did not rank a particular theme for that subset, the rank for that theme for that participant was coded as 0. We conducted a quantitative consensus analysis of participants' ranking of the most important themes for each question by calculating the weighted sum of centered ranks (WSCR) in Stata 13 IC [35] using the Skillings–Mack statistic (skilmack.ado, [36]). This flexible approach aggregates rankings across participants by combining the ranking for a specific question provided by each participant with the consensus on ranking for that question across all participants. With this approach, high consensus themes (those that are ranked more often or ranked very highly) will have a high and positive WSCR while low consensus themes, i.e., those that are ranked fewer times, ranked as less important, or show greater disagreement among respondents will have a low or negative WSCR. As we used rankings rather than raw numerical values in the analysis and replaced non-ranked themes with 0, standard errors are the same for all resulting WSCR for each question.

### 2.6. Presentation of Results

Qualitative results from the rapid thematic analysis are presented first, then qualitative and quantitative results are presented together to reflect the convergent design. Table 3 combines ranked themes with examples and important topics of discussion to illustrate how group processes affected participants' choices. We used these results to suggest ways that multiple stakeholder groups could help promote healthy gaming (Figure 1). This report follows standards for reporting qualitative, quantitative, and mixed methods research established by the American Psychological Association [27,28].

For game developers and industry

- Provide clear chapters or break points, even in open world games
- Force or reward play breaks
- Offer in-game reminders (game-breaking pop-ups are very effective)
- Allow autosave or quick save at any time
- Reward short gaming sessions
- Punish long gaming sessions (e.g., XP decay)
- Provide an on-screen clock
- Remove features that may promote excessive play (e.g., online multiplayer where players feel obligated to continue to support their team)

For players, family members and friends

- Play social games that depend on team members being present
- Use alarm clocks to keep track of and limit time
- Set limits for money spent on games
- Set clear activity goals for a gaming session (e.g., 3 quests, 1 hour)
- Schedule game play for after work or other life responsibilities

For clinicians and policymakers

- Discuss self-regulation with gamers and familiesSupport gamers and family/friends in setting appropriate goals around gaming
- Require games to offer features that promote self-regulation

**Figure 1.** Suggestions for regulating video game play.

**Table 3.** Ranked themes with examples of responses (n = 7).

| Theme as Categorized by Authors | Times Ranked [a] | WSCR [b] | WSCR/SE | Response Examples |
|---|---|---|---|---|
| Q1. What features of games make you want to play them or keep playing? | | | | |
| Immersion | 5 | 7.78 | 1.47 | *Visual/audio aesthetics, exploration of dynamic universe, known theme or IP, player/playstyle customization, great stories, color, sound* |
| Achievement | 5 | 3.54 | 0.67 | *Rewards, either literal ones in the form of items, unlocks, in-game money, OR psychological rewards such as a rewarding story pay off or resolution to a puzzle; well-balanced gameplay* |
| Game type | 4 | 0 | 0 | *Arcade-based games like racers or mech games.* |
| Mood | 3 | −0.71 | −0.13 | *Repeatable enjoyment* |
| Competition [c] | 1 | −10.61 | −2.00 | *Winning* |
| Q2. What features of games make you want to stop playing? | | | | |
| Social | 4 | 5.24 | 0.89 | *Online interaction with terrible people (most)* |
| Novelty | 5 | 5.24 | 0.89 | *Repetition/grinding with little variety* |
| Immersion | 4 | 1.96 | 0.33 | *Unclear control of avatar, Games that are crashy or slow* |
| Environment | 2 | −3.93 | −0.66 | *Out of time* |
| Achievement | 2 | −3.93 | −0.66 | *Unfair or unreliable game mechanics that result in "cheap" deaths/failures, games that are not balanced, games that are broken/not working* |
| Mood | 3 | −4.58 | −0.77 | *Not fun anymore* |
| Q3. What are some strategies people can use to regulate the amount of time they game? | | | | |
| Self-regulation | 7 | 5.2 | 1.39 | 2x[d,c]-*Limit time ... (60 min/session)*,2x[d]-*Use an alarm clock*, 2x-*Set firm goals for gameplay ex. "Just 3 quests", set a schedule for gaming after other responsibilities* |
| Social | 6 | 0 | 0 | *Play with others in a game that requires everyone to be present ... since the other players can effectively force you to stop* |
| Analyzing moves [c] | 5 | −5.2 | −1.39 | *Analyzing moves, moving slower* |
| Q4. What are some things the game industry could do to make it easier to regulate the amount that people play games? | | | | |
| Mechanics | 6 | 10.07 | 2.2 | *Clear delineations between missions/chapters which offer clear "break points" to the player, as opposed to open-ended/open world games which don't give an "excuse" to stop, autosave/quicksave, rewards that emphasize short sessions or have negative reinforcement mechanisms like XP delay, time allowed* |
| Environment | 5 | −0.77 | −0.17 | *Integrated health tips into game that use health points that players can use themselves* |
| Social | 5 | −2.32 | −0.51 | *Local multiplayer only- take away features of MO* |
| Novelty | 3 | −6.97 | −1.52 | *Augmented Reality Gaming—local multiplayer fun with new tech* |

[a] Number of times an item was ranked as one of a participant's top three choices. [b] Weighted sum of centered ranks statistic from the Skillings–Mack statistic, where high/positive ranks correspond to agreed-upon items and low/negative ranks correspond to items that were chosen less often or ranked as less important. SE were the same for each question: $SE_{Q1} = 5.29$, $SE_{Q2} = 5.92$, $SE_{Q3} = 3.74$, $SE_{Q4} = 4.58$. [c] New theme emerging from discussion. [d] More than one version/wording submitted by different respondents.

### 2.7. Methodological Integrity

To ensure fidelity and utility of our qualitative findings and address our research objectives, we address the adequacy, grounding, and context of data and how we used it to develop meaningful and coherent findings. First, we collected data from cultural insiders—those who had an interest in video gaming and self-regulation—grounding our data in their perspective. We used an emic approach to data collection, free listing, to elicit their cultural understanding and insider knowledge. We further grounded findings in evidence by using free-listed responses to illustrate themes. We included all audience members in our analysis, since all members identified as gamers. However, audience members also identified as members of other stakeholder groups. Although our sample was small, we aimed to gather insights/knowledge from gamers and other stakeholders; we feel the collected data are therefore adequate to capture a broad range of perspectives. Researchers' perspectives were used to determine an initial set of themes, facilitate rapid data analysis and guide group discussion.

We demonstrate consistency in our analysis by describing consensus development and discussion and when and how they were used in the analytic process. We used data displays (tables), author consensus on a priori themes, group discussion with participants, formal quantitative consensus, and participant feedback as checks to promote rigor in the qualitative analysis. We discuss the context of data collection and present findings coherently, reflecting on discrepancies and reporting according to mixed methods standards. Our results further the understanding of how gamers and other stakeholders can make insightful and meaningful contributions to a clinical- and policy-relevant research.

### 2.8. Ethics

The study protocol was approved by the institutional review board of the Johns Hopkins Bloomberg School of Public Health (IRB No. 00006931) and carried out in accordance with the Declaration of Helsinki. The need for written informed consent was waived by the institutional review board. Participants were fully informed about the study at the beginning of each study session and offered the opportunity not to participate.

## 3. Results

Six people participated in the free listing round and submitted between one and three answers per question. Seven people participated in the ranking round and six people completed demographic and gameplay questionnaires. Four questionnaires were complete, including rankings, while two were partially complete.

### 3.1. Qualitative

We initially identified nine themes from our brief review of several articles related to gaming engagement and design [8,9,29–32]. Our selection of themes was not meant to be exhaustive of all themes in the gaming literature, but rather a starting point for our discussion-based study design. Themes were chosen based on the authors' knowledge of game engagement and game design and how these factors contribute to problematic or self-regulated gaming. Categorization of responses to our four questions resulted in three to six themes for each question (Table 2). Some responses transcended themes, such as pop-up windows being a behavioral game mechanic that was "game-breaking", thus primarily having to do with the theme of immersion (Q4). Through discussion, some submissions categorized by the authors as having to do with one theme were reassigned to a different theme and one novel theme, analyzing moves, was suggested but did not end up being ranked highly by participants. Another theme, competition, was suggested as being different from achievement. The pre-determined theme of habit was not seen to match any of the responses. The full database of responses and assigned themes are available as Supplementary Materials.

### 3.2. Mixed Methods Synthesis

Table 3 presents results of nonparametric quantitative analysis that describe consensus on themes as they were ranked by participants. Immersion (e.g., *exploration of dynamic universe*) and achievement (e.g., *rewards*) emerged as important features of games that motivated playing (Q1), but there was less agreement on game type, mood and competition. Social factors (e.g., *online interactions with terrible people*) and novelty (e.g., *repetition/grinding with little variety*) were considered equally important reasons to stop playing (Q2). Immersion (e.g., *games that are crashy or slow*) was also agreed to be somewhat important, but achievement (*games that are not balanced*), environment (*out of time*), and mood (*not fun anymore*) were considered less important.

Social factors showed up again in Q3 as a strategy people could use to self-regulate (e.g., *play with others in a game that requires everyone to be present*). One response categorized as social described how online group play could limit gaming time. Participants debated this initially, but after deliberation agreed that choosing to play games online in groups might be an effective way to reduce time as other group members' leave, disrupting the group. Self-regulation strategies were also considered important. Responses focused on setting firm goals (*just three quests*) or limiting time (*setting an alarm, set a schedule for gaming time that is after your other work/responsibilities have been finished*) or money spent on gaming.

For Q4, there was strong agreement that the game industry could make it easier for players to self-regulate by changing or adding behavioral game mechanics (e.g., *clear break points, rewards for short sessions, negative reinforcement like XP decay*). Participants also offered social (*taking away features of online multiplayer and have local play only*) or environment-related (e.g., *integrated health tips into game that use health points that players can use themselves*) strategies, but these were less often ranked. The group also suggested benefits to new technology such as augmented reality games (e.g., Pokémon GO) that would offer novelty (*local multiplayer fun with new tech*), but there was low consensus on this theme. The group discussed this with regard to the benefits of staying grounded in the real world, especially when playing with others, which was thought to be useful for reducing the feeling of immersion that could lead to time loss.

## 4. Discussion

This study used a systematic, consensus-developing participatory approach with members of the gaming community to explore the importance gamers assigned to themes about self-regulating gaming. We found that even a small group (n = 7) was able to offer many specific suggestions that could form the basis of preventive interventions (Figure 1). These results support the emphasis on game mechanics and self-regulation identified in previous research [8,9,19], but add an additional dimension, social factors, that presents a new potential focus of prevention research. The findings also contribute to the importance of incorporating cultural insider knowledge about gaming and self-regulation into research and intervention development across disciplines.

The fact that gamers endorse the theme of self-regulation so strongly suggests that integrating specific techniques for promoting self-regulation (Figure 1) into preventive interventions may be a worthwhile approach. These strategies may be more palatable when endorsed by the gaming community itself. One possibility would be to have celebrity gamers (e.g., popular Twitch streamers) suggest or even discuss such strategies with their gaming audience. Hearing about risk from trusted individuals is important, and recent research shows that the general public may place greater trust in social media personalities than experts who may offer conflicting or confusing messages [37]. Streamers do address mental health topics in Twitch [38], so this may become an important mode for delivering preventive interventions relating to video game play.

Our small sample had many specific suggestions about features to include or leave out of games, such as exit points—places where they could leave the game without feeling that more had to be done. Exit points have been specifically mentioned as a factor of ethical game design that can be promoted in the video game industry [39]. Exit points may be unique to games and were not included in a recent expert-developed list of recommended tools for the prevention of problematic gambling that could be revised to address gaming disorder [14].

Another specific suggestion was to incentivize taking breaks. Our sample mentioned how games sometimes punish players for limiting their play, for example temporarily blocking players from team play if the leave a team abruptly. While games may do this to foster engagement, this also makes it more difficult for gamers to leave when competing opportunities or demands arise, such as a friend's request for a visit or the dawning recognition that time has passed and the dishes still need to be washed. Games can also reward breaks by manipulating experience gains, either by allowing players to progress faster when they return from a break or limiting progress after long sessions. While interventions related to experience gains have been implemented in several countries (experience decay), this approach may be less appealing to game developers [12]. In contrast, allowing faster progress when returning from a break (e.g., rested experience) may be a more palatable way to reward healthy amounts of gaming.

Social factors are an area brought up by our participants that seems to have little mention in suggestions for prevention interventions. Our sample found them important as a driver of disengaging (negative online interactions) and self-regulating (playing with others in a game that requires everyone to be present). In fact, this theme is a good example of the strength of a group reflection process as it reflected a single participant's suggestion. At the beginning of the discussion, most participants didn't understand or agree with the suggestion that choosing to "play with others in a game that requires everyone to be present ... since the other players can effectively force you to stop" would be a good way to self-regulate, but after a few minutes of discussion, six out of seven people ranked that as one of the most effective ways to limit time. This reveals the unique benefit to conducting a Delphi method approach with gamers as stakeholders—the perspective of an individual can be clarified within a group and ultimately recognized as a ground truth: Yes, if we choose to play games with that require a group, our time may be limited whether we choose to limit it (or are able to effectively limit it) or not.

Our findings suggest that focusing research and prevention efforts without involving insights from community members may unnecessarily limit the range of potential interventions decision-makers consider and impede progress toward implementation. The current epistemological approach toward research on gaming disorder places greater emphasis on clinical expertise rather than multiple perspectives [40]. The findings here challenge this traditional approach by considering gamers as vital co-creators of knowledge. For example, loot boxes have been the focus of much public health activity related to gaming disorder to date [13,41], yet loot boxes or other gambling-like mechanics were not mentioned by our sample. Other targets may be more palatable to multiple stakeholders, potentially easier to achieve, or more effective at preventing problematic gaming. Gamers are also useful in pointing out nuances of how we think about interventions. For example, while research may concentrate on immersion as a motivating factor for problematic gaming, our applied research here allowed gamers themselves to make a clear link between an example intervention (pop-ups) and the experience of losing immersion (pop-ups as game-breaking).

While this study was limited in sample size, it does reflect the gender (male) and age of gamers in the United States [42,43]. The small size does limit generalizability, and other sample makeups may suggest different responses. For example, our sample was self-selected for attending a science fiction and education convention and participating in a panel focused on gaming research. Other samples may prioritize different themes when ranking questions related to self-regulation. Our sample also felt the theme of Immersion to be more important than achievement—had we used a sample of gamers at a gaming tournament, for example, this would likely be different. In addition, our sample was English-speaking and based in the US, so findings may not transfer to other countries or cultures. However, one goal of this study was to demonstrate that the combination of perspective seeking, deliberation and systematic quantitative consensus analysis provides additional information beyond that of a survey, interview or focus group. Further research would benefit from systematic recruitment of a large sample of various stakeholders and a formal, multi-round consensus development technique in an online format to encourage transparency.

## 5. Conclusions

Formal consensus development techniques with gamers produced many specific examples of ways gamers can self-regulate and also emphasized the importance of game mechanics in fostering healthy gaming and preventing gaming disorder. These examples are supported by previous research and could serve as the basis for interventions to promote healthy gaming (Figure 1). Going forward, decision makers could increase the value of research on the prevention of problematic or disordered gaming by involving gamers, developers, clinicians and other stakeholders in co-learning about self-regulation strategies, game mechanics, and other features of game engagement.

**Author Contributions:** Conceptualization, M.C.C. and A.B.L.; data curation, M.C.; formal analysis, M.C.C., M.C. and A.B.L.; funding acquisition, M.C.C.; investigation, M.C.C.; methodology, M.C.C., M.C. and A.B.L.; project administration, M.C.C., M.C. and A.B.L.; resources, M.C. and A.B.L.; supervision, M.C.C. and A.B.L.; validation, M.C.C.; visualization, M.C.; writing—original draft, M.C.C.; writing—review and editing, M.C.C., M.C. and A.B.L. All authors have read and agreed to the published version of the manuscript.

**Acknowledgments:** The authors wish to thank Nico Pandi of the Museum of Science Fiction in Washington, D.C. for his extensive support.

## References

1. American Psychiatric Association. *Diagnostic and Statistical Manual of Mental Disorders*, 5th ed.; American Psychiatric Association: Arlington, VA, USA, 2013.
2. World Health Organization WHO. Gaming Disorder. Available online: http://www.who.int/features/qa/gaming-disorder/en/ (accessed on 28 May 2020).
3. Mihara, S.; Higuchi, S. Cross-sectional and longitudinal epidemiological studies of internet gaming disorder: A systematic review of the literature. *Psychiatry Clin. Neurosci.* **2017**, *71*, 425–444. [CrossRef] [PubMed]
4. González-Bueso, V.; Santamaría, J.J.; Fernández, D.; Merino, L.; Montero, E.; Ribas, J. Association between Internet Gaming Disorder or Pathological Video-Game Use and Comorbid Psychopathology: A Comprehensive Review. *Int. J. Environ. Res. Public Health* **2018**, *15*, 668. [CrossRef]
5. Männikkö, N.; Ruotsalainen, H.; Miettunen, J.; Pontes, H.M.; Kääriäinen, M. Problematic gaming behaviour and health-related outcomes: A systematic review and meta-analysis. *J. Health Psychol.* **2017**, *71*, 425–444. [CrossRef] [PubMed]
6. Przybylski, A.K.; Weinstein, N. A Large-Scale Test of the Goldilocks Hypothesis: Quantifying the Relations Between Digital-Screen Use and the Mental Well-Being of Adolescents. *Psychol. Sci.* **2017**, *28*, 204–215. [CrossRef] [PubMed]
7. World Health Organization WHO. Gaming behavior. Available online: https://www.who.int/substance_abuse/activities/gaming_disorders/en/ (accessed on 28 May 2020).
8. Van Rooij, A.J.; Daneels, R.; Liu, S.; Anrijs, S.; Looy, J.V. Children's Motives to Start, Continue, and Stop Playing Video Games: Confronting Popular Theories with Real-World Observations. *Curr. Addict. Rep.* **2017**, *4*, 323–332. [CrossRef]
9. Wood, R.T.A.; Griffiths, M.D.; Parke, A. Experiences of time loss among videogame players: An empirical study. *Cyber Psychol. Behav.* **2007**, *10*, 38–44. [CrossRef]
10. King, D.L.; Delfabbro, P.H. Predatory monetization schemes in video games (e.g. 'loot boxes') and internet gaming disorder. *Addiction* **2018**, *113*, 1967–1969. [CrossRef]
11. Snodgrass, J.G.; Lacy, M.G.; Francois Dengah, H.J., II; Fagan, J. Enhancing one life rather than living two: Playing MMOs with offline friends. *Comput. Hum. Behav.* **2011**, *27*, 1211–1222. [CrossRef]
12. Kiraly, O.; Griffiths, M.D.; King, D.L.; Lee, H.-K.; Lee, S.-Y.; Banyai, F.; Zsila, A.; Takacs, Z.K.; Demetrovics, Z. Policy responses to problematic video game use: A systematic review of current measures and future possibilities. *J. Behav. Addict.* **2018**, *7*, 503–517. [CrossRef]
13. Zendle, D.; Bowden-Jones, H. Loot boxes and the convergence of video games and gambling. *Lancet Psychiatry* **2019**, *6*, 724–725. [CrossRef]

14. Griffiths, M.D.; Pontes, H.M. The Future of Gaming Disorder Research and Player Protection: What Role Should the Video Gaming Industry and Researchers Play? *Int. J. Ment. Health Addict.* **2019**, 1–7. [CrossRef]
15. Booth, C. Facebook and Instagram officially announce new tools to fight social media addiction. Available online: https://thenextweb.com/facebook/2018/08/01/social-media-addiction-facebook-instagram/ (accessed on 17 February 2020).
16. Apple Use Screen Time on your iPhone, iPad, or iPod touch. Available online: https://support.apple.com/sl-si/HT208982 (accessed on 17 February 2020).
17. Derevensky, J.L.; Richard, J. Response to Commentary: The Future of Gaming Disorder Research and Player Protection: What Role Should the Video Gaming Industry and Researchers Play. *Int. J. Ment. Health Addict.* **2019**, 1–9. [CrossRef]
18. Kuss, D.J. Policy, prevention, and regulation for Internet Gaming Disorder. *J. Behav. Addict.* **2018**, *7*, 553–555. [CrossRef]
19. Colder Carras, M.; Porter, A.M.; Van Rooij, A.J.; King, D.; Lange, A.; Carras, M.; Labrique, A. Gamers' insights into the phenomenology of normal gaming and game "addiction": A mixed methods study. *Comput. Hum. Behav.* **2018**, *79*, 238–246. [CrossRef] [PubMed]
20. Shi, J.; Potenza, M.N.; Turner, N.E. Commentary on: "The Future of Gaming Disorder Research and Player Protection: What Role Should the Video Gaming Industry and Researchers Play?". *Int. J. Ment. Health Addict.* **2020**, 1–9. [CrossRef]
21. Claassen, C.A. The agenda development process of the United States' National Action Alliance for Suicide Prevention Research Prioritization Task Force. *Crisis* **2013**, *34*, 147–155. [CrossRef]
22. Khodyakov, D.; Savitsky, T.D.; Dalal, S. Collaborative learning framework for online stakeholder engagement. *Health Expect.* **2015**, *19*, 868–882. [CrossRef] [PubMed]
23. Dalal, S.; Khodyakov, D.; Srinivasan, R.; Straus, S.; Adams, J. ExpertLens: A system for eliciting opinions from a large pool of non-collocated experts with diverse knowledge. *Technol. Forecast. Soc. Chang.* **2011**, *78*, 1426–1444. [CrossRef]
24. Jones, L.; Wells, K. Strategies for academic and clinician engagement in community-participatory partnered research. *JAMA* **2007**, *297*, 407–410. [CrossRef]
25. Creswell, J.; Klassen, A.; Plano Clark, V.; Smith, K. *Best Practices for Mixed Methods Research in the Health Sciences*; National Institutes of Health: Rockville, MD, USA, 2011.
26. Morgan, D.L. Paradigms Lost and Pragmatism Regained: Methodological Implications of Combining Qualitative and Quantitative Methods. *J. Mix. Methods Res.* **2007**, *1*, 48–76. [CrossRef]
27. Levitt, H.M.; Bamberg, M.; Creswell, J.W.; Frost, D.M.; Josselson, R.; Suárez-Orozco, C. Journal article reporting standards for qualitative primary, qualitative meta-analytic, and mixed methods research in psychology: The APA Publications and Communications Board task force report. *Am. Psychol.* **2018**, *73*, 26–46. [CrossRef] [PubMed]
28. APA Style Journal Article Reporting Standards (APA Style JARS). Available online: https://apastyle.apa.org/jars/index (accessed on 4 May 2020).
29. King, D.; Delfabbro, P.; Griffiths, M. Video game structural characteristics: A new psychological taxonomy. *Int. J. Ment. Heal. Addict.* **2009**, *8*, 90–106. [CrossRef]
30. MDA: A Formal Approach to Game Design and Game Research. Available online: https://users.cs.northwestern.edu/~{}hunicke/MDA.pdf (accessed on 28 May 2020).
31. Ido, S. Using the Agential Structure Model to Classify Fun. Available online: https://www.gamasutra.com/blogs/SatoshiIdo/20170828/304503/Using_the_Agential_Structure_Model_to_classify_fun.php (accessed on 28 May 2020).
32. VandenBerghe, J. The 5 Domains of Play: Applying Psychology's Big 5 Motivation Domains to Games. In Proceedings of the 2012 Game Developers Conference (GDC), San Francisco, CA, USA, 25–29 March 2012.
33. Braun, V.; Clarke, V. Using thematic analysis in psychology. *Qual. Res. Psychol.* **2006**, *3*, 77–101. [CrossRef]
34. Museum of Science Fiction 2017 Museum of Science Fiction: Escape Velocity Prospectus and Program Guide. 2017. Available online: https://static1.squarespace.com/static/52615e54e4b051d1915a8890/t/5a15da39652dea2e1ac54cfb/1511381569778/MOSF+Prospectus+and+EV2017+Program+Guide+Web+Res.pdf (accessed on 1 May 2020).

35. StataCorp. *Stata Statistical Software: Release 13*; StataCorp LP.: College Station, TX, USA, 2013.
36. Chatfield, M.; Mander, A. The Skillings–Mack test (Friedman test when there are missing data). *Stata J.* **2009**, *9*, 299–305. [CrossRef] [PubMed]
37. World Health Organization. *Communicating Risk in Public Health Emergencies: A WHO Guideline for Emergency Risk Communication (ERC) Policy and Practice*; World Health Organization: Geneva, Switzerland, 2018; ISBN 92-4-155020-1.
38. Halberstadt, B. YouTubers and Streamers Speak up about Mental Health | GEMH Lab. Available online: https://gemhlab.com/blog/depression/lets-talk-about-mental-health-youtubers-and-twitch-streamers-speak/ (accessed on 15 February 2020).
39. Extra Credits Exit Points-Putting Down the Game Extra Credits. 2015. Available online: https://www.youtube.com/watch?v=GqjkWec61gQ (accessed on 17 September 2019).
40. Rumpf, H.-J.; Achab, S.; Billieux, J.; Bowden-Jones, H.; Carragher, N.; Demetrovics, Z.; Higuchi, S.; King, D.L.; Mann, K.; Potenza, M.; et al. Including gaming disorder in the ICD-11: The need to do so from a clinical and public health perspective. *J. Behav. Addict.* **2018**, *7*, 556–561. [CrossRef]
41. King, D.L.; Delfabbro, P.H. Video Game Monetization (e.g., 'Loot Boxes'): A Blueprint for Practical Social Responsibility Measures. *Int. J. Ment. Health Addict.* **2018**, *17*, 166–179. [CrossRef]
42. Duggan, M. Gaming and Gamers. Pew Research Center: Internet, Science & Tech. 2015. Available online: http://www.pewinternet.org/2015/12/15/gaming-and-gamers/ (accessed on 30 December 2015).
43. Entertainment Software Association Essential Facts about the Computer and Video Game Industry: 2018 Sales, Demographic and Usage Data. 2018. Available online: https://www.theesa.com/wp-content/uploads/2019/03/ESA_EssentialFacts_2018.pdf (accessed on 30 April 2019).

9

# Problematic Smartphone Use: Investigating Contemporary Experiences Using a Convergent Design

**Daria J. Kuss [1,*], Lydia Harkin [1], Eiman Kanjo [2] and Joel Billieux [3,4]**

1 International Gaming Research Unit, Psychology Department, Nottingham Trent University, Nottingham NG1 4FQ, UK; lydia.harkin02@ntu.ac.uk
2 Computing and Technology Department, Nottingham Trent University, Nottingham NG1 4FQ, UK; eiman.kanjo@ntu.ac.uk
3 Addictive and Compulsive Behaviour Lab., Institute for Health and Behaviour, Integrative Research Unit on Social and Individual Development (INSIDE), University of Luxembourg, Esch-sur-Alzette, L-4365 Luxembourg, Luxembourg; joel.billieux@uni.lu
4 Addiction Division, Department of Mental Health and Psychiatry, University Hospitals of Geneva, 44041 Geneva, Switzerland
* Correspondence: daria.kuss@ntu.ac.uk

**Abstract:** Internet-enabled smartphones are increasingly ubiquitous in the Western world. Research suggests a number of problems can result from mobile phone overuse, including dependence, dangerous and prohibited use. For over a decade, this has been measured by the Problematic Mobile Phone Use Questionnaire (PMPU-Q). Given the rapid developments in mobile technologies, changes of use patterns and possible problematic and addictive use, the aim of the present study was to investigate and validate an updated contemporary version of the PMPU-Q (PMPU-Q-R). A mixed methods convergent design was employed, including a psychometric survey ($N = 512$) alongside qualitative focus groups ($N = 21$), to elicit experiences and perceptions of problematic smartphone use. The results suggest the PMPU-Q-R factor structure can be updated to include smartphone dependence, dangerous driving, and antisocial smartphone use factors. Theories of problematic mobile phone use require consideration of the ubiquity and indispensability of smartphones in the present day and age, particularly regarding use whilst driving and in social interactions.

**Keywords:** smartphone; problematic mobile phone use; convergent design; focus group; survey

## 1. Introduction

The Western world has seen a significant increase in mobile technology use in the last decade. In 2016, the communications regulator Ofcom [1] referred to the UK as a "smartphone society"; 93% of the population own a smartphone, and users spend more time accessing the Internet via a phone than through other devices, such as laptops and desktop-computers. These recent trends suggest mobiles and the Internet have become intimately intertwined to enable "on-the-go" access to a range of facilities, including web-browsing, communication, shopping, banking, and gaming [1].

Recent research suggests a number of problems can result from smartphone overuse, including addiction-like symptoms and feelings of dependence [2,3], dangerous use, particularly whilst driving [4,5], and forbidden or prohibited use in areas such as libraries, classrooms, or public transport [6]. Accumulating evidence also connects excessive mobile phone use with increasing psychopathological symptoms, such as those related to depression and anxiety [7]. In other words, research suggests excessive mobile phone use can result from psychopathology and constitute a dysfunctional strategy to cope with adverse emotions. Similarly, King et al. [8] suggested that mobile phone checking can constitute a safety behaviour in anxious individuals. Internet-enabled devices may encourage checking behaviours by hosting a range of applications (or apps) with regular updates and notifications. Thus, mobile Internet use may increase habitual checking behaviours, which may contribute to developing and maintaining symptoms of psychopathology, such as addictive use [9]. Consequently, a growing number of studies are conducted to determine whether smartphone overuse constitutes a genuine addictive disorder (e.g., [10]), which is in line with the inclusion of a behavioural addiction category in the latest edition of the Diagnostic and Statistical Manual of Mental Disorders (DSM-5; [11]). Yet, to date, the evidence supporting problematic smartphone use as an addictive disorder is scarce, and the studies emphasizing behavioural and neurobiological similarities between problematic smartphone use and other types of recognised addictive disorders are limited [12].

### *1.1. Gaining a Contemporary View of Smartphone Behaviours*

Past research on problematic mobile phone and addictive smartphone behaviours employed quantitative methodologies to examine negative consequences associated with smartphone use. Various ways of measuring problematic smartphone use have been proposed considering different criteria and sources, including empirical evidence [13,14], substance abuse criteria [4,15–20], pathological gambling criteria [19,21], reviews of the relevant literature [2,17,18,22–24], or Internet addiction criteria [23]. When it comes to determining when smartphone use becomes problematic, it is important to be aware that time spent using these devices is not a sufficient indicator. For instance, it has been found that time spent socialising on mobile apps left users with positive mood [25]. Thus, the types of smartphone interactions appear to have varying impacts on user wellbeing. However, merely reading, removing, and scrolling through messages leaves users with negative emotions [25]. In addition to utilising a quantitative research approach, an experiential perspective based on users' own perceptions and understanding of their smartphone use may offer significant insights into what constitutes problematic smartphone use and how it is experienced on an individual level. User perceptions of smartphones can help to define what aspects of this technology are beneficial or problematic.

However, experiential evidence of mobile devices is outdated. Surveys capturing smartphone perspectives have failed to keep up with the speed of technological advancement and often do not reflect the full range of behaviours possible on modern smartphones [25]. Relatively recent smartphone interactions, particularly those which are supported by 'on-the -go' Internet technology, have not been accounted for and may influence problematic smartphone experiences. An experiential perspective based on users' own perceptions and understanding of their smartphone use may offer significant insights into what constitutes problematic use and how it is experienced on an individual level. The present research aims to fill this gap in knowledge by using a mixed methods convergent design incorporating a qualitative exploration of perspectives on contemporary smartphone use.

### *1.2. Existing Measures of Problematic Smartphone Use*

A theory of problematic mobile phone use [12] suggests that there are three pathways which may result in negative and pathological smartphone behaviours, namely (i) the excessive reassurance pathway, (ii) the impulsive-antisocial pathway, and (iii) an extraversion pathway. These pathways suggest that personality, psychopathological symptoms, and frequency of smartphone use can have particular problematic consequences. The Problematic Mobile Phone Use Questionnaire (PMPU-Q) [2] was developed to assess various facets of problematic mobile phone use. The original questionnaire included four subscales: (1) prohibited use; (2) dangerous use; (3) dependent use, and (4) financial problems resulting from use.

Contemporary publications and theoretical reflections on problematic smartphone use take different perspectives relative to Billieux et al.'s proposed model [12]. For instance, financial implications may no longer be considered a contemporary problematic use of smartphones. Recent evidence links the evolution of mobile phones to smart technology with many benefits; social applications such as WhatsApp and Skype can now facilitate communication with little cost to the user, and apps are available, which support financial and banking activities [26,27]. In addition, the US Department of Transportation reported smartphone technology as a key distractor which can deflect the attention of pedestrians and drivers, leading to potential collisions [28]. Considering this, previous survey measures of problematic behaviours excluding such contemporary activities may only partially record problematic experiences. Given the rapid developments in mobile technologies, changes of use patterns and possible problematic and addictive use, the aim of the present study was to test and validate an updated contemporary version of the original PMPU-Q using a rigorous and innovative convergent parallel design. In order to investigate the efficacy of the existing measure of these phenomena, a psychometric survey was included in this study which featured the PMPU-Q and validated measures of smartphone affect.

## 2. Methods

### 2.1. Design

This study used a mixed methods methodological approach with a convergent parallel design. A mixed methods approach allowed for bridging two research traditions regarding problematic smartphone use by means of integrating large-scale psychometric inquiry with a qualitative analysis on personalized experiences, allowing for a better understanding of the validity of the PMPU-Q-R. Fetters et al. [29] identified a convergent parallel design as a suitable mixed method for investigating the validity of quantitative measures. Design convergence in this case refers to decreasing PMPU-Q measurement uncertainty by using different methods [29]. The updated PMPU-Q (PMPU-Q-R) was administered to a sample of smartphone users, together with a number of relevant other validated psychometric measures, to determine the construct validity and internal consistency of the measure. In the second phase, perceptions and experiences of smartphone use, including the respective usages (i.e., dependent, dangerous and prohibited), were explored using focus groups. This concurrent procedure was time efficient, and meant that interpretive analysis of each individual dataset informed the other [29]. This was important in the present study as interpretation required innovative, evidence-based reconceptualising of an evolving technology. Figure 1 demonstrates the convergent design employed in this study.

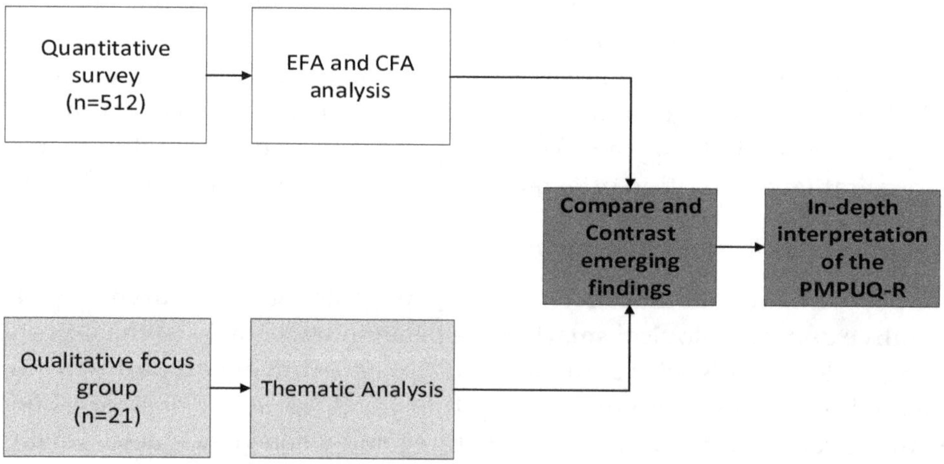


**Figure 1.** Convergent study design.

### 2.2. Study Recruitment

Smartphone users were recruited to the quantitative survey during December 2016 to March 2017 using opportunity and snowball sampling. Study advertisements encouraged smartphone users to follow a weblink to the survey hosted through Qualtrics in the UK. Offline advertisements were posted throughout university networks, and online advertisements were shared within student portals and social media networks, which focused on smartphone use. This social media dissemination included forums, Twitter, Facebook, and Reddit networks. Participants were considered eligible if they were smartphone users. Focus group participants were obtained from an opportunity sample of survey participants.

### 2.3. Study Procedures

#### 2.3.1. The PMPU-Q

The PMPU-Q was originally developed by Billieux and colleagues [2] and investigated four dimensions of problematic smartphone use: (1) prohibited use, (2) dangerous use, (3) dependent use, and (4) financial problems resulting from use. In this study, the financial problem scale was excluded as financial implications are no longer considered a contemporary problematic smartphone use [26,27]. In addition, items concerning pedestrian safety were included as dangerous items in the adapted PMPU-Q, as seen in Table 1. These adaptations produced the PMPU-Q-R, which was administered as a 17-item questionnaire. Responses were measured on a four-point Likert scale (ranging from 1 = strongly disagree to 4 = strongly agree).

**Table 1.** Items added to the PMPUQ.

| Item Question |
| --- |
| I use my mobile phone whilst crossing the road. |
| I have found myself in risky situations because I have used my mobile phone whilst walking. |

#### 2.3.2. Validated Measures for Comparative Analysis

1. Smartphone Addiction and Social Media Disorder

This survey included the Smartphone Addiction Scale (SAS) [16] and the Social Media Disorder Scale (SMD) [30]. These two scales measure excessive smartphone use as an addictive behaviour, and thus included items adapted from the substance abuse literature. The SAS consisted of ten items assessing symptoms of smartphone addiction. Statements relating to smartphone addiction were rated on a seven-point Likert scale ranging from 1 = strongly disagree to 7 = strongly agree. The SAS has previously demonstrated good internal consistency and concurrent validity [16]. Cronbach's alpha for this scale in the present study indicated good reliability ($\alpha = 0.88$). Recent research indicates a strong association between social media and smartphone use [31], supporting the inclusion of a psychometric tool assessing social media addiction. The SMD scale consisted of nine items representing eight aspects of social media disorder: preoccupation, tolerance, withdrawal, displacement, escape, problems, deception, displacement, and conflict. Participants were asked to rate, on a five-point Likert scale, how often they had experienced a symptom of social media disorder. The SMD scale has previously demonstrated appropriate internal consistency, good convergent and criterion validity, and sufficient test-retest reliability [30]. Cronbach's alpha in the present study indicated good reliability ($\alpha = 0.88$).

2. Psychopathology

The survey also included measures of psychopathological symptoms (depression, anxiety, stress, and ADHD), impulsivity, and the big five personality traits (i.e., neuroticism, extraversion, conscientiousness, agreeableness and openness) to assure content validity as the PMPU-Q has previously been linked to wellbeing and personality [2,4,32]. The Depression-Anxiety-Stress Scale (DASS-21; [33]) consisted of 21 measures of depression, anxiety, and stress symptoms experienced in the previous two weeks rated on a scale ranging from 0 (symptom did not apply to me at all) to 3 (applied to me very much, or most of the time). Impulsivity was rated using a short form of the Barratt Impulsiveness Scale (BIS-15) [34,35]. The DASS-21 and BIS-15 are both well established and highly cited scales, consistently demonstrating strong validity, reliability, and excellent internal validity [33,35,36]. Measures of Attention Deficit Hyperactivity Disorder (ADHD) symptoms approved by the World Health Organisation were included in the survey [37] as ADHD has been associated with smartphone addiction [38].

3. Focus Group Procedure

Three independent focus groups were used including two trained facilitators (LH and DK), and were scheduled for approximately 90 min, and held in a quiet university research room. Focus group questions were designed to ask general questions about smartphone experiences (e.g., "Can anyone tell us your favourite/least favourite smartphone uses, and why?") and to probe both beneficial and problematic aspects of smartphone experiences (e.g., "Can you tell us more about [experience]"). Eight prompt images were used on a PowerPoint slideshow to encourage discussion amongst participants, including images of smartphones used in different settings (e.g., on a train, in a library), and artistic depictions of smartphone use (e.g., cartoons and street art of smartphone use).

### 2.4. *Analyses*

#### 2.4.1. Quantitative Survey Analysis

The underlying structure of the PMPU-Q-R was assessed through exploratory factor analysis (EFA). This analysis was used to identify the latent constructs of smartphone experience underlying the variance in scores on measurements originally designed to measure mobile phone use. EFA analysis was conducted in IBM-SPSS with principle component analysis (PCA) and Direct Oblimin rotation, as recommended when establishing preliminary solutions [39,40].

CFA analysis was conducted to verify the factor structure of the variables. CFA was conducted in R package Lavaan using maximum likelihood estimators for CFA as they can effectively handle interactions between latent variables with multiple indicators [41,42]. To understand the fit of the model to the data, models were compared to threshold fit indices recommended by Hu and Bentler [43]. A model showing good fit to the data was expected to report CFI > 0.93, TLI > 0.93, RMSEA < 0.05 for very good fit, <0.084 for acceptable fit, and SRMR < 0.09.

The data set was randomly partitioned by a ratio 60:40 to run the factor analysis tests. Exploratory tests were performed on 60% of the data, and the proposed factor structure of the PMPUQ-R was examined on the remaining 40% of the data to test the proposed model on a second sample. This cross-validation approach is recommended to investigate the proposed model structure on independent datasets [44].

#### 2.4.2. Qualitative Thematic Analysis

Focus groups were audio recorded, and data were input into QSR-NVIVO, and analysed using thematic analysis [45] to explore smartphone experience. This involved familiarisation with the data by listening to and reading transcripts, generating initial codes for key features in the transcripts, searching for connections between codes (or themes), and reviewing and defining the identified themes based on the evidence presented across focus groups. Analysis was primarily conducted by Lydia Harkin. Themes were discussed amongst the wider team to assess the developing logic, in addition to discussing the apparent similarities and divergences within the qualitative and qualitative data.

### 2.5. *Ethical Considerations*

Participants provided informed consent to take part in this study. Only participants who agreed to be contacted for focus groups were invited for group interview. All contact information was stored securely, and after the study was completed, all identifying information was removed from the transcripts and destroyed. This study was given ethical approval by the Business, Law, and Social

Sciences Ethics Committee at Nottingham Trent University and abided by the ethical codes of the British Psychological Society.

## 3. Results

Participants in the quantitative survey were 512 smartphone users. The sample had a mean age of 25.5 (range = 13–68 years), were primarily female (78.5%), university students (67%), and from the United Kingdom (91.8%). Table 2 demonstrates the breakdown of demographics represented in this sample.

**Table 2.** Survey and Focus Group Participant Demographics.

| Participant Demographics | Survey Participants *N* (%) * | FG Participants *N* (%) |
|---|---|---|
| Gender | | |
| Male | 401 (20.9) | 10 (47.6) |
| Female | 107 (78.3) | 11 (52.4) |
| Prefer not to say | 3 (0.6) | 0 |
| Country of Origin | | |
| United Kingdom | 470 (91.8) | 21 (100) |
| USA | 10 (2) | |
| Ireland | 4 (0.8) | |
| Other | 49 (6.4) | |
| Level of Education | | |
| No formal qualifications | 4 (0.8) | 0 |
| GCSEs | 13 (2.5) | 0 |
| Further education | 286 (55.9) | 0 |
| Vocational qualification | 8 (1.6) | 10 (47.6) |
| Higher education | 122 (23.8) | 2 (9.5) |
| Postgraduate degree | 79 (15.4) | 9 (42.9) |
| Self-reported calls per day | | |
| 0–1 year | 262 (51.2) | |
| 2–5 years | 214 (41.8) | |
| 5–10 years | 27 (5.3) | |
| >10 years | 8 (1.6) | |
| Self-reported texts per day | | |
| 0–5 | 50 (9.8) | 1 (4.8) |
| 5–10 | 64 (12.5) | 6 (28.6) |
| 10–20 | 82 (16) | 4 (19) |
| 20–30 | 79 (15.4) | 2 (9.5) |
| 30–40 | 39 (7.6) | 3 (14.3) |
| >40 | 198 (38.7) | 4 (19) |
| Self-reported time spent on phone p/day | | |
| <30 min | 10 (2) | 0 |
| 30 min–1 h | 34 (6.6) | 4 (19) |
| 1–2 h | 134 (26.2) | 8 (38) |
| 3–5 h | 219 (42.8) | 7 (33.3) |
| 5–10 h | 92 (18) | 2 (9.5) |
| >10 h | 22 (4.3) | 0 |

* Note. Rounding may have led to percentages that do not equal 100.

### 3.1. Exploratory Factor Analysis

Firstly, 16 of the 17 items on the PMPU-Q-R correlated over 0.3 with at least one other item, indicating reasonable factorability [46,47]. Secondly, a Kaiser-Meyer-Olkin measure of sampling adequacy was 0.859, above the commonly recommended value of 0.6. Thirdly, Bartlett's test of sphericity was significant ($\chi^2$ (120) = 1682.441, $p < 0.001$), indicating the present sample had a suitable size for factor analysis. Finally, the communalities of 16 of the 17 items were above 0.3, confirming that these 16 items shared common variance with other items. One item from the original 'prohibited use' scale did not share variance with the body of items, and was excluded from further analyses ("When using my mobile phone on public transport, I try not to talk too loud"). The EFA revealed a three-factor solution which explained 54% of the variance in scores. Cronbach's alpha indicated the items consistently measured a closely related set of concepts ($\alpha = 0.86$). All latent variables positively correlated with one another. For factors one and two, this correlation was moderate to strong ($R^2 = 0.436$), whilst factor two correlated weakly with factor three ($R^2 = 0.172$). However, factor three correlated very weakly with factor one ($R^2 = 0.043$). Thus, the factors appeared to measure related, but distinct, concepts.

As Table 3 indicates, the pattern structure produced in the data did not correspond to the theoretical structure of the PMPU-Q-R. In line with the predefined PMPU-Q-R structure, all dependence items loaded highly together on one factor, with no cross-loadings onto factors two or three. The dependence factor explained 35% of variance in overall scores, and demonstrated high reliability ($\alpha = 0.89$). A combination of seven items from the original prohibited and dangerous mobile phone use subscales loaded highly onto one factor, explaining 12% of the variance, suggesting the factor labels of 'prohibited' and 'dangerous' smartphone use could not be applied to the items within the scale for this population. On face value, the items contributing to this factor did not demonstrate an immediately apparent underlying theoretical property as demonstrated in Table 3. However, alpha scores indicated a high level of shared variance in scores ($\alpha = 0.77$). Finally, two items from the dangerous subscale loaded highly onto factor three, explaining 8% of the score variance. A Cronbach's alpha calculation is not meaningful for a two item factor, and therefore a Pearson correlation coefficient was calculated, showing a significant low to moderate correlation ($R^2 = 0.33$, $p < 0.001$), indicating two distinct measures of a related concept. A review of these items revealed that they were the only PMPU-Q-R items to refer to driving behaviours: "I use my mobile phone while driving" and "I try to avoid using my mobile phone when driving on the motorway" ($R^2 = 0.43$, $p < 0.001$).

**Table 3.** Factor loadings for the PMPUQ-R items.

| Original Item Subscale | | Factor Loading | | |
|---|---|---|---|---|
| | | 1 | 2 | 3 |
| Dependence | I can easily live without my mobile phone * | 0.869 | | |
| Dependence | I feel lost without my mobile phone | 0.844 | | |
| Dependence | It is hard for me to turn my mobile phone off | 0.769 | | |
| Dependence | It is easy for me to spend all day not using my mobile phone | 0.747 | | |
| Dependence | I get irritated when I am forced to turn my mobile phone off | 0.699 | | |
| Dependence | I don't attach a lot of importance to my mobile phone * | 0.694 | | |
| Dependence | Is it hard for me not to use my mobile phone when I feel like it | 0.495 | | |
| Prohibited use | I don't use my mobile phone when it is completely forbidden to use it * | | 0.701 | |
| Prohibited use | I don't use my mobile phone in a library, cinema, or hospital * | | 0.700 | |
| Prohibited use | I use my mobile phone where it is forbidden to do so | | 0.673 | |
| Danger | I have found myself in risky situations because I have used my mobile phone whilst walking | | 0.583 | |
| Danger | I use my mobile phone whilst crossing the road | | 0.574 | |
| Prohibited use | I try to avoid using my mobile phone where people need silence * | | 0.568 | |
| Danger | I use my mobile phone in situations that would qualify as dangerous | | 0.563 | |
| Danger | I use my mobile phone while driving | | | 0.758 |
| Danger | I try to avoid using my mobile phone when driving on the motorway | | | 0.751 |

* Reversed item.

This factor structure was tested using a CFA. As expected, all items showed significant positive factor loadings with standardised coefficients ranging from 0.482 to 0.805 (see Table 4). Additionally, modification indices were low (<50), which indicated that items corresponded to the proposed structure of the PMPUQ-R and did not covary too strongly with other items. The model showed an adequate fit to the data, with most of the indices of model fit falling within the acceptable values for the CFA model to fit the variance in scores ($\chi^2$ (101) = 190.424, $p < 0.000$, CFI = 0.927, TLI = 0.906, RMSEA = 0.062, SRMR = 0.054).

**Table 4.** Beta coefficients and significance values of PMPUQ-R factor loadings.

| Latent Factor | Item | B | Standard Error | Beta (Standardised) | Sig |
|---|---|---|---|---|---|
| Dependence | x1 | 1.000 | | 0.504 | ** |
| Dependence | x2 | 0.941 | 0.278 | 0.485 | *** |
| Dependence | x3 | 1.000 | | 0.661 | *** |
| Dependence | x4 | 0.847 | 0.148 | 0.474 | *** |
| Dependence | x5 | 1.053 | 0.136 | 0.627 | *** |
| Dependence | x6 | 0.763 | 0.13 | 0.483 | *** |
| Dependence | x7 | 0.978 | 0.141 | 0.599 | *** |
| Factor 2 | x8 | 0.895 | 0.126 | 0.602 | *** |
| Factor 2 | x9 | 0.745 | 0.124 | 0.482 | *** |
| Factor 2 | x10 | 1.000 | | 0.79 | *** |
| Factor 2 | x11 | 0.570 | 0.07 | 0.568 | *** |
| Factor 2 | x12 | 0.797 | 0.075 | 0.72 | *** |
| Factor 2 | x13 | 0.774 | 0.073 | 0.714 | *** |
| Factor 2 | x14 | 0.954 | 0.075 | 0.805 | *** |
| Danger | x15 | 0.839 | 0.08 | 0.714 | *** |
| Danger | x16 | 0.849 | 0.075 | 0.752 | *** |

*** $p < 0.001$; ** $p = 0.001$.

### *3.2. Construct Analyses*

To shed light on the theoretical constructs underpinning the PMPUQ factor structure, Spearman's correlations were calculated with the new factor structure and validated measures connected to problematic technology and smartphone behaviours. These were summed measures of smartphone and addictive social media use, psychopathology (i.e., depression, stress, anxiety; and ADHD), and impulsivity. These scales were correlated with the three-factor structure emerging from our survey. Only correlations which were significant and within the low to high range (0.2–1) are reported here. Notably, no significant correlations were found for the dangerous driving-related item scores.

An increase in dependence-related items strongly correlated with increased smartphone addiction symptoms ($R^2$ = 0.67, $p < 0.001$), self-reported smartphone addiction ($R^2$ = 0.66, $p < 0.001$), and moderately correlated with social media addiction symptoms ($R^2$ = 0.44, $p < 0.001$). Additionally, dependence items weakly correlated with stress symptoms ($R^2$ = 0.22, $p < 0.001$), and attention impulsivity ($R^2$ = 0.26, $p < 0.001$).

Higher scores on the second, undefined factor strongly correlated with smartphone addiction symptom scores ($R^2$ = 0.52, $p < 0.001$), and with social media addiction symptoms ($R^2$ = 0.44, $p < 0.001$), self-reported smartphone addiction ($R^2$ = 0.42, $p < 0.001$), attention impulsivity symptoms ($R^2$ = 0.33, $p < 0.001$), motor impulsivity symptoms ($R^2$ = 0.25, $p < 0.001$), and ADHD symptoms ($R^2$ = 0.24, $p < 0.001$).

### *3.3. Thematic Analysis*

Three focus groups were attended by a total of 21 individuals (11 females). Focus groups lasted an average of 96 min. Participant self-reported smartphone use ranged considerably, as highlighted in Table 2. The focus groups produced lively discussions about the integration of smartphones in participants' lives. Thematic analysis of the focus group data revealed three distinct themes across perceptions of problematic smartphone use. These themes were smartphone dependence, dangerous driving, and antisocial smartphone use.

3.3.1. Smartphone Dependence

Across all three focus groups, participants discussed the dependence their lives had on smartphones and applications. This theme incorporated both problematic and beneficial use. Many participants awoke with their smartphone alarms, read news or played games as they travelled to work or university, used email apps to support out-of-hours' work, and to contact friends through social media. Thus, participants associated smartphones with many aspects of their day, much beyond the capabilities of traditional texting or calling. This was not perceived as necessarily problematic, and many participants emphasised that they benefitted from the integration of smartphones in day-to-day life.

> *P8: "My Smartphone is literally my life (laugh). Self-professed addict. I know the whole discussion has been generally negative, but erm, I still feel the positives outweigh any negatives that we get . . . (holds up phone) this is my calendar, this is how I communicate with everybody, how I organise my life, how I get up in the morning. It is my adult pacifier." Focus group 1.*

Smartphone dependence was discussed as an act of balancing benefits with potentially problematic aspects. Daily smartphone use could lead to habitual checking behaviours and wasted time. Therefore, several participants made attempts to delete particular apps or groups of apps. For instance, across two focus groups, discussions around the utility of *Facebook* and other social media arose. These apps were perceived as 'addictive' because participants compulsively checked their social media, despite limited beneficial interactions or information. Most participants were unsuccessful in attempts to reduce time on smartphones due to the convenience and functionality of the devices. One participant had successfully stopped using all social media for 29 days prior to the focus group, and yet he found himself searching for other apps to use on his phone in replacement of his prior social media use. Therefore, the dependence on smartphones in daily life seemed to have a profound impact on the thoughts and actions of participants.

> *P5: "I have moulded my phone around me. My music, my pictures, everything. And I would probably feel lost without it." Focus group 2.*

> *P1: (After quitting social media for 29 days) "So yeah my immediate reaction was like finding a replacement, not necessarily thinking oh I don't have social media I need a replacement for it, but it was kind of what can I go on now? So it didn't occur to me that I could just not go on my phone." Focus group 2.*

3.3.2. Dangerous Driving Behaviours

Of the problematic behaviours described by participants in the focus groups, driving whilst actively engaging with a smartphone was described as unequivocally problematic and dangerous. These types of actions were differentiated from some other potentially harmful smartphone uses. Participants were open to accepting smartphone use behaviours, such as crossing the road and walking, as an inevitable outcome of the proliferation of smartphone use. Discussions around emotionally dangerous behaviours, such as trolling online, were also perceived as a necessary evil of having constant exposure to the Internet. Thus, dangerous driving stood out distinctly as a problematic smartphone behaviour.

> *P2: "It (seeing people driving whilst on smartphones) infuriates you even when you see it and you know they are driving ridiculously." Focus group 1.*

> *P5: "My best friend always does that (uses smartphone) in the car. I am like . . . you are on Instagram. (Name) what are you doing? You are going to kill me. I have to take her phone, I am holding your phone." Focus group 3.*

*P3: "Maybe you should learn how to cross the road safely while using your phone because that is what adult people do. It is like crossing the road with the red light on. We all do it. I do it at least, and I think I do it safely ... I wouldn't say don't use it. I would say just be careful. Know how to use it." Focus group 1.*

### 3.3.3. Antisocial Smartphone Use

The antisocial properties of smartphone use emerged as a strong indicator of problematic behaviours, according to participants in this study. Participants were concerned that smartphone use often replaced face-to-face interactions. Groups of friends or couples were observed together in the 'real world', whilst seemingly disengaged from one another because they were using smartphones. This was perceived as indicative of poor social functioning. Similarly, several participants described feeling rejected or upset when their friends became distracted from their face-to-face conversations by their smartphones.

*P2: "I feel personally ... even if it's in a group and someone starts taking their phone out I feel like a sting of rejection, so I'll like sting them back. So I'm looking on my phone even if I've got no reason to. I'll just try and find a reason to look on my phone and then hope that they see that I don't need them either." Focus Group 2.*

*P6: "My partner absolutely drives me crazy on the phone. We go out for dinner ... and he just sits there like that (mime sitting with phone in front). And that is all he does. And it is a nightmare going for dinner. And he never used to do it. All I can see is him like that (mime holding phone in front of face) constantly. It drives me mad." Focus group 1.*

The antisocial properties of regular smartphone use seemed to govern and moderate participants' behaviours. In particular, participants were concerned about how they would be perceived by others. Using smartphones too frequently or in dangerous or prohibited situations was perceived as embarrassing and reflective of their character. Many participants did not want to be viewed as someone who 'needs' their smartphone. For this reason, a few participants had enforced rules on how they, their partner, or friends were allowed to use their smartphones. For instance, several participants 'banned' smartphone use in restaurants during romantic meals, and others endeavoured not to use their smartphones while walking in the street.

*P5: "I don't want to be seen as someone who, like in a restaurant me and my boyfriend never have ours out ... because I don't want people to look at me and be like 'oh god, she needs her phone out" Focus group 1.*

*P9: "I hate the idea of being thought of as somebody who can't put my phone down." Focus group 3.*

## 4. Discussion

The present study aimed to investigate and validate an updated contemporary version of the original PMPU-Q, the PMPU-Q-R, using a rigorous and innovative convergent design. The PMPU-Q-R was tested to determine how many factors emerged from the scale, and how this corresponded with the theoretical underpinnings of the original PMPU-Q subscales [2]. Construct validity of the PMPU-Q-R items was investigated, alongside existing contemporary measures of problematic smartphone behaviours, and psychopathology. The quantitative data inquiry using an EFA revealed the pattern structure did not correspond to the expected and predefined structure of the PMPU-Q. Whilst the dependence factor was explained well by the data, a second factor was made up by a combination of items of the prohibited and dangerous subscales, suggesting the factor labels of 'prohibited' and 'dangerous' smartphone use could not be applied to the items within the scale for this sample. An explanation for this may be the rapid expansion and development of mobile technology since the development of the original PMPU-Q [2], which may have contributed to the results. Smartphone functionality has significantly increased in this time period, including the availability of high-quality satellite navigation and location-based augmented reality games (e.g., *Pokémon-GO*), changing the possible risks related to engaging in smartphone activities.

An increase in dependence-related items strongly correlated with increased self-reported smartphone addiction symptoms (measured via items considering excessive smartphone use as addictive disorder), and moderately correlated with social media addiction symptoms. This provides support for the construct validity of the dependence subscale. Previous research [31] has suggested that addictive smartphone use may be part of social media addiction. According to the pathway model of problematic mobile phone use [12], an addictive pattern of smartphone use is characterized by the use of specific applications, including calls and instant messaging. This definition could be extended by evidence from the focus group discussions; participants found that features, such as social media, emails, and games, contributed to increased feelings of dependence. This suggests that rather than being an addictive medium per se, mobile technologies including smartphones and tablets are media that enable the engagement in potentially addictive activities, including social media use. Similarly, it has been argued that individuals do not become addicted to the medium of the Internet per se, but to the activities they engage in on the Internet [48], such as gaming [49] or social media use [50]. With the advent and ubiquity of mobile technologies, this supposition appears particularly pertinent. Using social networking sites is a particularly popular activity on smartphones, with around 80% of social media used via mobile technologies [51], and around 75% of *Facebook* users access *Facebook* via their smartphones [52]. Consequently, social media use and smartphone use appear inherently intertwined [31], suggesting future research should pay additional attention to the forms and functions of specific smartphone use.

Additionally, dependence items weakly correlated with stress symptoms, and attention impulsivity. With regards to stress, it has been shown that the increased use of smartphones was related to general distress, anxiety and depression [13,53,54]. Further research [9] also highlighted that stress predicts addictive smartphone use. Individuals may use their smartphones to cope with everyday stressors (e.g., social situations, relationship problems), and using smartphones as coping mechanism can be considered dysfunctional, similar to using the Internet to cope with life problems [55], resembling symptoms traditionally associated with substance-related addictions [56].

Considering attention impulsivity, previous research [2] has shown that impulsivity was a strong predictor of problematic smartphone use, specifically with regards to the subscales urgency, lack of premeditation and lack of perseverance, which appear related to attention impulsivity [57]. Similarly, the present research found that higher scores on the dependence factor strongly correlated with ADHD symptoms, which is in line with previous research [58] in children. Alternatively, it has been suggested that particular types of activities engaged in on smartphones, e.g., gaming, may lead to the development of ADHD symptoms, suggesting future research may be necessary to disentangle the differential impact of specific smartphone application use on possible dependence.

In addition to this, the thematic analysis applied in the present research revealed that there appears to be a strong awareness that using smartphones whilst driving can be dangerous both for the self and for others, which corroborates the quantitative data regarding the PMPU-Q-R dangerous driving factor. This suggests the driving factor is a valid and reliable factor that contributes to explaining contemporary problematic smartphone use, and should therefore be retained in future analyses of problematic smartphone use.

Findings from the qualitative and quantitative analysis suggested that dangerous driving stands out as a distinct form of problematic smartphone behaviour. This corroborates the US Department of Transportation's report showing smartphone use can distract pedestrians and drivers, leading to potential collisions [28]. In 2014, over 3000 individuals died in the US as a consequence of being distracted while driving, leading the US National Highway Traffic Safety Administration (NHTSA) to issue voluntary guidelines for smartphone developers, which aim to restrict the functions of smartphones being used by a driver. A recent report by the American Automobile Association

Foundation found that using smartphones, including Apple's voice control system Siri, is very dangerous in the context of driving as it leads to cognitive distraction [59].

The thematic analysis of the focus group data revealed three distinct themes across perceptions of problematic smartphone use, namely smartphone dependence, dangerous driving, and antisocial smartphone use. With regards to the first theme, smartphone dependence, the thematic analysis indicated smartphones are essential elements of individuals' lives as they are being used for their many functions, going beyond phone calls and texting, including other entertainment functions (e.g., music, pictures), as well as organisational functions (i.e., calendar, alarm). Participants perceived particular smartphone applications as being potentially addictive, including social media, which they were checking compulsively, although there were limited advantages of doing so. Participants found it difficult to reduce the time they spent on their smartphones as these were perceived to be very convenient and functional.

Antisocial smartphone use emerged as a key problematic behaviour, as evidenced through the thematic analysis. Importantly, when looking at the prohibited use items of the PMPU-Q-R, clear links between the qualitative and quantitative analyses emerged. Indeed, most of the prohibited items refer to situations where using smartphones is banned, implying that scoring highly on these items depicts engaging in antisocial behaviours. Beside prohibited use per se, this was a key observation as some individuals use their smartphones in social contexts, which may similarly appear as antisocial, and can consequently impact negatively on their overall social functioning, both in terms of the quality of interaction with others, and with regards to perceptions of rudeness and rejection in interpersonal contexts. Along the same lines, recent research focused on the "phubbing" phenomenon, defined as the act of snubbing someone in a social setting by using one's phone instead of interacting, and research has shown that such types of antisocial smartphone use are linked to lack of self-control [60] and lower relationship satisfaction among romantic partners [61].

In the current study, participants discussed how they disapproved of friends or couples disengaging from one another whilst engaging with their smartphones, leading to feeling devalued. Similar situations and behaviours have been observed in the context of young people disconnecting from their offline contacts for the sake of connecting online, which has been linked to a preference for online social interaction [62]. This was tied to an awareness of public perceptions on the individuals' smartphone use, often leading to behavioural change in terms of limiting use in particular situations and contexts, as found in the present research.

With regards to the integration of both methods using the adopted convergent design, the findings confirm that a combination of prohibited and dangerous items from the PMPU-Q-R may be explained by antisocial smartphone use. Further research is necessary to inquire about motivations for smartphone use, as well as the norms of smartphone use in public, given that stigma and public perceptions appear to significantly contribute to how smartphone use is perceived by the users regarding being prohibited or dangerous. The focus group data analysis furthermore revealed that public perceptions may lead to behavioural change in terms of how individuals engage with their smartphones, emphasising the need to assess problematic smartphone use within its sociocultural context, bearing in mind the cultural and behavioural norms associated with smartphone use. Using anthropological and cultural studies may aid our understanding and study of the impacts of technology use as it has been shown to be particularly insightful in the study of specific technology use, such as gaming, given it allows for an assessment of the behavioural norms and practices surrounding a concrete behaviour [63,64]. The individual's context is a significant factor that can mark the dividing line between problematic smartphone use and potential smartphone "addiction", and the smartphone use context can gain particular importance for users, depending on their life situation (i.e., the meaning they attach to their smartphone) and smartphone use preferences (i.e., particular types of apps used and activities engaged in). Moreover, the cultural context is significant because it embeds the smartphone user in a community with shared beliefs and practices, endowing their use with particular meaning as well as possible stigma. The context of the individual, the specific smartphone use and the smartphone use environment, as well as the broader framework of the respective culture the user is situated in are relevant in the study of problematic smartphone use and are therefore recommended to be used in the context of future smartphone use research [10].

Regarding the methodology that has been utilised in the present research, mixed methods have been employed, integrating quantitative with qualitative techniques. There was an existing body of theory to draw on [12], but it needed updating, so mixed methods allowed us to combine previous theory with present experiential understanding. The mixing of quantitative with qualitative methods is a challenging endeavour, particularly as these methods can be understood as separate scientific paradigms. One could claim these methods are incommensurate as their unit of analysis (i.e., words versus numbers), their epistemological position (i.e., knowledge derived from meaning versus behaviours), and their source of scientific knowledge (i.e., induction versus deduction) are inherently incompatible. Accordingly, the adherence to a single method could be seen as the epitome of normal science, indicating a scientific revolution is necessary to integrate the seemingly incongruous positions of quantitative and qualitative research. This integration overcomes the limitations of a single methodology, i.e., its inevitable incompleteness. The usage of mixed methods, on the other hand, allows for the corroboration, elaboration, and complementation of findings [65]. The present study corroborated the PMPU-Q-R structure in terms of the dependence factor, and suggested that dangerous driving is a distinct factor that needs considering when studying problematic smartphone use. Moreover, the qualitative element of this research complemented the quantitative findings with regards to the combination of the dangerous and prohibited factor by elaborating on how antisocial use and public perceptions may contribute to individual perceptions of norms surrounding smartphone use in different contexts.

## 5. Conclusions

The updated version of the PMPU-Q, the PMPU-Q-R, is a valid and reliable tool for measuring contemporary smartphone use and problems associated with this use, concerning dependence, antisocial use and dangerous driving. Future research is encouraged to discern user motivations and perceptions of usage norms and meanings applied to smartphone use to delineate the impact social stigma may have on smartphone use. The convergent design used in the present study appeared to offer a corroborative and complementary perspective on contemporary knowledge of problematic smartphone use, and has expanded the knowledge base in the field of behavioural technological addictions. Taken together, contemporary smartphone use may become problematic if engaged in excessively. Nonetheless, contemporary smartphone users often actively seek to modify their behaviours when they are being perceived as problematic, suggesting users appear aware and conscious of their usage patterns, which may limit the extent of problematic use.

**Acknowledgments:** We would like to acknowledge Nottingham Trent University (grant number Kickstarter_DK1), and the British Academy and the Leverhulme Trust (grant number SG162119) for funding this research.

**Author Contributions:** D.J.K. designed the study, collected the data and wrote the manuscript, including subsequent iterations. L.H. collected the data, completed the data analyses, and wrote the results section. E.K. co-designed the study. All authors contributed to the final write-up.

## References

1. The UK Is Now a Smartphone Society. Available online: http://media.ofcom.org.uk/news/2015/cmr-uk-2015/ (accessed on 28 August 2016).
2. Billieux, J.; Van der Linden, M.; Rochat, L. The role of impulsivity in actual and problematic use of the mobile phone. *Appl. Cogn. Psychol.* **2008**, *22*, 1195–1210. [CrossRef]
3. Chóliz, M. Mobile phone addiction: A point of issue. *Addiction* **2010**, *105*, 373–374. [PubMed]
4. Bianchi, A.; Phillips, J.G. Psychological predictors of problem mobile phone use. *Cyberpsychol. Behav.* **2005**, *8*, 39–51. [CrossRef] [PubMed]

5. White, M.P.; Eiser, J.R.; Harris, P.R. Risk perceptions of mobile phone use while driving. *Risk Anal.* **2004**, *24*, 323–334. [CrossRef] [PubMed]
6. Nickerson, R.C.; Isaac, H.; Mak, B. A multi-national study of attitudes about mobile phone use in social settings. *Int. J. Mob. Commun.* **2008**, *6*, 541–563. [CrossRef]
7. Elhai, J.D.; Levine, J.C.; Dvorak, R.D.; Hall, B.J. Non-social features of smartphone use are most related to depression, anxiety and problematic smartphone use. *Comput. Hum. Behav.* **2017**, *69*, 75–82. [CrossRef]
8. King, A.L.S.; Valença, A.M.; Silva, A.C.O.; Baczynski, T.; Carvalho, M.R.; Nardi, A.E. Nomophobia: Dependency on virtual environments or social phobia? *Comput. Hum. Behav.* **2013**, *29*, 140–144. [CrossRef]
9. Jeong, S.-H.; Kim, H.; Yum, J.-Y.; Hwang, Y. What type of content are smartphone users addicted to? SNS vs. games. *Comput. Hum. Behav.* **2016**, *54*, 10–17. [CrossRef]
10. Lopez-Fernandez, O.; Kuss, D.J.; Romo, L.; Morvan, Y.; Kern, L.; Graziani, P.; Rousseau, A.; Rumpf, H.J.; Bischof, A.; Gässler, A.K.; et al. Self-reported dependence on mobile phones in young adults: A European cross-cultural empirical survey. *J. Behav. Addict.* **2017**, *6*, 168–177. [CrossRef] [PubMed]
11. American Psychiatric Association. *Diagnostic and Statistical Manual of Mental Disorders (DSM-5)*; American Psychiatric Association: Arlington, VA, USA, 2013.
12. Billieux, J.; Maurage, P.; Lopez-Fernandez, O.; Kuss, D.J.; Griffiths, M.D. Can disordered mobile phone use be considered a behavioral addiction? An update on current evidence and a comprehensive model for future research. *Curr. Addict. Rep.* **2015**, *2*, 156–162. [CrossRef]
13. Ha, J.H.; Chin, B.; Park, D.H.; Ryu, S.H.; Yu, J. Characteristics of excessive cellular phone use in Korean adolescents. *Cyberpsychol. Behav.* **2008**, *11*, 783–784. [CrossRef] [PubMed]
14. Toda, M.; Monden, K.; Kubo, K.; Morimoto, K. Cellular phone dependence tendency of female university students. *Nihon Eiseigaku Zasshi* **2004**, *59*, 383–386. [CrossRef] [PubMed]
15. Chóliz, M. Mobile-phone addiction in adolescence: The Test of Mobile Phone Dependence (TMD). *Prog. Health Sci.* **2012**, *21*, 33–44.
16. Kwon, M.; Lee, J.; Won, W.; Park, J.; Min, J.; Hahn, C.; Kim, D. Development and validation of a Smartphone Addiction Scale. *PLoS ONE* **2013**, *8*, e56936. [CrossRef] [PubMed]
17. Lopez-Fernandez, O.; Honrubia-Serrano, L.; Freixa-Blanxart, M.; Gibson, W. Prevalence of problematic mobile phone use in British adolescents. *Cyberpsychol. Behav. Soc. Netw.* **2014**, *17*, 91–98. [CrossRef] [PubMed]
18. Walsh, S.P.; White, K.M.; Young, R.M. Needing to connect: The effect of self and others on young people's involvement with their mobile phones. *Aust. J. Psychol.* **2010**, *62*, 194–203. [CrossRef]
19. Xu, H.; Wu, X.; Lan, Y.; Chen, Y. Development of mobile phone dependence inventory for college students. *Chin. J. Clin. Psychol. Health* **2008**, *16*, 26–27.
20. Yen, C.F.; Tang, T.C.; Yen, J.Y.; Lin, H.C.; Huang, C.F.; Liu, S.C.; Ko, C.H. Symptoms of problematic cellular phone use, functional impairment and its association with depression among adolescents in Southern Taiwan. *J. Adolesc.* **2009**, *32*, 863–873. [CrossRef] [PubMed]
21. Jenaro, C.; Flores, N.; Gomez-Vela, M.; Gonzalez-Gil, F.; Caballo, C. Problematic internet and cell-phone use: Psychological, behavioral, and health correlates. *Addict. Res. Theory* **2007**, *15*, 309–320. [CrossRef]
22. Güzeller, C.O.; Cosguner, T. Development of a problematic mobile phone use scale for Turkish adolescents. *Cyberpsychol. Behav. Soc. Netw.* **2012**, *15*, 205–211. [CrossRef] [PubMed]
23. Kim, D.; Lee, Y.; Lee, J.; Nam, J.; Chung, Y. Development of Korean smartphone addiction proneness scale for youth. *PLoS ONE* **2014**, *9*, e97920. [CrossRef] [PubMed]
24. Martinotti, G.; Villella, C.; Di Thiene, D.; Di Nicola, M.; Bria, P.; Conte, G.; Cassano, M.; Petruccelli, F.; Corvasce, N.; Janiri, L.; et al. Problematic mobile phone use in adolescence: A cross-sectional study. *J. Public Health* **2011**, *19*, 545–551. [CrossRef]
25. Kanjo, E.; Kuss, D.J.; Ang, C.S. NotiMind: Responses to smartphone notifications as affective sensors. *IEEE Access* **2017**. [CrossRef]
26. Hanafizadeh, P.; Keating, B.; Khedmatgozar, H.R. A systematic review of Internet banking adoption. *Telemat. Inform.* **2014**, *31*, 492–510. [CrossRef]
27. Lyman, T.; Pickens, M.; Porteous, D. *Regulating Transformational Branchless Banking: Mobile Phones and Other Technology to Increase Access to Finance*; CGAP & Deparment for International Development: London, UK, 2008.
28. Scopatz, R.A.; Zhou, Y. *Effect of Electronic Device Use on Pedestrian Safety: A Literature Review*; National Highway Traffic Safety Administration: Washington, DC, USA, 2016.

29. Fetters, M.D.; Curry, L.A.; Creswell, J.W. Achieving integration in mixed methods designs—Principles and practices. *Health Serv. Res.* **2013**, *48*, 2134–2156. [CrossRef] [PubMed]
30. Van den Eijnden, R.J.J.M.; Lemmens, J.S.; Valkenburg, P.M. The Social Media Disorder Scale: Validity and psychometric properties. *Comput. Hum. Behav.* **2016**, *61*, 478–487. [CrossRef]
31. Kuss, D.J.; Griffiths, M.D. Social Networking Sites and Addiction: Ten lessons learned. *Int. J. Environ. Res. Public Health* **2017**, *14*, 311. [CrossRef] [PubMed]
32. Billieux, J. Problematic Mobile Phone Use: A literature review and a pathways model. *Curr. Psychiatry Rev.* **2012**, *8*, 299–307. [CrossRef]
33. Lovibond, S.H.; Lovibond, P.F. *Manual for the Depression Anxiety Stress Scales*, 2nd ed.; Psychological Foundation: Sydney, Australia, 1995.
34. Patton, J.H.; Stanford, M.S.; Barratt, E.S. Factor structure of the Barratt Impulsiveness Scale. *J. Clin. Psychol.* **1995**, *51*, 768–774. [CrossRef]
35. Spinella, M. Normative data and a short form of the Barratt Impulsiveness Scale. *Int. J. Neurosci.* **2007**, *117*, 359–368. [CrossRef] [PubMed]
36. Henry, J.D.; Crawford, J.R. The short-form version of the Depression Anxiety Stress Scales (DASS-21): Construct validity and normative data in a large non-clinical sample. *Br. J. Clin. Psychol.* **2005**, *44*, 227–239. [CrossRef] [PubMed]
37. Kessler, R.C.; Adler, L.; Ames, M.; Demler, O.; Faraone, S.; Hiripi, E.; Howes, M.J.; Jin, R.; Secnik, K.; Spencer, T.; et al. The World Health Organization Adult ADHD Self-Report Scale (ASRS): A short screening scale for use in the general population. *Psychol. Med.* **2005**, *35*, 245–256. [CrossRef] [PubMed]
38. Khang, H.; Kim, J.K.; Kim, Y. Self-traits and motivations as antecedents of digital media flow and addiction: The Internet, mobile phones, and video games. *Comput. Hum. Behav.* **2013**, *29*, 2416–2424. [CrossRef]
39. Beavers, G.A.; Iwata, B.A.; Lerman, D.C. Thirty years of research on the functional analysis of problem behavior. *J. Appl. Behav. Anal.* **2013**, *46*, 1–21. [CrossRef] [PubMed]
40. Pett, M.A.; Lackey, N.R.; Sullivan, J. *Making Sense of Factor Analysis: The Use of Factor Analysis for Instrument Development in Health Care Research*; Sage: London, UK, 2003.
41. Muthén, L.K.; Muthén, B.O. *Mplus User's Guide*, 6th ed.; Muthén & Muthén: Los Angeles, CA, USA, 2011.
42. Rosseel, Y. lavaan: An R Package for Structural Equation Modeling. *J. Stat. Softw.* **2012**, *48*, 1–36. [CrossRef]
43. Hu, L.T.; Bentler, P.M. Cutoff criteria for fit indexes in covariance structure analysis: Conventional criteria versus new alternatives. *Struct. Equ. Model. Multidiscip. J.* **1999**, *6*, 1–55. [CrossRef]
44. Bandalos, D.L. Factors influencing cross-validation of confirmatory factor analysis models. *Multivar. Behav. Res.* **1993**, *28*, 351–374. [CrossRef] [PubMed]
45. Braun, V.; Clarke, V. Using thematic analysis in psychology. *Qual. Res. Psychol.* **2006**, *3*, 77–101. [CrossRef]
46. Tabachnick, B.G.; Fidell, L.S. *Using Multivariate Statistics*, 4th ed.; Allyn and Bacon: Boston, MA, USA, 2001.
47. Williams, B.; Onsman, A.; Brown, T. Exploratory factor analysis: A five-step guide for novices. *J. Emerg. Prim. Health Care* **2010**, *8*, 1–13.
48. Starcevic, V.; Billieux, J. Does the construct of Internet addiction reflect a single entity or a spectrum of disorders? *Clin. Neuropsychiatry* **2017**, *14*, 5–10.
49. Kuss, D.J.; Griffiths, M.D. Internet gaming addiction: A systematic review of empirical research. *Int. J. Ment. Health Addict.* **2012**, *10*, 278–296. [CrossRef]
50. Kuss, D.J.; Griffiths, M.D. Online social networking and addiction—A review of the psychological literature. *Int. J. Environ. Res. Public Health* **2011**, *8*, 3528–3552. [CrossRef] [PubMed]
51. Marketing Land Nearly 80 Percent of Social Media Time Now Spent on Mobile Devices. Available online: http://marketingland.com/facebook-usage-accounts-1-5-minutes-spent-mobile-171561 (accessed on 29 January 2017).
52. Statista Share of Facebook Users Worldwide Who Accessed Facebook via Mobile from 2013 to 2018. Available online: https://www.statista.com/statistics/380550/share-of-global-mobile-facebook-users/ (accessed on 29 January 2017).
53. Hong, F.-Y.; Chiu, S.-I.; Huang, D.-H. A model of the relationship between psychological characteristics, mobile phone addiction and use of mobile phones by Taiwanese university female students. *Comput. Hum. Behav.* **2012**, *28*, 2152–2159. [CrossRef]

54. Panova, T.; Lleras, A. Avoidance or boredom: Negative mental health outcomes associated with use of Information and Communication Technologies depend on users' motivations. *Comput. Hum. Behav.* **2016**, *58*, 249–258. [CrossRef]
55. Kuss, D.J.; Dunn, T.J.; Wölfling, K.; Müller, K.W.; Hędzelek, M.; Marcinkowski, J. Excessive Internet use and psychopathology: The role of coping. *Clin. Neuropsychiatry* **2017**, *14*, 73–81.
56. Kuss, D.J.; Shorter, G.W.; van Rooij, A.J.; Griffiths, M.D.; Schoenmakers, T. Assessing Internet addiction using the parsimonious Internet addiction components model—A preliminary study. *Int. J. Ment. Health Addict.* **2014**, *12*, 351–366. [CrossRef]
57. Billieux, J.; Van der Linden, M.; D'Acremont, M.; Ceschi, G.; Zermatten, A. Does impulsivity relate to perceived dependence on and actual use of the mobile phone? *Appl. Cogn. Psychol.* **2007**, *21*. [CrossRef]
58. Byun, Y.H.; Ha, M.; Kwon, H.J.; Hong, Y.C.; Leem, J.H.; Sakong, J.; Kim, S.Y.; Lee, C.G.; Kang, D.; Choi, H.D.; et al. Mobile phone use, blood lead levels, and attention deficit hyperactivity symptoms in children: A longitudinal study. *PLoS ONE* **2013**, *8*, e59742. [CrossRef] [PubMed]
59. Strayer, D.L.; Turrill, J.; Coleman, J.R.; Ortiz, E.V.; Cooper, J.M. *Measuring Cognitive Distraction in the Automobile II: Assessing in-Vehicle Voice-Based Interactive Technologies*; American Automobile Association Foundation: Salt Lake City, UT, USA, 2014.
60. Chotpitayasunondh, V.; Douglas, K.M. How "phubbing" becomes the norm: The antecedents and consequences of snubbing via smartphone. *Comput. Hum. Behav.* **2016**, *63*, 9–18. [CrossRef]
61. Roberts, J.A.; David, M.E. My life has become a major distraction from my cell phone: Partner phubbing and relationship satisfaction among romantic partners. *Comput. Hum. Behav.* **2016**, *54*, 134–141. [CrossRef]
62. Caplan, S.E. Theory and measurement of generalized problematic Internet use: A two-step approach. *Comput. Hum. Behav.* **2010**, *26*, 1089–1097. [CrossRef]
63. Karlsen, F. *A World of Excesses; Online Games and Excessive Playing*; Ashgate: Farnham, UK, 2013.
64. Kuss, D.J. *For the Horde! How Playing World of Warcraft Reflects Our Participation in Popular Media Culture*; LAP LAMBERT Academic Publishing: Saarbrücken, Germany, 2013.
65. Brannen, J. Mixing methods: The entry of qualitative and quantitative approaches into the research process. *Int. J. Soc. Res. Methodol.* **2005**, *8*, 173–184. [CrossRef]

# 10

# The Effect of Solution-Focused Group Counseling Intervention on College Students' Internet Addiction

**Xinhe Zhang [1], Xiaoxuan Shi [1], Shuowei Xu [1], Jingwen Qiu [1], Ofir Turel [2] and Qinghua He [1,3,4,5,*]**

1 Faculty of Psychology, Ministry of Education Key Laboratory of Cognition and Personality, Southwest University, Chongqing 400715, China; guhong15@126.com (X.Z.); shixx@email.swu.edu.cn (X.S.); adson2688@gmail.com (S.X.); qjw990130@email.swu.edu.cn (J.Q.)

2 Information Systems and Decision Sciences, California State University, Fullerton, CA 92831, USA; oturel@fullerton.edu

3 Chongqing Collaborative Innovation Center for Brain Science, Chongqing 400715, China

4 Southwest University Branch, Collaborative Innovation Center of Assessment toward Basic Education Quality at Beijing Normal University, Chongqing 400715, China

5 Institute of Psychology, Key Laboratory of Mental Health, Chinese Academy of Sciences, Beijing 100101, China

* Correspondence: heqinghua@swu.edu.cn

**Abstract:** This pilot study aimed to explore the effect of solution-focused group counseling intervention on Internet addiction among college students. Eighteen college students participated in this study, out of which nine subjects were assigned into the experimental group and the rest ($n = 9$) to a control group. The experimental group received group counseling for five weeks, while the control group did not receive any intervention. The revised version of the Chinese Internet Addiction Scale (CIAS-R) was used to capture pre-test and post-test excessive use in the two groups. The experimental group was also subjected to a follow-up test and self-reported Internet addiction scores six months after the end of group counseling. Results showed that after the five-week solution-focused group counseling, the scores of four dimensions of the CIAS-R in the experimental group had CIAS-R decreased, and the reduction trend of the total score of CIAS-R was similar across all subjects in this group. The treatment effect was larger than the placebo reduction in the control group in two dimensions: compulsive and withdrawal (Sym-C & Sym-W) and tolerance (Sym-T) symptoms. Qualitative research confirmed the conclusions from the quantitative data, showing that the experimental group reduced its Internet addiction symptoms. Overall, the findings suggested that solution-focused group counseling had positive intervention effects on Internet addiction.

**Keywords:** Internet addiction; solution-focused group counseling; intervention; college students

## 1. Introduction

The Internet can serve as a double-edged sword. On the one hand, it provides many benefits and increases convenience. On the other, its use can be highly alluring, which may result in excess consumption, which manifests in behavioral addiction-like symptoms [1]. Since Goldberg [2] proposed the concept of "Internet Addiction Disorder", many researchers have used similar concepts, such as Pathological Internet Use, Problematic Internet Use, Excessive Internet Use, and Internet Addiction [3].

Although these concepts are slightly different, they all have two common characteristics: (1) addiction-like symptoms: compulsive use of Internet, withdrawal reactions, and tolerance, combined with inability of users to effectively control themselves; (2) as a result, their daily functions such as academic and social activities, as well as sleep and food intake, are impaired [4]. We believe that the concept of Internet Addiction (IA) can best reflect the above characteristics and is widely used. While the term is controversial [5], for convenience reasons, we will use in this study the term Internet Addiction to describe this phenomenon, while acknowledging the need of future research to fine tune its definition and boundaries. IA has been recognized as a public health concern [6], which can correlate with poor health outcomes such as higher likelihood of being overweight [7], impaired sleep [8], increased suicidal ideation and attempt [9], and increased depressive symptoms [10].

College students can be highly susceptible to IA [11]. Once freed from the strict control of high school and family, they tend to have free time at their disposal, which when coupled with easy access to the Internet can lead to IA [12]. In addition, these students are experiencing changes in the environment with which they must learn to cope. For example, they face pressures on handling new interpersonal relationships and balancing learning and social activities [13]. Consequently, students may seek to relieve these pressures via Internet use, which can result in IA [14]. Among Chinese college students, IA is prevalent. Between 6.56% and 13.5% of Chinese college students may be classified as addicted to the Internet [15]. Therefore, paying close attention to issues related to college students' use of the Internet, and intervening if necessary, is critical for preventing IA and its adverse impacts [16].

Various schools of psychotherapy have been applied to alleviate IA. Among them, solution-focused brief therapy (SFBT), as a relatively new paradigm of post-modern constructivism, has also been applied to IA cases. Specifically, Yang [17] provided psychotherapy with an emphasis on SFBT and comprehensive family intervention to teenagers with IA, and reported positive results showing that SFBT can be an effective therapy for treating IA. SFBT evolved out of the clinical practice of Steve de Shazer, Insoo Kim Berg, and colleagues at the Brief Family Therapy Center in Milwaukee, Wisconsin, in the early 1980s [18]. SFBT change processes were originally grounded in the constructivist approaches to communication and social interactional theories [19]. Over time, SFBT also became associated with social constructionism and the philosophical, post-structural views of language such as in Wittgenstein's language games [20,21]. The main components of SFBT include looking for previous solutions, acknowledging problems but identifying that exceptions to the problem are key to the solution, focusing on present and future, as opposed to past-orientated questions, using validation, and utilizing techniques such as miracle questions, scaling questions, and coping questions [22].

Due to the high cost of psychotherapy, people strive for a faster and more effective treatment, which has led to the widespread application of SFBT, such as for treating students' emotional behavior problems [23], substance abuse [24], adolescent crisis events, suicide and self-harm [25]. SFBT is not only applied to psychotherapy and counseling, but also applied in school class management, enterprise management and other fields [26]. SFBT emphasizes using a positive perspective to comprehend people, expressing their affirmation, and fully trusting that people will understand the methods that suit them. It is complementary to traditional Confucian culture [27] and compatible with it [28]. As such, it is highly suitable for application in China, as demonstrated by large effects in Chinese populations [29].

Comparing SFBT with Cognitive Behavioral Therapy (CBT), Jordan, Froerar, & Brovelas [30] argue that professionals using CBT assume the expert role, aiming to identify problems in people's thinking and behavior. But professionals using SFBT regard their patients as already having all the resources they need, defining their own role as supportive in eliciting the individuals' strengths, and empowering people to articulate these into achievable goals for the future. Therefore, SFBT enables patients to look for possible behaviors to change, and puts patients in control as regulators of their behavioral changes. It is not only beneficial for patients to maintain behavioral change, but also helps them to improve self-efficacy, thus making it more suitable for college students' self-exploration and continuous transformation. In addition, some studies have shown that SFBT used more of the client's exact words, and used more positive language, than other therapies such as CBT and Motivational Interviewing (MI) [30,31]. Therefore, SFBT may be more beneficial to relieve patients' anxiety and their concerns towards the issue, thereby making it easier for college students who are sensitive and care about others' evaluation and social pressures to accept this method and reduce their resistance.

In addition, group counseling is an effective intervention for IA [32]. Compared to solution-focused individual counseling, applying SFBT to group counseling makes the process lively, encourages group members to share their experiences and promotes psychological growth with mutual support and encouragement from the group. Nevertheless, the efficacy of SFBT in group counseling to reduce IA in Chinese populations is not fully established. We aim at ameliorating this gap in this pilot study.

Specifically, we focused on applying SFBT in group counseling and explored the intervention effects of solution-focused group counseling on IA in college students. By examining immediate and long-term post-intervention effects, we aim at clarifying if solution-focused group counseling improves IA in college students. Based on the above mentioned findings of prior intervention studies applying SFBT in different contexts, we hypothesized that participants in the experimental group (i.e., those who will accept five-week solution-focused group counseling aimed at alleviating Internet Addiction core symptoms, such as compulsive use, withdrawal and tolerance, and Internet Addiction related problems such as interpersonal, health-related, and time management problems) will show significant changes in these aspects, beyond the placebo effects observed in a control group.

## 2. Materials and Methods

### 2.1. Study Design and Participants

Participants were screened from a sample of 27 college students who presented high IA symptomology, recruited through flyers on campus. Based on an initial interview and the Revised Chinese Internet Addition Scale (CIAS-R), we selected 18 subjects with scores ≥53. The other 9 had score <53 and were excluded. The final 18 participants were randomly assigned to experimental or control groups with inclusion criteria CIAS-R score ≥53, which represents moderate to high levels of IA. There were 9 in the experimental group, (male = 3, female = 6; age = 20.11 ± 1.45) and 9 in the control group (male = 3, female = 6; age = 20 ± 1.56). Non-parametric Mann-Whitney U tests showed that there was no significant difference in CIAS-R score between the two groups [$Z = -0.71$, $p > 0.05$]. We also used a self-reported Symptom Checklist-90 (SCL-90) questionnaire as an auxiliary selection tool, and the scores of each factor of the students in the two groups were less than 5, showing no symptoms of serious mental disorders. The study was given ethical approval by the Institutional Review Board of the Southwest University (No. 20180030).

### 2.2. Procedures

Closed semi-structured group counseling was conducted on the experimental group once a week for five weeks. Every counseling session lasted about two and a half hours. There were one leader and two assistants in the group. The leader is a certified psychotherapist, and the assistants are psychology graduate students trained for group counseling. Their roles followed basic procedures that were designed in advance. Participants were given free interaction space. The leader regulated and navigated the group process according to the needs of the members. The control group did not receive any intervention. Both groups completed surveys at t1 and t2 (t1 + 5 weeks). The intervention group also completed a t1 + 6 months survey. Instruments included in the survey are outlined in the next section.

### 2.3. Instruments

#### 2.3.1. Revised Chinese Internet Addiction Scale (CIAS-R)

The scale [33,34] consists of 19 items, on a four-point Likert scale. Two subscales are Internet Addiction Core Symptoms (IA-Sym) and Internet Addiction Related Problems (IA-RP). Core symptoms include four dimensions: Compulsive and Withdrawal Symptoms of Internet addiction (Sym–C&Sym-W), Tolerance Symptoms of Internet Addiction (Sym-T), Interpersonal and Health-Related Problems of Internet Addiction (RP-IH), and Time Management Problems (RP-TM).

The experimental group and the control group completed the scale before and after group counseling, and the experimental group also carried out follow-up measurement six months after group counseling. The higher the score, the greater the risk of IA is. CIAS-R is widely used in the measurement of IA. Several studies show that CIAS-R has good reliability, with Cronbach's alpha ranging from 0.85 to 0.90 [34–36]. In this study, Cronbach's alpha was 0.86, 0.89 and 0.83 in the three rounds of administration.

#### 2.3.2. Symptom Checklist-90 (SCL-90)

The Symptom Checklist-90 (SCL-90) has a total of 90 items rated on a five-point Likert scale. It includes 9 factors, such as depression and anxiety. Studies have found that IA may be comorbid with depression and anxiety disorders [37,38]. If comorbidity exists, it is very important to evaluate and treat related mental disorders. However, our group counseling mainly focused on Internet addiction and had no strong pertinence to other mental disorders. Therefore, SCL-90 is used to screen whether the subjects had major comorbid mental disorders.

#### 2.3.3. Scaling Questions Form

Scaling questions are representative questions of SFBT. Members of the experimental group are required to evaluate the current state of Internet use with a 10-point score, which increases successively from 0 ("the worst state of Internet use") to 10 ("the most ideal state of Internet use"). The experimental group completed the evaluation at the pre- and post-group counseling.

#### 2.3.4. Satisfaction Survey

The experimental group was asked to evaluate the overall satisfaction with group counseling at the end of each session on a 10-point Likert scale (from 0 = "very unsatisfied" to 10 = "very satisfied").

#### 2.3.5. Change Questionnaire after Group Counseling

Six months after group counseling, the experimental group members were tracked by a change questionnaire, to examine the sustainability of changes after receiving the group counseling. The questionnaire employed open-ended questions that asked whether there was any change in the behavior of members after they participated in group counseling compared with before, such as Internet use time, attitude towards Internet use, behaviors related to Internet use, and changes in other life aspects beyond Internet use.

### 2.4. *Data Analysis*

Quantitative data were analyzed with SPSS 23.0 (IBM Corp. Released, Armonk, NY, USA). We used the non-parametric Mann-Whitney U test and Friedman test for analyses. Qualitative data were sorted based on the Kawakita Jiro (KJ) method which is used to organize data into useful categories. It adopts the bottom-up sorting process and is very useful for classifying data. Based on the statement of significance of "Change after group counseling", researchers summarized, coded and recorded responses with concise, independent and clear phrases, extracted representative topics, and formed a comprehensive database of self-reported parsed statements from group members.

### 2.5. *Solution-Focused Group Counseling Programs*

The Solution Focused Brief Therapy Association listed three elements of SFBT [39]. First, there are the overall topics. SFBT conversations are centered on client concerns: who and what are important to the clients; a vision of a preferred future; clients' exceptions, strengths, and resources related to that vision; scaling of clients' motivational level and confidence in finding solutions; and ongoing scaling of clients' progress toward reaching the preferred future. Second, SFBT conversations involve a therapeutic process of co-constructing altered or new meanings in clients. Third, therapists use a number of specific responding and questioning techniques that invite clients to construct a vision of a preferred future and draw on their past successes, strengths, and resources to make that vision a reality. Based on the above factors we designed five focused-solution group counseling sessions (Table 1), with the purpose of assisting college students to establish the goal of alleviating IA (e.g., Ask group members: what changes about IA do you want to make after our group counseling sessions?), reconstruct the problem (e.g., Let group members reflect on the pros and cons of the internet through the group counseling sessions, discussing and sharing with each other), expand positive resources and exceptional experience (e.g., Ask group members: in your past life, to some extent, did you ever think that your internet usage has reached the target state?), and actively seek and enrich solutions (e.g., Let the group members list obstacles they may encounter when using the internet in the future, proving better solutions, after brainstorms.). In group counseling, the leader encouraged and assisted group members to share their experiences (e.g., All members were invited to participate in the group counseling sessions, freely expressing their views and feelings.), and actively adopt a variety of questions (e.g., When group members share twice regarding their changes, the leader will ask more details about what caused these changes.), compliments (e.g., At the end of each session, praise is given to the group members on their efforts to solve and conquer the problems of IA.), other techniques in SFBT (e.g., miracle question: When you go back to sleep in the dormitory tonight, a miracle will happen and all the problems that you brought here have all been solved. (Pauses) But because you are sleeping, you don't know that a miracle has happened. When you wake up the next day, what will you pay attention to, in order to know that a miracle has happened?).

**Table 1.** Solution-Focused Group Counseling Programs.

| Theme | Objective | Activity Process |
|---|---|---|
| You and I together | Preliminary understanding between group members; Clarify and establish a group contract to be observed by all members of the group; Arouse the interest of individuals in participating groups; Clarify members' expectations of the group and define members' personal goals. | 1. Warm up: The wind blows<br>2. Serial self-introduction<br>3. Form a group contract<br>4. Clarify members' personal goals<br>5. Complete the scaling question form<br>6. Feedback and homework: try to improve your score on scaling questions by 1 point; Think about and document the positive aspects of the Internet<br>7. Complete the satisfaction survey |
| When miracles happen | Reconstruct the problem of IA, discuss the change between group counseling interventions and a vision of a preferred future, and dig out the materials to solve the problem. | 1. Members share their change<br>2. Warm up: In the same boat<br>3. Share homework, reconstruct the problem of IA<br>4. Progressive muscle relaxation and miracle question<br>5. Feedback and homework: Think about and document the positive aspects of the Internet use<br>6. Complete the satisfaction survey |
| Look for a successful self | Explore exceptional experiences and successful experiences that have been achieved, expand positive resources, and gain confidence. | 7. Members share changes based on homework<br>8. Warm up: Trip to trust<br>9. Explore the exceptional experiences associated with internet use by group members<br>10. Feedback and homework: Replicate the exceptional experience<br>11. Complete the satisfaction survey |

**Table 1.** *Cont.*

| Theme | Objective | Activity Process |
|---|---|---|
| Make friends with the future | Discuss potential obstacles in the future and find and enrich solutions. | 1. Members share changes based on homework<br>2. Warm up: Break through the dilemma<br>3. Brainstorming: Discuss solutions to obstacles in the future<br>4. Leader gives a keynote speech: The content aims at the common trouble of the members of the previous three sessions—procrastination<br>5. Feedback and homework: Replicate the exceptional experience<br>6. Complete the satisfaction survey |
| Common agreement | Deal with the parting mood, discuss and summarize the changes brought by the group counseling to the members, praise the members and end the group. | 1. King and angel: assign roles<br>2. Warm up: Copy the human body<br>3. Share the overall changes from five sessions of group counseling<br>4. The angel wanted to talk to the king: Members compliment each other<br>5. End group counseling: Invite members to finish outcome questionnaire after six months<br>6. Complete the satisfaction survey and scaling question form |

## 3. Results

### 3.1. *Effects of Group Counseling Programs*

The change in scores between t1 and t2 was used to compare the treatment and the control group changes (△= post-test score − pre-test score). We compared the scores with the non-parametric Mann-Whitney U test. The changes in both groups are shown in Table 2. As can be seen, both groups showed reduction in IA symptoms, but the reductions in the experimental group were larger. Specifically, the intervention produced significantly larger reductions, compared to the control group, in two IA symptoms: compulsive use and withdrawal (Sym-C & Sym-W) and tolerance (Sym-T), as well as in the total IA score. The small reduction in the control group may manifest from learning and social desirability.

**Table 2.** Comparison between the Experimental and Control Groups.

| Measures | Experimental Group ($n$ = 9) | Control Group ($n$ = 9) | Z |
|---|---|---|---|
| Sym-C & Sym-W | −2.67 ± 2.17 | −0.88 ± 1.05 | −1.99 * |
| Sym-T | −2.78 ± 1.72 | −0.78 ± 1.20 | −2.48 * |
| RP-IH | −2.00 ± 2.83 | −0.11 ± 2.15 | −1.48 |
| RP-TM | −2.00 ± 2.45 | −0.89 ± 1.54 | −0.82 |
| Total IA | −9.44 ± 6.13 | −2.67 ± 4.24 | −2.26 * |

Note: Sym-C: compulsive use; Sym-W: withdrawal; Sym-T: tolerance; RP-IH: interpersonal and health-related problems; RP-TM: time management problems; * $p < 0.05$.

### 3.2. *Long-term Effects of the Intervention*

To examine long-term effects of the intervention, beyond the immediate post-intervention effects, we followed up with participants six months after t1. The results of the non-parametric Friedman test showed that significant effects existed in all dimensions of IA (Table 3). Statistical analysis of the data using the Wilcoxon signed-rank test revealed that the IA scores in the pre-test were significantly higher than those in the post-test and follow-up tests for three dimensions of IA: compulsive and withdrawal

(Sym-C & Sym-W), tolerance (Sym-T) and time management problems (RP-TM), as well as for the total IA score. In the dimension of interpersonal and health-related problems (RP-IH), the scores of the pre- and post-test were significantly higher than those of the follow-up test. As shown in Figure 1, the change trend of the total score of the CIAS-R was similar for all subjects in the experimental group.

**Table 3.** Comparison of the Differences among Pre-test, Post-test and Tracking Scores in the Experimental Group ($x \pm s$).

| Measures | Pre-Test (T1) | Post-Test (T2) | Follow-up Test (T3) | χ2 | Multiple Comparisons |
|---|---|---|---|---|---|
| Sym-C & Sym-W | 17.44 ± 1.67 | 14.78 ± 1.86 | 13.89 ± 2.67 | 11.46 ** | T1 > T2, T1 > T3 |
| Sym-T | 12.78 ± 1.72 | 10.00 ± 1.94 | 9.89 ± 2.20 | 13.15 ** | T1 > T2, T1 > T3 |
| RP-IH | 15.89 ± 2.09 | 13.89 ± 2.57 | 11.67 ± 2.78 | 13.24 ** | T1 > T3, T2 > T3 |
| RP-TM | 12.67 ± 1.73 | 10.67 ± 2.29 | 10.33 ± 1.32 | 11.53 ** | T1 > T2, T1 > T3 |
| Total IA | 58.78 ± 6.12 | 49.33 ± 6.63 | 45.78 ± 7.12 | 14.80 ** | T1 > T2, T1 > T3 |

Note: Sym-C: compulsive use; Sym-W: withdrawal; Sym-T: tolerance; RP-IH: interpersonal and health-related problems; RP-TM: time management problems; ** $p < 0.01$.

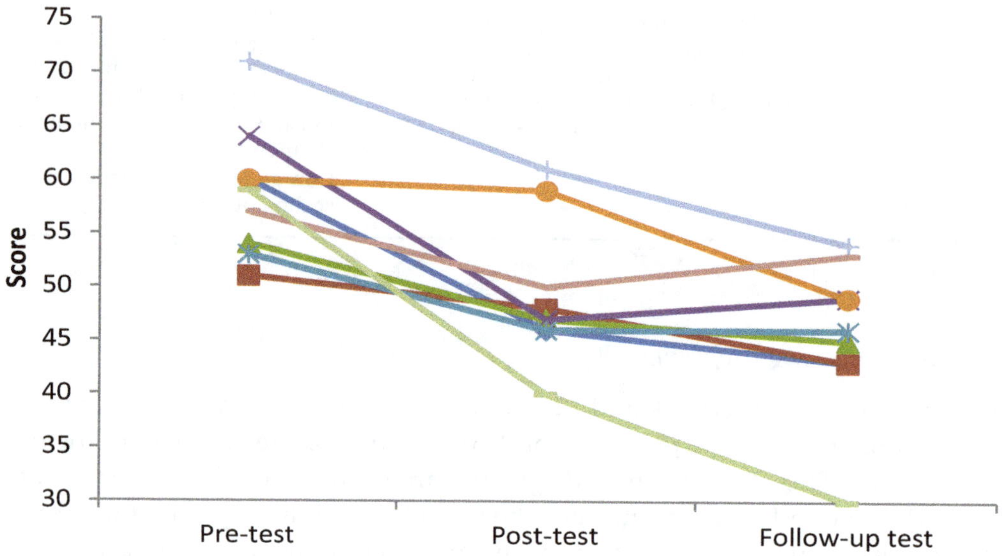


**Figure 1.** The Total IA Score in the Experimental Group ($n = 9$).

### 3.3. *Survey Score in Group Counseling of Experimental Group*

As shown in Table 4, the satisfaction degree of the experimental group for each group counseling was above 8.5. Paired-samples t-test revealed that the score of the experimental group on the scaling question at the last group counseling was significantly improved, compared with the first group counseling session ($t = 8.00$, $p < 0.01$).

**Table 4.** Satisfaction Survey Score of Experimental Group.

| Measures | Week 1 | Week 2 | Week 3 | Week 4 | Week 5 |
|---|---|---|---|---|---|
| Satisfaction Score | 8.78 ± 0.63 | 8.75 ± 0.83 | 9.67 ± 0.47 | 9.33 ± 0.47 | 9.78 ± 0.42 |
| scaling question Score | 3.11 ± 0.57 | / | / | / | 5.78 ± 0.92 |

### 3.4. *The Change Questionnaire after Group Counseling of Experimental Group*

Based on the change questionnaire after group counseling, the changes of college students can be summarized as "changes related to Internet use" (i.e., changes are directly related to Internet use, including Internet use time, Internet use attitude, Internet use form, etc.) and "changes related to daily life" (i.e., changes in other aspects of daily life that are not directly related to Internet use, such as schedule, interpersonal communication, studying, etc.) (Table 5).

**Table 5.** Benign Changes after Group Counseling of Experimental Group Members.

| Third-Level Coding | Second-Level Coding | First-Level Coding (Number of People Mentioned & Examples of Group Members' Changes) |
|---|---|---|
| Changes related to the Internet use | Changes in Internet use time | Time spent on Internet reduced (4; e.g., Time reduced by about an hour or two) |
| | | Reasonable planning and control of Internet use time (2; e.g., Able to put the phone down in time) |
| | | Reasonably allocate time for online entertainment and learning (3; e.g., Study for about 40 minutes, and take a 10-minute break to play on the phone) |
| | | Time spent on games reduced (1) |
| | Changes in Internet use attitude | Objective view on Internet use (4; e.g., Understand my own Internet use behavior) |
| | | When surfing the Internet, my mentality is more peaceful (2; e.g., Not experiencing dilemmas like before on using internet) |
| | | The appeal of my mobile phone declined (1) |
| | | More focused on other things (1) |
| | | It doesn't matter if I don't surf the Internet (2; e.g., It's no big deal not to be online) |
| | Changes in Internet use form | The Internet becomes a relaxation tool (3 e.g., Occasionally watch videos to relax) |
| | | The Internet becomes a learning tool (1) |
| | | The Internet becomes a tool of daily life (2; e.g., Now usually use Internet to chat) |
| | | More meaningful content browsed on the Internet (1) |
| | | Dialectical view of Internet point (1) |
| Changes related to daily life | Changes in schedule | Schedule more regular (2; e.g., Meals on times) |
| | | Internet use will not overly affect sleep (1) |
| | | More days to get up early (1) |
| | | The number and timing of getting up lately adjusted (1) |
| | Changes in work and study | Spent time on reflection (1) |
| | | More time spent on study (1) |
| | | The number of visits to the library increased (1) |
| | Changes in interpersonal communication | More activities with friends (2; e.g., Spend more time out with friends for studying and playing) |
| | | Internet use will not affect interpersonal communication (1) |
| | Changes in life planning | Re-adjust life planning (1) |
| | | Life plan is clearer (1) |
| | Changes in whole life | Use time to adjust life (1) |
| | | Life is more organized (1) |
| | Changes in other aspects | The amount of exercise increased (1) |
| | | Internet use will not affect walking (1) |
| | | Began to pay attention to clothing collocation (1) |
| | | Pay more attention to observing emotions (1) |
| | | Continuous counseling (1) |

## 4. Discussion

This pilot study explored the intervention effect of solution-focused group counseling for college students' IA. The results of the comparison between the two groups found that the change in total IA scores as well as in the dimensions of compulsive use, withdrawal (Sym-C & Sym-W) and tolerance

(Sym-T) were significantly larger in the intervention compared to the control group. Within the experimental group, the scores in the four IA dimensions were significantly decreased and the change trend of the total IA score was similar for all subjects in the experimental group. In the dimension of time management problems (RP-TM), the follow-up test was significantly lower than the scores in the pre- and post-tests. In the other dimensions, the post-test was significantly lower than the pre-test, and the follow-up test was significantly lower than the pre-test. The score on the scaling question in the post-test in the experimental group was significantly higher than that in the pre-test, indicating that the members of the group subjectively felt improvements in IA after the group counseling. In addition, the open-ended responses revealed that Internet use time, attitudes toward Internet use and Internet use form, as well as many aspects of daily life of group members, have changed. Moreover, the satisfaction score of the experimental group for every-week group counseling was above 8.5 points, which showed that members valued the provided group counseling. Overall, the results described above indicated that solution-focused group counseling intervention has a positive effect on college students' IA and can lead to healthier Internet use and lifestyles.

After group counseling, the experimental group experienced more significant changes than the control group in IA-Sym, including but not limited to compulsion and withdrawal symptoms (Sym-C & Sym-W), and tolerance symptoms (Sym-T). However, there were no significant differences between the experimental group and the control group with regards to interpersonal and health-related problems (RP-IH), time management problems (RP-TM), and other related IA issues. These results indicated that the characteristics and advantages of SFBT make this therapeutic approach highly targeted, symptom specific, and efficient. Specifically, SFBT helps group members to clarify their goals and find clues to realize their goals by helping them visualize themselves after they use the Internet in a healthier and responsible fashion and avoid IA symptoms. SFBT is effective for several reasons. It guides group members to actively think about the function of the Internet, and to restructure their negative attitudes about the Internet towards more positive views of Internet use. SFBT encourages members to actively explore positive experiences and coping strategies for rational uses of the internet, and to search for past successful experiences to help discover and replicate effective methods of overcoming IA and uncontrolled use. All of this is done in combination with brainstorming, interpersonal communication and sharing, and other related processes to enrich the treatment milieu. SFBT stimulates group members to put various methods into practice through homework, thus gradually boosting changes in members' core IA symptoms. It should be noted here that the change in the experimental group is more significant and may be related to the effect of social desirability. Specifically, in the process of participating in group counseling, the experimental group establishes relationships with leaders and other members, and become eager for recognition and praise. This, coupled with clear goals of group counseling, may stimulate members to actively perform in line with group goals. Of course, this is also one of the motivations of the group. From the perspective of SFBT, the socially desirable responding of the parties is an important psychological resource, which can be used for achieving better results. Through asking questions, the parties can express their abilities and efforts in the process of answering, so that the parties can have a clearer understanding of how to make progress.

Research findings within the groups showed that the experimental group experienced positive significant changes in IA. The classification we employed is based on a study of a sample of 388 college students who completed the CIAS-R revised. They found that a cutoff of 46 separates normal from at-risk groups, and a cutoff of 53 separates at-risk from the Internet addiction group [32]. According to this standard, the average Internet addiction score of the experimental group in this study belongs to the range of Internet addiction before intervention, the range of Internet addiction risk after intervention, and the normal range after six months. Although it is only a rough comparison of the average value, it reflects the clinical significance of the intervention effect to a certain extent. However, the experimental group showed different changes in different aspects of Internet addiction. In terms of core IA symptoms (IA-Sym), such as compulsion (Sym-C), withdrawal (Sym-W) and tolerance symptoms (Sym-T), and time management problems (RP-TM), the immediate effect of group counseling was quite positive and lasted to the follow-up test, six months later. In the Interpersonal and health-related problems (RP-IH) domain, there was no significant change after group counseling, but there was a significant improvement six months later. In addition, the open-ended reports after the follow-up period supported the quantitative data, indicating that experimental group members had experienced positive changes in Internet use and daily life. An earlier study [29] found that the application of SFBT in China can have positive immediate effect. Extending this view, the current study demonstrated that in the form of group counseling SFBT can have both short-term and long-term effects. Additionally, the solution-focused group counseling of this study first stimulated changes in core problems, and those changes were mostly maintained after group counseling. While changes in other dimensions were not as rapid and obvious as changes in core problems, there was still the possibility of change after the group counseling. De Jong and Berg [40] suggested that the professional value of SFBT is multidimensional. It encourages clients' involvement, improves clients' self-determination, maximizes their sense of empowerment, and promotes transferability. Specifically, SFBT helps clients to help themselves, maximizes client potential and resources in solving problems, and makes clients responsible for their own lives by applying what they got from the counseling to other scenarios through the process of creating solutions with counselors. Therefore, solution-focused group counseling not only achieved significant outcomes in treating core IA symptoms, but also had positive longer-lasting impacts on interpersonal relationships, learning, work and other life domains.

Many researchers have also conducted intervention studies on college students' Internet addiction, but follow-up tests are often conducted within six or eight weeks after the intervention [34,41]. We extend such studies in this paper, by focusing on long-term follow-up changes. Moreover, Cognitive-Behavioral Therapy has been widely applied to treatment of IA [42], but the existing cognitive behavioral therapies mostly draw on results of well-developed studies in substance addiction and intervention treatments of other mental disorders. These treatments may not be as efficacious with college students, which is a specific clinical group that needs to use the Internet, but needs to learn to do so responsibly, even under conditions of total freedom. These reasons may account for the limited success of these therapies with IA cases [43]. Besides shedding factors that have controlled their life, many college students lack self-control and behavior-selection strategies. Even if students make positive changes, these can be difficult to maintain. Moreover, each relapse to an addictive behavior will further undermine their self-efficacy [44], thus leading to increased engagement in addictive behaviors and further loss of control. Based on the concept of SFBT, the current pilot study respected the subjectivity of college students and helped them dig deeper into their own resources and strengths to solve the problem. In addition, the form of group counseling promoted positive feedback among members. This is not only conducive to the improvement in the core IA symptoms, but also helps to maintain the change and to generalize the change to other life domains.

Several limitations of the current study are noteworthy. First, the sample size is small. The reliability and validity of major measurement tools such as CIAS-R cannot be fully verified, and the generalizability of the results may be limited. Future studies can consider increasing the sample size to verify the reliability and validity of the measurement tools and improve generalization of the research results. Second, the variables in this study are all self-reported, subjective and easy to be influenced by the effect of social desirability. Future research can consider obtaining more objective data from different approaches such as multi-subject evaluation by consultants, classmates, etc., and/or control for social desirability bias. Third, the sample included college students. The design of the focus solution group counseling program is based on college students' cognitive development level and other psychological characteristics, and the Internet addiction level of the subjects is controlled. In the future, when the group counseling program is applied to other age, identity or Internet addiction level groups, it needs to be revised according to the specific situation. Fourth, changes brought by group counseling may be subtle and even unconscious. More sensitive indicators, such as using neurophysiology related technologies to explore brain structure and functions following SFBT [43], can be used in future research to lay a foundation for improving IA interventions.

## 5. Conclusions

In sum, this pilot study used solution-focused group counseling to treat college students with moderate to high levels of IA symptoms. The results suggested that solution-focused group counseling had positive effects on IA and some of its core dimensions, and was generally positively valued by participants. SFBT has the characteristics of high-efficiency, simplicity and durability in intervening with college students' Internet use. We call for further studies to apply this approach and examine its merits.

**Author Contributions:** Conceptualization, X.Z., O.T., and Q.H.; methodology, X.Z. and S.X.; formal analysis, X.Z. and X.S.; investigation, X.Z., X.S., S.X., and J.Q.; resources, X.Z., S.X., and J.Q.; data curation, J.Q.; writing—original draft preparation, X.Z., X.S., S.X., J.Q.; writing—review and editing, O.T. and Q.H.; supervision, X.Z. and Q.H.; project administration, X.Z.; funding acquisition, Q.H. All authors have read and agreed to the published version of the manuscript.

**Acknowledgments:** We are grateful to all the volunteers for participating in the present study.

## References

1. Young, K. *Internet Addiction Test (IAT)*; Stoelting: Wood Dale, IL, USA, 2017.
2. Goldberg, I. Internet Addiction Disorder: Diagnostic Criteria, 1996. Available online: http://users.rider.edu/~{}suler/psycyber/supportgp.html (accessed on 3 April 2020).
3. Turel, O.; Serenko, A.; Giles, P. Integrating technology addiction and use: An empirical investigation of online auction users. *Mis. Q.* **2011**, *35*, 1043–1061. [CrossRef]
4. Turel, O.; Romashkin, A.; Morrison, K.M. Health Outcomes of Information System Use Lifestyles among Adolescents: Videogame Addiction, Sleep Curtailment and Cardio-Metabolic Deficiencies. *PLoS ONE* **2016**, *11*, e0154764. [CrossRef] [PubMed]
5. He, Q.; Turel, O.; Bechara, A. Brain anatomy alterations associated with Social Networking Site (SNS) addiction. *Sci. Rep.* **2017**, *7*, 1–8. [CrossRef] [PubMed]
6. Kumar, N.; Kumar, A.; Mahto, S.K.; Kandpal, M.; Deshpande, S.N.; Tanwar, P. Prevalence of excessive internet use and its correlation with associated psychopathology in 11th and 12th grade students. *Gen. Psychiatry* **2019**, *32*, 84–91. [CrossRef] [PubMed]
7. Ding, Y.J.; Lau, C.H.; Sou, K.L.; Abraham, A.A.; Griffiths, S.M.; Kim, J.H. Association between internet addiction and high-risk sexual attitudes in Chinese university students from Hong Kong and Macau. *Public Health* **2016**, *132*, 60–63. [CrossRef]
8. Canan, F.; Yildirm, O.; Sinani, G.; Ozturk, O.; Ustunel, T.Y.; Ataoglu, A. Internet addiction and sleep disturbance symptoms among adolescents. *Eur. Psychiatry* **2013**, *28*, 1. [CrossRef]
9. Lin, I.H.; Ko, C.H.; Chang, Y.P.; Liu, T.L.; Wang, P.W.; Lin, H.C.; Huang, M.F.; Yeh, Y.C.; Chou, W.J.; Yen, C.F. The association between suicidality and Internet addiction and activities in Taiwanese adolescents. *Compr. Psychiatry* **2014**, *55*, 504–510. [CrossRef]
10. Ozgul, O.; Ozlem, O.; Alaettin, U.; Sinan Ozalp, S. Evaluation of Internet Addiction and Depression among University Students. *Procedia-Soc. Behav. Sci.* **2013**, *82*, 445–454.
11. Turel, O.; Serenko, A. Cognitive biases and excessive use of social media: The facebook implicit associations test (FIAT). *Addict. Behav.* **2020**, *105*, 106328. [CrossRef]
12. Rui, G.L.; Wang, W.; Liu, X.M. An epidemiological survey of Internet addiction among College Students. *Chin. J. Behav. Med. Sci.* **2004**, *13*, 333.
13. Li, Q. The Research about the Relationship of college student Psychological Capital, Stress and creativity. Master's Thesis, Zhejiang University of science and technology, Hangzhou, China, 2014.
14. Ye, B.J.; Zheng, Q. The Effects of Stress on College Students' Internet Addiction. *J. Psychol. Sci.* **2016**, *39*, 621–627.
15. Deng, L.Y.; Fang, X.Y.; Wan, J.J.; Zhang, J.T.; Xia, C.C. The Relationship of Psychological Needs and Need Gratification with Internet Addiction Among College Students. *J. Psychol. Sci.* **2012**, *35*, 123–128.
16. Turel, O.; Mouttapa, M.; Donato, E. Preventing problematic Internet use through video-based interventions: A theoretical model and empirical test. *Behav. Inform. Technol.* **2015**, *34*, 349–362. [CrossRef]

17. Yang, F.R.; Hao, W. The Effect of Integrated Psychosocial Intervention on 52 Adolescents with Internet Addiction Disorder. *Chin. J. Clin. Psychol.* **2005**, *13*, 343–352.
18. Gingerich, W.J.; Eisengart, S. Solution-focused brief therapy: A review of the outcome research. *Fam. Process.* **2000**, *39*, 477–498. [CrossRef] [PubMed]
19. de Shazer, S. *Putting Difference to Work*; Norton: New York, NY, USA, 1991.
20. de Shazer, S. *Words were Originally Magic*; WW Norton &, Co.: New York, NY, USA, 1994.
21. Bavelas, J.B.; De Jong, P.; Jordan, S.; Korman, H. The theoretical and research basis of co-constructing meaning in dialogue. *Solut.-Focus. Brief Ther.* **2014**, *2*, 1–24.
22. Shazer, S.D. *Clues: Investigating Solutions in Brief Therapy*; W.W. Norton Polishers: New York, NY, USA, 1988.
23. Wilmshurst, L.A. Treatment programs for youth with emotional and behavioral disorders: An outcome study of two alternate approaches. *Ment. Health Serv. Res.* **2002**, *4*, 85–96. [CrossRef]
24. Froeschle, J.G.; Smith, R.L.; Ricard, R. The efficacy of a systematic substance abuse program for adolescent females. *Prof. Sch. Couns.* **2007**, *10*, 498–505. [CrossRef]
25. Lamprecht, H.; Laydon, C.; Mcquillan, C.; Wiseman, S.; Reilly, J. Single-session solution-focused brief therapy and self-harm: A pilot study. *J. Psychol. Ment. Health Nurs.* **2010**, *14*, 601–602. [CrossRef]
26. Franklin, C.; Trepper, T.S.; Gingerich, W.J.; McCollum, E.E. *Solution-Focused Brief Therapy: A Handbook of Evidence-Based Practice*; Oxford University Press: Oxford, UK, 2012.
27. Li, Y.C.; Lin, S.L.; Hong, L.Z.; Zhang, D.C.; Zhang, J.W.; Ye, Z.P.; Fan, X.C. *Multiple Applications of Focus Solution Consultation*; Teach. Zhang Cult: Taipei, China, 2006.
28. Xu, W.S. The representative of paradigm shift — the philosophy of Solution-focused Brief Therapy. *Psycho: Tech. Appl.* **2014**, *13*, 41–44.
29. Gong, H.L.; Xu, W.S. A Meta-analysis on the Effectiveness of Solution-focused Brief Therapy. *Psychol. Behav. Res.* **2015**, *13*, 799–803.
30. Jordan, S.S.; Froerer, A.S.; Bavelas, J.B. Microanalysis of positive and negative content in solution focused brief therapy and cognitive behavioral therapy expert sessions. *J. Syst. Ther.* **2013**, *32*, 46–59. [CrossRef]
31. Korman, H.; Bavelas, J.B.; De Jong, P. Microanalysis of formulations in solution-focused brief therapy, cognitive behavioral therapy, and motivational interviewing. *J. Syst. Ther.* **2013**, *32*, 31–45. [CrossRef]
32. Bai, Y.; Fan, F.M. The Effects of Group Counseling on Internet Dependent College Students. *Chin. J. Ment. Health* **2007**, *21*, 247–250.
33. Chen, S.H. Development of Chinese Internet Addiction Scale and Research on Psychometric Characteristics. *Chin. Psychol.* **2003**, *45*, 279–294.
34. Bai, Y.; Fan, F.M. A Study on the Internet Dependence of College Students: The Revising and Applying of a Measurement. *Psychol. Dev. Educ.* **2005**, *4*, 99–104.
35. Gao, F.Q.; Geng, J.Y.; Ren, Y.Q.; Yang, H.Y.; Han, L. Mediating effect of perceived social support and relative deprivation among life events and internet addiction in college students. *Chin. Ment. Health J.* **2017**, *31*, 734–738.
36. Zhang, J.; Zhang, Y.J.; Shen, L.J. Attentional bias characteristics of different levels of over-users in mobile network under different time-course conditions. *Chin. Ment. Health J.* **2019**, *33*, 545–549.
37. Ha, J.H.; Yoo, H.J.; Cho, I.H.; Chin, B.; Shin, D.; Kim, J.H. Psychiatric comorbidity assessed in korean children and adolescents who screen positive for internet addiction. *J. Clin. Psychiatry* **2006**, *67*, 821–826. [CrossRef]
38. Luo, K.L.; Meng, H.Q.; Fu, Y.X. Depression and Anxiety as well as the comorbid of them in adolescents with internet addiction disorder. *Chin J. Clin. Rehabil.* **2005**, *8*, 5–6.
39. Trepper, T.S.; McCollum, E.E.; De Jong, P.; Korman, H.; Gingerich, W.; Franklin, C. *Solution-Focused Therapy Treatment Manual for Working with Individuals*; Research Committee of the Solution Focused Brief Therapy Association, 2010; Available online: https://www.andrews.edu/sed/gpc/faculty-research/coffen-research/trepper_2010_solution.pdf (accessed on 3 April 2020).
40. De Jong, P.D.; Berg, I.K. Interviewing for solutions. *J. Marital. Fam. Ther.* **1998**, *26*, 117.
41. Fang, H.Z.; Dai, Y.Z. Psychological intervention of positive psychology on internet addiction of college students. *Chin. J. Health Psychol.* **2019**, *27*, 1906–1909.
42. Young, K.S. CBT-IA: The first treatment model for internet addiction. *J. Cogn. Psychother.* **2011**, *25*, 304. [CrossRef]

43. Fang, X.Y.; Liu, L.; Deng, L.Y.; Liu, Q.X.; Su, W.L.; Lan, J. The Prevention and Intervention on Adolescent Internet Addiction. *Psychol. Dev. Educ.* **2015**, *31*, 100–107.
44. He, J.F. Effects of group counseling on internet using and study management in college students. *Chin. J. Ment. Health* **2013**, *27*, 496–501.

# 11

# Exploring the Opportunities and Challenges of the Digital World for Early Childhood Services with Vulnerable Children

**Leona Harris [1,2], Niki Davis [1,2,*], Una Cunningham [3], Lia de Vocht [1], Sonja Macfarlane [4], Nikita Gregory [2], Saili Aukuso [1,2], Tufulasifa'atafatafa Ova Taleni [2] and Jan Dobson [5]**

1 E-Learning Research Lab, University of Canterbury, Christchurch 8041, New Zealand; leona.harris@canterbury.ac.nz (L.H.); lia.devocht@canterbury.ac.nz (L.d.V.); saili.aukuso@pg.canterbury.ac.nz (S.A.)
2 Child Well-being Research Institute, University of Canterbury, Christchurch 8041, New Zealand; nikita.gregory@pg.canterbury.ac.nz (N.G.); tufulasi.taleni@canterbury.ac.nz (T.O.T.)
3 Department of Education, Uppsala University, 75236 Uppsala, Sweden; una.cunningham@edu.uu.se
4 Te Rū Rangahau: The Māori Research Laboratory, University of Canterbury, Christchurch 8041, New Zealand; sonja.macfarlane@canterbury.ac.nz
5 Sector Enablement and Support, Ministry of Education, Christchurch 8013, New Zealand; jan.dobson@education.govt.nz
* Correspondence: niki.davis@canterbury.ac.nz

**Abstract:** Potentially addictive behaviours supported by the internet and mobile phones raise concerns in education services for early childhood. Although there is evidence that screen media can distract the attention of young children, there was a massive uptake of digital devices by early childhood centres (ECCs). We investigated practices of families ($n$ = 85) and of six ECCs serving vulnerable children in New Zealand, many of whom are emergent bilinguals. Descriptions of the limited and exemplary choice of screen media of the ECCs include digital portfolios containing children's learning stories in multiple languages illustrated with digital photos. This was facilitated by increasing partnership with the families and the inclusion of their languages in the physical and digital landscapes of the ECCs. However, these families and the ECCs are seeking additional guidance to face the complex challenges of the digital world. These early findings from our national research programme, A Better Start, E Tipu E Rea, already informed significant changes in the ECCs; we also identified the potential for young children to act as agents of change.

**Keywords:** internet addiction; mobile phone (or smartphone) use; young children; early childhood education; parenting; emergent bilinguals; intergenerational language transmission

---

## 1. Introduction

Childhood today is increasingly technologically constructed [1] with digital technologies such as computers, tablets, and smartphones now commonplace in many education systems and homes worldwide [2]. While the ubiquity of these technologies has beneficial outcomes for youngsters' learning and socialisation, it contributes also, among other detrimental outcomes, to the loss of minority languages and cultures [3]. This loss is of concern given the increasing body of evidence that bilingualism and multilingualism can have lifelong cognitive, health, and economic benefits (see, for example, Reference [4]).

Addictive behaviours supported by technologies, such as the internet and mobile phones, raise concerns, particularly in health services for early childhood. The bold claims of the American Academy of Paediatrics Committee on Education in 2001 included recommendations reducing the exposure of children under six years of age to screen media. These arose from concerns about overuse of digital devices, resulting in young children missing developmentally appropriate activities and/or not getting enough exercise; in other words, typical activities in childhood are displaced by the adoption of digital media. Evidence that media can distract the attention of young children increased since those recommendations were published [5]). However, directives to simply reduce time spent with digital devices are unhelpful and impractical in a world in which digital devices have become ubiquitous, and when a range of devices with apps and digital environments now marketed include some supporting developmentally appropriate activities that were adopted by early childhood educators and other experts in the field [2].

In addition to the concerns about the exposure of young children to digital media, concerns about the influence of digital media on the behaviour of family members emerged over the last decade. Given the complexity of effective parent and sibling interaction with young children [6], it is possible that increasing the use of mobile phones and other devices can adversely impact child development, particularly in families suffering from some form of media addiction.

The study documented in this paper was partly prompted by these concerns. It describes the linguistic landscapes, as well as the deployment of digital technologies within them, of six early childhood education (ECE) centres (ECCs) in New Zealand to explore how such centres contribute to young children's language development. The provision of high-quality early childhood education was shown to have a beneficial impact on the development of young children, particularly those from low-income families [7].

We set our study within these centres because the children attending them are of an age (four to six years) when they are rapidly developing their language and social skills. We also wanted to gain a better understanding of how digital technologies might further support the evolution of linguistic landscapes in ways that provide a better start within education systems for young children, particularly those who acquire more than one language (emergent bilinguals; cf. [8]), and for whom an enriched linguistic landscape, visibly valuing their home language, has the potential to make the most impact [9].

New Zealand is, for several reasons, a particularly interesting location in which to explore the interface between digital technology use in ECE and the effort to support emergent bilinguals attending ECCs.

1. Opportunities and challenges linked with the digital world recently grew in New Zealand with the rollout of ultrafast broadband nationwide and the consequent expanded internet access in schools, a great many homes, community facilities, and workplaces [10]; from 2015 to 2017, the "frequency, range of activities, and the number of devices people use to access the internet all increased" [11].
2. New Zealand's ECE curriculum, Te Whāriki [12], is grounded in the country's founding document from 1840, te Tiriti o Waitangi (Treaty of Waitangi), which is highly respectful of cultural and linguistic diversity. Written in both Māori and English, Te Whāriki is based on four principles (empowerment, holistic development, family and community, and relationships) woven together with five strands (wellbeing, belonging, contribution, communication, and exploration). The term "oral language" used within Te Whāriki refers to any method of communication that "the child uses as a first language" (p. 42). The culturally safe development of children's language skills is essential (e.g., Reference [13]).
3. New Zealand's awareness of the lifelong benefits of bilingualism and multilingualism is relatively recent [14]. Māori did not become one of the country's three official national languages until 1987 (the other two are English and New Zealand sign language), and despite New Zealand's increasingly multilingual population, migrants are generally encouraged to adopt English at the expense of their heritage languages [15]. English remains the language most commonly spoken in New Zealand and is the de facto language of nearly all educational provision in the country.

4. New Zealand is recognised as a linguistically "superdiverse" country with over 160 languages, in addition to English and Māori, with Samoan, Hindi, and Northern Chinese more commonly spoken [16]. Te reo Māori words are included in this article in line with common practice.

We aimed to gather evidence in a way that spread good practice in regard to enhancing the linguistic landscapes in the ECCs and minimising the risks that come with the digital world.

## 2. Growing Up in a Digital World

Hsin, Li, and Tsai's comprehensive review of studies on information and communications technology (ICT) use in ECE [17] found positive associations between children's language and literacy development and their use of digital tools and toys, although the learning outcomes generally depended on how the children used the technology. Chaudron's Europe-wide study investigating the digital technology behaviours of children (0–8 years) [18] showed children typically using digital devices on their own, with parental management restricted to limiting length and frequency of use. Parents had little knowledge of what their children were actually doing in the digital world, however. Aubrey and Dahl [19] found ECE educators likewise lacked detailed knowledge of children's digital experiences, and that parents rarely shared information with educators about how their children were using digital technologies at home. Marklind and Dunkels examined the introduction of tablets by early childhood teachers in Sweden [20], sometimes in the face of opposition from colleagues or parents, to develop children's literacy and school-oriented language development, which is especially relevant for multilingual children.

Adult and adolescent addictive behaviours relating to problematic mobile phone use (PMPU) [21], have been found to be "positively associated with stress, depression, sleep disturbances, extraversion, female gender, young age, and poor academic or professional competence or performance" (p. 1213) and to affect learning [22]. However, it remains important to be cautious when applying the label addiction using the connection with substance abuse as a way of categorising online behaviour as disordered [23]. In the context of early childhood, the poor competence or performance of particular concern is around parenting and the contribution of siblings to the healthy development of young children. Kildare and Middlemiss's comprehensive literature review [24] identified that there was a range of both parenting benefits and complications with the integration of mobile devices in their day-to-day lives, suggesting that the impact on any particular child was wide-ranging and complex. The common themes that emerged included "parent's level of absorption with their mobile devices, child safety in the presence of parents' mobile distractions and parents conflicted attitudes regarding device use, and decreased parental responsiveness and sensitivity towards children while distracted." (p. 590). Perhaps most interestingly, they note that children's screen time increases with parents' screen time [25].

The findings from these studies highlight the importance of adults (most notably parents and educators) as mediators of children's learning via ICT, as well as role models. Research by McPake, Plowman, and Stephen [26] found that young children's use of digital technology at home tended to expand children's early communicative and creative experiences. They also observed that maximisation of this learning once the children were in more formal educational settings relied on educators' knowledge of these home-based learning experiences (including digital), and on their ability to carefully and creatively help the children build on those experiences.

However, adults cannot be effective mediators if they do not know how children are using these technologies at home and in formal educational settings, and if they do not understand how that use might be influencing the children's holistic (including linguistic) development.

## 3. Emergent Bilinguals

Recent findings in neuroscience and from longitudinal cohort studies indicate that young children who acquire more than one language and retain them into adulthood have significantly better lifetime outcomes [27,28]. Research also shows that children learn a new language more effectively when they continue to use and develop their heritage language [29], and that pre-schoolers develop more positive identities as learners and are more engaged in literacy activities when their ECE settings include their home cultures and experiences [30].

Increasing opportunities in ECE settings for young children to engage in their family's languages and cultures is important not only for reasons such as these, but also because the children's respective languages and cultures encapsulate their heritage and enhance their mana (a word used in Māori to denote power, prestige, acumen, and efficacy). However, while children's ability to develop and retain more than one language is challenging in educational contexts that are largely monolingual [31], proficiency in their parents' language is important for the children of migrants [32].

Dressler [33] found that, as children move around their educational settings, they draw conclusions about the relative importance of the languages evident in the signs and artefacts around them, because it is these that indicate what is socially supported within those places. Thus, the presence of signs in more than one language and of culturally based artefacts in ECCs prompts and supports the use of multiple languages, enabling children and adults to co-build multilingual language and social skills [9,34].

Early childhood educators can value and support children's use of their heritage languages by working in partnership with the children's whānau (families, including extended family members) to ensure the authenticity of these inclusions in the linguistic landscapes of the centres. Bridging language practices between home and educational settings through parental participation, such as being expert partners in bi-literacy development through the co-creation of dual-language texts, reinforces children's bilingual language development, as well as building their self-confidence, and strengthening their bilingual identities and their English language competencies [35–38].

However, there is very little research into the duration of internet and/or mobile phone use in educational contexts that aim to provide holistic support for young children, including ECCs. The benefits for emergent bilinguals are particularly relevant for vulnerable children.

## 4. Materials and Methods

Our main research question was "How are ECCs contributing to the development of the languages of young bilingual children who are growing up in a digital world?" In addition, for whānau with children who have lower levels of oral language ability in English, (i) How long do children spend on digital media? (ii) What are whānau views on the importance of their child's multilingualism?

The study presented in this article conformed to the provisions of the Declaration of Helsinki in 1995, revised in Edinburgh in 2000 [39]. Ethical approval was granted by the University's committee for human ethics (number 2016/21/ERHEC). For this paper, we bring together two complementary datasets of vulnerable emergent bilinguals who grew up in one locality, at a time when the digital world blended into their physical world: (1) qualitative ethnographic case studies of the linguistic landscapes of six ECCs in 2016 and in 2017, and (2) a multidisciplinary survey of families that included some of the same children during their first year of primary school in the same locality ($n$ = 85). It may also be important to note that this multidisciplinary mixed-methods study was conducted within our national research programme's Vision Matauranga, which braids western scientific methods with indigenous kaupapa Māori principles [40]. The research was also associated with a multi-agency initiative called "You Matter to Us" that emerged to support young children in an area with some of the most complex challenges faced in this country [41].

These children were situated within three suburbs of a large city purposefully selected because of its cultural diversity and over-representation of low-income families. Around 22% of people in this area speak more than one language compared with 15.8% across the city [42]. The languages other than English most commonly spoken in this area are Māori and Samoan. The details of our approach and methods are provided in other publications [43,44]; thus, in this paper, we provide a brief summary along with details of the participants. We begin with the methodology used with the ECC before describing the survey methodology.

*4.1. Case Studies of Six Early Childhood Centres*

The first set of evidence was linguistic ethnographies [45] gathered in collaboration with six mainstream English medium ECCs. Reports from the national government department responsible for reviewing the quality of ECCs in New Zealand, called the Education Review Office, considered five of the ECCs "well placed" and the sixth ECC "very well placed" to promote positive learning outcomes for children (the highest two levels) [46]. To acknowledge the value of their participation, each ECC received a report of their linguistic landscape to use for their own purposes (plus advising edits). In addition, some development time was gifted on request. Figure 1 is derived from an image that was created as koha (a gift).

**Figure 1.** An example of innovative practice co-constructed with the pilot Māori early childhood centre (ECC) in response to parents' need for support to sing along in the Māori language with their children at home [44]. The image of the child was retrieved from https://pixabay.com, which is released under the Creative Commons, as is this image CC BY SA3.

The ethnographic data for each linguistic landscape consisted of images in the form of still pictures, videos, and online screenshots. Still pictures and two videos (child height and adult height) captured the displays on the walls within each centre. Videos and screenshots (of publicly accessible pages online) were used to support interviews. Sixteen interviews were conducted with 18 staff (15 with individuals and one with a small group), as well as a few with whānau. In most ECCs, there was one interview with the head teacher and other teachers, and one interview with member(s) of a bilingual child's whānau. In addition, there was one interview with the outreach librarian who provided library services for those with limited ability to visit community libraries. She visited many of these ECCs to promote the library services through storytelling, songs, and digital storytelling.

Linguistic content in the photos was classified by the language(s) visible. Selected artefacts (for example, the e-portfolio) were used to discuss each centre's language and digital technology policies and practices, and to identify each centre's engagement with whānau and the communities that supported the language development of its emergent bilingual children. The interviews were semi-structured and conversational, and questions about what they did to support the language development of their emergent bilinguals stemmed from the participants' narratives and explanations of the physical and digital artefacts. The interviews elicited reflections on adults' practices with emergent bilinguals and prompted ideas for future strategies. Interviews were transcribed and analyses were both inductive and deductive. Firstly, a short report was produced for the ECCs to verify and use for their own purposes, such as an annual review and future planning. Then themes around policies and practices relating to language and digital media were identified through coding references to the use of digital technologies and/or languages other than English. Other themes also emerged, such as teachers prioritizing social competencies, physical play, and the development of relationships over digital technology use, and the challenges faced engaging whānau when whānau were under increased pressures in everyday life. Expert researchers then validated the evidence for each theme, applying their expertise in ECE, linguistics, and/or the digital world.

*4.2. The Survey of Families*

Our overarching programme of research focuses on vulnerable children because our aim is to give them a better start [47]. As a proxy for vulnerability, we chose to focus on those with lower language levels. These children were in the first year of schooling in the same suburbs as the ECC and included children who previously attended the six participating ECCs. A questionnaire was developed to ask whānau (extended family) about the hauora (health and wellbeing), hononga (reading together at home), hinengaro (reading practices), and harikoa (positive identities) of their children, who were identified with lower levels of oral language ability.

These children were selected from all 247 children in their first year attending the seven participating primary schools (see Figure 2). The screening employed two sub-tests from the Clinical Evaluation of Language Fundamentals Preschool, Second Edition (CELF-P2) [48], and the initial phoneme identity task from the New Zealand Computer-Based Phonological Awareness Database (CBPA) [49]. The 152 children who scored less than eight on the CELF-P2 subtest and/or less than six on the CBPA assessment were identified with lower levels of oral language ability.

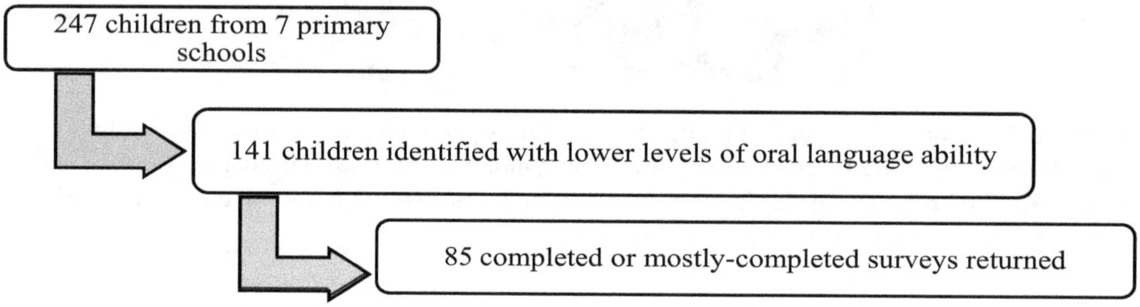


**Figure 2.** Visual representation of staged recruitment process of the whānau survey.

All 141 whānau of those children with lower levels of oral language ability were invited to complete the questionnaire. Subsequently, 85 (60%) of these whānau questionnaires were returned, and the demographics of participants are shown in Table 1. There was unlikely to be much difference with those who did not complete the survey, because they had a similar demographic makeup to the 141 children identified with lower levels of language ability (see Table 1). Whānau completing a survey or interview were given a $15 New Zealand dollar (NZD) voucher for groceries to acknowledge the gift of their time. Various follow-up methods were employed to reach this number, including community workshops, one-on-one meetings (occasionally with a researcher who spoke their home language), phone calls, and emails. Only items related to multilingualism and the digital world are considered in this paper; another article will report in full on this survey [43].

**Table 1.** Demographic information of the 85 children whose whānau participated in the survey compared with national demographics for children of the same age. NZ—New Zealand.

| Characteristic | Surveys Returned (%) ($n$ = 85) | Children Who Entered School with Lower Levels of Oral Language Ability ($n$ = 141) | Percentage Nationwide of Children Aged 5–6 Years of Age in 2013 [42] |
|---|---|---|---|
| Gender | | | |
| Male | 50 (58.8%) | 49.60% | 50.90% |
| Female | 35 (41.2%) | 50.40% | 49.10% |
| Ethnicity | | | |
| NZ European and other ethnicity | 48 (56.5%) | 54.50% | 62.80% |
| Pasifika | 15 (17.64%) | 21% | 8.80% |
| Māori | 22 (25.9%) | 24.50% | 20.10% |

## 5. Findings

### *5.1. Linguistic Landscapes of Six ECC*

An overview of the languages that could be seen in the physical and digital landscapes of the six ECCs is followed by a discussion of themes relating to the perception and use of digital media, ending with a review of challenges. Table 2 provides a summary of the languages in the six ECE centres that was evident in their signs and artefacts. Of the 469 images taken of all wall displays across the six centres, 354 contained linguistic items. These signs and artefacts were categorised as containing only one language (e.g., English only), as having an equal presence of two languages (e.g., English and Māori), or as having the majority of one language and some presence another language (e.g., English with some Māori). This indicated that these centres were reflecting Te Whāriki curriculum guidelines relating to commitment and work within the bilingual (Māori and English) context of Aotearoa New Zealand. Other languages were also represented, with these typically responsive to the languages and cultures of the children attending the centres and purposively chosen to meet centre policies and practices, such as collaboration (see Table 2 and Figures 3 and 4).

**Table 2.** Pictures containing linguistic items across the six early childhood education centres (ECCs) classified on the basis of the language(s) they contained.

| Language(s) in the Items | Number of Items ($n$ = 354) |
|---|---|
| English only | 171 |
| English with some Māori | 43 |
| English and Māori | 50 |
| Māori with some English | 30 |
| Māori only | 22 |
| Samoan only | 10 |
| Samoan and English | 9 |
| English/Samoan/Māori | 8 |
| Multilingual | 11 |

Most teachers interviewed said that the main purpose of the linguistic landscape was to engage whānau in their children's learning and development. This engagement facilitated face-to-face conversations with whānau, making it easier to communicate centre aims and plans, discuss children's activities, and promote conversations, collaboration, and language development. It was notable that all ECCs had a multilingual welcome near the entrance and online (see Figure 3).

**Figure 3.** Screenshot of one early childhood education (ECE) centre website with bilingual welcome.

Crucially, teachers emphasised that centres relied on whānau support and collaboration with respect to children's bilingual language development. Multilingual languages were most commonly seen in basic greetings used in displays, e-portfolios, and written communication to welcome, respect, and celebrate culture, identity, and language. A Whānau Aspirations Tree was observed in most ECCs. The one illustrated in Figure 4 was particularly rich in languages and culture. All the children's photos taken with a digital camera were place on the tree, an image that echoes Māori culture, and beside each photo was the family's aspirations in their home languages that focused mainly on the social aspects. A copy was placed within each child's e-portfolio. Pictures of the co-construction surrounded this large display.

**Figure 4.** The Whānau Aspirations Tree echoes Māori culture. It was co-constructed by centre staff and whānau and set within the ECC's main learning area. The photos were taken with a digital camera.

After English, the Māori language, along with cultural symbols and references, was most prevalent with evidence in artefacts such as signs, labels, songs, commands, books, portfolios, and communications to the children's whānau. The writing on the walls also served as reminders and prompts for the teachers to use languages with their emergent bilingual children. Pasifika languages were also used in songs, instructions, resources, and books that also contained cultural symbols and references; some were obtained through digital technologies such as iPads and computers.

The outreach librarian stressed the importance of supporting emergent bilinguals by creating an environment which welcomed the use of all children's languages beyond the context of the child's home by stretching across the contexts of the home and ECC through the child's digital world. "It's really interesting that [bilingual children] actually can't translate for you and they usually won't speak that language when they're at preschool. It is out of context, this isn't where that happens, [the bilingual children] are just not old enough to put that in place. [The digital world] is a huge part of who [the child] is and who their family is and it doesn't just belong in that house, it can actually exist everywhere else." (Outreach librarian interview, 2016).

### 5.1.1. Blended and Digital Resources Were Used Purposefully

Table 3 provides an overview of the way in which physical and digital resources were commonly used in all ECCs. The key digital resource was the e-portfolio, often used alongside paper portfolios. The e-portfolio was used to collate children's learning stories and compile observational records of children's competencies and learning dispositions, as recommended in Te Whāriki. Portfolio content, which included digital photos, videos, and text in English, Māori, and the children's home languages, was shared with centre colleagues, homes, and whānau residing elsewhere, and it provided an opportunities for whānau to contribute in their home languages. The portfolios prompted children to reflect on, share, and talk about their activities across contexts.

From one centre's perspective, the e-portfolio had both benefits and disadvantages. One advantage to using the e-portfolio was the ability to connect, engage, and collaborate with family/whānau and a platform to use home languages. "In our learning stories and children's [portfolio] books we're really encouraging the partnership between whānau, the teaching team, and the kindergarten, so that we are encouraging them to contribute photos of things that are of cultural significance to them, things that are important to their family. So, photos are a really good way of doing that. We're trying to use greetings as we are writing the story and maybe some images." (Teacher interview, 2016). The disadvantage was that some parents chose not to access their computer until after their children went to bed; thus, the child missed the sharing experience. The teacher told us, "So, we've gone back to redoing them, we are still loading them electronically, but we are doing it in the book as well." (Teacher interview, 2016).

**Table 3.** Representative sample of resources commonly observed in the six ECCs, classified by purpose(s) and an illustrative use. Figures refer to the examples of ECC artefacts.

| Resource | Example of Use |
|---|---|
| Physical resource | |
| Whiteboards | Multilingual greetings and sentences in Māori and other languages (Figure 3) |
| Paper portfolio | Multilingual greetings and learning stories with Māori words and concepts |
| Labels | Prompt for teachers to use languages and welcomes |
| Cultural protocols | Normal practice in ECC, e.g., songs and prayers; mostly sung in Māori and Samoan (Figure 1) |
| Displays, national events | Resources supporting Samoan language week, Diwali Festival, etc. |
| Digital/blended resource | |
| E-portfolios | Children's learning stories included multilingual greetings, Māori words and concepts, and family languages (e.g., Educa ePortfolio) |
| iPads | Cloud-based games supporting curriculum carefully managed; most apps in English |
| E-newsletters | Instead of or complementing paper version, these included multilingual greetings, and Māori words and concepts |
| Email | Used to send newsletters and photos to family (Figure 1) |
| Texting | Used occasionally for quick communication with families (e.g., to update a parent on their child) |
| Facebook | Produced by national organisations for their ECC; one had multilingual greetings |
| Websites | Produced by national organisations for their ECC; one had multilingual greetings (Figure 3) |
| Digital cameras | Extensive use by teachers for displays and artefacts to take home (Figures 1 and 4) |

All centres had a digital camera and used digital photos extensively, enabling teachers, children, and whānau to share experiences across environments and generate conversations regardless of language. Digital photos were displayed on walls, in portfolios (both types) on iPads, and on a large screen in the mat or seating areas. Each centre had one of these screens, and teachers played videos (recorded on the digital camera) of the children's activities on it and occasionally multicultural stories and celebrations. Whānau could send digital photos via email to the centre or place them in the e-portfolios. Teachers often added text to the photos and asked whānau if they could translate the text into home languages. One teacher interviewed said, "I gave (the family) some photos of their two children, two boys, what they were doing, and then asked them to take them home and talk to the boys about those (photos). So, they've come back with some of their own dialect (written on them)."

Despite the ability to connect language and experiences across the children's environments of home and the ECCs, there were concerns that digital media could be distracting. Teachers in all ECCs expressed concerns about the impact digital media may have that reduces the real-world experiences that children have, which generate the conversations of shared experiences that are necessary for language development. For example, "I don't hear our children talk about those experiences ... So if they are not talking about them to us, then I would guess that the parents aren't talking to the children about doing them ... So they might be doing them but there's not a lot of language going on while they are doing them, (adults) are not mediating for (young children)." (Teacher interview 2016).

The outreach librarian also reflected that parents were not engaged with the literacy activities, as was hoped. However, she noted that many parents approached her asking about the apps she used during the story time session to download themselves. This response was different from that to physical books. She believed it was the instant accessibility and the desire for access to quality apps that was motivating (Researcher journal, 2016).

All the centres had iPads, used for games (in English), music, and accessing content stemming from the children's interests. One ECC also had apps in Samoan and Māori. Centres carefully managed children's access to iPads. For one centre, this entailed the use of a booking system that allowed the child 10 min of iPad use controlled with the input of a passcode. This system was self-managing, and the next child on the booking schedule would prompt the transfer of the iPad. At the time of the study, two of the centres were not actively using the iPads, due to technical issues. Neither prioritised funding for maintaining them, partly due to the difficulties in managing them, as well as the teachers' stated belief that whānau preferred children to play outdoors and socialise with one another rather than spend time on screens.

Because all of the centres deemed (through policy and practice) the children's emotional regulation and social competency a priority, their staff took care to ensure that digital technology use and associated language artefacts were meaningful to the children and likely to engage their whānau in supporting that child's development. The majority of teachers thought that most of the children attending the centres had access to at least one digital device at home. If teachers knew that a whānau did not have home-based access, they typically encouraged them to use the free internet at a public library. However, and crucially, all teachers said they did not know how the children used devices at home and what content they could access on them, one said "I haven't had any experiences [of children's digital worlds]. I have to say it is not something that has been a passion for me or really interested me, so unless somebody is really struggling or there is a child that I haven't spent time with and I think that the only time that I'll be able to spend with them is on an iPad, then for me it's not one of the top priorities."

#### 5.1.2. Issues and Access

There was concern about digital media distracting from young children's social and physical development, particularly mobile devices, and a number of adults mentioned that controlling their use was problematic in all locations, including arguments at home among siblings. However, there was no mention of any "screen addiction". However, fear of being judged, lack of shared information about how much is too much, and limited knowledge of such addictions may be why the term addiction was avoided. Alternatively, it may be less likely among families with low incomes. Indeed, in the previous year during the stakeholder meeting that informed the research design so that ECCs were included, one of the teachers passionately objected to the "Bring Your Own Device" policy that was being introduced in the neighbouring schools, because of the stress that it placed on families that already struggled to feed and clothe their children.

### 5.2. Survey Findings

As introduced earlier, the whānau survey enabled us to extend our findings relating to digital world and whānau perceptions of their children's multilingualism. Despite the small sample size ($n = 85$) of the survey, there were some significant findings. The 85 questionnaires returned by whānau described the selected 50 boys and 35 girls with low language abilities attending their first year of schooling (age mean = 68.13 months, SD = 3.46 months) including many of the children that previously attended an ECC described earlier. Table 1 outlines the demographics of the children surveyed, as well as that for all the children with lower levels of oral language ability and the same nationwide demographics from the most recent census [42]. To aid in interpreting our results, we also compared our finds with the Growing Up in New Zealand (GUiNZ) cohort study of four year olds in 2013/2014 [50], while also noting that our findings are limited and not generalizable.

One of the questions in the survey asked, "During a typical week at home, approximately how many hours would your tamaiti/child/tama spend on digital media?". In order to improve the cultural relevance of the survey, the questions inter-languaged English between Māori and Samoan words, e.g., "tamaiti/child/tama". As shown in Table 4, we found that 6.8% of children did not engage with any digital media. When compared to the GUiNZ findings that 5% of four year olds did not engage with digital media, this suggests the proportion of cautious parents does not appear to be increasing, despite the increasing access to digital devices reported by the World Internet Project for New Zealand [11]. We also found that nearly one-third (32%) of children engaged with digital media for more than 5 h per week, equivalent to an average of more than 43 min per day. When comparing this result to GUiNZ data (41% of four year olds spending one or more hours a day on digital devices), our findings suggest that there is less use reported by whānau of these children than for the four year olds of the GUiNZ study. A limitation of our survey data was the way in which the question was asked and answered, and its variation with respect to the categories in GUiNZ survey, which also allowed open ended answers. These differences in survey design may be the cause for the differences in findings between our questionnaire and that in the GUiNZ study. As discussed later, any simple measure of time is problematic given the blending of physical and digital worlds.

**Table 4.** Frequency table of hours spent of digital media and of the importance of bilingualism.

| | | Frequency | Percent | Valid Percent |
|---|---|---|---|---|
| Hours on digital media per week | Never | 5 | 5.9 | 6.8 |
| | Less than an hour | 11 | 12.9 | 14.6 |
| | 1–3 h | 18 | 21.2 | 24.3 |
| | 3–5 h | 16 | 18.8 | 21.6 |
| | More than 5 h | 24 | 28.2 | 32.4 |
| | Sub total | 74 | 87.1 | 100 |
| Missing | | 11 | 12.9 | |
| Total | | 85 | 100 | |
| Importance of bi- and multilingualism | Not at all important | 17 | 20 | 20.5 |
| | Not that important | 24 | 28.2 | 29.9 |
| | Quite important | 22 | 25.9 | 26.5 |
| | Very important | 20 | 23.5 | 24.1 |
| | Sub total | 83 | 97.6 | 100 |
| Missing | | 2 | 2.4 | |
| Total | | 85 | 100 | |

Our statistical analysis to investigate potential relationships with this use of digital devices identified a two negative associations that were nearing significance: the number of hours on digital media and the whānau report of whether the child slept well through the night ($r = -0.184$, $p = 0.122$)

and also with the whānau report of amount of sleep ($r = -0.196$, $p = 0.09$). Most of these children appear to be having the recommended 10–12 h of sleep (mean = 10 h 57 min, SD = 57 min), with only 4.9% having less than 10 h sleep per night. This result was similar to the hours of sleep per night (mean = 10 h 45 min) for four year olds in the GUiNZ study.

Whānau indicated that there were 54 multilingual children in this sample who spoke one or more languages in addition to English. In order to look into whānau perceptions, the importance of bi- or multilingualism was scaled from 0, not important at all, through to 3, very important. Counts are shown in Table 4; further analysis showed that whānau of multilingual children were the most affirmative. When looked at with reading practices, a positive correlation was found with children's ability to read words that were pointed to ($r = 0.315$, $p = 0.012$). We also found that speaking more than one language was positively associated with children's ability to read words that were pointed to ($r = 0.308$, $p = 0.014$), children's ability to point and say words without being asked ($r = 0.279$, $p = 0.027$), and children's ability to write their own surname ($r = 0.471$, $p < 0.01$). These findings may indicate the value for multilingualism in a child's literacy development, such as richer language exchanges with whānau.

## 6. Discussion

Our descriptions of the linguistic landscapes of six mainstream ECE centres are reassuring in the way that they indicate purposeful integration of the digital world in the experiences of the children and the adults who support them, including the use of multilingual e-portfolios to share with whānau and to develop the children's learning stories across time and space. Evidence from our survey also supported previous research indicating parental care of children. All the ECCs respected the children's rights to access digital media and also controlled that access to ensure a healthy balance of activities in the knowledge that most children had a lot of exposure at home. This is exemplary, including the recognition of the need for further organisational and professional development.

Of particular value to multilingual children and their whānau, the teachers used languages other than English in the physical and digitally mediated linguistic landscape to welcome, respect, and celebrate the cultures and identities of all the children attending. The diverse languages presented in signs and artefacts also reminded and prompted teachers to use diverse languages with their emergent bilingual children. Teachers created most of the displays in the centres, especially the bilingual or multilingual ones, and this effort reflected their motivation for supporting emergent bilingual children.

Teachers and whānau prioritised social competencies, interaction, and emotional regulation as foundational for the development of their children's languages. Centres carefully managed digital resources as an additional means of strengthening connections between the centre and home. Our later research showed that whānau engagement with the e-portfolio grew significantly from 2016 to 2017, along with the teachers' skills and confidence in engaging with the software to collaborate on their children's linguistic and other experiences. The linguistic landscapes nurtured reciprocal relationships with families and their communities to support children's language development, including intergenerational transmission of language that is likely to result in a better start [36], particularly for the more vulnerable children who grow up with whānau speaking more than one language.

Incorporation of the digital world in the centres was not without concern, however, with teachers expressing interest in professional development and guidance in this area, particularly in terms of strategies that enable adults to share and shape children's experiences in the digital world across both home and centre environments. Although early exemplars of learning stories to guide assessment practice in New Zealand ECE included resources such as digital cameras, email, and home languages [51], our study suggests that, as the complexity of the digital world increases, teachers and children's families are likely to need more guidance to mediate that world for young children in ways that support both the children's linguistic and holistic development.

While centres found it relatively easy to share children's learning stories with the children's whānau by encouraging them to add images and translations to the children's e-portfolios, development of these portfolios created challenges for teachers, such as increased workload. The portfolios also highlighted issues relating to digital equity. For example, lack of technology or data to access e-portfolios at home reduced the opportunity to work with ECC staff to support their child. This lack of access could also potentially compromise the cultural safety interface between an ECC and homes [52].

Of most concern is the widespread knowledge that many young children are overexposed to digital media outside ECCs. Paudel et al.'s systematic literature review [53] suggests that children growing up in families with addictions such as those related to mobile screen media are at most risk and identified the following correlates: "older children, children better skilled in using mobile screen media devices, and those having greater access to such devices at home and whose parents had high mobile screen media use were more likely to have higher use of mobile screen media devices." According to Lindenberg et al. [54], who identified prevalence rates of over 5% among adolescents in Germany, the World Health Organisation recently listed gaming disorder in addition to internet use disorder, indicating that the rising rates of various types of overuse of screen media are an increasing cause of health concerns. Our study updates our understanding of the protective factor of quality ECE [7]. Our study also raises the possibility that ECCs can guide and support families coping with these addictive behaviours to reduce that impact on these young children.

The writing of this article prompted us to consider ways in which to guide ECC. Concerns about the influence of digital media on the behaviour of family members emerged over the last decade. For example, Raman et al., whose detailed study [55] of screen exposure during young children's daily routines explored the risk of having social-emotional delay, showed that children were exposed to screens throughout daily routines that would typically involve face-to-face interaction and conversational turn-taking, such as eating and sleeping routines. This persistent exposure to digital screens has the potential to distract attention away from the daily conversational interactions between adults and young children, which are necessary for healthy early development. Several teachers were concerned that parents were not mediating the use of digital media for their children, with one teacher saying that there was "not a lot of language going on".

Digital distraction may cause these and other conversations to become shallow, thus reducing young children's opportunities. Given the complexity of effective parent and sibling interaction with young children [6], it is possible that the increasing use of mobile phones and other devices can adversely impact child development, particularly in families suffering from some form of media addiction. For example, the Tizard and Hughes study [56] of the interactions of four-year-old girls with their mother at home in the 1980s contradicted the Piagetian thinking, which was prevalent at the time of their research, that the young child is illogical or whimsical (p. xiv). Instead, they concluded that children have an intense need to understand the world, which is reflected in the many "why" questions they asked at home (averaging 26 questions per hour). The analysis also showed that the turn-taking of the children and their mother supporting them to ask questions in a persistent and logical way in order to extend their understanding.

This unexplored relationship between digital distraction and young children's need for interaction with parents indicates the need for additional research. It is also worth noting that Raman et al.'s methodology [55] clarified our understanding of how children experience the impact of the digital world for themselves and their whānau. This impact is spread across the entire day, from waking up until going to sleep, so that it becomes misleading to describe it in a unit of time, such as the 2.1 h from the GuiNZ study [50]. It will be important to apply this to the interpretation of the literature and in the design of future research, policy, and guidance that we share on our web sites (see Supplementary Materials).

## 7. Recommendations and Conclusions

The invitation to write this article in response to the IJERPH special issue on "Internet and Mobile Phone Addiction: Health and Educational Effects" led us to reflect deeply on that topic, and we now plan to apply this to our mission. The mission of our national programme of multidisciplinary research includes a strand on mental health within which Merry and her colleagues are developing e-health interventions, e.g., Reference [57]. "To predict, prevent, and treat vulnerability in obesity, poor literacy, and mental health through research excellence that will achieve healthy, well-adjusted, and well-educated tamariki and young people. We aim to achieve our mission by taking both a life-course and a "braided river" approach to integrate themes, research disciplines, and both western and indigenous models of knowledge and practice, as well as incorporating the use of digital technology into our proposed solutions" [47].

We identified the need for additional research into the effects of addictions related to the internet and mobile devices. In particular, there is a need to provide more nuanced guidance for parents and siblings so that these young children have more opportunities for deep learning of languages, concepts, and social behaviour. Such research could identify mitigating strategies to include policy guidance for health and educational services, an action that we previously recommended within our national "Better Start" programme of research.

Drawing on the findings presented, this policy guidance is recommended to include strategies that enable adults to share children's experiences in the digital world. Vaughan and Beers' account of iPad-related professional development for ECE teachers [58] could be adapted to integrate strategies that benefit emergent bilinguals.

Improvements in software and interface design are also needed. Miller and Kocurek's five principles for the design and development of educational games for children under five years of age [59] could apply equally well to the development of digitally based multilingual activities and artefacts: (1) developmentally appropriate content; (2) reference to theoretical frameworks from the learning science field; (3) embedding learning in socially rich contexts; (4) ensuring diversity of content; and (5) creating a balance between play and real-world learning opportunities. To these five principles, we would add (6) opportunities for adults to engage alongside the children in their digital world(s) and to use all their languages.

We also have a recommendation with regards to multilingualism and the intergenerational transfer of languages. In Aotearoa New Zealand, Māori is recognised as a national language, and the ECE curriculum promotes its use as a living language. We found that it was often present in the six ECC landscapes as a language additional to English. Similar approaches could be extended to support the over 160 other languages in this linguistically "superdiverse" country [16], particularly for the more commonly spoken Samoan, Hindi, and Northern Chinese. Because the wider ecosystems influence the practices within ECE centres and homes [60], we recommend that policy documents, curricula, and related web resources be improved by weaving into them relevant languages and cultural images to support the enrichment of linguistic landscapes. Increased guidance and professional development is also recommended to strengthen language practices in ECE so that they are inclusive of linguistically diverse children. This approach was one that whānau and the community members who participated in our study and related workshops identified and endorsed.

Our future work includes the following commitments: (1) to expand our collection of evidence to describe changes in the landscapes in the first year of school in our target area; (2) to disseminate research-informed guidance for policy-makers locally nationally and globally that addresses the complexity of the digital world in which young children are growing up, including the support of intergenerational languages transmission. We also plan to further align our research with the "You Matter To Us" (YMTU) consortium which is exploring how inter-agency action combined with community development can influence the evolution of organisational policies and practices (system change) to enhance wellbeing of children aged 0–5 years.

*Conclusions*

This research indicates that vulnerable children in quality ECC do have a better start in the digital world. ECE is improving multilingualism in Aotearoa New Zealand through its Te Whāriki curriculum, which ECCs are applying to evaluate and develop such practice. This practice limits "screen time" while also promoting strategies that deliberately deploy the digital world to serve the purposes of ECE in appropriate sociocultural ways. In addition to improving the quality of engagement, ECC staff deployed the digital world to increase the range and strength of their partnerships with whānau. As Taylor et al. [36] found, such purposeful strategies leverage the diverse languages of whānau with cultural support for their children, so it is also likely to have a positive impact on these families and their minority communities, which may result in a virtuous circle back to support all the children in the ECCs. In our research, the Whānau Aspirations Tree increased the sense of belonging, participation, and safety; mostly, it gave a strong presence in the ECC of the whānau voices. Given the fact that the area of the city in which the ECCs were located included one of the three most deprived suburbs in the country [61], this could have increased participants' feelings of safety. Multiple sources of evidence evaluated for the related community project "You matter to Us" indicate that such improvements are possible [41].

Therefore, there is evidence that ECCs can contribute to the resilience of vulnerable children and given them a better start in the digital world. The increased thoughtfulness of the adults and siblings of young children is also likely to lead to increases in resilience to potential internet and mobile phone addictions. For example, United States guidance [62] (p. 77) recommends media mentors to guide children and states, "As the primary role models for technology and media use, adults should be aware of and set limits on their own technology and media use when children are present, and focus on children having well-rounded experiences, including moderate, healthy media use."

The actions of these ECCs to deploy the digital world purposefully with developmentally appropriate sociocultural strategies included partnership with families. Projects by the World Organisation for Early Childhood Education (OMEP) [63] provide evidence that young children can act agents of change in their families to promote health and wellbeing. In the future, young children and their ECCs may be recognised as change agents redressing the challenges of addiction that are associated with growing up in a digital world.

**Author Contributions:** L.H. was the lead research assistant for "emergent bilinguals in a digital world" (EBinDW), and piloted the data collection design, collected all of the linguistic landscapes, analysed most of the EBinDW data, and led the writing of that methodology and findings. N.D. is co-principal investigator for the EBinDW strand of research; she co-conceived, co-designed, and co-analysed the EBinDW study, and she also collaborated on most aspects of the survey study. N.D. also conceptualised this article and led its writing. U.C. was the other co-principal investigator for the EBinDW research (2015–2017) who co-conceived, co-designed, and co-analysed the study, and she contributed to writing of the article. L.d.V. contributed her expertise in early childhood education, including application of literature to the analysis and writing of this article. S.M. was the principal investigator for the survey research, who led its conception, design and analysis. N.G. undertook the statistical analysis of the survey data and drafted that methodology and findings section. S.A. and T.O.T. gathered data volunteered by Pacific participants and also contributed to the analysis in both parts of the study. J.D. supported engagement of the whole project with stakeholders and contributed the fifth future strategy in this article.

**Acknowledgments:** The data were collected within the project "Eke pānui, eke tamaiti: Braiding health and education services to ensure early literacy success and healthy well-being for vulnerable children" co-led by Gail Gillon and Angus Macfarlane. We acknowledge the collaborative community of researchers in our National Science Challenge. No conditions were imposed by the financing beyond the Vision Matauranga cited in this article. We thank all the participants in the study, including the leaders of the ECC, community library, and schools. In addition, we acknowledge the support of the Ministry of Education.

## References

1. Fleer, M. Technologically constructed childhoods: Moving beyond a reproductive to a productive and critical view of curriculum development. *Aust. J. Early Child.* **2011**, *36*, 16–24.
2. Stephen, C.; Edwards, S. *Young Children and Learning in a Digital Age: A Cultural and Critical Perspective*; Routledge: Abingdon, UK, 2018.

3. UNESCO. *Recognizing the Potential of ICT in Early Childhood Education*; UNESCO Institute for Information Technologies in Education: Moscow, Russia, 2010.
4. Cunningham, U. *Growing up with Two Languages*, 3rd ed.; Routledge: London, UK, 2011.
5. Pempek, T.A.; Kirkorian, H.L.; Richards, J.E.; Anderson, D.R.; Lund, A.F.; Stevens, M. Video comprehensibility and attention in very young children. *Dev. Psychol.* **2010**, *46*, 1283–1293. [CrossRef] [PubMed]
6. Bornstein, M.H. Parenting science and practice. In *Handbook of Child Psychology: Child Psychology in Practice*, 6th ed.; Renniger, K.A., Sigel, I.E., Eds.; Wiley: Hoboken, NJ, USA, 2006; Volume 4, pp. 893–949.
7. Lamb, M.E.; Ahnert, L. Nonparental child care: Context, concepts, correlates, and consequences. In *Handbook of Child Psychology: Child Psychology in Practice*, 6th ed.; Renniger, K.A., Sigel, I.E., Eds.; Wiley: Hoboken, NJ, USA, 2006; Volume 4, pp. 950–1016.
8. García, O.; Kleifgen, J.A.; Falchi, L. *From English Language Learners to Emergent Bilinguals: Equity Matters Research Review No. 1*; Campaign for Educational Equity; Teachers College, Columbia University: New York, NY, USA, 2008.
9. Brown, K.D. The linguistic landscape of educational spaces: Language revitalization and schools in southeastern Estonia. In *Minority Languages in the Linguistic Landscape*; Gorter, D., Marten, H.F., Van Mensel, L., Eds.; Palgrave-Macmillan: Basingstoke, UK, 2012; pp. 281–298.
10. Crothers, C.; Smith, P.; Urale, P.W.B.; Bell, A. *The Internet in New Zealand 2015*; Institute of Culture, Discourse & Communication, Auckland University of Technology: Auckland, New Zealand, 2016.
11. Díaz Andrade, A.; Hedges, M.R.; Karimikia, H.; Techatassanasoontorn, A. *World Internet Project: The Internet in New Zealand 2017*; New Zealand Work Research Institute: Auckland, New Zealand, 2018.
12. Ministry of Education. *Te Whāriki: He Whāriki Mātauranga mō ngā Mokopuna o Aotearoa Early Childhood Curriculum*; Learning Media: Wellington, New Zealand, 2017.
13. Education Council. *Our Code, Our Standards*; Education Council: Wellington, New Zealand, 2017.
14. King, J.; de Vocht, L.; Cunningham, U.; Davis, N.E. *Languages Policy Development: A Guidance Note. He Kupu Āwhina kia Whakaritea He Kaupapa mō Ngā Reo*; Unpublished note to Minister of Education, University of Canterbury: Christchurch, New Zealand, 2017.
15. Office of Ethnic Affairs. Language and Integration in New Zealand. Available online: https://ethniccommunities.govt.nz/story/language-information-and-advice (accessed on 30 July 2018).
16. Royal Society of New Zealand. *Languages in Aotearoa New Zealand*; Royal Society of New Zealand: Wellington, New Zealand, 2013.
17. Hsin, C.-T.; Li, M.-C.; Tsai, C.-C. The influence of young children's use of technology on their learning: A review. *J. Educ. Technol. Soc.* **2014**, *17*, 85–99.
18. Chaudron, S. *Young Children (0–8) and Digital Technology: A Qualitative Exploratory Study across Seven Countries*; Publications Office of the European Union: Luxembourg, 2015.
19. Aubrey, C.; Dahl, S. The confidence and competence in information and communication technologies of practitioners, parents and young children in the early years foundation stage. *Early Years* **2014**, *34*, 94–108. [CrossRef]
20. Marklund, L.; Dunkels, E. Digital play as a means to develop children's literacy and power in the Swedish preschool. *Early Years* **2016**, *36*, 289–304. [CrossRef]
21. Lopez-Fernandez, O.; Kuss, D.; Pontes, H.; Griffiths, M.; Dawes, C.; Justice, L.; Männikkö, N.; Kääriäinen, M.; Rumpf, H.J.; Bischof, A.; et al. Measurement invariance of the short version of the problematic mobile phone use questionnaire (PMPUQ-SV) across eight languages. *Int. J. Environ. Res. Public Health* **2018**, *15*, 1213. [CrossRef] [PubMed]
22. Rozgonjuk, D.; Saal, K.; Tahl, K. Problematic smartphone use, deep and surface approaches to learning, and social media use in lectures. *Int. J. Environ. Res. Public Health* **2018**, *15*, 92. [CrossRef] [PubMed]
23. Van Rooij, A.J.; Ferguson, C.J.; Colder Carras, M.; Kardefelt-Winther, D.; Shi, J.; Aarseth, E.; Bean, A.M.; Bergmark, K.H.; Brus, A.; Coulson, M.; et al. A weak scientific basis for gaming disorder: Let us err on the side of caution. *J. Behav. Addict.* **2018**, *7*, 1–9. [CrossRef] [PubMed]
24. Kildare, C.A.; Middlemiss, W. Impact of parents mobile device use on parent-child interaction: A literature review. *Comput. Hum. Behav.* **2017**, *75*, 579–593. [CrossRef]
25. Lauricella, A.R.; Wartella, E.; Rideout, V.J. Young children's screen time: The complex role of parent and child factors. *J. Appl. Dev. Psychol.* **2015**, *36*, 11–17. [CrossRef]

26. McPake, J.; Plowman, L.; Stephen, C. Pre-school children creating and communicating with digital technologies in the home. *Br. J. Educ. Technol.* **2013**, *44*, 421–431. [CrossRef]
27. Bak, T.H.; Nissan, J.J.; Allerhand, M.M.; Deary, I.J. Does bilingualism influence cognitive aging? *Ann. Neurol.* **2014**, *75*, 959–963. [CrossRef] [PubMed]
28. Olsen, R.K.; Pangelinan, M.M.; Bogulski, C.; Chakravarty, M.M.; Luk, G.; Grady, C.L.; Bialystok, E. The effect of lifelong bilingualism on regional grey and white matter volume. *Brain Res.* **2015**, *1612*, 128–139. [CrossRef] [PubMed]
29. Cummins, J. *Language, Power, and Pedagogy: Bilingual Children Caught in the Crossfire*; Multilingual Matters Ltd.: Clevedon, UK, 2000.
30. Rowe, D.W.; Miller, M.E. Designing for diverse classrooms: Using iPads and digital cameras to compose eBooks with emergent bilingual/biliterate four-year-olds. *J. Early Child. Lit.* **2016**, *16*, 425–472. [CrossRef]
31. King, J.; Cunningham, U. Intergenerational transmission of minority languages in New Zealand: Methodological issues. In *Advances in Understanding Multilingualism: A Global Perspective*; Grucza, S., Olpińska-Szkielko, M., Romanowski, P., Eds.; Peter Lang Verlag: Frankfurt, Germany, 2016; pp. 61–77.
32. Cunningham, U.; King, J. Language, ethnicity, and belonging for the children of migrants in New Zealand. *SAGE Open* **2018**, *8*. [CrossRef]
33. Dressler, R. Sign geist: Promoting bilingualism through the linguistic landscape of school signage. *Int. J. Multiling.* **2015**, *12*, 128–145. [CrossRef]
34. Cenoz, J.; Gorter, D. Linguistic landscape and minority languages. *Int. J. Multiling.* **2006**, *3*, 67–80. [CrossRef]
35. Sneddon, R. Young bilingual children learning to read with dual-language books. *Engl. Teach. Pract. Crit.* **2008**, *7*, 71–84.
36. Taylor, L.K.; Bernhard, J.K.; Garg, S.; Cummins, J. Affirming plural belonging: Building on students' family-based cultural and linguistic capital through multiliteracies pedagogy. *J. Early Child. Lit.* **2008**, *8*, 260–294. [CrossRef]
37. Gorter, D. Linguistic landscapes and trends in the study of schoolscapes. *Linguist. Educ.* **2017**, *44*, 80–85. [CrossRef]
38. Cooper, M.; Hedges, H. Beyond participation: What we learned from Hunter about collaboration with Pasifika children and families. *Contemp. Issues Early Child.* **2014**, *15*, 165–175. [CrossRef]
39. World Medical Association. Declaration of Helsinki. Ethical principles for medical research involving human subjects. *Bull. World Health Organ.* **2001**, *79*, 373–374.
40. A Better Start, E Tipu E Rea. Vision Mātauranga and He Awa Whiria Guide Our Research and Operations. Available online: https://www.abetterstart.nz/the-science/vision-matauranga/ (accessed on 1 September 2018).
41. Dobson, J. (Ed.) *You Matter to Us (YMTU)*, Unpublished Concept Paper. 2017.
42. Statistics New Zealand. *2013 Census QuickStats about a Place*; Statistics New Zealand: Wellington, New Zealand, 2013.
43. Schaughency, E.; Riordan, J.; Reese, E.; Derby, M.; Wilson, L.; Gillon, G. Developing a community-based oral language shared book reading program: Exploring feasibility and social validity. Submitted. 2018.
44. Harris, L. An Ethnographic Case Study of the Linguistic Landscape of an Award-Winning Māori Immersion Early Childhood Centre. Master's Thesis, University of Canterbury, Christchurch, New Zealand, 2016.
45. Copland, F.; Creese, A.; Rock, F.; Shaw, S. *Linguistic Ethnography: Collecting, Analysing and Presenting Data*; SAGE: Los Angeles, CA, USA, 2015.
46. Education Review Office. Early Childhood and School Reports. Available online: http://www.ero.govt.nz/review-reports/ (accessed on 30 July 2018).
47. A Better Start National Science Challenge E Tipu e Rea. Revised Research and Business Plans. Available online: http://www.abetterstart.nz/about/ (accessed on 30 July 2018).
48. Wiig, E.H.; Secord, W.; Semel, E. *Clinical Evaluation of Language Fundamentals—Preschool*, 2nd ed.; Harcourt Assessment: London, UK, 2006.
49. Carson, K.; Gillon, G.; Boustead, T. Computer-administered versus paper-based assessment of school-entry phonological awareness ability. *Asia Pac. J. Speech Lang. Hear.* **2011**, *14*, 85–101. [CrossRef]
50. Morton, S.M.B.; Grant, C.C.; Berry, S.D.; Walker, C.G.; Corkin, M.; Ly, K.; de Castro, T.G.; Atatoa Carr, P.E.; Bandara, D.K.; Mohal, J.; et al. *Growing Up in New Zealand: A Longitudinal Study of New Zealand Children and Their Families. Now We Are Four: Describing the Preschool Years*; Growing Up in New Zealand: Auckland, New Zealand, 2017.

51. Carr, M.; Lee, W.; Jones, C. Information and communication technology (ICT). In *Kei Tua o te Pae: Assessment for Learning: Early Childhood Exemplars*; Ministry of Education; Learning Media: Wellington, New Zealand, 2009.
52. Conteh, J.; Brock, A. 'Safe spaces'? Sites of bilingualism for young learners in home, school and community. *Int. J. Biling. Educ. Biling.* **2011**, *14*, 347–360. [CrossRef]
53. Paudel, S.; Jancey, J.; Subedi, N.; Leavy, J. Correlates of mobile screen media use among children aged 0–8: A systematic review. *BMJ Open* **2017**, *7*, e014585. [CrossRef] [PubMed]
54. Lindenberg, K.; Halasy, K.; Szász-Janocha, C.; Wartberg, L. A phenotype classification of internet use disorder in a large-scale high-school Study. *Int. J. Environ. Res. Public Health* **2018**, *15*, 733. [CrossRef] [PubMed]
55. Raman, S.; Guerrero-Duby, S.; McCullough, J.L.; Brown, M.; Ostrowski-Delahanty, S.; Langkamp, D.; Duby, J.C. Screen exposure during daily routines and a young child's risk for having social-emotional delay. *Clin. Pediatr.* **2017**, *56*, 1244–1253. [CrossRef] [PubMed]
56. Tizard, B.; Hughes, M. *Young Children Learning*, 2nd ed.; Blackwell Publishing: Malden, MA, USA, 2002.
57. Fleming, T.; Bavin, L.; Lucassen, M.; Stasiak, K.; Hopkins, S.; Merry, S. Beyond the trial: Systematic review of real-world uptake and engagement with digital self-help interventions for depression, low mood, or anxiety. *J. Med. Int. Res.* **2018**, *20*, e199. [CrossRef] [PubMed]
58. Vaughan, M.; Beers, C. Using an exploratory professional development initiative to introduce iPads in the early childhood education classroom. *Early Child. Educ. J.* **2017**, *45*, 321–331. [CrossRef]
59. Miller, J.L.; Kocurek, C.A. Principles for educational game development for young children. *J. Child. Media* **2017**, *11*, 314–329. [CrossRef]
60. Davis, N.E. *Digital Technologies and Change in Education: The Arena Framework*; Routledge: New York, NY, USA, 2018.
61. Schluter, P.J.; Audas, R.; Kokaua, J.; McNeill, B.; Taylor, B.; Milne, B.; Gillon, G. The efficacy of preschool developmental indicators as a screen for early primary school-based literacy interventions. *Child. Dev.* **2018**, in press. [CrossRef] [PubMed]
62. Donohue, C.; Shomburg, R. Technology and Interactive Media in Early Childhood Programs. What We've Learned from Five Years of Research, Policy, and Practice. *Young Children* **2017**, *72*, 72–78.
63. Engdahl, I. Early childhood education for sustainability: The OMEP world project. *Int. J. Early Child.* **2015**, *47*, 347–366. [CrossRef]

# 12

# Emotional Regulation in Young Adults with Internet Gaming Disorder

**Ju-Yu Yen [1,2], Yi-Chun Yeh [1,3,4], Peng-Wei Wang [1,4], Tai-Ling Liu [3,4], Yun-Yu Chen [1] and Chih-Hung Ko [1,3,4,5,*]**

[1] Department of Psychiatry, Faculty of Medicine, College of Medicine, Kaohsiung Medical University, Kaohsiung City 807, Taiwan; yenjuyu@cc.kmu.edu.tw (J.-Y.Y.); y7552156@gmail.com (Y.-C.Y.); wistar.huang@gmail.com (P.-W.W.); li52030tw@gmail.com (Y.-Y.C.)
[2] Department of Psychiatry, Kaohsiung Municipal Ta-Tung Hospital, Kaohsiung Medical University, Kaohsiung City 801, Taiwan
[3] Graduate Institute of Medicine, College of Medicine, Kaohsiung Medical University, Kaohsiung City 807, Taiwan; dai32155@gmail.com
[4] Department of Psychiatry, Kaohsiung Medical University Hospital, Kaohsiung Medical University, Kaohsiung City 807, Taiwan
[5] Department of Psychiatry, Kaohsiung Municipal Hsiao-Kang Hospital, Kaohsiung Medical University, Kaohsiung City 812, Taiwan
* Correspondence: chihhungko@gmail.com

**Abstract:** People diagnosed with Internet gaming disorder (IGD) have been frequently reported to experience depression, anxiety, and hostility. Emotional regulation contributes to these mood symptoms. This study evaluated emotional regulation in subjects with IGD and examined relationships between emotional regulation, depression, anxiety, and hostility in young adults with IGD. We recruited 87 people with IGD and a control group of 87 people without a history of IGD. All participants underwent a diagnostic interview based on the IGD criteria of the Diagnostic and Statistical Manual of Mental Disorders, Fifth Edition, and they completed a questionnaire on emotional regulation, depression, anxiety, and hostility. We found that subjects with IGD were less likely to practice cognitive reappraisal and were more likely to suppress their emotions. Linear regression revealed the higher cognitive reappraisal and lower expressive suppression associated with depression, anxiety, and hostility among subjects with IGD. The emotional regulation strategies that characterize those with IGD could be contributing factors to the depression and hostility tendencies of these people. When treating patients with IGD, in addition to providing appropriate interventions to relieve depression and hostility, practitioners should effectively assess emotional regulation strategies and provide emotional regulation therapy to prevent a vicious cycle of negative emotions.

**Keywords:** Internet gaming disorder; IGD; emotional regulation; cognitive reappraisal; suppression; depression; hostility

## 1. Introduction

Diagnostic criteria for Internet gaming disorder (IGD), defined as an addiction to Internet games, are proposed as research criteria in section III of the Diagnostic and Statistical Manual of Mental Disorders, Fifth Edition (DSM-5) [1]. IGD is one type of internet addiction and has been associated with mood-related psychopathological symptoms, such as depression and irritability [2,3]. This comorbidity could contribute to treatment difficulties and a poor prognosis of addictive disorder [4], for example, the comorbidity of depression associated with the higher psychosocial burden among subjects with IGD [5]. Further, comorbidity could indicate a causal relationship between the disorders [6] or a common factors model [7], wherein a shared mechanism generally accounts for increased comorbidity. To intervene, the shared mechanism might benefit both disorders. Therefore, understanding the shared mechanism causing comorbidity between IGD and psychopathological symptoms could contribute to successfully developing treatments for them.

### 1.1. Association between IGD and Emotional Difficulties

The amount of time spent playing online games has been positively correlated with depressive symptoms [8,9]. The association between IGD, depression, and hostility were also demonstrated in recent studies [10,11]. Gentile et al. reported that IGD could be a cause of depression in adolescents [12]. Further, Ciarrochi et al. also reported that compulsive internet use predicted poor mental health among adolescents in longitudinal investigation [13]. These results might indicate that repeatedly excessive online gaming could contribute to emotional difficulties, possibly though impaired daily life functions or their negative consequences. On the other side, addictive behavior, such as online gaming [14], could be a way of coping with pre-existing emotional difficulties, such as depression [6]. Depression was reported to predict the incidence of internet addiction and support this claim [15]. This might suggest that emotional difficulties could possibly contribute to IGD; however, this has not been proved. The possible bidirectional effect between IGD and emotional difficulties deserves future prospective study. On the other hand, an underlying factor, such as emotional regulation, might be associated with both IGD and emotional difficulties, and could contribute to the comorbidity of IGD.

### 1.2. Emotional Regulation and Depression, Anxiety, Hostility, and IGD

Emotional regulation, also known as emotional self-regulation, was defined by [16] as the set of cognitive processes that influence emotional responses. Emotional regulation is a complex process that includes the initiation, inhibition, or modulation of aspects of emotion functioning. A previous review demonstrated that interventions that specifically target emotional regulation can not only promote positive emotional regulation but also attenuate associated psychopathological symptoms [17].

Two strategies are commonly used for downregulating emotion. The first, reappraisal, comes early in the emotion-generative process and entails changing how a situation is construed in order to reduce its emotional impact. The second, suppression, comes later in the emotion-generative process and entails the inhibition of outward signs of inner feelings [18]. The two types of emotional regulation are evaluated in The Emotional Regulation Questionnaire, which measures the habitual use of expressive suppression and cognitive re-evaluation. The scale includes items related to the regulation of positive and negative emotions [19]. According to this measurement, practicing reappraisal is associated with greater positive emotion, improved interpersonal functioning, and well-being. By contrast, practicing suppression is associated with negative emotions and poorer interpersonal functioning. These results suggest that strategies that act early in the emotion-generative process have a different profile of consequences than strategies that act later.

Emotional regulation was associated with depression [20] and anxiety [21]. The employment of adaptive emotional regulation strategies (e.g., reappraisal) causes a reduction in stress-induced emotions. Conversely, dysfunctional emotional regulation strategies, such as emotion suppression, appear to influence the pathogenesis of depression. For example, a structural equation modeling study found that expressive suppression mediated the relationship between intensity of negative affect and psychological distress [22]. In addition, emotional regulation therapy has been reported to be an effective treatment of emotional dysfunctions, such as anxiety or depression [17,23,24]. The literature demonstrates the role for emotional regulation in the development or maintenance of depression and anxiety [20,21].

Fewer studies have evaluated the relationship between emotional regulation and hostility than the relationship between emotional regulation and depression or anxiety. People with lower anger control can reasonably be assumed to display more aggressive behaviors [25]. A previous study demonstrated the relationship between emotional regulation and anger reactivity [26]. Hostile cognition is a major factor contributing to anger and aggressive behavior [27]. However, whether cognitive appraisal can attenuate the role of hostile cognition in depression has not been evaluated.

Depression and emotional regulation are considered risk factors for the development of addictive disorders [28]. Emotional regulation was reported to predict substance use disorder (specifically, alcohol use disorder [29]) and has been suggested to have a moderating role in addiction development [30]. IGD has been reported to be associated with depression, irritability, and anxiety [2,3,31]. Difficulties with emotional regulation are associated with these associated psychopathological symptoms [20,21]. Furthermore, poor emotional regulation might contribute to depression [20] that predicts IGD [15,32]. Moreover, excessive online gaming could have negative consequences that could result in stress for individuals with IGD. Appropriate emotional regulation mediates negative effects and psychological stress [22], whereas impaired emotional regulation might contribute to mood symptoms, such as depression and anxiety. Loton et al. revealed that the coping strategy had been reported to account for the association between video gaming addiction and depression [14]. It supported the claim that inappropriate emotional regulation might contribute to the association between psychopathological symptoms of IGD. However, the association between emotional regulation and these psychopathological symptoms has not been evaluated among subjects with IGD.

### 1.3. Study Hypothesis and Objectives

We hypothesized that emotional regulation, cognitive reappraisal, and suppression are associated with IGD, and that individuals with IGD practice less emotional regulation, use fewer reappraisal strategies, and tend to suppress emotions more than does the average person. Furthermore, the deficit in emotional regulation might be correlated with depression, hostility, and anxiety among subjects with IGD. Accordingly, this study evaluated the following: (1) cognitive reappraisal and expressive suppression among individuals with and without IGD, and (2) the associations among cognitive reappraisal, expressive suppression, depression, hostility, and anxiety among subjects with IGD.

## 2. Materials and Methods

### 2.1. Participants

Our participants, namely individuals with current IGD (the IGD group) and those with no history of IGD (the control group), were recruited through advertisements that demonstrated our recruitment critieria on campuses and bulletin board systems at universities in Taiwan between September 2012 and October 2013. Our recruitment criteria for the IGD group, which were based on an fMRI study for young adults with IGD, were as follows [32]: (1) aged 20–30 years with education of >9 years; (2) played Internet games for $\geq$4 h per day on weekdays and $\geq$8 h per day on weekends or for $\geq$40 h per week; and (3) had maintained an Internet gaming pattern for >2 years. The recruited participants spent most of their free time on Internet gaming. For participants fulfilling these criteria, a psychiatrist conducted an interview, during which the DSM-5 diagnostic criteria for IGD was used [1] in the interviewing room at laboratory. Participants that fulfilled the DSM-5 criteria of IGD were classified in the IGD group.

For every participant enrolled in the IGD group, a gender-, age- (within a range of 1 year), and education level-matched control participant was recruited according to the criteria that their nonessential Internet use was of <4 h per day in their daily life. The limitation on internet use was designed to prevent recruiting subjects with internet addiction in control group. Then, these participants also underwent a diagnostic interview with the psychiatrist based on DSM-5 criteria of IGD to confirm their recruitment in control group.

The diagnostic interview comprised two parts: (1) a diagnostic interview based on the Chinese version of the Mini-International Neuropsychiatric Interview (MINI) to reveal existing psychotic disorders, bipolar I disorder, and substance use disorders; and (2) a history-taking interview to determine psychotropic medication use, mental retardation, severe physical disorder, and brain injury. Individuals with psychotic disorders, bipolar I disorder, substance use disorders, psychotropic medication use, mental retardation, severe physical disorder, or brain injury were excluded. In total, 174 participants—87 in each group—were included after diagnostic interviewing and their informed consent was obtained. Then, study participants completed the assessment in this present study. This study was approved by the Institutional Review Board of Kaohsiung Medical University Hospital.

### 2.2. Measures

DSM-5 diagnostic criteria for IGD [1]. The DSM-5 IGD diagnostic criteria include comprises nine items: preoccupation, withdrawal, tolerance, unsuccessful attempts to control, loss or decrease of other interests, continued excessive use despite psychosocial problems, deceiving, escapism, and functional impairment [1]. We developed a semistructured interview for examining the DSM-5 criteria for IGD. Participants fulfilling ≥5 criteria were included in classified as the IGD group.

Chinese version of the MINI [33]. We conducted a diagnostic interview to rule out psychiatric disorders by using the modules of psychotic disorders, bipolar I disorder, and substance use disorders in the Chinese version of the MINI. Those with existing disorders were excluded from the study.

Emotional regulation questionnaire. The emotional regulation questionnaire (ERQ) is a 10-item scale designed to measure respondents' tendency to regulate their emotions in two ways: (1) cognitive reappraisal, assessed using a reappraisal scale (six items such as "When I want to feel less negative emotion (such as sadness or anger), I change what I'm thinking about"), and (2) expressive suppression, assessed using a suppression scale (four items such as "I control my emotions by not expressing them"). Respondents answer each item on a 7-point Likert-type scale from 1 (strongly disagree) to 7 (strongly agree). The alpha reliabilities were averaged 0.79 and 0.73 for the reappraisal and suppression scales, respectively. Test–retest reliability over 3 months was 0.69 for both scales in its original study [19]. There are several scales assessing emotional regulation. We utilized ERQ to assess the most important two strategy of emotional regulation because of its brief and convenient nature.

Depression, hostility, and anxiety were assessed by the Center for Epidemiological Studies' Depression Scale (CES-D) [34,35] Penn State Worry Questionnaire (PSWQ) [36] and the Buss–Durkee Hostility Inventory Chinese Version—Short Form (BDHIC-SF) [37]. Cronbach's alpha of CES-D, PSWQ, and BDHIC-SF in the present study were 0.92, 0.90, and 0.92, respectively. Higher score of CES-D, BDHIC-SF, and PSWQ indicates higher depression, hostility, and anxiety, respectively.

### 2.3. Statistical Analysis

We first evaluated the differences in cognitive reappraisal and expressive suppression between the IGD and control groups. Logistic regression was used to regress the diagnosis of IGD on the reappraisal and suppression while controlling for gender, age, and educational level. Then, linear regression was used to regress the depression on the cognitive reappraisal, and expressive suppression with control of gender, age, and educational level in both IGD and control group. The gender was set as female = 0 and male = 1 in the linear regression. The same method was used to evaluate the associations between reappraisal, suppression, and hostility or anxiety. $p < 0.05$ was considered significant in the analyses, all of which were performed using SPSS. The significant threshold of multiplicity was corrected using the Holm–Bonferroni methods. The Holm–Bonferroni method controls the familywise error rate (Type I errors) by adjusting the $p$ value of the individual comparison [38].

## 3. Results

### 3.1. Gender, Age, and Education Levels

Eighty-seven people were recruited for each group. Their gender ($X^2 = 0$, $p = 1$), age ($t = 0.26$, $p = 0.80$), and education levels ($t = 1.15$, $p = 0.25$) did not differ significantly (Table 1).

**Table 1.** Age, educational level, emotional regulation, hostility, depression, and severity for the IGD and control groups.

| Variables | IGD Diagnosis | | $X^2$ |
|---|---|---|---|
| | Yes ($N$ = 87) | No ($N$ = 87) | |
| | Mean ± SD | Mean ± SD | $t$-Test |
| Gender | | | |
| Male | 70 (80.5%) | 70 (80.5%) | 0.00 |
| Female | 17 (19.5%) | 17 (19.5%) | |
| Age | 23.29 ± 2.34 | 23.38 ± 2.40 | 0.26 |
| Education level | 15.93 ± 1.15 | 16.14 ± 1.22 | 1.15 |
| Cognitive reappraisal [1] | 31.09 ± 5.43 | 33.16 ± 4.87 | −2.64 ** |
| Expressive suppression [2] | 19.22 ± 3.40 | 17.98 ± 3.74 | 2.292 * |

* $p < 0.05$; ** $p < 0.01$; [1] Score of cognitive reappraisal subscale of *ERQ*; [2] Score of expressive suppression subscale of *ERQ*.

### 3.2. Emotional Regulation and IGD

The IGD group had significantly lower cognitive reappraisal strategies ($t = -2.64$, $p = 0.009$) and greater expressive suppression strategies ($t = 2.29$, $p = 0.02$) than did the control group (Table 1). Logistic regression (Table 2) revealed that cognitive reappraisal negatively predicts IGD (odds ratio; OR = 0.91; 95% CI = 0.85–0.97) and that expressive suppression positively predicts IGD (OR = 1.14; 95% CI = 1.04–1.25).

**Table 2.** Logistic regression to evaluate the predictive value of emotional regulation in IGD with control of gender, age, and educational level.

| Variables | Wald | Exp(β) | 95% CI |
|---|---|---|---|
| Among all subjects | | | |
| Gender | 0.01 | 1.05 | 0.47–2.32 |
| Age (year) | 0.43 | 1.0550 | 0.91–1.22 |
| Education level (year) | 1.11 | 0.86 | 0.64–1.14 |
| Cognitive reappraisal [1] | 8.97 ** | 0.91 | 0.85–0.97 |
| Expressive Suppression [2] | 7.28 ** | 1.14 | 1.04–1.25 |

** $p < 0.01$; [1] Score of cognitive reappraisal subscale of *ERQ*; [2] Score of expressive suppression subscale of *ERQ*.

### 3.3. Within-Group Analysis for Emotional Regulation

Multiple linear regression analysis was used to test if the emotional regulation significantly predicted depression, anxiety, or hostility of subjects in IGD group (Table 3). The results indicated the model explained 19% of the variance in depression ($R^2 = 0.19$, $F_{(5,81)} = 3.74$). Cognitive reappraisal significant predicted depression ($B = -0.72$, $t = -3.66$, $p < 0.001$), as did expressive suppression ($B = 1.02$, $t = 3.24$, $p = 0.002$). Further, the model explained 18% of variance in anxiety ($R^2 = 0.18$, $F_{(5,81)} = 3.59$). Cognitive reappraisal significant predicted anxiety ($B = -0.69$, $t = -3.20$, $p = 0.002$), as did expressive suppression ($B = 0.91$, $t = 2.66$, $p = 0.01$). The model also explained 12% of variance in hostility ($R^2 = 0.12$, $F_{(5,81)} = 2.2$). Cognitive reappraisal significantly predicted hostility ($B = -0.75$, $t = -2.79$, $p = 0.007$), as did expressive suppression ($B = 1.09$, $t = 2.53$, $p = 0.01$). These results suggested that IGD subjects with lower cognitive reappraisal and higher expressive suppression had higher depression, anxiety, and hostility. We also provide the result in control group. It demonstrated the similar association between emotional regulation and depression, anxiety, and hostility in control group (Table 3).

**Table 3.** Multiple linear regression analysis for the predictive value of emotional regulation in depression, hostility, and CGI score among IGD group or control group.

| Variables | IGD B | IGD t | IGD p | Control B | Control t | Control p |
|---|---|---|---|---|---|---|
| Depression [1] | | | | | | |
| Gender | 0.78 | 0.31 | 0.76 | −1.76 | −1.06 | 0.29 |
| Age (year) | 0.24 | 0.52 | 0.61 | −0.24 | −0.77 | 0.44 |
| Education level (year) | −0.19 | −0.20 | 0.84 | 0.21 | 0.34 | 0.73 |
| Cognitive reappraisal [2] | −0.72 | −3.66 | <0.001 | −0.73 | −5.21 | <0.001 |
| Suppression [3] | 1.02 | 3.24 | 0.002 | 1.06 | 6.01 | <0.001 |
| | $F_{(5,81)} = 3.74$ | $R^2 = 0.19$ | | $F_{(5,81)} = 12.90$ | $R^2 = 0.44$ | |
| Anxiety [4] | | | | | | |
| Gender | −1.86 | −0.68 | 0.50 | −2.75 | −1.29 | 0.20 |
| Age (year) | −0.79 | −1.57 | 0.12 | −0.72 | −1.78 | 0.08 |
| Education level (year) | 1.39 | 1.34 | 0.19 | 1.58 | 1.98 | 0.05 |
| Cognitive reappraisal | −0.69 | −3.20 | 0.002 | −0.96 | −5.28 | <0.001 |
| Suppression | 0.91 | 2.66 | 0.01 | 1.13 | 4.93 | <0.001 |
| | $F_{(5,81)} = 3.59$ | $R^2 = 0.18$ | | $F_{(5,81)} = 11.71$ | $R^2 = 0.42$ | |
| Hostility [5] | | | | | | |
| Gender | −1.19 | −0.34 | 0.73 | −3.61 | −1.52 | 0.13 |
| Age (year) | 0.13 | 0.20 | 0.84 | 0.09 | 0.21 | 0.84 |
| Education level (year) | −0.60 | −0.46 | 0.65 | 0.15 | 0.17 | 0.87 |
| Cognitive reappraisal | −0.75 | −2.79 | 0.01 | −0.72 | −3.55 | 0.001 |
| Suppression | 1.09 | 2.53 | 0.01 | 1.45 | 5.69 | <0.001 |
| | $F_{(5,81)} = 2.20$ | $R^2 = 0.12$ | | $F_{(5,81)} = 8.87$ | $R^2 = 0.35$ | |

[1] Score of cognitive reappraisal subscale of *ERQ*; [2] Score of expressive suppression subscale of *ERQ*; [3] Score of Center for Epidemiological Studies' Depression Scale; [4] Score of PSWQ; [5] Score of the Buss–Durkee Hostility Inventory—Chinese Version—Short Form.

## 4. Discussion

People with poor emotional regulation often engage in maladaptive behavior to escape from their emotions, creating risks of a range of mood disorders and addictive disorders [39]. Thus, such people have been associated with various addictive disorders [29,30]. To our knowledge, no previous study has assessed emotional regulation among subjects with IGD. As expected, the present study demonstrated that subjects with IGD have lower cognitive reappraisal and higher expressive suppression. This result is similar to a previous report demonstrating lower cognitive reappraisal in gambling disorder [39]. Further, our study demonstrated that lower cognitive reappraisal and higher expressive suppression were associated with depression, anxiety, and hostility among subjects with IGD.

Our literature review suggested that those individuals experiencing depression or anxiety have ineffective emotional regulation and difficulties in processing negative emotions [20,21]. Cognitive reappraisal is a cognitively-oriented strategy for redefining emotional stimuli in unemotional terms or for reimagining depressive situations [40]. It comes early in the emotion-generative process and effectively decreases the experience of negative emotions [18]. By contrast, expressive suppression, coming later in the emotion-generative process, entails the inhibition of outward signs of inner feelings. Suppression is ineffective for down-regulating negative emotions, and people with a history of depression have been reported to spontaneously use this strategy [41]. Like these previous results, our results demonstrated that subjects with higher depression have lower cognitive reappraisal and higher expressive suppression among both subjects with IGD and controls.

People with IGD experience negative psychosocial consequences from excessive online gaming [42]. They also experience depression, anxiety, or irritation when they are prohibited from playing games online [1]. Thus, previous prospective study had suggested that internet gaming disorder or excessive online gaming [8,12] contributes to depression. They could reappraisal that this is a logical result of ceasing an excessive, self-gratifying behavior, and that the depression and restlessness could be avoided if they engaged in an alternative, appropriate activity such as exercise. However, without appropriate reappraisal, subjects with IGD could experience depression. Further, continuing to suppress negative emotions rather than reappraising them could leave these emotional difficulties unresolved. Thus, the lower cognitive reappraisal and higher suppression of subjects with IGD could partly account for their vulnerability to depression.

Although there is no report demonstrating the predictive effect of depression on internet gaming disorder, previous reports had suggested that depression predicted incidence of internet addiction [32]. Subjects with lower cognitive reappraisal that were habituated to use suppression could experience depression under stress [20,22]. Online gaming could provide a virtual world for people to escape from their negative emotions [43] and could buffer stress [44]. However, if the gaming time could not be well controlled, the repeatedly excessive gaming could result in further negative consequences among vulnerable subjects. It could create a vicious cycle and lead to repeated engagement in online gaming, resulting in increased addiction risk. Anyway, this claim should be further evaluated in prospective study.

Subjects with higher anxiety were more likely to pay attention to threat-related stimuli rather than neutral stimuli [45]. The continued attention to threat increases their cognitive and emotional response, contributing to anxiety symptoms. The manner in which information was processed in emotional regulation could determine anxiety severity [24]. The use of suppression as a regulatory mechanism and limited access to emotional regulation strategies, such as cognitive reappraisal, were associated with anxiety [46]. Thus, dysfunctional emotional regulation contributes to the development of anxiety disorder [24]. In this study, the anxiety of subjects with IGD is negatively associated with cognitive reappraisal and positively associated with expressive suppression.

In addition, reappraisal facilitates the adaptive processing of anger-inducing situations and contributes to anger regulation [47]. However, the suppression of anger could increase hostility under stress [48]. As expected, subjects with IGD habitually suppress emotions, or those unlikely to reappraise their negative cognition exhibited higher levels of hostility in this study. Moreover, suppression of hostility could increase sympathetic activity [49], as well as the risk of cardiovascular disorder [50]. Thus, emotional suppression and hostility of subjects with IGD might result in not only emotional difficulty but also cardiovascular risk.

Cognitive control ability is essential and contributes to emotional regulation, such as reappraisal [40]. Subjects with IGD had impaired cognitive control [51], similar to people with gambling disorders [52] and addictive disorder, such as cocaine use disorder [53]. The impaired cognitive control ability could associate with their impaired cognitive reappraisal in subjects with IGD. Further study is necessary to understand the neurocognitive mechanism of the impaired emotional regulation, such as cognitive control, among subjects with IGD.

### *4.1. Clinical Implication*

The dysfunctional emotional regulation of subjects with IGD was associated with depression, anxiety, and hostility [32]. Emotional regulation should be well assessed and intervened in among young adults with IGD. Three key steps—emotional awareness, emotional regulation, and exchanging one emotion for another—help people to modify the state, the belief, and the behavior in response to emotion-eliciting events. These interventions for emotional regulation [23] have been recommended for the treatment of depression [20]. Evidence-based emotion management strategies, such as emotion-focused therapy [54], could be provided to young adults with IGD to promote cognitive reappraisal and attenuate expressive suppression strategies and responses. They must become aware that their negative emotions result from the negative consequences of gaming or from the conflicts in their lives. Alternative activities, physical exercise, and further psychological support should be offered to help relieve negative emotions. Furthermore, information and guidance on reappraisal should be provided so that positive thinking can replace negative thinking. This intervention to promote reappraisal and prevent suppression may attenuate their depression, anxiety, and hostility, and prevent the vicious cycle of IGD. However, these claims for the effects of emotional regulation therapy should be evaluated with future clinical research.

### 4.2. Limitations

This study has three limitations. First, emotional regulation was assessed using a questionnaire only and not through the investigation of real situations. Second, IGD was diagnosed only through diagnostic interviews with the participants, and supplementary information from family members or partners, which could have contributed to verifying the validity of the diagnoses, was not collected. Third, our cross-sectional research design could not confirm causal relationships between emotional regulation and IGD. Besides, the structure equation model had not been utilized to test hypothesized model because of unconfirmed causal relationship.

## 5. Conclusions

People with IGD practice less cognitive reappraisal and more suppression. In this study, people practicing less cognitive reappraisal and more suppression had more symptoms of depression, anxiety, and hostility, suggesting that impaired emotional regulation might exacerbate negative mood symptoms in people with IGD. Thus, emotional regulation should be effectively assessed when treating people with IGD. Furthermore, this group should be given interventions to promote cognitive reappraisal and attenuate expressive suppression in order to avoid a vicious cycle of negative emotions.

**Acknowledgments:** This study was supported by grants from the National Science Council (MOST105-2314-B-037-027-MY2), Kaohsiung Municipal Ta-Tung Hospital (kmtth-102-016; kmtth-103-018), and the Kaohsiung Medical University Hospital (KMUH103-3R62). These institutions had no role in the design, process, analysis, and production of the present study.

**Author Contributions:** Chih-Hung Ko conceived and designed the experiments; Tai-Ling Liu and Yun-Yu Chen performed the experiments; Yi-Chun Yeh and Peng-Wei Wang analyzed the data; Ju-Yu Yen wrote the paper.

## References

1. American Psychiatric Association. *Diagnostic and Statistical Manual of Mental Disorders*, 5th ed.; American Psychiatric Association: Arlington, TX, USA, 2013.
2. Ko, C.H.; Liu, T.L.; Wang, P.W.; Chen, C.S.; Yen, C.F.; Yen, J.Y. The exacerbation of depression, hostility, and social anxiety in the course of Internet addiction among adolescents: A prospective study. *Compr. Psychiatry* **2014**, *55*, 1377–1384. [CrossRef] [PubMed]
3. Ko, C.H.; Yen, J.Y.; Yen, C.F.; Chen, C.S.; Chen, C.C. The association between Internet addiction and psychiatric disorder: A review of the literature. *Eur. Psychiatry* **2012**, *27*, 1–8. [CrossRef] [PubMed]
4. Benaiges, I.; Prat, G.; Adan, A. Neuropsychological aspects of dual diagnosis. *Curr. Drug Abuse Rev.* **2010**, *3*, 175–188. [CrossRef] [PubMed]
5. Wang, H.R.; Cho, H.; Kim, D.J. Prevalence and correlates of comorbid depression in a nonclinical online sample with DSM-5 internet gaming disorder. *J. Affect. Disord.* **2017**, *226*, 1–5. [CrossRef] [PubMed]
6. Kessler, R.C. The epidemiology of dual diagnosis. *Biol. Psychiatry* **2004**, *56*, 730–737. [CrossRef] [PubMed]
7. Mueser, K.T.; Drake, R.E.; Wallach, M.A. Dual diagnosis: A review of etiological theories. *Addict. Behav.* **1998**, *23*, 717–734. [CrossRef]
8. Hellstrom, C.; Nilsson, K.W.; Leppert, J.; Aslund, C. Effects of adolescent online gaming time and motives on depressive, musculoskeletal, and psychosomatic symptoms. *Upsala J. Med. Sci.* **2015**, *120*, 263–275. [CrossRef] [PubMed]
9. Wei, H.T.; Chen, M.H.; Huang, P.C.; Bai, Y.M. The association between online gaming, social phobia, and depression: An internet survey. *BMC Psychiatry* **2012**, *12*, 92. [CrossRef] [PubMed]
10. Yeh, Y.C.; Wang, P.W.; Huang, M.F.; Lin, P.C.; Chen, C.S.; Ko, C.H. The procrastination of Internet gaming disorder in young adults: The clinical severity. *Psychiatry Res.* **2017**, *254*, 258–262. [CrossRef] [PubMed]

11. Yen, J.Y.; Liu, T.L.; Wang, P.W.; Chen, C.S.; Yen, C.F.; Ko, C.H. Association between Internet gaming disorder and adult attention deficit and hyperactivity disorder and their correlates: Impulsivity and hostility. *Addict. Behav.* **2017**, *64*, 308–313. [CrossRef] [PubMed]
12. Gentile, D.A.; Choo, H.; Liau, A.; Sim, T.; Li, D.; Fung, D.; Khoo, A. Pathological video game use among youths: A two-year longitudinal study. *Pediatrics* **2011**, *127*, e319–e329. [CrossRef] [PubMed]
13. Ciarrochi, J.; Parker, P.; Sahdra, B.; Marshall, S.; Jackson, C.; Gloster, A.T.; Heaven, P. The development of compulsive internet use and mental health: A four-year study of adolescence. *Dev. Psychol.* **2016**, *52*, 272–283. [CrossRef] [PubMed]
14. Loton, D.; Borkoles, E.; Lubman, D.; Polman, R. Video game addiction, engagement and symptoms of stress, depression and anxiety: The mediating role of coping. *Int. J. Mental Health Addict.* **2016**, *14*, 14. [CrossRef]
15. Ko, C.H.; Yen, J.Y.; Chen, C.S.; Yeh, Y.C.; Yen, C.F. Predictive values of psychiatric symptoms for internet addiction in adolescents: A 2-year prospective study. *Arch. Pediatr. Adolesc. Med.* **2009**, *163*, 937–943. [CrossRef] [PubMed]
16. Gross, J.J. Antecedent- and response-focused emotion regulation: Divergent consequences for experience, expression, and physiology. *J. Personal. Soc. Psychol.* **1998**, *74*, 224–237. [CrossRef]
17. Sloan, E.; Hall, K.; Moulding, R.; Bryce, S.; Mildred, H.; Staiger, P.K. Emotion regulation as a transdiagnostic treatment construct across anxiety, depression, substance, eating and borderline personality disorders: A systematic review. *Clin. Psychol. Rev.* **2017**, *57*, 141–163. [CrossRef] [PubMed]
18. Gross, J.J. Emotion regulation: Affective, cognitive, and social consequences. *Psychophysiology* **2002**, *39*, 281–291. [CrossRef] [PubMed]
19. Gross, J.J.; John, O.P. Individual differences in two emotion regulation processes: Implications for affect, relationships, and well-being. *J. Personal. Soc. Psychol.* **2003**, *85*, 348–362. [CrossRef]
20. Compare, A.; Zarbo, C.; Shonin, E.; Van Gordon, W.; Marconi, C. Emotional Regulation and Depression: A Potential Mediator between Heart and Mind. *Cardiovasc. Psychiatry Neurol.* **2014**, *2014*, 324374. [CrossRef] [PubMed]
21. Amstadter, A. Emotion regulation and anxiety disorders. *J. Anxiety Disord.* **2008**, *22*, 211–221. [CrossRef] [PubMed]
22. Lynch, T.R.; Robins, C.J.; Morse, J.Q.; Krause, E.D. A mediational model relating affect intensity, emotion inhibition, and psychological distress. *Behav. Ther.* **2001**, *32*, 519–536. [CrossRef]
23. Mennin, D.S.; Fresco, D.M.; Ritter, M.; Heimberg, R.G. An Open Trial of Emotion Regulation Therapy for Generalized Anxiety Disorder and Cooccurring Depression. *Depress. Anxiety* **2015**, *32*, 614–623. [CrossRef] [PubMed]
24. Esbjorn, B.H.; Bender, P.K.; Reinholdt-Dunne, M.L.; Munck, L.A.; Ollendick, T.H. The development of anxiety disorders: Considering the contributions of attachment and emotion regulation. *Clin. Child Fam. Psychol. Rev.* **2012**, *15*, 129–143. [CrossRef] [PubMed]
25. Sullivan, T.N.; Helms, S.W.; Kliewer, W.; Goodman, K.L. Associations between Sadness and Anger Regulation Coping, Emotional Expression, and Physical and Relational Aggression among Urban Adolescents. *Soc. Dev.* **2010**, *19*, 30–51. [CrossRef] [PubMed]
26. Harrist, A.W.; Hubbs-Tait, L.; Topham, G.L.; Shriver, L.H.; Page, M.C. Emotion regulation is related to children's emotional and external eating. *J. Dev. Behav. Pediatr.* **2013**, *34*, 557–565. [CrossRef] [PubMed]
27. DeWall, C.N.; Twenge, J.M.; Gitter, S.A.; Baumeister, R.F. It's the thought that counts: The role of hostile cognition in shaping aggressive responses to social exclusion. *J. Personal. Soc. Psychol.* **2009**, *96*, 45–59. [CrossRef] [PubMed]
28. Nikmanesh, Z.; Kazemi, Y.; Khosravy, M. Study role of different dimensions of emotional self-regulation on addiction potential. *J. Fam. Reprod. Health* **2014**, *8*, 69–72.
29. Wilens, T.E.; Martelon, M.; Anderson, J.P.; Shelley-Abrahamson, R.; Biederman, J. Difficulties in emotional regulation and substance use disorders: A controlled family study of bipolar adolescents. *Drug Alcohol Depend.* **2013**, *132*, 114–121. [CrossRef] [PubMed]
30. Wills, T.A.; Pokhrel, P.; Morehouse, E.; Fenster, B. Behavioral and emotional regulation and adolescent substance use problems: A test of moderation effects in a dual-process model. *Psychol. Addict. Behav.* **2011**, *25*, 279–292. [CrossRef] [PubMed]

31. Yu, H.; Cho, J. Prevalence of Internet Gaming Disorder among Korean Adolescents and Associations with Non-psychotic Psychological Symptoms, and Physical Aggression. *Am. J. Health Behav.* **2016**, *40*, 705–716. [CrossRef] [PubMed]
32. Ko, C.H.; Hsieh, T.J.; Wang, P.W.; Lin, W.C.; Yen, C.F.; Chen, C.S.; Yen, J.Y. Altered gray matter density and disrupted functional connectivity of the amygdala in adults with Internet gaming disorder. *Prog. Neuropsychopharmacol. Biol. Psychiatry* **2015**, *57*, 185–192. [CrossRef] [PubMed]
33. Sheehan, D.V.; Lecrubier, Y.; Sheehan, K.H.; Amorim, P.; Janavs, J.; Weiller, E.; Herqueta, T.; Baker, R.; Dunbar, G.C. The Mini-International Neuropsychiatric Interview (M.I.N.I.): The development and validation of a structured diagnostic psychiatric interview for DSM-IV and ICD-10. *J. Clin.* **1998**, *59*, 22–33.
34. Chien, C.P.; Cheng, T.A. Depression in Taiwan: Epidemiological survey utilizing CES-D. *Seishin Shinkeigaku Zasshi* **1985**, *45*, 335–338.
35. Radloff, L.S. The CES-D Scale: A self-report depression scale for research in the general population. *Appl. Psychol. Meas.* **1977**, *1*, 16. [CrossRef]
36. Meyer, T.J.; Miller, M.L.; Metzger, R.L.; Borkovec, T.D. Development and validation of the Penn State Worry Questionnaire. *Behav. Res. Ther.* **1990**, *28*, 487–495. [CrossRef]
37. Lin, T.K.; Weng, C.Y.; Wang, W.C.; Chen, C.C.; Lin, I.M.; Lin, C.L. Hostility trait and vascular dilatory functions in healthy Taiwanese. *J. Behav. Med.* **2008**, *31*, 517–524. [CrossRef] [PubMed]
38. Aickin, M.; Gensler, H. Adjusting for multiple testing when reporting research results: The Bonferroni vs. Holm methods. *Am. J. Public Health* **1996**, *86*, 726–728. [CrossRef] [PubMed]
39. Williams, A.D.; Grisham, J.R.; Erskine, A.; Cassedy, E. Deficits in emotion regulation associated with pathological gambling. *Br. J. Clin. Psychol.* **2012**, *51*, 223–238. [CrossRef] [PubMed]
40. Joormann, J.; Gotlib, I.H. Emotion Regulation in Depression: Relation to Cognitive Inhibition. *Cogn. Emot.* **2010**, *24*, 281–298. [CrossRef] [PubMed]
41. Ehring, T.; Tuschen-Caffier, B.; Schnulle, J.; Fischer, S.; Gross, J.J. Emotion regulation and vulnerability to depression: Spontaneous versus instructed use of emotion suppression and reappraisal. *Emotion* **2010**, *10*, 563–572. [CrossRef] [PubMed]
42. Ko, C.H.; Yen, J.Y.; Chen, S.H.; Wang, P.W.; Chen, C.S.; Yen, C.F. Evaluation of the diagnostic criteria of Internet gaming disorder in the DSM-5 among young adults in Taiwan. *J. Psychiatr. Res.* **2014**, *3*, 103–110. [CrossRef] [PubMed]
43. Kazakova, S.; Cauberghe, V.; Pandelaere, M.; De Pelsmacker, P. Players' expertise and competition with others shape the satisfaction of competence needs, gaming gratifications, and contingent self-esteem in a gaming context. *Cyberpsychol. Behav. Soc. Netw.* **2014**, *17*, 26–32. [CrossRef] [PubMed]
44. Reinecke, L. Games and recovery: The use of video and computer games to recuperate from stress and strain. *J. Media Psychol. Theor. Methods Appl.* **2009**, *21*, 126–142. [CrossRef]
45. Bar-Haim, Y.; Lamy, D.; Pergamin, L.; Bakermans-Kranenburg, M.J.; van Ijzendoorn, M.H. Threat-related attentional bias in anxious and nonanxious individuals: A meta-analytic study. *Psychol. Bull.* **2007**, *133*, 1–24. [CrossRef] [PubMed]
46. Campbell-Sills, L.; Barlow, D.H.; Brown, T.A.; Hofmann, S.G. Acceptability and suppression of negative emotion in anxiety and mood disorders. *Emotion* **2006**, *6*, 587–595. [CrossRef] [PubMed]
47. Denson, T.F.; Moulds, M.L.; Grisham, J.R. The effects of analytical rumination, reappraisal, and distraction on anger experience. *Behav. Ther.* **2012**, *43*, 355–364. [CrossRef] [PubMed]
48. Quartana, P.J.; Burns, J.W. Painful consequences of anger suppression. *Emotion* **2007**, *7*, 400–414. [CrossRef] [PubMed]
49. Giese-Davis, J.; Conrad, A.; Nouriani, B.; Spiegel, D. Exploring Emotion-Regulation and Autonomic Physiology in Metastatic Breast Cancer Patients: Repression, Suppression, and Restraint of Hostility. *Personal. Individ. Differ.* **2008**, *44*, 226–237. [CrossRef] [PubMed]
50. Vogele, C.; Jarvis, A.; Cheeseman, K. Anger suppression, reactivity, and hypertension risk: Gender makes a difference. *Ann. Behav. Med.* **1997**, *19*, 61–69. [CrossRef] [PubMed]
51. Cai, C.; Yuan, K.; Yin, J.; Feng, D.; Bi, Y.; Li, Y.; Yu, D.; Jin, C.; Qin, W.; Tian, J. Striatum morphometry is associated with cognitive control deficits and symptom severity in internet gaming disorder. *Brain Imaging Behav.* **2016**, *10*, 12–20. [CrossRef] [PubMed]

52. Moccia, L.; Pettorruso, M.; De Crescenzo, F.; De Risio, L.; di Nuzzo, L.; Martinotti, G.; Bifone, A.; Janiri, L.; Di Nicola, M. Neural correlates of cognitive control in gambling disorder: A systematic review of fMRI studies. *Neurosci. Biobehav. Rev.* **2017**, *78*, 104–116. [CrossRef] [PubMed]
53. Ide, J.S.; Hu, S.; Zhang, S.; Yu, A.J.; Li, C.S. Impaired Bayesian learning for cognitive control in cocaine dependence. *Drug Alcohol. Depend.* **2015**, *151*, 220–227. [CrossRef] [PubMed]
54. Greenberg, L. *Emotion-Focused Therapy, Coaching Client to Work through Their Feelings*; American Psychiatric Association: Washington, DC, USA, 2002.

13

# Aligning the "Manifesto for a European Research Network into Problematic Usage of the Internet" with the Diverse Needs of the Professional and Consumer Communities Affected by Problematic Usage of Pornography

**Darryl Mead [1,2,*] and Mary Sharpe [1,3]**

1 The Reward Foundation, The Melting Pot, Edinburgh EH2 2PR, UK; mary@rewardfoundation.org
2 Digital Humanities, Information Studies, University College London, London WC1E 6BT, UK
3 Lucy Cavendish College, University of Cambridge, Cambridge CB3 0BU, UK
* Correspondence: info@rewardfoundation.org

**Abstract:** The Manifesto for a European research network into Problematic Usage of the Internet was published in May 2018. It was written from the perspective of the COST Action Network, a programme of the European Cooperation in Science and Technology CA16207 and is expected to have significant influence on research funding priorities over the next decade. The Manifesto identified nine key research priorities to advance understanding in the field. Our analysis shows that while at the most general level it identified problematic usage of pornography (PUP) as a key research priority, it then barely mentioned it again within the body of the report. This paper uses the Manifesto's framework to suggest research areas into the problematic usage of pornography which are of particular relevance to clinicians and other professionals working in the field who want to develop approaches to assist individuals and target groups affected by PUP. It also looks at potential research opportunities inspired by the lived-experience of users withdrawing from PUP. A large number of opportunities are identified for new work on PUP across all nine key research areas of the Manifesto.

**Keywords:** problematic usage of pornography; manifesto; problematic usage of the internet; COST action network; behavioural addiction research.

## 1. Introduction

The publication of the Manifesto for a European research network into Problematic Usage of the Internet (PUI) [1] in May 2018 was a milestone in planning the roadmap for the behavioural addictions' community. It provided an international focus for developing policy across different elements of the research landscape for behavioural addiction over the next decade. The Manifesto was written from the perspective of the framework of the COST Action Network, a programme of the European Cooperation in Science and Technology CA16207.

The Manifesto identified nine key research priorities to advance the understanding of PUI (Table 1).

The Manifesto identifies pornography usage as a potential PUI. We have called this activity problematic usage of pornography (PUP).

**Table 1.** Summary of key research priorities to advance the understanding of PUI [1]

| | |
|---|---|
| 1. | *"Reliable consensus-driven conceptualisation of PUI (defining main phenotypes and specifiers, related comorbidities and brain-based mechanisms)* |
| 2. | *Age- and culture-appropriate assessment instruments to screen, diagnose and measure the severity of different forms of PUI* |
| 3. | *Characterise the impacts of different forms of PUI on health and quality of life* |
| 4. | *Define the clinical courses of different forms of PUI* |
| 5. | *Reduce obstacles to timely recognition and interventions* |
| 6. | *Clarify the possible role of genetics and personality features in different forms of PUI* |
| 7. | *Consider the impact of social factors in the development of PUI* |
| 8. | *Generate and validate effective interventions, both to prevent PUI, and to treat its various forms once established* |
| 9. | *Identify biomarkers, including digital markers, to improve early detection and intervention".* |

*Problematic Use of Pornography*

Since 2008 pornography consumption has transitioned from the model where a market supplied physical media such as magazines and DVDs to consumers through retail networks, to a transnational, Internet-based system mainly operating on a freemium trading model [2–4]. In the process it has scaled from predominantly national businesses reaching an audience of millions through shops and mail-order, to a world-wide online one with perhaps a billion customers [5–8]. Today, pornography is generally accessed on smartphones and other devices. Its consumption has the potential to develop into a large-scale form of PUI [9–11]. This technology-driven progression has massively increased the number of people potentially exposed to PUP, while simultaneously removing barriers moderating individual levels of consumption.

Some consumers uncomfortable with the apparent impacts of their pornography use have now gathered together in large-scale, online recovery communities [12,13]. Many of these are self-help groups who try to support individuals to manage their consumption, or to end it all together. A growing community of professional therapists [14–17], coaches [18] and mental health experts [19] has developed to support these self-help groups, as well as people accessing mental and physical health services through more mainstream medical, psychological and psychiatric routes.

Academic research and public policy to support consumers, recovery communities and professionals is still at an early stage of development. Much of the motivation for writing the current paper comes from the opportunity the Manifesto offers when it says:

> *"Additionally, through an interactive Dissemination Plan (including website, social media, blogs) we are reaching out to relevant stakeholders at international and national levels with an emphasis on encouraging people with the lived experience of PUI to become involved in the Action"* [1] p. 1235.

This paper is a result of the authors heeding this call to action. First, it discusses the extent to which the topic of pornography usage is carried through in the nine key research themes. Next it considers how the Manifesto tries to address the diverse needs of the professional and consumer communities affected by PUP. It then goes on to suggest additional areas of research to bridge any identified gaps.

Our research question is "what topics should be included within future research proposals under the Manifesto to meet the diverse needs of consumers, recovery communities and professionals impacted by the problematic use of pornography"?

## 2. Materials and Methods

The current study has used the content of the Manifesto [1] as its target document. Its authors created the Manifesto both in the hope of influencing future research directions around PUI and to improve the availability of funding to support those aspirations. As far as the authors are aware, the Manifesto is the only research planning and policy document of its type currently available, which is relevant to the field of PUI.

Rather than developing a mechanism to choose to include some parts of the Manifesto and to exclude other portions, the target document is sufficiently short for it to be analysed as a single entity. Each and every paragraph referencing pornography within the Manifesto has been identified and is reproduced in this paper to provide context to allow consideration of both what has been said, and just as importantly, what has been omitted.

The Manifesto began by setting a level playing field for different problematic Internet usage behaviours. It also introduced the central focus on health impacts.

> *"We use the umbrella term PUI to encompass all potentially problematic Internet related behaviours, including those relating to gaming, gambling, buying, pornography viewing, social networking, "cyber-bullying," "cyberchondria" among others. PUI may have mental and physical health consequences"* [1] p. 1234.

The nature of the health impacts is then developed further.

> *"Disordered online behaviours, such as excessive video gaming, pornography viewing, buying, gambling, or streaming and social networks use (Ioannidis et al., 2018) have been associated with marked functional impairment including loss of productivity (or reduced scholastic achievement), and mental health sequelae including mood and anxiety disorders (Derbyshire et al., 2013; Ho et al., 2014)"* [1] p. 1234.

The next step was to contextualise the behaviours according to their form, their place within the international medical diagnostic frameworks and as issues affecting identifiable user populations.

> *"As noted, PUI envelops a wide range of activities including video gaming, pornography viewing (and other compulsive sexual behaviours), buying, gambling, web-streaming, social media use and other behaviours. Some of these behaviours may fall into an existing mental disorder in psychiatric nomenclature (e.g., gambling disorder), whereas others are likely to be formally recognized in future DSM/ICD revisions, notably Internet Gaming Disorder (Kim et al., 2016b). Different types of PUI often start in childhood or adolescence (Volpe et al., 2015), but broad age ranges can be affected (Ioannidis et al., 2018). Age and gender relate importantly to PUI behaviours, with younger people typically having problems with gaming and media streaming, males with gaming, gambling and pornography viewing and females with social media and buying (Andreassen et al., 2016)"* [1] p. 1234.

The manifesto then moves into a process of exploring the individual research priorities according to the list above.

> ***"1.1. Reliable consensus-driven conceptualisations of different forms of PUI (phenomenologies, comorbidities and brain-based mechanisms)***
>
> *The clinical aspects of some Internet-related behaviours appear phenomenologically much like addiction (e.g., gambling or viewing pornography), and demonstrate impaired control (unsuccessful attempts to reduce or cease the behaviour), preoccupation (craving), associated functional impairment (neglect of other areas of life), and persistence despite damaging effects (Billieux et al., 2015; Ioannidis et al., 2016; Kardefelt-Winther, 2017). However, it remains less clear whether, apart from gambling disorder, these other forms of PUI meet the physiological criteria relating to addiction (tolerance, withdrawal). (Fineberg et al., 2018)"* [1] p. 1235.

This section starts to indicate at least one area of potential future research. Is viewing pornography a PUI that meets the physiological criteria for addiction? It then adds:

> *"Interestingly, obsessive-compulsive personality traits are common in excessive Internet users and are associated with problematic Internet use (Chamberlain et al., 2017b), hinting that compulsive*

*behaviours contribute to some forms of PUI. Some forms of online shopping or cybersex, on the other hand, may closely resemble ICD-10 or DSM-IV impulse control or sexual disorders (Volpe et al., 2015)"* [1] p 1236.

However, after this fairly strong opening, placing pornography viewing into the PUI research context, we do not hear about pornography again until Research Priority 7.

***"7. Consider the impact of social factors in the development of PUI***

*For problematic online sexual behaviour (e.g., cybersex), three structural elements have been highlighted as being important contributors per the so-termed Triple A Model involving: accessibility, affordability, and anonymity (Cooper, 1998; Cooper et al., 1999), though more research is needed on this topic (Brand et al., 2016a; Wery and Billieux, 2017). Another similar proposed framework is the ACE Model (anonymity, convenience, and escape) (Young, 2008). For excessive streaming (watching videos excessively), important structural features may include the ability of given programmes to grab attention by activating a biological 'orientating response', mediated through techniques including the use of attention-grabbing noises, zooming/panning, and presentation of rewarding stimuli (e.g., of a sexual or thrilling nature) (Flayelle et al., 2017, 2018). Collectively, public research into the structural elements that may promote PUI in different contexts is lacking"* [1] p. 1241.

However, this is the only mention of pornography after Section 1. So what is missing and what areas of research would be useful to the consumer, recovery and professional communities affected by problematic usage of pornography?

## 3. Results

This paper sets out to determine "what topics should be included within future research proposals under the Manifesto to meet the diverse needs of consumers, recovery communities and professionals impacted by the problematic use of pornography"?

The Manifesto tells us that PUP is a part of PUI and provides some discussion on phenomenologies, comorbidities and brain-based mechanisms. It introduces pornography in the context of how to classify it as a disorder. Some early models of pornography consumption are discussed in Research Priority 7.

Beyond these initial pointers, direct reference to the Manifesto provides little specific guidance for policy-makers considering the research environment for PUP. Unlike other behavioural disorders such as gambling and gaming, which were referred to repeatedly in the Manifesto, with pornography the Manifesto was mostly silent. It did not try linking PUP to assessment instruments, characterisation, defining clinical forms and removing obstacles to recognition and treatment. Equally it did not recommend directly relevant research on issues around genetics, personality features, interventions for prevention and/or treatments, or the field of biomarkers.

### *Pornography and the Manifesto*

Is the absence of more mentions of pornography viewing as a PUI in the Manifesto accidental or driven by other factors? We will not attempt to answer this. We recognise that the Manifesto's authors covered a great deal of ground in 7000 words and some omissions were always likely. Several of the authors have published widely in the field of PUP. While still limited in comparison with research in areas such as gambling and gaming, the scale of literature investigating pornography viewing as a PUI is growing rapidly. During 2018 we read over 200 papers on pornography usage, about 90% of them published in 2017–2018.

New work which has appeared since the Manifesto was published revealed previously unquantified consumer patterns. The diagnostic category of compulsive sexual behaviour disorder (CSBD) was published in ICD-11, two months after the Manifesto appeared [20]. Over 80% of people now seeking treatment for CSBD have a pornography-use related issue, a statistic not widely known when the Manifesto was published [21]. Subsequent pornography-consumer behaviour has also been significantly influenced by entirely new factors such as the COVID-19 pandemic [22].

## 4. Discussion

So, where does an analysis of the Manifesto leave policy-makers, funders, researchers and other interested parties? Our discussion now approaches this from two separate, though linked, directions. First, we consider how PUP can be researched to meet the needs of the different stakeholder communities. We then consider the potential for future research, as seen through the lens of the nine priorities set out in the Manifesto.

### *4.1. Community-Focused Issues*

Pornography accessed for free via the Internet is now used on a frequent basis by hundreds of millions of people. For most users any problems only emerge slowly over time. However, the scale of the consumer population suggests that problematic pornography usage has the potential to impact the health of millions of people across the nine key research priorities set out in the Manifesto. To make wise choices for research resource allocation, policy-makers and funders need to have sight of a research landscape that addresses each priority. What might it look like?

The following is a pragmatic assessment based on a consideration of the existing literature, mediated by the constraints set within the Manifesto. This assessment is supported by the author's wide-ranging dialogues with professional, recovery and consumer communities. Since 2016 we have had face-to-face discussions on pornography consumption with over 9000 people in the United Kingdom, the Republic of Ireland, France, Germany, Croatia, Hungary, the Ukraine, Turkey, Japan, Australia and the United States [23,24].

#### 4.1.1. Professional Communities Affected by Problematic Usage of Pornography

What else do therapists, medical practitioners, counsellors and sex educators want to know about the mental and physical health implications of problematic pornography usage? What are the issues that their clients, the problematic pornography users, want to have investigated? It is unhelpful that the diagnostic manuals do not mention the word "pornography" when over 80% of people seeking treatment for compulsive sexual behaviour have a pornography-related issue [21]. Further, the nature of the condition for many meets the criteria for addictive disorders and should be clearly categorised as such to enable healthcare professionals to respond with appropriate treatments. Both groups have an interest in distinguishing between classifying pornography usage as a potentially addictive disorder versus it being considered as an impulse control disorder. At any rate, there is clear desire in both lay people and professionals to have the word "pornography" appear in any given classification of a future edition of the International Classification of Diseases [20] and the Diagnostic and Statistical Manual of Mental Health Disorders [25].

It is apparent from our experience in meeting researchers from all parts of the world [23,24] that the therapists' own knowledge, attitudes and prejudices are very important issues in terms of delivering access to appropriate treatment services. While the Internet brings PUP to all parts of the world, different cultures have different taboos and even blind spots about what is PUP, what is unacceptable behaviour and what sorts of treatment might be considered appropriate. The legal systems of different countries are also relevant, and there are no universal standards for most sexual behaviours.

For the last four years the authors have been teaching healthcare professionals about Internet pornography and behavioural addiction. These audiences have consistently expressed a desire for the health and social implications arising from pornography usage to be taught as a component of general medical education. Clinicians have also expressed interest in integrating the management of compulsive sexual behaviour disorder into the regular functioning of national healthcare systems.

#### 4.1.2. Issues within the Pornography Recovery Communities

It would be desirable for the Manifesto to address the concerns of the online pornography recovery communities and members of 12-step programmes such as Sex Addicts Anonymous [18,19,26]. So far, we know of no quantitative research that has investigated elimination of digital porn use to reverse sexual dysfunction and a variety of mental health disorders reported by those who quit [27].

The focus within recovery communities begins with recognition/identification/diagnosis of problematic pornography usage. The first question is "do I have a problem?" If they do have a problem, this quickly becomes "how do I stop?" with a focus on tools, techniques and support. It then becomes "how do I maintain my desired level of sexual sobriety?" Here we need more longitudinal research on the mechanisms and techniques for overall programmes of quitting pornography usage, on abstaining from pornography viewing, and the issue of managing masturbation. Unlike most PUIs such as gambling, shopping or gaming, pornography viewing is linked to very deep biological sexual and reproductive drives, with the option of the interactive reinforcement by masturbation. The pornography, masturbation and orgasm (PMO) cycle reinforces the viewing behaviour, making simple abstinence strategies difficult to maintain for many former users. When you stop gaming you can get rid of your game console or you can have yourself banned from gambling venues, but you cannot stop being a sexual being.

There are some specific characteristics of problematic pornography viewing which merit more research, particularly issues around triggering and flatlining. A deeper understanding of PUP triggering factors would be useful to help individuals and clinicians build better strategies and models for avoiding problematic usage. Flatlining is the term for the severe and sustained, short to medium-term loss of libido some users report upon quitting a cycle of problematic pornography viewing. While widely reported in community forums such as NoFap [12] and RebootNation [13], it is not well-covered by the academic literature [28].

The medical establishment has an ongoing interest in the development of new approaches to support quitting pornography viewing by identifying effective drug treatments. Naltrexone is a medication that is used often in drug and alcohol addiction. It blocks the effects of drugs known as opiates. It competes with these drugs for opioid receptors in the brain. Naltrexone can reduce a patient's desire for drinking thereby helping them remain abstinent. Three papers have looked at the effect of naltrexone on problematic pornography use [29–31]. Given the similarity of brain changes in substance abuse disorders and behavioural addictions, this could prove a fruitful area for further research. Very recently transcranial magnetic stimulation has been suggested as a novel treatment [32]. Investment in research to try to demonstrate the value of such approaches to clinical populations at scale would be very helpful.

Therapists operating within the context of organisations such as the Association for the Treatment of Sexual Addiction and Compulsivity (ATSAC) in the United Kingdom [16] and the Society for the Advancement of Sexual Health (SASH) in the United States [15] would benefit from more research into behavioural modification techniques to help their clients stop Internet-based behaviours. This might include the creation of apps and other Internet tools. Very recently metacognitive therapy has claimed to be three-times as effective as traditional cognitive behavioural therapy. It deals successfully with 'desire thinking' and rumination, a behaviour that often predicts relapse. Extending new work on this to clinical populations of recovering pornography users would be helpful [33,34].

#### 4.1.3. Consumer Communities Affected by Problematic Usage of Pornography

Pornography viewing is now a widespread behaviour in most countries where there is good quality access to the Internet [8]. To have a protective effect on health and wellbeing, consumer-facing academic research on PUP needs to have impact in the wider community. This is a science communication issue. Little published research has looked at the ecology of spreading this type of message. There is scope for developing a very diverse array of effective communication strategies and toolkits. More research is needed on what would help adults to avoid situations and behaviours that might lead to PUP.

There is more active research focused on schools and adolescents. The Manifesto could support the sort of educational work The Reward Foundation does in schools to help equip young people with the knowledge about the reward system of the brain and the skills they need to avoid not just

PUP, but PUI in all its forms [35]. Other educational programmes are available from an array of non-governmental organisations such as Culture Reframed, eChildhood, and the Naked Truth Project. Common to all programmes is a lack of longitudinal studies evaluating their effectiveness over time, across cultures and among varying age groups.

We also need to recognise that PUP is not just a first-world issue. The Reward Foundation website operates in English, but uses the machine translations system GTranslate to make all pages available in over 100 languages. As a result, a significant proportion of our traffic is now in African languages such as Hausa and Somali. These people have a need for information about PUP, but it is not readily available from within their own language communities.

World-wide data from Pornhub shows that heaviest usage of pornography is by people in the 18 to 34 years age brackets. It is strongly tilted towards male consumers, but supply-side drivers are slowly pushing consumption towards gender parity [5–8].

Research over the past decade has shown that pornography viewing correlates with higher levels of sexual assaults and dating violence, pathways into domestic violence and reduced levels of bystander intervention [36–39]. The next generation of research should help move us from noting these as correlations to investigating questions of causation (or not) in these fields.

*4.2. Future Research Seen Through the Lens of the Nine Priorities*

The categories in the following discussion are directly based on the Manifesto's nine research priorities, simply substituting 'problematic usage of pornography' for the wider PUI category. They map out some of the ways the Manifesto could respond to the needs of the professional and consumer communities.

- Research area 1: Reliable consensus-driven categorization of Problematic Usage of Pornography (defining main phenotypes and specifiers, related comorbidity and brain-based mechanisms) [1].

Separate and interlocking strands of research would be useful in the two main fields analysing sexual behaviour; compulsive sexual behaviour towards people and the usage of pornography. In particular, the overlap between them needs more work. There would also be considerable value in research on the overlap of pornography viewing with other PUI's involving sexual behaviour-related activity, especially dating apps and social media.

- Research area 2: Age- and culture-appropriate assessment instruments to screen, diagnose and measure the severity of different forms of Problematic Usage of Pornography [1].

The number of screening, diagnostic and measuring tools for pornography usage keeps expanding. There would be considerable value in testing and calibrating the best of the existing crop of tools, such as the Brief Pornography Screener and Problematic Pornography Use Scale, across genders, age groups and societies [14,40]. Extending field trials would materially improve the ease with which these tools can then be rolled out for widespread adoption by clinicians and other people who are in the first line of contact by individuals concerned about PUP. Even among the experts the Brief Pornography Screener is not universally known [41]. Separately, major international reviews of erectile dysfunction have not referred in any way to the behavioural addiction field for data [42].

Tolerance and escalation are classic behavioural symptoms of the journey towards an addictive disorder. Each contributes to some consumers developing problematic usage. More research would be useful in relating the roles of tolerance and escalation in the PUP of viewers who escalate to viewing child abuse material. This seems to have become a wide and growing aspect of cybercrime around the world [43,44]. More knowledge of effective crime-fighting strategies could lead to better policy-making on prevention and to better risk-based advice for the courts and judges around sentencing and disposal. Standardised and tested risk assessment tools would be particularly useful.

Problematic usage of pornography seems to be creating a new separate sub-population of consumers who choose to view child abuse material without having any particular sexual interest in children in real life. They appear to be a separate clinical population to individuals with a paedophilic sexual orientation.

Another area where screening tools are woefully lacking is in the categorisation of the use of pornography by people on the autistic spectrum. Whereas about 1% of the population have autism spectrum disorders, crime statistics suggest that a disproportionately large number of the people (circa 30%) who escalate to viewing child abuse material come from specific vulnerable communities such those with as autism spectrum disorders, ADHD and those with learning difficulties [35]. These vulnerable populations are often considered 'asexual', and not requiring any sex education. This is wrong as many use the Internet as a substitute for relationships that they find so difficult to negotiate in real life. People with ASD are rarely represented in other crime categories. Their emotional immaturity and inability to interpret social rules can result in an attraction to younger people online who match their emotional age better. More research needs to be done on this group to improve prevention of access to child abuse material and to consider their special needs in terms of disposal following a conviction. For example, they do not function well in groups, which are the typical types of setting for sex offender rehabilitation [45].

- Research Area 3: Characterise the impacts of problematic Usage of Pornography on health and quality of life [1].

#### 4.2.1. Is Problematic Pornography Usage a Primary Disorder?

This question can be explored by research into the pornography, masturbation and orgasm cycle. In turn, this line of work could lead to consideration of the extent to which PMO may be driving depression, social isolation and other mental health issues in the wider population. Is it a bi-directional process – to what extent are these mental health issues powering the PMO cycle? Work in this space to test causation was recommended as far back as 2016 [27], but has yet to gain funding.

Bi-directional work would also be helpful for studies exploring health links or problematic pornography usage and the Big-5 personality factors. First, factors such as narcissism are regularly shown as correlates of heavy pornography usage [46], but few studies look at what happens to personality factors after people end problematic pornography use. Do they remain constant or is there an individual and/or population tendency for them to revert to what they were before the individual began engaging in PUP [27]. Other recent studies have highlighted the need for longitudinal studies in this area [47].

Similarly, conference reports [23,24] and our informal discussions with both individual problematic pornography users in the community [26] and among sex therapists [15,16], suggest that there are co-morbidities with other addictions, both to substances and behaviours. Developing new and/or improved strategies for treating complex webs of problematic usage are always of value.

More literature would be helpful on the impact of problematic pornography use at different points in the human life-cycle. Most research published to date has focused on teens or university students, though around half of all pornography viewers are older [8]. This makes case studies or more specific work on older people very rare [48,49]. It would also allow us to look at the potentially very different trajectories of younger populations who began with access to unlimited, free streaming videos in or around 2008, and older users who may have transitioned through several successive modes of access to pornography such as magazines and DVDs, to Internet use.

#### 4.2.2. Individual, Relationship and Community Impacts

The many roles of pornography in forming, sustaining and ending couple relationships would benefit from further research. The majority of research to date has been on users, and to a lesser extent their sexual partners. There would be value in unpacking the factors relating to pornography consumption as they impact on various aspects of an individual's health and quality of life in the context of a dyad [18,19,28]. This focus on couple relationships naturally tends to exclude work on the lack of relationships among young heavy users, around 50% of whom are virgins and not in relationships [12]. The other area needing more work is on the way pornography creates expectations of "how partnered sex will be" [35,46]. The literature of wider family and community impacts of pornography use across the human lifespan is also limited [48].

Additional research into the impact of accessibility would be valuable, as problematic pornography usage would seem to be a case where the PUI strongly links to private viewing. This is especially true for mobile platforms which can be used alone or with sexual partners. Smartphones are also now used widely for technology-enabled flirting including "sexting" with diverse relationship, social and potentially legal implications.

How does pornography consumption relate to the health and quality of life in a couple or a family? The authors frequently train social workers and criminal justice professionals who report that consumption of pornography, particularly violent pornography, is a consistent negative factor in the out-of-control domestic situations they encounter in their work. Unlike mainstream television where intimate partner violence in programmes tends to be simulated, most violence depicted in pornography is real [37,50]. It is not simulated and may offer viewers ethically challenging issues while they are viewing. It may also lead to post traumatic stress disorder and related symptoms after they stop. Once seen, real violence and intimate partner violence shown in pornography cannot be unseen. Where the real rape of minors is being streamed as entertainment by major commercial pornography sites, the legal and ethical challenges can be even more complex [51].

To what extent does acting out violent, coercive or controlling pornography scripts with real partners drive domestic violence and a growing appetite for dangerous practices such as sexual strangulation [52]? These questions are key in many different cross-disciplinary approaches to understanding PUI and PUP.

- Research Area 4: Define the Clinical Courses of Different Forms of Problematic Usage of Pornography [1].

  The Manifesto noted that:

  *"Remarkably little prospective research has been conducted on the courses of different forms of PUI and we remain relatively ignorant of key factors affecting long-term out-comes. Such data are of crucial importance in understanding aetiology, planning treatment and improving prognostication. For example, for some individuals PUI may represent a temporary phenomenon and spontaneously resolve (e.g., in some young people as brain systems mature), whereas for others PUI may become chronic."* [1] p. 1238.

These observations apply very strongly to PUP. There are many areas where we have little data.

In simple terms, PUP can lead to the individual failing to stop their use when faced with consequences, following the model set out in the diagnosis for compulsive sexual behaviour disorder [20]. However, ICD-11 is careful not to set out the details of the specific sexual behaviours that are causing the distress. Equally it is vague about the progression of the disorder from the perspectives of screening, assessment and diagnosis. This gives considerable scope to clearly define the clinical courses of each and every form of PUP.

We suggest that there are two fundamental classes of PUP, and each needs more research. The first is where the consumption of pornography leads to problems directly attributable to the consumption process. The user cannot stop their use and it is leading to negative consequences. This is applicable to CSBD as an impulse control disorder [20] and would also apply if a future version of the International Classification of Diseases gave it an entry in the addictive disorders section.

We propose that the second category is where the development of a PUP comes from the ideas it introduces into a viewer's mind and life. These can range across a whole spectrum from requiring to replay sexual scripts from pornography in your head to get aroused during partnered sex, to learning to ignore the need for consent in sexual activities, to promoting rape myths, the diminution of bystander intervention and the promotion of practicing dangerous activities such as autoerotic asphyxiation. Other problematic uses can encompass escalation to criminal activities around viewing or creating images of child sexual abuse. It can also lead individuals to engage in sextortion, 'capping', and other illegal activities towards minors [35]. Other new populations are the technology-enabled voyeurs whose illegal activities are also directed at adults, encompassing upskirting, hidden cameras, revenge porn and sharing sexual material without permission. Pornography has also appeared that was secretly recorded on baby monitors lacking password protection.

Pornography-induced erectile dysfunction (PIED) [28,53] has been identified as a key factor that causes male sufferers of PUP to seek treatment [54], but this area still lacks clear before and after brain-imaging studies [27]. PIED has also been linked to escalation to child abuse material. As desensitisation, tolerance and hypofrontality develop, a problematic pornography user needs more shocking material to feel any arousal.

Therapists need to know how long it can take for a PUP to develop and what external or internal factors can act as triggers. Reports from the recovery communities talk about the triggering influence of everything from life events and rites of passage, to social networks and the manipulation of viewer's taste by the algorithms used by the commercial pornography suppliers.

The withdrawal process from PUP, both physical and mental, seems generally similar to that of other PUIs. The only unique characteristic of PUP identified so far is 'flatlining'. The literature does not adequately characterise the features of flatlining as a symptom across the population of users withdrawing from PUP. This means that when it happens, problematic users can relapse to try to feel aroused again and overcome their feeling that their sexuality might be permanently 'broken'.

More studies of co-morbidity, both between PUP and other behavioural or substance addictions, and with other compulsive sexual behaviours, would also be welcome.

There are other elements research could reveal about the general characteristics of PUP. What are the characteristics of the incubation periods of PUP at both the individual and population levels? Do they have characteristics driven by gender or other factors? This in turn leads to the need for wider studies looking at gender, lifestyle and sexuality-based approaches to tease apart key elements in the PUP process. What commonalties and differences exist across the LGBTQI++ spectrum? In parallel, is PUP in the chemsex community driving addiction, or is its influence bi-directional [55]?

Existing brain-imaging studies [56,57] hint that both the quantity of pornography viewed and the period the viewing is spread across can have impacts on the development of PUP. However, the current crop of brain studies on pornography are restricted to people in their 20s and 30s and they also draw on very narrow demographic and cultural samples. In a world where an average age for boys' first exposure is 12 years or younger, brain development issues need investigation [2].

More women-focused studies would be beneficial. How is PUP the same for women as for men, and how is it different? Are the genders the same in the etiology of compulsive use? To what extent is sex toy used [58] a component of women's PUP? Some research has suggested that pornography usage by women has influenced their behaviour in couple relationships [59,60]. Are there differences according to ages and points in the lifecycle? We are unaware of any PUP studies in women controlling for stages across the menopause as a variable.

Age and stage of life should also be addressed from other perspectives. Virgins make up perhaps 50% of the recovery community [12]. What are the longer-term implications of early PUP across their lives as sexual beings? Separately, how do the challenges faced by older addicts, who used a lot of pornography before the Internet, compare to those of purely Internet-based consumers?

What are the impacts of PUP on relationship formation, sustainability and sexual health? A study of Korean men in stable relationships suggested they had developed a preference for viewing violent pornography as an alternative to real sex with their dyadic partner [61]. This also raises the issue of the nature of the content of the pornography being viewed. In line with the self-reports from the recovery community, a Swedish and Italian study of university students demonstrated that unusual sexual content creates more excitement. It also concluded that lots of the acts considered "unusual" by the researchers in 2015, already had become mainstream to many viewers and did not seem "unusual" at all [62].

- Research Area 5: Reduce Obstacles to Timely Recognition and Interventions [1].

Obstacles around the timely recognition of PUP and in delivering interventions exist both within the user population and among professionals. The interests of the groups overlap where there is a desire to develop, test and deploy more public health intervention strategies to draw the attention of pornography users across society to indicators of problematic usage.

At the widest level there is value in developing strategies to have the issue of PUP accepted by national healthcare systems. It can now be diagnosed as compulsive sexual behaviour disorder, coded 6C72 under the parent category of impulse control disorders [20]. Some clinicians are using this categorisation, but there will be considerable lags before it is adopted by nations world-wide. In some countries such as the United States, the need for clinicians to have a code for CSBD to allow patients to claim on medical insurance is paramount.

A separate issue revolves around making effective training for professionals more widely available. There is a need for the right balance of availability of practitioners (numbers, skills, geographical spread) to the scale of needs of people with issues.

Training can be built into continuing education programmes for professionals, as it is in the United States through the Society for the Advancement of Sexual Health and the International Institute for Trauma and Addiction [15,17]. In the UK this is done through the Association for the Treatment of Sexual Addiction and Compulsivity and the College of Sexual and Relationship Therapists [11,16]. However, CSBD and PUP are very new ideas and they have not become part of general medical training in most tertiary institutions.

- Research Area 6: Clarify the Possible Role of Genetics and Personality Features in Different Forms of Problematic Usage of Pornography [1].

This area of PUP research is still very immature. There would be value in developing a broad literature looking at the relationship between genetic factors and the natural history of problematic pornography usage. Are particular individuals or populations especially vulnerable? Key dimensions might include gender, sexual orientation and exploring health links to Big-5 personality factors.

Proof of concept was demonstrated by a 2017 paper [63] examining links between gene methylation and hypersexual disorder. The study found that the epigenetic state in the CRH gene may contribute to explaining the biological mechanisms of hypersexual disorder. Thus, some genes appear to play a role in hypersexual disorder.

Within the recovery community there is a strong desire to find answers to the 'why me' question. What is the relationship between predisposition to PUP versus acquiring it through consumer behaviour in a changed technological environment? Epigenetic factors need to be further researched. Informal evidence from the online recovery communities indicates that certain character traits or personality types thought to be fixed actually change when regular use of a supernormal stimulus such as hardcore pornography ceases. For example, in some users out of control hypersexual or narcissistic or sensation seeking or aggressive behavioural traits remit or disappear when the stressor is removed.

- Research Area 7: Consider the Impact of Social Factors in the Development of Problematic Usage of Pornography [1].

Several separate, but overlapping strands of research around social factors would be useful. Five are highlighted here as requiring more investigation: the technologies of the attention economy; women's changing role as consumers; environmental impacts; social acceptability; and the potential for early exposure to pornography to be considered as an Adverse Childhood Experience.

First, the Manifesto in Research area 7, in Section 2 above, identified

> *"For excessive streaming (watching videos excessively), important structural features may include the ability of given programmes to grab attention by activating a biological 'orientating response', mediated through techniques including the use of attention-grabbing noises, zooming/panning, and presentation of rewarding stimuli (e.g., of a sexual or thrilling nature)"* [1] p. 1241.

This neatly summarises the core behaviour of people engaged in PUP, where watching is generally accompanied by the viewer masturbating. This is absolutely an area where public research is required into the structural elements of commercial pornography sites as a part of the attention economy. Commercial sites seem to have adopted the structural concepts pioneered by B.J. Fogg at Stanford University and the behavioural design work of Nir Eyal [64,65]. This allows them to build websites and apps that change users' thoughts and behaviour without their knowing. In particular, the pornographers target the unconscious mind via dopamine pathways in the reward centre to stimulate cravings that keep users coming back for more, resulting in PUP for increasing numbers of consumers. Artificial intelligence is being deployed by the commercial pornography suppliers to learn about user's sexuality to deliver the most engaging experience possible. This has implications for privacy. As some research suggests that pornography viewing can change a person's sexual tastes, this is a very slippery area. Do we really want a big-porn machine algorithm to reshape our sexual templates [66]?

Another area ripe for research is the issue of intentional manipulation of consumption patterns by commercial interests in the pornography industry. In particular, since 2016 there has been a sustained increase of usage by women as a world-wide phenomenon [5–8,67]. To what extent has this resulted from deliberate female-focused promotional strategies of the commercial pornography suppliers and what are its implications for dyadic relationships, family structures and society in general?

Pornography sites get heavy, repeat traffic from users. The largest supplier, Pornhub, streamed 115 billion videos in 2019 to a world-wide audience of perhaps 1 billion individual viewers [8]. It would be extremely helpful to have reliable calculations for the world-wide use of pornography. The industry is now so large that it has been calculated to consume 27% of the energy used by the Internet and is currently responsible for 0.2% of all greenhouse gas emissions world-wide, roughly equivalent to the domestic energy use of every household in France [68]. The environmental impact is large enough for researchers to calculate a quantifiable contribution to rising sea levels.

Across cultures and within cultures, the phenomenon of "normalisation" of pornography consumption as a socially acceptable activity has grown rapidly. Since the arrival of the iPhone in June 2007, supported by high-speed network services, the smartphone supplying "free" commercial pornography has removed barriers and increased temptation through its Triple-A model of effectively unlimited access, affordability and anonymity [69]. The speed of this adoption has outstripped the capacity of researchers to place it in context and to include it in theoretical models. It is clear that the arrival of smartphones, Wi-Fi and 4G networks leads to most societies adopting pornography as a more acceptable form of recreation, especially among the young. The trajectory of this change can be unique to each country [2].

Many stories circulate within the recovery community suggesting that childhood exposure to pornography in general, and Internet pornography in particular, should be considered an adverse childhood experience (ACE). However, at present this cannot happen. The list of definitions of ACEs pre-dates the arrival of problematic usage of pornography from the Internet. It would mean revisiting the research field of defining, testing and verifying the validity of PUP as an ACE. This would be a very worthwhile project.

- Research Area 8: Generate and Validate Effective Interventions, both to prevent Problematic Usage of Pornography, and to Treat its Various Forms once Established [1].

#### 4.2.3. Supply-Side Preventative Interventions

These tend to revolve around whole-population approaches to changing the ease of access to Internet pornography. After three false starts, will age verification legislation in the UK prove to be a successful intervention? How and where might it be tried in other countries? How will it be validated and will it achieve the intended outcomes?

There is an established and diverse commercial ecosystem of blocking technologies now available for individuals and groups to prevent access to Internet pornography. Their characteristics tend to be specific to their local geographies. They can operate at the individual level, usually by subscription. Many Internet Service Providers (ISPs) offer filtering on either an opt-in or opt-out basis. Academic analysis of the effectiveness of these measures would be helpful.

PUP research could also look to public health models used for other areas of addiction, particularly online gambling, where the business models and delivery mechanisms are often quite similar. Policy research into new models of control, monitoring and product delivery limitation involving the government, commercial and voluntary sectors could be developed. This remains minimally charted territory.

A recent development in pornography delivery (and sometimes production) is the increasing role of social media as a point of access. While games delivery platforms are now a significant source of pornography for some consumers, we have also encountered adolescents getting around parental controls via the Internet of Things. A poorly protected smart refrigerator could get a grounded teen online.

#### 4.2.4. Supply-Side Treatment Interventions

Individual or community approaches to treatment from counsellors, schools, churches or other local units can be successful, especially when linked to demand-side reduction measures. Accountability partners are popular in some communities [26]. Again, more external validation of success, or not, of different approaches would be valuable.

#### 4.2.5. Demand-Side Preventative Interventions

Are all pornography consumers at risk of developing PUP? The simple answer is probably not, but we do not know for certain. If the general characteristics of PUP are broadly similar to other better studied behaviours with a propensity to lead to behavioural addiction, the answer is 'no'. A proportion of users will be likely to move first into problematic use and then addictive use. Some studies suggest that all pornography consumption generates brain changes, even at quite low durations [56,57]. So far, the World Health Organization only considers the research base is strong enough to support the diagnosis of compulsive sexual behaviour disorder under the parent category of impulse control [20]. At the same time, few pornography consumers have been exposing themselves to large volumes of online erotica for longer than two decades, so we have only explored it as a factor for, at most, half of the duration of a human beings' sexual life-cycle. We do know that the more pornography some people consume, the more likely they are to develop compulsive behaviours as a result. It is the sort of issue that could respond well to the development of a risk-managed framework. Such a framework could balance benefits of pornography consumption at the individual and society levels with the inevitable side-effects from some individuals being unhappy with the consequences arising from their use.

Where consumers do develop concerns, many practitioners believe that the solution to PUP is rooted in consumer education. As a society we can choose to try to reduce the strength of demand for access to pornography. Some individuals who see pornography as a valuable part of a sex positive culture would be uncomfortable about this, but it is up to each society to consider what restrictions may or may not be appropriate if some individuals may be harmed by excessive consumption.

More systematic assessments of the success of educational strategies would show how effective they can be as risk-reduction strategies. What role will learning about the addictive potential of PUP play in reducing demand? Does learning about porn-induced erectile dysfunction reduce consumption? Thousands of anonymous self-reports on the recovery websites show that the availability of knowledge of the effects of Internet pornography on the brain was sufficient to encourage users to experiment with quitting porn [12,13]. When they did, a range of mental and physical health problems remitted or cleared up. Only when heavy users quit porn did they realise that those conditions were related to their porn use. Formal research into this phenomenon would be valuable.

A separate investigation into the issues of prevention versus cure would be interesting. We are suggesting research to compare the benefits of never beginning pornography usage versus treating the problem when it has been 'cured'. At a population level, are people who quit ultimately as mentally and physically healthy as those who never engaged in PUP in the first place? What methodologies might help unpack this question?

#### 4.2.6. Demand-Side Treatment Interventions

The development of possible drug treatments is still at an early stage. In theory adjusting brain chemistry with substances could reduce libido and cravings for pornography. The most common approach is to look at substances that are already approved for clinical use and to begin the process of taking them through stages from case reports and on to small and then large-scale clinical trials. What drugs might discourage PUP and what pathways should be targeted? A major review was published by Sniewski and colleagues in 2018 [70]. Early work focused on possible similarities to obsessive compulsive disorder and suggested trying drugs known as selective serotonin re-uptake inhibitors (SSRIs). Recent case reports have been published for Paroxetine [71], Nalmefene [49] and Aripiprazole [72], with mixed results.

- Research Area 9: Identify Biomarkers, Including Digital Markers, to Improve Early Detection and Intervention [1].

This is a new area, but it may have real potential to help improve health at the individual and population levels. As far as we are aware, biomarkers are not currently in use for detecting or diagnosing PUP. Would there be value in their introduction?

Research might be able to separate out the underlying tendency of some individuals or groups to be susceptible to problematic usage. This could be contrasted to the potential for Internet pornography to lead to problematic usage as a natural characteristic in and of itself. The issue here is "are you the problem?" versus "is pornography the problem". Co-morbidity studies involving other PUIs would also be helpful—many users find themselves trying to unhook from gaming or recreational drugs and pornography at the same time.

Biomarkers are a high-tech intervention. In face-to-face situations, such as a doctor's surgery or a counsellor's office, are they a better solution than simply asking a person about their level of pornography consumption? The brief pornography screener with five questions on a single A4 sheet of paper can be administered in three minutes and seems to be both sensitive and reliable [14].

A different line of research would be to look at the potential for widescale interventions using Internet data. It might even extend to artificial intelligence algorithms at commercial pornography suppliers or the ISP level. It would mean monitoring people for signs of problematic usage and then invoking a warning or even a cut-off protocol. This has privacy and data management implications, but the reality seems to be that monitoring rather like this is already at the core of the business model of major commercial pornography suppliers. Could governments consider introducing national level intervention programmes? How would they operate and what would be the success criteria?

At the same time, the pornography supply companies are very reluctant to share their data. In this they follow the lead of other industries supplying addictive substances like tobacco and alcohol. The commercial pornography suppliers are quite vulnerable to a 'smoking gun' which showed that were trying to induce addictive behaviour as a part of their business model.

## 5. Conclusions

When you consider the conclusions in the Manifesto [1] in the light of the current paper, there is nothing recommended for research into PUI that does not equally apply to the sub-discipline of PUP.

To come back to our research question, "what topics should be included within future research proposals under the Manifesto to meet the diverse needs of consumers, recovery communities and professionals impacted by the problematic use of pornography"?

The comments in this section have been grouped to answer these questions individually, but there is, and should be, overlap between them, so we begin by looking at general questions about the field of research. The management and treatment of PUP requires the right approaches to meet the specific needs of everybody in this mental and physical health ecosystem.

### 5.1. General Research

Given the massive scale of use of pornography and its potentially negative outcomes for some users, it is important for the European Union's Problematic Usage of the Internet (EU-PUI) Network to have a visible and trusted champion for PUP, just as it should for other behaviours. Linked to this, Europe should hold a planning conference under the umbrella of COST Action to design its response. The opportunity for PUP data to be made accessible to researchers through shared multinational databases is extremely attractive.

To assist the World Health Organization in improving the classification of compulsive sexual behaviour disorder in future to include the word pornography, research is required to separate out the natural history of PUP from compulsive sexual behaviours focused on people.

Experimental work to investigate causation through longitudinal studies would provide a better strategic foundation for PUP. This would be stronger if it included large-scale brain imaging studies to gather evidence before and after people have quit or have been given treatment. It is essential to develop a wider evidence-base covering all ages and stages of the human life-cycle for people engaging in PUP. There should be much more research focus on women as they are now the main sector of growth for PUP. Equally our data should embrace sexual diversity and investigate the usage among LGBTQI++ communities where levels of mental health disorders and chemical dependencies are higher than in the mainstream heterosexual population. Could PUP be a contributing factor?

### 5.2. Research for the Professional and Therapist Community

The 2020s is the decade when training of health and social care professionals should begin to incorporate a deep and broad understanding of all PUIs as a matter of course. This will be a communication and public relations programme. It should be recognised that within the field of PUP we are starting from a low-base with modest levels of training or resources available for people working as professionals and therapists. New research should be leading towards giving professionals a wider toolkit to support treatment of all the different forms of PUP.

Ideally the next ten years will see a rising quality of research into PUP, moving us towards a landscape with more double-blind placebo trials for drugs and longitudinal studies covering time periods that allow us to take a broader view on PUP. It is a disorder that is slow to develop and potentially also slow to heal.

We should encourage better and deeper validation of a few assessment tools across diverse populations. Standardisation is helpful and surely two proven ones are sufficient. Link this to a strong communication programme to make them known widely in communities from general practitioners (MDs) and urologists to sex therapists, relationship counsellors, school counsellors and parents.

The next decade should see the debate around pornography use and erectile health fully resolved. Dialogues about the impact of pornography use in the context of violence against women and children also require more experimental approaches if the discussion is going to be able to move from correlation to causation.

The next few years will clearly be a time of great advances in linking genetic data and behaviour and we will monitor the contributions that this form of high-technology can make to epigenetic changes in humans.

### *5.3. Research for Consumers*

At the low-tech end, the most important thing is to initiate a research and development programme to determine if early exposure to Internet pornography can be recognised as an adverse childhood experience (ACE). Success in that project could have a profound impact on raising awareness of the need to reduce early exposure and thereby reduce the risk of subsequent PUP.

Work monitoring the success, or otherwise, of age verification legislation around the world will be important for policy development. For individuals and communities, it is important that we learn which interventions are sustainable and cost effective.

Could commercial pornography suppliers be encouraged to take a pro-active role in heading off the development of PUP, rather than following their current laissez faire view that a customer can never have too much pornography? It will be important to have research to boost the accountability of suppliers. Accountability can be achieved through government intervention or industry self-regulation. So far the latter does not seem to be working in the consumer's favour. In general the access to pornography is free, but the consumption risks are all transferred to the user.

The powerful position of commercial pornography suppliers within the context of the attention economy leaves the average consumer poorly informed about how their tastes and behaviour are being influenced by 'free' pornography. Commercial pornography suppliers use the data that gather to develop a deep understanding of consumer behaviour. Commercial players also benefit from the access to artificial intelligence and other data-mining tools to build market share and develop new markets.

### *5.4. Research for the Recovery Community*

Good academic studies of the recovery communities, be they NoFap, Sex Addicts Anonymous or others, could be revolutionary. Recovery communities are a cheap solution to a potentially very expensive medical problem. However, often the communities do not really want to be studied. Members just want to be healed or to help others to heal. There is some acceptance that good research could help. There is also a recognition that for some PUP members, recovery communities are only part of the answer and that they may also need help from therapists and other professionals.

Quantitative research looking at the elimination of pornography is the highest priority. Does it really reverse sexual dysfunctions and have a positive impact on a variety of mental health disorders? The field currently has extensive anecdotal evidence to support these suggestions, but that is not a substitute for large-scale, well-grounded studies.

### *5.5. Moving Forward*

It is now nearly two years since the Manifesto was published. In that time there has been a continuing growth world-wide in the volume of research appearing on pornography use in general and PUP in particular. However, most of the work being done tends to be at the easier, cheaper end of the scale. As far as we can tell as frequent observers of this field, there remains a general lack of vision and large-scale co-ordination between the many research groups around the world. The future needs to be more about designing investigations to test causation, not just to demonstrate yet more correlations.

The time is right for the COST Action team and the EU-PUI Network to create, fund and promote a visible and trusted champion for PUP research. Europe has sufficient resources to support such a role. Perhaps the research ideas sketched in this paper could be a positive contribution towards COST Action accepting it should deliver a leadership role in the field of PUP.

### *5.6. Limitations*

Focusing on the Manifesto is a limiting strategy, in that many researchers in the pornography field around the world are unlikely to be familiar with it. Our approach has been to work with what is already available to build a more coherent research environment. At the same time, focusing on the Manifesto is essential. It is the only major published document which deals with the whole policy context of problematic use of the Internet. It is Europe-wide in its reach and is designed to endure for a decade.

By writing a response homing in on the issues around PUP, we hope to encourage researchers to have conversations to advance the field in ways that will benefit the continent's taxpayers and publicly funded research programmes.

Our methodology of simply analysing all of the Manifesto as a whole through the particular lens of PUP is a limitation. This approach was taken to balance achieving the clearest level of understanding of what readers could infer from the document with an open agenda to build the strongest possible set of recommendations to shape the future of PUP research in Europe over the next decade.

**Author Contributions:** Conceptualisation, D.M. and M.S.; Writing—original draft preparation, D.M.; Writing—review and editing, D.M. and M.S. All authors have read and agreed to the published version of the manuscript.

**Acknowledgments:** The authors would like to thank Julius Burkauskas, the Science Communications Manager of the COST Action Dissemination Plan for encouraging the preparation of this paper.

## References

1. Fineberg, N.; Demetrovics, Z.; Stein, D.; Ioannidis, K.; Potenza, M.; Grünblatt, E.; Brand, M.; Billieux, J.; Carmi, L.; King, D.; et al. Manifesto for a European Research Network into Problematic Usage of the Internet. *Eur. Neuropsychopharmacol.* **2018**, *28*, 1232–1246. [CrossRef] [PubMed]
2. Mead, D. The Risks Young People Face as Porn Consumers. *Addicta- Turk. J. Addict.* **2016**, *3*, 387–400. [CrossRef]
3. Döring, N.M. The Internet's impact on sexuality: A critical review of 15 years of research. *Comput. Hum. Behav.* **2009**, *25*, 1089–1101. [CrossRef]
4. Döring, N.; Daneback, K.; Shaughnessy, K.; Grov, C.; Byers, E.S. Online sexual activity experiences among college students: A four-country comparison. *Arch. Sex. Behav.* **2017**, *46*, 1641–1652. [CrossRef] [PubMed]
5. Pornhub Insights. 2016 Year in Review. Available online: https://www.pornhub.com/insights/2016-year-in-review (accessed on 27 February 2020).
6. Pornhub Insights. 2017 year in Review. Available online: https://www.pornhub.com/insights/2017-year-in-review (accessed on 27 February 2020).
7. Pornhub Insights. 2018 Year in Review. Available online: https://www.pornhub.com/insights/2018-year-in-review (accessed on 27 February 2020).
8. Pornhub Insights. The 2019 Year in Review. Available online: https://www.pornhub.com/insights/2019-year-in-review (accessed on 27 February 2020).
9. Brand, M.; Blycker, G.R.; Potenza, M. When pornography becomes a problem: Clinical insights. *Psychiatric Times* **2019**, *36*, 12.
10. Stark, R.; Klucken, T.; Potenza, M.N.; Brand, M.; Strahler, J. A current understanding of the behavioral neuroscience of compulsive sexual behavior disorder and problematic pornography use. *Curr. Behav. Neurosci. Rep.* **2018**, *5*, 218–231. [CrossRef]
11. College of Sexual and Relationship Therapists. Available online: https://www.cosrt.org.uk/ (accessed on 30 April 2020).
12. NoFap.com. Available online: https://www.nofap.com (accessed on 27 February 2020).
13. RebootNation.org. Available online: http://www.rebootnation.org/ (accessed on 27 February 2020).
14. Kraus, S.W.; Hoff, R.A.; Gola, M.; Kowalewska, E.; Potenza, M.N. Clinical Characteristics of Compulsive Pornography Users: A Military Sample. *J. Behav. Addict.* **2018**, *7*, 98.
15. Society for the Advancement of Sexual Health. Available online: https://www.sash.net/ (accessed on 30 April 2020).
16. Association for the Treatment of Sexual Addiction and Compulsivity. Available online: https://atsac.org.uk/ (accessed on 30 April 2020).
17. International Institute for Trauma and Addiction Professionals. Available online: https://iitap.com/default.aspx (accessed on 30 April 2020).
18. Church, N. *Wack: Addicted to Internet Porn*; Bvrning Qvestions LLC: Portland, OR, USA, 2014.

19. Hall, P. *Understanding and Treating Sex and Pornography Addiction: A Comprehensive Guide for People Who Struggle with Sex Addiction and Those Who Want to Help Them*; Routledge: Abingdon-on-Thames, UK, 2018.
20. World Health Organization. International Classification of Diseases, 11th Revision (ICD-11). Available online: https://www.who.int/classifications/icd/en/ (accessed on 15 February 2020).
21. Bőthe, B.; Tóth-Király, I.; Potenza, M.N.; Griffiths, M.D.; Orosz, G.; Demetrovics, Z. Revisiting the Role of Impulsivity and Compulsivity in Problematic Sexual Behaviors. *J. Sex Res.* **2019**, *56*, 166–179. [CrossRef]
22. Mestre-Bach, G.; Blycker, G.R.; Potenza, M.N. Pornography use in the setting of the COVID-19 pandemic. *J. Behav. Addict.* **2020**. Available online: https://akjournals.com/view/journals/2006/aop/article-10.1556-2006.2020.00015/article-10.1556-2006.2020.00015.xml (accessed on 27 April 2020). [CrossRef]
23. Mead, D.; Sharpe, M. Pornography and Sexuality Research Papers at the 4th International Conference on Behavioral Addictions. *Sex. Addict. Compulsivity* **2017**, *24*, 217–223. [CrossRef]
24. Mead, D.; Sharpe, M. Pornography and Sexuality Research Papers at the 5th International Conference on Behavioral Addictions. *Sex. Addict. Compulsivity* **2018**, *25*, 248–268. [CrossRef]
25. American Psychiatric Association. *Diagnostic and Statistical Manual of Mental Disorders (DSM-5®)*; American Psychiatric Pub: Washington, DC, USA, 2013.
26. Anonymous. *Sex Addicts Anonymous*; International Service Organization of SAA: Houston, TX, USA, 2017.
27. Wilson, G. Eliminate Chronic Internet Pornography Use to Reveal Its Effects. *Addicta Turk. J. Addict.* **2016**, *3*, 1–13. [CrossRef]
28. Park, B.Y.; Wilson, G.; Berger, J.; Christman, M.; Reina, B.; Bishop, F.; Klam, W.P.; Doan, A.P. Is Internet Pornography Causing Sexual Dysfunctions? A Review with Clinical Reports. *Behav. Sci.* **2016**, *6*, 17. [CrossRef] [PubMed]
29. Bostwick, J.M.; Bucci, J.A. *Internet Sex Addiction Treated with Naltrexone. Mayo Clinic Proceedings*; Elsevier: Amsterdam, The Netherlands, 2008; Volume 83, pp. 226–230.
30. Capurso, N.A. Naltrexone for the Treatment of Comorbid Tobacco and Pornography Addiction. *Am. J. Addict.* **2017**, *26*, 115–117. [CrossRef]
31. Kraus, S.W.; Meshberg-Cohen, S.; Martino, S.; Quinones, L.J.; Potenza, M.N. Treatment of Compulsive Pornography Use with Naltrexone: A Case Report. *Am. J. Psychiatry* **2015**, *172*, 1260–1261. [CrossRef]
32. Blum, A.W.; Grant, J.E. Positive Response of Compulsive Sexual Behavior to Transcranial Magnetic Stimulation. *Prim. Care Companion CNS Disord.* **2020**, *22*, 19l02469. [CrossRef]
33. Caselli, G.; Spada, M.M. Desire Thinking: A New Target for Treatment of Addictive Behaviors? *Int. J. Cogn. Ther.* **2016**, *9*, 344–355. [CrossRef]
34. Wells, A. Advances in Metacognitive Therapy. *Int. J. Cogn. Ther.* **2013**, *6*, 186–201. [CrossRef]
35. The Reward Foundation - Love, Sex and the Internet. Available online: https://rewardfoundation.org (accessed on 27 February 2020).
36. Rodenhizer, K.A.E.; Edwards, K.M. The Impacts of Sexual Media Exposure on Adolescent and Emerging Adults' Dating and Sexual Violence Attitudes and Behaviors: A Critical Review of the Literature. *Trauma Violence Abuse* **2019**, *20*, 439–452. [CrossRef]
37. Bridges, A.J. Pornography and Sexual Assault. In *Handbook of Sexual Assault and Sexual Assault Prevention*; O'Donohue, W.T., Schewe, P.A., Eds.; Springer International Publishing: Cham, Switzerland, 2019; pp. 129–149. [CrossRef]
38. Foubert, J.D.; Blanchard, W.; Houston, M.; Williams, R.R. Pornography and Sexual Violence. In *Handbook of Sexual Assault and Sexual Assault Prevention*; O'Donohue, W.T., Schewe, P.A., Eds.; Springer International Publishing: Cham, Switzerland, 2019; pp. 109–127. [CrossRef]
39. Brem, M.J.; Garner, A.R.; Grigorian, H.; Florimbio, A.R.; Wolford-Clevenger, C.; Shorey, R.C.; Stuart, G.L. Problematic Pornography Use and Physical and Sexual Intimate Partner Violence Perpetration Among Men in Batterer Intervention Programs. *J. Interpers. Violence* **2018**, 088626051881280. [CrossRef]
40. Bőthe, B.; Tóth-Király, I.; Zsila, Á.; Griffiths, M.D.; Demetrovics, Z.; Orosz, G. The Development of the Problematic Pornography Consumption Scale (PPCS). *J. Sex Res.* **2018**, *55*, 395–406. [CrossRef] [PubMed]
41. de Alarcón, R.; de la Iglesia, J.I.; Casado, N.M.; Montejo, A.L. Online Porn Addiction: What We Know and What We Don't—A Systematic Review. *J. Clin. Med.* **2019**, *8*, 91. [CrossRef] [PubMed]
42. Goldstein, I.; Goren, A.; Li, V.W.; Tang, W.Y.; Hassan, T.A. Epidemiology Update of Erectile Dysfunction in Eight Countries with High Burden. *Sex. Med. Rev.* **2020**, *8*, 48–58. [CrossRef] [PubMed]

43. Nowak, M. Promotion and Protection of All Human Rights, Civil, Political, Economic, Social and Cultural Rights, Including the Right to Development. Report of the Special Rapporteur on Torture, and Other Cruel, Inhuman or Degrading Treatment or Punishment. Available online: https://www.refworld.org/docid/47c2c5452.html (accessed on 15 February 2020).
44. Knack, N.; Holmes, D.; Fedoroff, J.P. Motivational Pathways Underlying the Onset and Maintenance of Viewing Child Pornography on the Internet. *Behav. Sci. Law* **2020**, *37*, 100–116. [CrossRef]
45. Hackett, S.; Phillips, J.; Masson, H.; Balfe, M. Individual, Family and Abuse Characteristics of 700 British Child and Adolescent Sexual Abusers. *Child Abuse Rev.* **2013**, *22*, 232–245. [CrossRef]
46. Efrati, Y.; Amichai-Hamburger, Y. Are Adolescents Who Consume Pornography Different from Those Who Engaged in Online Sexual Activities? *Child. Youth Serv. Rev.* **2020**, *111*, 104843. [CrossRef]
47. Borgogna, N.C.; Aita, S.L. Problematic Pornography Viewing from a Big-5 Personality Perspective. *Sex. Addict. Compulsivity* **2019**, *26*, 293–314. [CrossRef]
48. Herbenick, D.; Fu, T.-C.; Wright, P.; Paul, B.; Gradus, R.; Bauer, J.; Jones, R. Diverse Sexual Behaviors and Pornography Use: Findings From a Nationally Representative Probability Survey of Americans Aged 14 to 60 Years. *J. Sex. Med.* **2020**, S1743609520300473. [CrossRef]
49. Yazdi, K.; Fuchs-Leitner, I.; Gerstgrasser, N.W. Nalmefene in the Treatment of Internet Pornography Addiction—A Case Report and Review of Literature. *J. Addict. Med.* **2020**, 1. [CrossRef]
50. Bridges, A.J.; Wosnitzer, R.; Scharrer, E.; Sun, C.; Liberman, R. Aggression and Sexual Behavior in Best-Selling Pornography Videos: A Content Analysis Update. *Violence Women* **2010**, *16*, 1065–1085. [CrossRef]
51. McDonald, S. Florida man arrested after 58 porn videos, photos link him to missing underage teen girl. Available online: https://www.newsweek.com/florida-man-arrested-after-58-porn-videos-photos-link-him-missing-underage-teen-girl-1467413 (accessed on 22 February 2020).
52. Chapple, L. Characteristics of Individuals Who Participate In Autoerotic Asphyxiation Practices: An Exploratory Study. PhD thesis, University of North Dakota, Grand Forks, North Dakota, August.
53. Retzler, K. Erectile Dysfunction: A Review of Comprehensive Treatment Options for Optimal Outcome. *J. Restor. Med.* **2019**, *8*. [CrossRef]
54. Wilson, G. *Your Brain on Porn: Internet Pornography and the Emerging Science of Addiction*, 2nd ed.; Commonwealth Publishing: Margate, UK, 2018.
55. Corkery, J.M.; Loi, B.; Claridge, H.; Goodair, C.; Corazza, O.; Elliott, S.; Schifano, F. Gamma Hydroxybutyrate (GHB), Gamma Butyrolactone (GBL) and 1,4-Butanediol (1,4-BD.; BDO): A Literature Review with a Focus on UK Fatalities Related to Non-Medical Use. *Neurosci. Biobehav. Rev.* **2015**, *53*, 52–78. [CrossRef] [PubMed]
56. Kühn, S.; Gallinat, J. Brain Structure and Functional Connectivity Associated with Pornography Consumption: The Brain on Porn. *JAMA Psychiatry* **2014**, *71*, 827–834. [CrossRef] [PubMed]
57. Voon, V.; Mole, T.B.; Banca, P.; Porter, L.; Morris, L.; Mitchell, S.; Lapa, T.R.; Karr, J.; Harrison, N.A.; Potenza, M.N. Neural Correlates of Sexual Cue Reactivity in Individuals with and without Compulsive Sexual Behaviours. *PloS ONE* **2014**, *9*, e102419. [CrossRef] [PubMed]
58. Davis, C.M.; Blank, J.; Lin, H.; Bonillas, C. Characteristics of Vibrator Use among Women. *J. Sex Res.* **1996**, *33*, 313–320. [CrossRef]
59. Wright, P.J.; Sun, C.; Miezan, E. Individual Differences in Women's Pornography Use, Perceptions of Pornography, and Unprotected Sex: Preliminary Results from South Korea. *Personal. Individ. Differ.* **2019**, *141*, 107–110. [CrossRef]
60. Bélanger Lejars, V.O.; Bélanger, C.H.; Razmak, J. Exploring New Measures of Online Sexual Activities, Device Use, and Gender Differences. *Comput. Hum. Behav.* **2020**, *108*, 106300. [CrossRef]
61. Sun, C.; Miezan, E.; Lee, N.-Y.; Shim, J.W. Korean Men's Pornography Use, Their Interest in Extreme Pornography, and Dyadic Sexual Relationships. *Int. J. Sex. Health* **2015**, *27*, 16–35. [CrossRef]
62. Tripodi, F.; Eleuteri, S.; Giuliani, M.; Rossi, R.; Livi, S.; Petruccelli, I.; Petruccelli, F.; Daneback, K.; Simonelli, C. Unusual online sexual interests in heterosexual Swedish and Italian university students. *Sexologies* **2015**, *24*, e84–e94. [CrossRef]
63. Jokinen, J.; Boström, A.E.; Chatzittofis, A.; Ciuculete, D.M.; Öberg, K.G.; Flanagan, J.N.; Arver, S.; Schiöth, H.B. Methylation of HPA Axis Related Genes in Men with Hypersexual Disorder. *Psychoneuroendocrinology* **2017**, *80*, 67–73. [CrossRef]
64. Fogg, B.J. *Tiny Habits: The Small Changes That Change Everything*; Houghton Mifflin Harcourt: Boston, MS, USA, 2019.

65. Eyal, N. *Hooked: How to Build Habit-Forming Products*; Penguin: New York, NY, USA, 2014.
66. Wéry, A.; Billieux, J. Online Sexual Activities: An Exploratory Study of Problematic and Non-Problematic Usage Patterns in a Sample of Men. *Comput. Hum. Behav.* **2016**, *56*, 257–266. [CrossRef]
67. The Official xHamster 2019 Trend Report. Available online: https://xhamster.com/blog/posts/911001 (accessed on 1 May 2020).
68. Efoui-Hess, M. *Climate Crisis: The Unsustainable Use of Online Video*; The Shift Project: Paris, France, 2019.
69. Cooper, A. Sexuality and the Internet: Surfing into the New Millennium. *Cyberpsychol. Behav.* **1998**, *1*, 187–193. [CrossRef]
70. Sniewski, L.; Farvid, P.; Carter, P. The Assessment and Treatment of Adult Heterosexual Men with Self-Perceived Problematic Pornography Use: A Review. *Addict. Behav.* **2018**, *77*, 217–224. [CrossRef] [PubMed]
71. Gola, M.; Potenza, M.N. Paroxetine Treatment of Problematic Pornography Use: A Case Series. *J. Behav. Addict.* **2016**, *5*, 529–532. [CrossRef] [PubMed]
72. Mousailidis, G.; Mehboob, R.; Papanna, B.; Bhan-Kotwal, S.; Shoka, A. Hypersexuality and New Sexual Orientation Following Aripiprazole Use. *Prog. Neurol. Psychiatry* **2020**, *24*, 14–16. [CrossRef]

# Permissions

All chapters in this book were first published by MDPI; hereby published with permission under the Creative Commons Attribution License or equivalent. Every chapter published in this book has been scrutinized by our experts. Their significance has been extensively debated. The topics covered herein carry significant findings which will fuel the growth of the discipline. They may even be implemented as practical applications or may be referred to as a beginning point for another development.

The contributors of this book come from diverse backgrounds, making this book a truly international effort. This book will bring forth new frontiers with its revolutionizing research information and detailed analysis of the nascent developments around the world.

We would like to thank all the contributing authors for lending their expertise to make the book truly unique. They have played a crucial role in the development of this book. Without their invaluable contributions this book wouldn't have been possible. They have made vital efforts to compile up to date information on the varied aspects of this subject to make this book a valuable addition to the collection of many professionals and students.

This book was conceptualized with the vision of imparting up-to-date information and advanced data in this field. To ensure the same, a matchless editorial board was set up. Every individual on the board went through rigorous rounds of assessment to prove their worth. After which they invested a large part of their time researching and compiling the most relevant data for our readers.

The editorial board has been involved in producing this book since its inception. They have spent rigorous hours researching and exploring the diverse topics which have resulted in the successful publishing of this book. They have passed on their knowledge of decades through this book. To expedite this challenging task, the publisher supported the team at every step. A small team of assistant editors was also appointed to further simplify the editing procedure and attain best results for the readers.

Apart from the editorial board, the designing team has also invested a significant amount of their time in understanding the subject and creating the most relevant covers. They scrutinized every image to scout for the most suitable representation of the subject and create an appropriate cover for the book.

The publishing team has been an ardent support to the editorial, designing and production team. Their endless efforts to recruit the best for this project, has resulted in the accomplishment of this book. They are a veteran in the field of academics and their pool of knowledge is as vast as their experience in printing. Their expertise and guidance has proved useful at every step. Their uncompromising quality standards have made this book an exceptional effort. Their encouragement from time to time has been an inspiration for everyone.

The publisher and the editorial board hope that this book will prove to be a valuable piece of knowledge for researchers, students, practitioners and scholars across the globe.

# List of Contributors

**Juan M. Machimbarrena**
Faculty of Psychology, University of the Basque Country (UPV/EHU), 20018 Donostia-San Sebastian, Spain

**Joaquín González-Cabrera, Jéssica Ortega-Barón, Marta Beranuy-Fargues, Aitor Álvarez-Bardón and Blanca Tejero**
Faculty of Education, Universidad Internacional de la Rioja (UNIR), 26006 Logrono, Spain

**Sulki Chung**
Department of Social Welfare, Chung-Ang University, Seoul 06974, Korea

**Jaekyoung Lee**
Korea Center on Gambling Problems, Research and Development Team, Seoul 04554, Korea

**Hae Kook Lee**
Uijeongbu St. Mary's Hospital, The Catholic University of Korea, Uijeongbu-si 11765, Korea

**Melina A. Throuvala, Mark D. Griffiths and Daria J. Kuss**
International Gaming Research Unit, Psychology Department, Nottingham Trent University, Nottingham NG1 4FQ, UK

**Mike Rennoldson**
Psychology Department, Nottingham Trent University, Nottingham NG1 4FQ, UK

**Verónica Marín-Díaz, Juan Manuel Muñoz-González and Begoña-Esther Sampedro-Requena**
Education department, University of Cordoba, 14071 Córdoba, Spain

**Vega González-Bueso, Juan José Santamaría, Marta Baño and Joan Ribas**
Atención e Investigación en Socioadicciones (AIS), Mental Health and Addictions Network, Generalitat de Catalunya (XHUB), 08014 Barcelona, Spain

**Ignasi Oliveras and Elena Montero**
Department of Psychiatry & Forensic Medicine, Institute of Neurosciences, Universitat Autònoma de Barcelona, Bellaterra, 08193 Barcelona, Spain

**Daniel Fernández**
Research and Development Unit, Parc Sanitari Sant Joan de Déu, Fundació Sant Joan de Déu, Sant Boi de Llobregat, 08830 Barcelona, Spain
Department of Statistics and Operations Research, Polytechnic University of Catalonia-BarcelonaTech, 08028 Barcelona, Spain
Centro de Investigación Biomédica en Red de Salud Mental (CIBERSAM), Instituto de Salud Carlos III, 28029 Madrid, Spain

**Susana Jiménez-Murcia**
Pathological Gambling Unit, Department of Psychiatry, Bellvitge University Hospital-IDIBELL, 08907 Barcelona, Spain
Ciber Fisiopatología Obesidad y Nutrición (CIBERObn), Instituto de Salud Carlos III, 28029 Madrid, Spain
Department of Clinical Sciences, School of Medicine and Health Sciences, University of Barcelona, 08907 Barcelona, Spain

**Amparo del Pino-Gutiérrez**
Pathological Gambling Unit, Department of Psychiatry, Bellvitge University Hospital-IDIBELL, 08907 Barcelona, Spain
Nursing Department of Mental Health, Public Health, Maternal and Child Health, Nursing School of the University of Barcelona, 08907 Barcelona, Spain

**Élodie Verseillié, Stéphanie Laconi and Henri Chabrol**
Centre d'Etudes et de Recherches en Psychopathologie et Psychologie de la Santé (CERPPS) EA7411, Université de Toulouse, 5, Allées Antonio Machado, 31058 Toulouse Cedex, France

**Michelle Colder Carras**
Department of International Health, Johns Hopkins Bloomberg School of Public Health, 615 N. Wolfe St. W5501, Baltimore, MD 21205, USA

**Matthew Carras**
Carras Consulting, 1407 Scanlan Drive, Glen Burnie, MD 21205, USA

**Alain B. Labrique**
Departments of International Health, Epidemiology, and Health Policy and Management, Johns Hopkins Bloomberg School of Public Health, 615 N. Wolfe St. W5501, Baltimore, MD 21205, USA

**Lydia Harkin**
International Gaming Research Unit, Psychology Department, Nottingham Trent University, Nottingham NG1 4FQ, UK

**Eiman Kanjo**
Computing and Technology Department, Nottingham Trent University, Nottingham NG1 4FQ, UK

**Joel Billieux**
Addictive and Compulsive Behaviour Lab., Institute for Health and Behaviour, Integrative Research Unit on Social and Individual Development (INSIDE), University of Luxembourg, Esch-sur-Alzette, L-4365 Luxembourg, Luxembourg
Addiction Division, Department of Mental Health and Psychiatry, University Hospitals of Geneva, 44041 Geneva, Switzerland

**Xinhe Zhang, Xiaoxuan Shi, Shuowei Xu and Jingwen Qiu**
Faculty of Psychology, Ministry of Education Key Laboratory of Cognition and Personality, Southwest University, Chongqing 400715, China

**Ofir Turel**
Information Systems and Decision Sciences, California State University, Fullerton, CA 92831, USA

**Qinghua He**
Faculty of Psychology, Ministry of Education Key Laboratory of Cognition and Personality, Southwest University, Chongqing 400715, China
Chongqing Collaborative Innovation Center for Brain Science, Chongqing 400715, China
Southwest University Branch, Collaborative Innovation Center of Assessment toward Basic Education Quality at Beijing Normal University, Chongqing 400715, China
Institute of Psychology, Key Laboratory of Mental Health, Chinese Academy of Sciences, Beijing 100101, China

**Lia de Vocht**
E-Learning Research Lab, University of Canterbury, Christchurch 8041, New Zealand

**Leona Harris, Niki Davis and Saili Aukuso**
E-Learning Research Lab, University of Canterbury, Christchurch 8041, New Zealand
Child Well-being Research Institute, University of Canterbury, Christchurch 8041, New Zealand

**Tufulasifa'atafatafa Ova Taleni and Nikita Gregory**
Child Well-being Research Institute, University of Canterbury, Christchurch 8041, New Zealand

**Una Cunningham**
Department of Education, Uppsala University, 75236 Uppsala, Sweden

**Sonja Macfarlane**
Te Rū Rangahau: The Māori Research Laboratory, University of Canterbury, Christchurch 8041, New Zealand

**Jan Dobson**
Sector Enablement and Support, Ministry of Education, Christchurch 8013, New Zealand

**Yun-Yu Chen**
Department of Psychiatry, Faculty of Medicine, College of Medicine, Kaohsiung Medical University, Kaohsiung City 807, Taiwan

**Ju-Yu Yen**
Department of Psychiatry, Faculty of Medicine, College of Medicine, Kaohsiung Medical University, Kaohsiung City 807, Taiwan
Department of Psychiatry, Kaohsiung Municipal Ta-Tung Hospital, Kaohsiung Medical University, Kaohsiung City 801, Taiwan

**Yi-Chun Yeh**
Department of Psychiatry, Faculty of Medicine, College of Medicine, Kaohsiung Medical University, Kaohsiung City 807, Taiwan
Graduate Institute of Medicine, College of Medicine, Kaohsiung Medical University, Kaohsiung City 807, Taiwan
Department of Psychiatry, Kaohsiung Medical University Hospital, Kaohsiung Medical University, Kaohsiung City 807, Taiwan

**Peng-Wei Wang**
Department of Psychiatry, Faculty of Medicine, College of Medicine, Kaohsiung Medical University, Kaohsiung City 807, Taiwan
Department of Psychiatry, Kaohsiung Medical University Hospital, Kaohsiung Medical University, Kaohsiung City 807, Taiwan

**Tai-Ling Liu**
Graduate Institute of Medicine, College of Medicine, Kaohsiung Medical University, Kaohsiung City 807, Taiwan
Department of Psychiatry, Kaohsiung Medical University Hospital, Kaohsiung Medical University, Kaohsiung City 807, Taiwan

**Chih-Hung Ko**
Department of Psychiatry, Faculty of Medicine, College of Medicine, Kaohsiung Medical University, Kaohsiung City 807, Taiwan
Graduate Institute of Medicine, College of Medicine, Kaohsiung Medical University, Kaohsiung City 807, Taiwan
Department of Psychiatry, Kaohsiung Medical University Hospital, Kaohsiung Medical University, Kaohsiung City 807, Taiwan
Department of Psychiatry, Kaohsiung Municipal Hsiao-Kang Hospital, Kaohsiung Medical University, Kaohsiung City 812, Taiwan

**Darryl Mead**
The Reward Foundation, The Melting Pot, Edinburgh EH2 2PR, UK
Digital Humanities, Information Studies, University College London, London WC1E 6BT, UK

**Mary Sharpe**
The Reward Foundation, The Melting Pot, Edinburgh EH2 2PR, UK
Lucy Cavendish College, University of Cambridge, Cambridge CB3 0BU, UK

# Index

www.ingramcontent.com/pod-product-compliance
Lightning Source LLC
LaVergne TN
LVHW082220200926
848484LV00008B/2279